THE AGE OF EMPIRES

THE AGE OF
EMPIRES

EDITED BY ROBERT ALDRICH

First published in 2007 in hardcover in the
United States of America by Thames & Hudson Inc.,
500 Fifth Avenue, New York, New York 10110

thamesandhudsonusa.com

Chapters by Jean-Luc Vellut, Walter Sauer,
Jacques Frémeaux and Joachim Zeller
translated by David H. Wilson

Chapter by Esther Captain and Guno Jones
translated by Lorna Dale

Chapter by Josep Fradera
translated by Matthew Clarke

© 2007 Thames & Hudson Ltd, London

PICTURE RESEARCH:
Wendy Gay and Elizabeth Moore

EDITOR: Ian Sutton

ASSISTANT EDITOR: Robert Shore

DESIGN, TYPOGRAPHY AND MAPS:
Isambard Thomas, London

PRODUCTION: Susanna Friedman

Printed and bound in Singapore by CS Graphics
Pte Limited

Library of Congress Catalog Card Number
2006940557

ISBN 978-0-500-25136-2

ON THE TITLE PAGE:
Recuperación de Bahia de Brasil by Fray Juan Bautista
Maino (Museo del Prado, Madrid). The painting
celebrates the recovery by Spain and Portugal of the
town of Bahia in Brazil, which had been captured by
the Dutch in 1625. General Don Fadrique de Toledo
is unveiling a tapestry showing Philip IV trampling
on Heresy, Discord and War. Behind him Victory
crowns him with the laurel wreath and on his other
side stands Count-Duke Olivares. In the background
wounded men are being tended.

Introduction: Imperial Overview

ROBERT ALDRICH

AMERICAN SCHOOLCHILDREN for long recited the mnemonic celebrating the 'discovery' of the New World by chanting: 'In fourteen hundred and ninety-two Columbus sailed the ocean blue.' Their British counterparts celebrated Empire Day, and French pupils reeled off the poetic names – Chandernagor, Mahé, Karikal, Pondichéry, Yanaon – of the French enclaves in India. Spaniards retained memories of the heroic conquistadors, and nurtured relations with the South American republics considered part of a large Hispanic family of nations. Camoens' saga of the Portuguese 'discoverers', *The Lusiads*, was as famous to Lusophones as Kipling's or Conrad's novels to Anglophones. Stanley and Livingstone, Brazza and Lyautey stood tall in the colonial gallery of great men of history. The heritage of trade in the East Indies suffused Dutch culture, from 'Delft' ware modelled on Chinese porcelain to the searing novel of colonialism in Java, *Multatuli*. The Germans and Italians were less familiar with their short-lived overseas empires (though some Italians yearned for the grandeur of ancient Rome), while Americans and Russians often claimed, contrary to the evidence, that the United States and the Soviet Union were not imperialistic states. The disappearance of the Austro-Hungarian and Ottoman empires obscured some of the imperial dimensions of those deceased states.

Nevertheless, the colonial world, receding further into the past with each decade, has returned to the consciousness of both the former colonizers and the formerly colonized: in recent years, partly thanks to perspectives introduced by the new cultural history, and the approaches of post-modernism, gender studies, cultural studies, subaltern studies and post-colonialism. A spate of films – ranging from cinematic versions of E.M. Forster's *A Passage to India* to Marguerite Duras' *Indochine* – brought colonialism to the big screen and a wider audience, while television series such as *Queen Victoria's Empire* presented colonialism in prime time. Anniversaries – the 500th anniversary of Columbus' voyage, then the anniversary of Vasco da Gama's expedition – in the 1990s provided the occasion for celebrations, contestations and scholarly reassessments of Spanish and Portuguese expansion, followed by commemorations of the

400th anniversary of the setting up of the Dutch East India Company in 2002. The bicentenary of British settlement in Australia in 1988, the fiftieth anniversary of the independence of Indonesia in the 1990s, the fiftieth year since the end of the Franco-Indochinese War in 2004: all these dates gave opportunities for revisiting the colonial period, a backward glance sometimes tinged with fond remembrances of colonies past, at other times with recriminations at the sometimes still officially unacknowledged exactions of colonialism.

IMAGES OF EMPIRE

'Empire', 'emperor' or 'imperial' in a word association game would conjure up a variety of images. Some might think of the Roman empire with its roads and aqueducts, the Forum and the Colosseum, toga-clad legionnaires and gladiators. To others, the words would evoke figures from European continental empires, Napoleon crowning himself in Paris, a bemedalled Austrian archduke or a Russian tsarina. Still others might picture an exotic potentate – the glamorously infamous Dowager Empress Cixi of China, the long-lived Emperor Hirohito of Japan or the ill-fated Emperor Haile Selassie of Ethiopia. Asked about 'empire', however, many would immediately think of the colonial empires: Christopher Columbus and Vasco da Gama, planters in the West Indies and spice-traders in the East Indies, pith-helmeted adventurers hacking their way through equatorial forests in Africa or grand memsahibs presiding over tiffin in India. Interrogated about what 'empire' means, respondents – especially those not of European heritage – might also speak of slavery, indentured labour, transported prisoners, conquest and war, and genocide.

'Empire' is not an easy word to define, though it may be seen at its most basic as the rule by a particular group in a political centre over a diverse and different set of other, often distant countries and peoples, generally as a result of military conquest. But if 'empire' is not a precise word or an easily identifiable political regime, neither is it a colourless word. Promoters of empire, in whatever time and place, championed its merits and the benefits that it brought to both the colonizing and the colonized. Anti-colonialists, by contrast, saw in imperial rule humiliating battlefield defeat, unwarranted political domination, economic exploitation, social disenfranchisement and cultural alienation. Present-day observers are apt to take a more anti-colonial than pro-colonial perspective on empire, though a nostalgia for imperial days can be discerned in some quarters, and there have been attempts to rehabilitate imperial actions. If few would raise three cheers for imperialism, a generation after most European colonies gained independence, whether colonial expansion might be given one (or even two) cheers is a matter of historical debate and public disagreement. A comparative study of empires, across continents and historical periods, sheds light on colonial ambitions and accomplishments, and on imperial achievements and failures.[1]

Empire is one of the key topics in human history, and tracing its origins involves returning to the earliest historical epochs. The ancient Egyptian pyramids were constructed for empire-builders, pharaohs who conquered Nubia and used coerced labour to raise their mausolea. The biblical Nebuchadnezzar ruled an empire in Babylon. The Greeks established colonies of settlers around the Mediterranean, and the Hellenistic Alexander the Great pushed his empire towards the Himalayas and the Ganges. The Roman empire spread from the borders of Scotland to Syria, from Spain to the Black Sea. Indeed, the Caesars left such a profound imperial imprint on the world that later colonizers would study their writings and try to emulate their deeds. Roman administration, many subsequent colonial theorists argued, provided a template for the rule of distant provinces and different peoples, while the highways and trading networks of Rome's empire survived as models for economic development. The spread of Latin formed an integral part of the classical civilizing mission, and the granting of prized Roman citizenship showed how worthy men from barbarous lands might be assimilated into the ruling body politic.[2]

The 'rise and fall' of the Roman empire, especially in Edward Gibbon's eighteenth-century rendition, became a mainstay of historical study. However, the ancient imperial idea did not die with the decline of Rome, but lived on for a thousand years in Byzantium. In western Europe, Charlemagne in 800 meanwhile took on an imperial mantle, and though his empire was later fragmented among his sons, the vacuous title of Holy Roman Emperor that he invented endured until the beginning of the nineteenth century. Clashes of civilization in the long Middle Ages created new empires. Muslims expanding from Arabia created an empire in North Africa that crossed the Straits of Gibraltar to southern Spain, stopped only by the Christian Charles Martel at Poitiers in 732. The Crusaders, departing on what they believed to be a God-blessed mission to liberate their Holy Land from the Infidels, surged into the Middle East, setting up puppet kingdoms in Cyprus and the Levant. In different types of expansion, Venice created a trading empire around the Adriatic, and Norsemen sailed to Britain, Normandy, Russia and Sicily, leaving Viking settlements wherever they landed.

Early empires were not restricted to Europe. The Han Chinese created an empire in East Asia, only to be conquered in turn by the Mongols and then Manchurians, and Chinese imperial influence ultimately covered a vast expanse of eastern Asia, from Tibet to Vietnam to Mongolia. The Srivijaya empire spread through insular southeast Asia, while the rulers of the Champa, Pagan and Khmer empires battled over mainland southeast Asia. The Mughal emperor gained control of much of south Asia. The Japanese emperor – the only sovereign who still uses the title of emperor today – ruled the huge Japanese archipelago and, at times, extended his domains much further. The Ottomans came from the East to conquer a tri-continental empire in Asia, Africa and Europe that proved one of the most persistent in the modern world. In South America, the Aztecs and Incas ruled domains that might well be called empires, as did various chieftains in sub-Saharan Africa. Manifestations of imperialism, thus, have appeared throughout the world.

MODERN EMPIRES

In the modern period of Western history, from the Renaissance until the present, empires in one form or another have been a constant feature of the political landscape. Early European experiences, not limited to the Roman empire, provided examples for empire-builders to follow in conquering new domains, settling expatriate populations, channelling trade and setting up structures of government. Colonizers claimed a natural or divine right to take over unoccupied lands or those inhabited by people whom they considered their cultural or biological inferiors. They raised flags, read proclamations and brandished symbols of their new suzerainty over what they branded primitive societies in Africa or Oceania or over the 'decadent' cultures in the Middle East or Asia. They arrogated to themselves the right to spread their version of civilization, whether Christian or secular, monarchical or republican, mercantilist or capitalist or socialist. They saw foreign places as sites for the settlement of transported prisoners, free migrants or servile labourers that they recruited around the world – including, for many centuries, those in Africa whom they reduced to slavery in order to ship them to distant domains as the cheapest possible sort of labour. They restructured 'native' societies, exporting their systems of administration, frequently replacing local rulers and laws with ones brought from home, or reducing sultans, rajahs and chiefs to vassal status within their orbit. If land despoliation, and social and economic marginalization were often the lot of indigenous populations, the colonizers promised good governance, law and order, modernization, and the advantages of European technology, medicine and education. The colonizers also hoped their newly acquired possessions would yield treasure troves of foodstuffs, coveted precious metals and other useful raw materials. They thought that decades, perhaps centuries or more in the case of the most 'backward' populations, would be necessary before political power might be devolved back to non-white people. Seldom if ever did they imagine that their rule would come to an end, though it did so almost everywhere, often in only two or three generations, in some cases with alacrity, through war, revolution and the sea change of decolonization.

The expansion of imperial powers from the sixteenth century through the early nineteenth century is one of the 'big issues' in history, and much ink has been expended debating empire. Indeed, there was little consensus even at the height of the imperial age. Though most Europeans (and others in colonizing countries) probably supported their nations' overseas endeavours, at least in a vague sort of way, numerous voices were raised in dissent. Critics often felt that expansion wasted the 'blood and gold' of Europe for dubious benefits, and that concern with faraway places diverted attention from pressing issues at home. Particular anti-colonial campaigns were waged against some of the worst excesses of imperialism, notably in the anti-slavery movement from the late eighteenth century until the abolition of slavery, and then in opposition at the turn of the twentieth century to the horrific exactions visited on labourers (especially in the Congo Free State). Regular exposés of colonial conditions were published, and when a giant *Exposition Coloniale* was held in Paris in 1931, opponents of imperialism, including Surrealists and Communists, organized an anti-colonial exhibition. Anti-colonial nationalist movements led by figures ranging from Gandhi to Ho Chi Minh gained much support in Europe, and prolonged attempts to retain colonial control, for example, by the French in Algeria or in a later military action that some deemed imperialistic, the Americans in Vietnam, provoked widespread opposition at home and abroad.

Historians, too, have debated empire; imperial and colonial studies have been a prominent branch of history that have seen a renascence in the last two decades. Scholars have suggested many interpretations of empire. Probably the single most contested topic, prompted by the writings of John Hobson in 1902, was whether economics formed the 'taproots' of imperial expansion and whether imperialism was a product of modern industrial and finance capitalism.[3] More recently, triggered by Edward Said's *Orientalism*, published in 1978, attention has turned to the cultural bases of imperialism, the way in which certain ethnocentric assumptions underpinned expansion and the way in which imperial culture did or did not suffuse Europe itself.[4] Historical theories abound on every issue of relevance to colonialism, for instance, about 'formal' versus 'informal' empire – areas of political sovereignty compared to those of hegemonic influence. Some historians make a difference between 'colonialism', seen as the foundation of settler societies, and 'imperialism', political, economic and cultural expansion into areas where Europeans did not achieve a large-scale demographic presence. The 'imperialism of free trade', commercial primacy without political control, is sometimes contrasted with an imperialism that mandated formal political overlordship. 'Sub-imperialism' has been suggested as the autonomous expansion of one colony elsewhere in its region, and 'internal colonization' has been used to describe the way that heartlands of a country exploitatively treat peripheral regions of the same state. 'Neo-colonialism' has been propounded as the type of influence that imperial countries continued to exercise over possessions once they gained formal independence.[5] In the present volume, still other variations on the imperial nomenclature appear. The welter of names and theories underlines above all the importance of the phenomenon of expansion (and its seemingly inevitable corollary, contraction), and emphasizes the interest that it provokes in scholars.

New developments in historical research lead students to raise new questions about the colonial past. One of the biggest areas of interest nowadays is gender and empire, though a generation ago few studied issues relating to the gendered nature of expansion, the differing roles of women and men in empire, and such areas as sexuality and private life.[6] Ecology has been another fertile growth area in colonial studies, with scholars looking at how colonials remoulded the physical

GREENLAND

ICELAND

Reykjavik

San Francisco

Los Angeles
San Diego

New York

NEW SWEDEN

PORTUGAL

Lisbon

MEXICO
(NEW SPAIN)

New Orleans

Monterrey

Miami

WESTERN SAHARA
(RIO DEL ORO)

Guadalajara

Havana

CUBA

HISPANIOLA

Mexico City
(Tenochtitlan)

JAMAICA

San Juan
PUERTO RICO

Acapulco

BELIZE

GUATEMALA
EL SALVADOR

HONDURAS

GUINÉ-BISSAU

NICARAGUA

GUINEA

COSTA RICA

PANAMA

VENEZUELA

Bogotá

Belém

COLOMBIA

ECUADOR

Quito

The Portuguese, Spanish, Austro-Hungarian and Scandinavian Empires

The shading indicates all territories that were at any time – not necessarily at the same time – ruled by the colonial powers.

The Portuguese Empire

Portuguese settlements and outposts. (The shading does not imply that Portugal controlled the whole coastline of Africa, only that Portuguese explorers and traders were granted the right to occupy those lands.)

The Spanish Empire

Scandinavian empires

The Austro-Hungarian Empire

Recife

Lima

Bahia

BRAZIL
(NEW PORTUGAL)

Porto Seguro

La Paz
BOLIVIA
Potosí

PERU

PARAGUAY

Rio de Janiero

São Paulo

CHILE

Cordoba

Porto Alegre

URUGUAY

Santiago

Buenos Aires

Montevideo

ARGENTINA

LAS MALVINAS
(FALKLAND ISLANDS)

SPITZBERGEN

SWEDEN

FINLAND

Helsinki

Stockholm

ESTONIA

St Petersburg

LATVIA

LITHUANIA

nhagen

BOHEMIA

SLOVAKIA

enna

Budapest

STRIA

HUNGARY

BOSNIA

ROMANIA

ITALY

me

Muscat

Daman

Diu

Hughli

INDIA

Macao

Goa

Manila

Calicut

Tranquebar

PHILIPPINES

Cochin

Colombo

SRI LANKA
(CEYLON)

Galle

Kuala Lumpur

MALAYSIA

SUMATRA

Singapore

Malindi

Mombasa

Zanzibar

INDONESIA

da

PAPUA
NEW
GUINEA

ANGOLA

JAVA

EAST TIMOR

MOZAMBIQUE

MADAGASCAR

Matatane

Durban

Cape Town

landscape of places they ruled by depredations on the natural environment leading to the extinction of such animals as the unfortunate dodo, the import and acclimatization of new species, land clearance, the building of dams and roadways.[7] How European artists saw the landscapes of faraway places and people has provided an immense subject for historians and curators.[8] Studies of culture contact between East and West, and between North and South, various types of imperial encounters and how they appeared in painting, literature, music, film, fashion and food, have broadened the range of perspectives on empire. Imperial health and hygiene provide yet another major area of contemporary research, focusing on disease and prophylaxis, provisions for health care and the biological revolutions that took place in many colonized regions.[9] A particular area of interest has been how imperial ambitions, experiences and culture helped to form national identities both in the colonial and the post-colonial periods.[10] All sorts of specific topics – the great hedgerows set up by the British in India, or the development of the spice trade between Europe and Asia – have been the subjects of popular books.[11]

THROUGH THE EYES OF THE COLONIZED
Victims of colonialism have increasingly put forward their views, demanding redress of grievances inherited from colonial rule or symbolic recognitions of wrongs done to their ancestors. Aboriginals demanded land rights in Australia, claims given a judicial imprimatur with the Mabo decision by the High Court in Canberra in 1992. Groups of African-Americans and other descendants of enslaved Africans claimed reparations for the evils of the slave trade, and cultural leaders of many formerly colonized people have asked for the restitution of sacred items (and human remains) enshrined in Western museums. The reception of such demands has proved ambivalent, and leaders have been reluctant to say 'sorry' for colonial misdeeds or to offer anything other than symbolic compensation for injustices. Nevertheless, the Dutch erected a monument in memory of the enslaved peoples in Amsterdam, the French parliament declared that slavery and slave-trading constituted a 'crime against humanity', and the Germans officially recognized a 'genocide' of the Herero people in 1904 in what is now Namibia: steps towards coming to terms with the colonial past and perhaps also to effecting a reconciliation between the former colonizers and colonized.

Debates continue to rage on such topics as the extent of systematic torture practised by French troops in colonial Algeria, the level of cruelty of Belgians in the Congo, and the role of colonialism in creating an inequitable and iniquitous disparity in wealth between the North and the South (or, in an earlier nomenclature, the First and Third Worlds). Arguments about the benefits and demerits of contemporary globalization perpetuate claims of development and underdevelopment. Commentators have found in colonial conditions the origins of bloody post-colonial conflagrations in recent years from Northern Ireland to Palestine, from Rwanda to Aceh, from the Sudan to East Timor. Meanwhile, European countries have faced difficult and pressing issues, particularly linked to migration, the emergence of societies of multiple cultures, and the economic and political gaps between various ethnic groups in their midst, especially when many of the disadvantaged are descendants of those who came from former colonies. Urban riots in Britain and France, ethnic tensions in the Netherlands and Germany, and conflicts between Italy and Spain and their neighbours across the Mediterranean, resonate with issues tied to colonial conquest and the uneasy situations they produced. Civil war in the Balkans in the 1990s was ascribed both to the inheritance of Austro-Hungarian imperialism and to a new Serbian imperialism. In Russia, nationalists in Chechnya and Nagorno-Karabakh accuse Moscow of unreconstructed Russian imperialism; critics of the Iraq war that began in 2003 allege the United States, the world's remaining superpower, is reinventing a new imperialistic dominion. The colonial legacy, the volatile accusations of 'colonialism' and 'imperialism', public interest in empire and scholarly debates about overseas expansion are manifestly issues of the present, not just the past.

Involved in this interest, for both scholars and the general public, is a host of questions. Did colonial administration create the economic underdevelopment that became such a handicap to much of sub-Saharan Africa or, at least in some parts of Asia, did it, by contrast, lay the groundwork for the extraordinary economic growth that marked the 1980s and afterwards, despite several notable downturns in that continent? Did foreign overlordship, by combining diverse cultural groups into one polity and for long limiting the exercise of self-determination and representative government, underlie political dictatorship and corruption, or did it rather plant the seeds of pluralism, democracy and parliamentarianism? Did European cultural expansion have a 'fatal impact' on local societies and their cultures and traditions, or introduce a potential conduit for emancipation from gendered, hierarchical and inegalitarian 'feudalism'? Was the Western impulse behind expansion primordially one of greed justified by racism, or were there higher ideals and less deleterious results to the enterprise of expansion? Were imperialists heroes or villains, or something in between? Were the colonized always victims, sometimes collaborators or even beneficiaries in the colonial project?

Colonial history, thus, is not limited to maps of explorations, chronologies of conquests, pantheons of explorers, settlers and administrators, and balance sheets of commercial activities. It touches on the fundamentals of Western culture itself: ideas of governance and the ways that political rights and powers were (or were not) extended throughout populations; notions of race, ethnicity, culture and ideology; types of economic relationships and models for development; moral codes and standards of personal conduct; the roles of religion, education, science and technology in the modern world. The study of colonialism is an investigation of the effect of Europeans (and other colonizers) on distant lands and peoples, but also of the impact of the Americas, Asia, Africa and the South Seas on Europe itself. It is, too, a study of the ideas and ideologies that motivated Europeans to leave their native lands and take over much of the rest of the world.

EMPIRES AND THE WORLD

The extent of modern imperialism since the 1500s truly encompasses the globe, and indeed imperialism has been the most important contributor to contemporary globalization. One need only recall that in the mid-eighteenth century, the islands of the Caribbean and the North and South American continents were coming under the control of European powers, which had also established numerous trading outposts around the coast of Africa and the Indian subcontinent and onwards to East Asia. Although almost all of the American countries gained independence by the early decades of the nineteenth century, imperialists soon expanded into the hinterlands of their Asian and African beachheads, and they had already found other domains for expansion, stretching from Australasia to North Africa. In the early twentieth century, the British monarch reigned over between a quarter and a fifth of humanity and the planet; France claimed an empire of 11 million sq km (4.25 million sq miles) and 100 million citizens and subjects; the Belgian Congo was seventy-three times the size of Belgium. By the mid-1930s, the zenith of the 'new' imperialism, all of southern and southeast Asia was ruled by Europeans, except for such largely inaccessible Himalayan regions as Bhutan, as well as Thailand, maintained as a buffer between the French and British colonies. Most of China and Japan had escaped European takeover, though from the mid-nineteenth-century Opium Wars onwards, Westerners had demanded concessionary trade and political privileges from China, where imperial and then republican authorities struggled to maintain their centralized control over the world's most populous conglomeration of peoples. Japan, forcibly opened to the West by 'gunboat

CANADA

Vancouver   Calgary

Quebec

Montreal   NEWFOUNDLAND

Chicago   Toronto   Boston

New York (New Amsterdam)

UNITED STATES   Philadelphia
OF AMERICA

St Louis   Washington DC

LOUISIANA

New Orleans

Port-au-Prince   VIRGIN ISLANDS   Nouakchott
                                              MAURITANIA
HAITI
                      GUADELOUPE   Dakar
NETHERLANDS   MARTINIQUE   SENEGAL
ANTILLES
                                             GUINÉ-BISS.
                      TOBAGO

                                             Cor
Georgetown   Paramaribo

GUYANA   Cayenne

SURINAME   FRENCH GUIANA

The Ottoman, French, Dutch, Italian, Belgian and German Empires

The shading indicates all territories that were at any time – not necessarily at the same time – ruled by the colonial powers. At its greatest extent the Ottoman Empire included territories later absorbed into the empires of Austria-Hungary, France and Italy; these territories included parts of North Africa and the Levant, which are shown here with dual shading.

TAHITI

The Ottoman Empire

The French Empire

The Dutch Empire

The Italian Empire

The Belgian Empire

The German Empire

Kaliningrad

Berlin (PRUSSIA)

ERLANDS

LITHUANIA

GERMANY

POLAND

LGIUM

Vienna

AUSTRIA

RANCE

THE BALKANS

Edirne

Istanbul

Rome

ITALY

GREECE

TURKEY

Algiers

Bursa

Tunis

TUNISIA

Damascus

SYRIA

Tehran

nca

Tripoli

LEBANON

Baghdad

IRAN
(PERSIA)

ISRAEL

IRAQ

Alexandria

LIBYA

EGYPT

SAUDI ARABIA

NCH
FRICA

Medina

stu

Jeddah

Mecca

NIGER

CHAD

Chandannagar

Chinsura

(FRENCH
EQUATORIAL
AFRICA)

Khartoum

ERITREA

Hanoi

INDIA

LAOS

N'Djamena

Asmara

Yanam

VIETNAM

DJIBOUTI
(FRENCH SOMALILAND)

Mahé

Pulicat

Bangkok

Angkor Wat

Lagos

CENTRAL
AFRICAN
REPUBLIC

Fashoda

Calicut

Pondicherry

CAMBODIA

Karikal

Addis Ababa

CEYLON

Saigon

ETHIOPIA
(ABYSSINIA)

Colombo

Mogadishu

FRENCH
CONGO

DEMOCRATIC
REPUBLIC OF
CONGO
(BELGIAN
CONGO)

UGANDA
(BUGANDA)

Kuala Lumpur

Leopoldville

SUMATRA

Singapore

Mombasa

Luanda

TANZANIA
(GERMAN
EAST
AFRICA)

Zanzibar

INDONESIA
(DUTCH EAST INDIES)

Batavia

JAVA

PAPUA
NEW GUINEA

NAMIBIA
(GERMAN
WEST
AFRICA)

Antananarivo

MAURITIUS

Walvis Bay

Windhoek

MADAGASCAR

RÉUNION

AUSTRALIA
(NEW HOLLAND)

Johannesburg

SOUTH
AFRICA

Durban

Cape Town

TASMANIA
(VAN DIEMAN'S LAND)

diplomacy', had then learned from European government and economics, and also imitated European imperialism by taking over Korea, Taiwan and islands in Micronesia; leaders in Tokyo by the 1930s were formulating plans for further expansion. The new Communist rulers of the Soviet Union after 1917 had essentially recreated the old Tsarist empire along new Marxist lines, all the way from the Baltic to Central Asia and the Pacific Ocean. The United States, after fulfilling its 'manifest destiny' to spread from the Atlantic to the Pacific, replaced Spain as imperial overlord in the Philippines. Further south, every single island in the Pacific Ocean, from relatively large Papua New Guinea and New Caledonia to myriads of tiny coral atolls, fell under the sway of colonial governments; Australia and New Zealand, proud of their continued 'late-colonial' affiliation to Britain, had joined the imperial powers ruling in Melanesia and Polynesia. In Africa, the story of colonial rule was the same. With Mussolini's conquest of Ethiopia in the mid-1930s, the entire continent – barring Liberia, though it, too, came under the influence of the Americans when they established it as a colony for emancipated slaves – was effectively ruled by colonial powers. In the Middle East, the victorious Allies divided up the Ottoman domains after 1918; though technically territories administered under League of Nations auspices, they were treated as colonies. The colonizers had even scrambled for uninhabited places in the world, from minuscule rocky outcrops in the North Atlantic to immense ranges of Antarctica.

The achievements of empire, at least in a technical sense, were no less remarkable than the extent of imperial control. Transport is a prime example. The French built the Suez Canal in the hopes of increasing international trade, though Britain proved the primary beneficiary of this new maritime route to India and further east. Throughout the colonial world, a vast infrastructure was put into place: the Canadian-Pacific and the Indian-Pacific railways across North America and across Australia, the great system of trunk roads in India, the parallel French and Belgian rail links from the African interior to the coast of the Congo. Shipping companies, such as the Messageries Maritimes and P&O, joined together colonial ports, and telegraph cables created an international communications network. Along the transport routes, European manufactured goods, capital and migrants poured into the empire. The colonies sent to Europe foodstuffs and other consumer goods – France even imported wine from Algeria. New industrial demands increased markets for primary resources. Phosphate from Morocco, Christmas Island and Nauru was useful for fertilizer, nickel from New Caledonia and Canada supplied an important alloy in steel. Rubber became essential for tyres and insulation – the British developed rubber plantations in Malaya, as did the Dutch in the East Indies and the French in Indochina, while the Belgians harvested rubber from the Congo. Coconut oil from tropical islands was the key ingredient in industrially produced soap. The busy ports of Rotterdam, Marseille and Liverpool handled the 'colonial wares' as the geographical interfaces between Europe and the wider world, and large numbers of shippers, merchants and financiers depended on the colonies for their wealth.

MEN, WOMEN AND IDEAS

Like goods, men and women too moved around the empire. By the early twentieth century, the British dominions of Canada, Australia, New Zealand and South Africa were such successful white settler societies that they had been granted self-government under the Crown. Substantial British settler communities lived in Rhodesia, in the highlands of Kenya and in the trading ports of Asia. The French had made Algeria a settler society, though Italians, Spaniards and Maltese for long outnumbered French migrants, and on a smaller scale New Caledonia saw itself as an austral France. German colonial authorities hoped (in vain, it turned out) that the African colonies would attract some of the millions of Germans who would migrate overseas, while the Italians conceived of colonial Libya as a 'fourth shore' for settlement of poor peasants from the

Mezzogiorno.[12] Batavia, capital of the Dutch East Indies, boasted a thriving European population until the Second World War. Thousands of mixed-race Eurasians moved to the Netherlands from Indonesia in the 1940s; when Algeria became independent in 1962, a million French citizens were 'repatriated' to France; and when Portugal withdrew from Angola and Mozambique in 1975, some 500,000 settlers and their descendants moved back to Portugal. In the midst of 'permanent' settlers in the colonies lived business people on short-term contracts, government officials, soldiers and the large number of Protestant and Catholic missionaries who counted among the key groups in colonialism. Europeans were proud of turning such cities as Hanoi, Léopoldville (Kinshasa), New Delhi and Addis Ababa into European-style capitals; the government houses, cathedrals and warehouses were architectural symbols of European colonialism at its most triumphant.

Ideas, too, circulated through colonial networks. Europeans hoped to spread their notions of 'commerce and Christianity', among other pillars of 'civilization'. However, ideas of 'liberty, equality and fraternity', the notion of the 'nation' as an independent state, the merits of representative democracy, and the call to class struggle also echoed around the empire: European concepts that could be used against the colonial overlords. Christian theology, a prime European export, became an essential part of the cultures of the American countries, the Philippines and many islands in the South Pacific and Caribbean. Most ex-colonies have institutions – parliaments, law courts and universities – modelled on European prototypes. At the same time, ideas from the wider world were taken to Europe. Whole scientific disciplines, such as ethnology and anthropology, owed their origins to fieldwork carried out in distant places. Esoteric religions, from nineteenth-century Theosophy to contemporary 'new age' beliefs, borrowed eclectically from non-European cosmologies. The artistic styles of 'primitive' cultures worked an enormous influence on Picasso and others of the early twentieth-century avant-garde who saw African masks and Oceanic sculptures in European galleries. The political ideas of Gandhi influenced Martin Luther King in the United States, and the independence struggles in colonial Vietnam and Algeria inspired many later 'liberation fronts'.

The international movement of ideas, people and trade goods, along the new lines of transport and communication, made of imperialism a complex international system of multilateral connections. By the 1920s and 1930s, when the exchanges were quicker, information was more rapidly disseminated, and perhaps European countries were more open to foreign influences – fascination with African and African-American cultures, or 'Negrophilia', is an example[13] – the imperial system had reached its most 'perfect' expression, though the seeds of discontent and crisis were rapidly germinating. The sweep of imperialism in the interwar years of the twentieth century is breathtaking, and the cast of imperialistic powers is equally remarkable. By the 1930s, only the Germans and Ottomans had been eliminated as imperial overloads (as had Austria-Hungary, if one considers the colonial aspects of Habsburg rule in the Balkans), and countries such as Denmark and Spain had just residues and memories of their former imperial holdings.

LOWERING THE FLAGS

Throughout the course of colonial history since the 1500s, all of the great powers of Europe, and some of the smaller ones, have been players in the imperial game. Many were involved for centuries, and some would cling to their far-flung domains even after the liberation or secession of most formal colonies. The flags have long been lowered over the British Raj and French Indochina, the Belgian Congo and the Dutch East Indies, but some fifty territories today remain in a state of constitutional dependency on distant powers, incorporated through a baffling variety of statutes. America's former colonies of Alaska and Hawaii are states, Puerto Rico and the Mariana Islands are 'commonwealths', Palau and the Federated States of Micronesia are 'associated states', Guam and American

ALASKA

CANADA

Vancouver

Quebec
Montreal
MASSACHUSETTS
UNITED STATES
OF AMERICA
Boston
New York
Philadelphia
Washington DC
VIRGINIA

Havana   CUBA

BRITISH VIRGIN
ISLANDS
● ● ANGUILLA
BRITISH
HONDURAS   JAMAICA

SENEGAL
GAMBIA

SIERRA LEO

TRINIDAD
AND TOBAGO
Georgetown   BRITISH GUYANA

ASC

The British and
Russian Empires

The shading indicates all territories
that were at any time – not necessarily
at the same time – ruled by the
colonial powers. The eastern states of
North America, for instance, ceased
to be British in 1776, and Alaska
ceased to be Russian in 1867.

The British Empire,
colonies, protectorates,
mandates and dominions

The Russian Empire

Soviet-aligned states

FIJI

Auckland
NEW
ZEALAND
Christchurch

FALKLAND ISLANDS

SOUTH GEORGIA

Samoa are 'unincorporated' territories. French overseas territories encompass Martinique and Guadeloupe in the Caribbean, Saint-Pierre et Miquelon in the North Atlantic and French Guyana in South America, Mayotte and Réunion in the Indian Ocean, and French Polynesia, New Caledonia and Wallis and Futuna in the Pacific. The Netherlands administers six small islands in the Antilles; the geographically enormous Greenland is still linked to Denmark. Spain claims Ceuta and Melilla, two enclaves within Morocco. Britain's overseas outposts include Bermuda – formally ruled by London since 1684 – and other Atlantic islands, including the Falklands, which Margaret Thatcher's government successfully fought to recapture from Argentina in 1982, and folkloric St Helena and Tristan da Cunha, as well as a host of West Indian islands. Gibraltar in Europe, the British Indian Ocean Territory (rented to the United States as a navy base) and minuscule Pitcairn in the southeastern Pacific still form part of Her Majesty's 'realms and territories'.[14] (Meanwhile, various subject peoples still campaign for independence from the successor states to the old colonial empires.)

Despite the survival of these 'confetti of empire',[15] decolonization, which occurred in different colonies at various stages, was in sum quick and thorough. The United States, Haiti and the Spanish and Portuguese South American colonies gained independence from the 1780s through the 1820s. Most of the latter-day Asian colonies won independence within a decade after the Second World War – India, Pakistan and Burma in 1947, Sri Lanka the following year, Indonesia and the Philippines by the end of the 1940s as well, the countries of French Indochina, after a bloody war, in 1954. By the end of the 1950s, most of the larger countries of the Middle East and North Africa were independent, with France holding out in Algeria for several more years. The 1960s saw the independence of the majority of African colonies, though in this arena Portugal held out, and the case of Rhodesia remained intractable. Even the smallest countries were on the road to independence, and by the 1970s sovereign microstates were proliferating in the Caribbean and the Pacific. The subject countries of the Baltic, eastern Europe and Central Asia had to await the falling apart of the Soviet Union to get their independence.

Changed international conditions partly explain the final round of decolonization of the empires of western European states. Japan and Italy lost their colonies after the Second World War, and the war had distended ties between European colonial masters and their Asian possessions. Gandhi's non-violent struggle played the major role in forcing the British to quit India. The Dutch were simply unable to re-establish colonial control over the East Indies after the Japanese occupation in the face of Sukarno's nationalism, and Ho Chi Minh's Marxist-inspired nationalists dealt a humiliating defeat to the French at Dien Bien Phu. Nationalism in Africa – liberal constitutionalism, more radical brands of socialism, blatant or disguised authoritarianism – pushed forward the separation between the Europeans and their African subjects. During the decade after 1945, post-war recovery and rebuilding focused European energies on home countries, and the boom years of the 1950s and 1960s provided ample opportunities for growth in domestic economies. Though Europeans were then pouring ever-larger amounts of money into their dwindling colonies, policy-makers were concerned about the costs of administration, 'pacification' of nationalist movements, and infrastructural investment, and were not always willing to shoulder such onerous financial responsibilities. The racialist assumptions on which imperialism had been based were less tenable after the defeat of Fascism and Nazism. Extension of democratic rights, education and political enfranchisement in the colonial world undermined monopolies of European rule. Such institutions as the United Nations and, ostensibly, the USA and the USSR opposed the maintenance of colonial rule. Anti-colonial forces in the overseas possessions gained strength almost everywhere, using the media, elected assemblies, direct action and, sometimes, violence to pursue their ends. Authorities in European capitals ultimately faced the inevitable. Winston

Churchill remarked in the 1940s that he had not become the prime minister of Britain in order to preside over the dissolution of the British empire, but Harold Macmillan spoke only a few years later of the 'wind of change' buffeting the British colonies. A French parliamentarian immediately after the war argued that, without its empire, France would only be a parcel of Europe, but by the beginning of the 1960s Charles de Gaulle affirmed that decolonization was French policy because it was in the French interest. Neither the Dutch nor the Belgians suffered dramatically from the loss of their colonies. A combination of guerrilla warfare in Africa and regime change in Europe, the 1974 'revolution of the carnations' in Portugal, provoked the end of the last major overseas empire. Somewhat ironically, European states that once proclaimed colonies necessary for their economic and political well-being have thrived in the absence of empire. Yet while the European imperial sun was setting, the United States assumed Britain's place as the leading Western power, further trying to extend its role throughout the Caribbean, in eastern Asia and in the Middle East.[16]

THE LEGACY OF EMPIRE

Extreme longevity nevertheless marked some colonial establishments. Portugal ruled Macao from the 1550s to 1999, and the Dutch presence in parts of the East Indies covered three centuries. In other cases, the formal colonial period was relatively brief, though its impact ran deep. The French were in Algeria for 132 years and in southern Vietnam for under a century; they ruled Morocco as a protectorate for less than forty-five years. Britain's official rule of the Raj ranged from 1858 to 1947, although the East India Company had established a commercial, political and cultural presence in South Asia two centuries before the 'Mutiny'. Formal European colonial rule in most parts of sub-Saharan Africa (other than in South Africa and Western African trading posts) lasted for about seven decades. Germany ruled overseas colonies for barely thirty years, France and Britain administered their mandated territories in the Middle East for a similar span, and Italy's Ethiopian empire lasted only a decade. However, these spans of time belie the important transformations that foreign rule effected wherever the Europeans established themselves, and the imprint on the colonized countries represents the clearest legacy of the colonial epoch.

In Europe, too, the legacy of empire remains prominent. As the British sit down to a meal of curry, or the French to couscous, or the Dutch to a *rijstafel*, they are consuming the products of trade in commodities and cuisines that began with colonial encounters. Even more ubiquitous, coffee, tea and many spices are products of Europe's encounter with the East, and tomatoes, maize and chocolate (as well as tobacco) were brought to Europe's shores from the new worlds of the Americas, while sugar was the precious export of plantation colonies in the West Indies and Indian Ocean, São Tomé, Fiji, Natal and colonial Queensland. A European menu without 'colonial' foodstuffs would hardly be palatable, and the porcelain and china on which Europeans eat their meals are also souvenirs of the voyage to the Orient.[17]

European wardrobes and sitting rooms also have (or at least had) a colonial legacy. The fashion for *chinoiserie* was big business in the eighteenth century, as traders in China sought silks for clothing, upholstery and wall decorations.[18] 'Nankeen' came from China, and 'madras' and 'calico' from India. Wool from Australasia and cotton from South Asia were woven into cloth in the factories of the Industrial Revolution. Nineteenth-century furnituremakers liked tropical hardwoods such as teak and mahogany, and decorators cluttered houses with rugs from Persia and Turkey, and knickknacks made from African ivory or mother-of-pearl from the South Pacific. Those who had been on safari decorated their walls with hunting trophies, and the odd elephant-foot table or lion-skin rug still appears in dusty antique shops. Women bejewelled themselves with gold and diamonds from South Africa and sapphires from Ceylon. Children collected colonial coins and stamps, and soldiers proudly pinned on their colonial medals.

Europeans today view the art and artefacts of foreign cultures in their

ALASKA

Portland

Minneapolis

San Francisco

Chicago
Detroit
Boston
New York
St Louis
Washington DC

Los Angeles
Phoenix
San Diego

UNITED STATES
OF AMERICA

Atlanta

Dallas
New Orleans

Houston

MEXICO

HAWAII

Miami

Havana

Guantanamo
Bay

CUBA

DOMINICAN
REPUBLIC

San Juan

Mexico City

BELIZE

HAITI
PUERTO
RICO

US VIRGIN ISLANDS

HONDURAS

EL SALVADOR

NICARAGUA

Managua

PANAMA

Paramaribo

Bogotá

SURINAME

COLOMBIA

ECUADOR

Quito

PERU

Lima

La Paz

BOLIVIA

PARAGUAY

Asunción

The United States of America

The USA exercises its power in ways
quite unlike those of traditional empires
and has relatively rarely occupied
overseas territories.

The United States of America

Countries that have come into military
conflict with the USA since 1840
(excluding the two world wars)

Independent and self-governing countries that
host American air, naval or military
bases (2007)

Countries under military surveillance
and/or with US troop activity

THE
NETHERLANDS

M

Berlin

GERMANY

GIUM

Rome   Moscow   RUSSIA

ITALY   BOSNIA   SERBIA

MACEDONEY   BULGARIA

Tripoli   Istanbul   Beijing   NORTH
                                                                                              KOREA
              TURKEY   UZBEKISTAN   KYRGYZSTAN
LIBYA   JAPAN
                            Baghdad   Tehrān   TAJIKISTAN   CHINA   Seoul
              ISRAEL   Hiroshima
                            IRAQ   IRAN   Kabul   SOUTH   Tokyo
                                                      AFGHANISTAN   KOREA   Nagasaki
                            Kuwait   PAKISTAN

                                                                                   Hanoi
                                                                          LAOS   NORTH
SUDAN   VIETNAM   Manila

                                                                          CAMBODIA   PHILIPPINES
         DJIBOUTI   SOUTH
                                                                                  VIETNAM
         SOMALIA   Saigon

              Mogadishu

                                        DIEGO GARCIA

                                                                                  Geraldton

                                                                                        Sydney

museums – Benin bronzes at the British Museum, Khmer statues at the Musée Guimet, Indonesian textiles at the Tropenmuseum.[19] 'Colonial' motifs appear in buildings, the symbols of age-old European fascination for faraway places, whether in the Indian pastiche of the Royal Pavilion at Brighton or the statues of a Turk and an American Indian on the façade of the bakers' guild house in Brussels' Grand' Place.[20] Botanical gardens – Kew outside London, the Jardin des Plantes and the former Jardin Colonial in Paris, similar botanical gardens in Florence and Lisbon – testify to the collection and acclimatization of colonial flora, and zoos as well are reminders of the European desire to tame the wild and collect the exotic. Monuments, statues, memorials and other 'sites of memory' continue to testify to the way that colonialist promoters imprinted the empire on metropolitan landscapes and national consciousness.[21]

The new British Empire and Commonwealth Museum in Bristol, the soon-to-be-opened colonial museum in Marseille, and revamped displays in old colonial museums in Amsterdam and in the suburbs of Brussels illustrate the rediscovered interest in the history of imperialism. In other ways, too, the legacy of Europe's links with the wider world and, more specifically, with their old colonial possessions, is evident. Europeans listen to the world music recorded in Paris or London: Algerian *rai* or Indian *bhangra*. They read the diasporic literature coming forth from major European publishing houses, often written by authors who have elected to live in Europe, such as Salman Rushdie and Tahar Ben Jelloun. Sports teams, especially in European football, are line-ups of players of diverse backgrounds – the Algerian-born Zinedine Zidane captained France's World Cup-winning team in 1998 but proved ill-fated in the competition eight years later – and cricket and the Commonwealth Games continue to tie together Britain's old dominions and colonies more certainly than any political instance.

The major cities of Europe have become cosmopolitan juxtapositions of populations from many horizons, including the South Asians in Britain, and the North and West Africans in France, as well as, though in fewer numbers, the Surinamese and Javanese in Holland and the Ethiopians and Libyans in Italy. Mosques and Hindu and Buddhist temples provide sites of worship and of cultural identity for many, and issues of integration, assimilation and exclusion, both socially and culturally, underscore the complexities of cultural intermingling that owes much to the channels of migration created during the colonial period. Forced and free migration has, both literally and figuratively, changed the demographic complexion of host societies, including former colonies themselves. Brazil champions its *mestiço* coupling of Amerindian, European and African peoples and cultures; the United States claims to be a 'melting pot', though it remains a country marked by exclusive self-identification among such groups as the African-American descendants of enslaved peoples. Many of the former colonies of the Caribbean and Indian Ocean are home to a spectrum of cultures and ethnic groups – in Mauritius, the descendants of French planters, African slaves, indentured Indian workers, Chinese traders and those whose family trees included many of those roots.

The societies of the colonizing peoples, however, have faced particular, and sometimes forbidding, challenges in their own itinerary from relative cultural homogeneity to the incorporation of men and women who, whatever their individual or collective memories of the colonial pasts, have often looked to the old colonizing countries as sources of new opportunities or of potential refuge. The post-colonial predicament offers a chance, perhaps a necessity, for the self-redefinition of societies once arrogantly sure about the superior verities of Greco-Roman and Christian precepts, the white race, and European technological and commercial superiority. Cultural *métissage* and hybridity are quintessential post-colonial conditions.

In chronological length, geographical breadth and thematic complexity, the age of empires covers much of modern history, an inexhaustible reservoir for research and debate. This volume examines a particular set of empires: those in which European states expanded around the world from the sixteenth century onwards – cases of the 'classic' and extensive overseas empires of Portugal, Spain, Britain, France, Belgium and the Netherlands, the lesser-known outposts of Scandinavian countries, and those of the short-lived imperial late-comers, Germany and Italy. To these examples are added the continental empire of Austria-Hungary (and the interests of Habsburg leaders in the wider world), which shows some surprising parallels with the more widely flung empires. The empires of tsarist Russia (and its successor states, the Soviet Union and the Russian Federation), the Ottoman sultanate and the United States have all been both continental and inter-continental manifestations of the imperial phenomenon, and they, too, offer fascinating parallels and some contrasts with the other cases of expansion. Covering hundreds of years of history and most of the globe, these empires are not the only ones in the modern world, though it is beyond the brief of this book to look at empires constructed by other powers, such as China or Japan. This book, therefore, examines a restricted group of empires in the modern world, those where promoters of continental and overseas expansion shared some basic ideas associated with Europe and its culture, the economic system of mercantilistic then industrial capitalism (though socialist in the case of the USSR), the development of certain types of technology (including the weaponry that facilitated conquest), and the ideology of big-power conflict that pitted one imperial master against another.

The aim of this volume is to provide accessible overviews of these imperial experiences. The focus is on the imperial countries themselves, looking at the modes and cycles of expansion and contraction, the ideologies that prompted them and some of the repercussions of colonial expansion that rebounded on the metropolitan states. Most authors have adopted a chronological approach, though adapted to the very significant differences among the various empires. Different chapters focus attention variously on geopolitical, economic, social or cultural issues. Several of the writers have laid emphasis on historiographical and interpretive debates, while others have preferred a more narrative framework of imperial advance and retreat. Those who have contributed chapters on the largest and longest-lived of empires – those of Portugal, Spain, Britain and France – have met the particular challenges posed by word limits to provide succinct summaries of diverse imperial experiences on which literally thousands of full-scale works have been published. Those writing on more limited empires, for instance, the Scandinavian countries, Germany and Italy, may introduce readers to less familiar cases of expansion. The chapters on American and Russian/Soviet expansion argue for the inclusion of those cases within the broad framework of colonial and imperial history, as does the essay on Austria-Hungary.

The chapters provide introductions to different issues, offer synopses of current research and debate, indicate leads to further reading and are intended to inspire discussion about the extremely rich and fascinating issues raised by colonial history. Without either misplaced nostalgia for the colonial past or an angry and polemical castigation of imperial objectives, they seek not so much to draw authoritative conclusions as to provoke further questions. In its own fashion, each chapter also underlines the significance of the colonial past in the post-colonial present, as those in countries that were colonizers and those that were colonized struggle to make sense of a past that inextricably tied them together. The legacy of imperialism continues to contribute to the metamorphosis of social and cultural structures, to the articulation of their national identities and ideologies, and to the globalization considered a hallmark of our own world.

I

The Ottoman Empire: A Resilient Polity

NICHOLAS DOUMANIS

CONSTANTINOPLE FELL after a siege of two months at the end of May 1453. Though painted only two years later, this manuscript illumination (*opposite*) is not particularly accurate (where is Hagia Sophia, for instance?), but it shows the barriers closing the Golden Horn and teams of Turkish soldiers transporting boats across the land.

'EITHER I SHALL TAKE this city or the city will take me,' said Mehmet II (*above*), who had grown up with the conviction that he was destined to capture Constantinople. When it fell in 1453, he acquired the name of 'the Conqueror'. A man of wide culture, he summoned the Venetian artist Gentile Bellini to his court to paint his portrait.

IN THE SPRING OF 1453, as the Ottoman Turks worked doggedly to breech the walls of Constantinople, both the besiegers and the besieged were constantly looking for omens. For the Byzantines within, losing the city to the infidel could only mean that God had forsaken his chosen people. Certain death or enslavement awaited them. For Mehmet II (ruled 1444–46, 1451–81), victory would mean the heavens had fated him for imperial greatness. As the legitimate capital of the Roman Empire and, according to the Byzantines, the earthly counterpart to the Kingdom of Heaven, the city carried exceptional symbolic significance. As one Italian contemporary reported, Mehmet now claimed it was his right to 'extend his rule over the whole Christian world'.[1] For Mehmet, who also drew inspiration from Central Asian and Islamic warrior traditions and from the equally youthful Alexander the Great, possession of Constantinople meant he was entitled to a universal empire. Over the next two centuries, Mehmet and his successors proceeded to build an empire that was suitably massive, from the Mahgreb (Algeria) to Mesopotamia (Iraq), and from Hungary down to the Indian Ocean.

Ottoman history thereafter experienced two successive, and quite distinct, phases. For much of the early modern age, the Ottomans were the world's most formidable military power. During the reign of Süleyman the Magnificent (1520–66), the greatest of all Ottoman rulers, Constantinople was recognized across the entire Sunni Muslim world as the seat of the Khalifa (caliph), or 'deputy of the prophet of God', that is, of Muhammad. The Ottoman sultan assumed responsibility for overseeing the *hajj* (pilgrimage), he was custodian of the holy cities of Mecca and Medina, and he held the ultimate temporal authority for Muslims as far away as Senegal and Sumatra. The empire's second career started from the mid-eighteenth century, when it gradually succumbed to European powers that had found the means to exercise global political and economic domination. By that stage, the Ottomans had acquired the disreputable image of a ramshackle anachronism: the empire was now the principal site for Western fantasies of 'Oriental' decadence. To survive, the

le siege du grant turc auec ij deses principaulx conseillers
le liure du capiteine general de la turquie

THE OTTOMANS never forgot their nomadic pastoral roots. A late 15th-century manuscript from Tabriz, in Persia, showing a prince listening to a dervish, surrounded by his horses, food and weapons, found its way into the Topkapi Palace.

empire struggled to renew itself, and but for the intervention of the First World War it might well have survived in a workable, albeit truncated, form.

Founded in 1300 and dissolved in 1922, the Ottoman Empire was one of the most durable in world history. How does one account for its durability? How did it assert such firm control over the Balkans and the Middle East, perhaps the most militarily contested zone in world history?

PASTORAL BACKGROUND

Some answers can be found among the semi-arid steppes of Central Asia, the ancestral homeland of the Ottoman Turks. As with the Huns and Mongols, the Turks were pastoral nomads who formed tribal confederations and created vast (albeit short-lived) empires from the sixth century CE. Around the eleventh century, Turks migrated south and formed a series of powerful states from the Mediterranean through to India, including the Delhi Sultanates (1206–1526) and the great Mughal Empire (1526–1707).

That nomads should be able to produce such formidable military states had much to do with the exceptionally unstable nature of the pastoral economy of the steppes. As the Chinese historian Ssu-ma Ch'ien noted, 'It is the custom to herd their flocks in times of peace and make their living by hunting, but in periods of crisis they take up arms and go off on plundering and marauding expeditions.'[2] Periods of crisis were so common, however, that hunting and plundering were routine. Extreme climatic conditions, the unpredictable nature of livestock reproduction, and fierce competition for pastureland forced nomadic groups to supplement their pastoral activities with trade, hunting game and raiding other groups. War was intrinsic to the pastoral way of life, and nomads were not unlike professional soldiers, spending much of their lives honing their riding and martial skills. Many great empires, from Rome across to China, suffered at the hands of Central Asian tribal confederations that used their great mobility and supreme archery skills to disperse and annihilate enemy formations.

The chronically insecure nature of pastoral life also conditioned the peoples of Central Asia to be versatile when formulating survival strategies. As mobile peoples they mingled frequently with different cultures, and became accustomed to adopting and modifying ideas to meet their own needs. Such qualities were extremely important when pastoral armies encountered unfamiliar challenges, such as sophisticated stone fortifications and naval power. Like the Mongols, the Turks were quick to master military techniques (e.g. siege warfare) and technologies (e.g. catapults, gunpowder weapons), so as to eliminate the advantages enjoyed by more sophisticated sedentary states. Pastoral empires therefore managed to grow to impressive sizes. In 1280, for example, much of Asia and Europe, between the Sea of China and Poland, was ruled by four such empires or 'khanates'.

In most cases, however, the khanates were unstable political states that collapsed within a generation or two. What set the Ottoman Turks apart was their unique ability to extend that pastoralist virtuosity to state-building. In its quest to expand, consolidate and survive, the Ottoman Empire seemed to be constantly reinventing itself throughout its long history.

THE EARLY OTTOMAN EMPIRE

The Ottoman state began life as a minor principality or emirate in northwestern Anatolia, along the frontier with the Byzantine Empire, a Christian state that for centuries acted as a barrier between Christian Europe and Islam. As with the other Muslim principalities that dominated the Anatolian hinterland, the Ottoman emirate consisted of warrior tribesmen committed to perpetual holy war, or *gaza*, against the infidel. Its founder, Osman (*c.*1300–24), revived a languishing struggle against the Byzantines and, after a series of military campaigns, created a sizeable domain centred on the city of Bursa. His

WHEN HE CONQUERED the city, Mehmet II also took possession of what was the world's largest church. The Hagia Sophia was immediately designated to become a mosque, complete with towering minarets.

immediate successors, Orhan (1324?–62), Murat I (1362–89) and Bayezit I (1389–1402), built upon his achievements and transformed the House of Osman into a major regional power. Orhan's main feat was to establish a foothold on European soil, while Murat I captured the city of Adrianople (Edirne), the gateway to the Balkans, and followed up by conquering much of Thrace and Macedonia. Under Murat and Bayezit, the Ottomans consolidated their power in the Balkans, making the Bulgarian king a vassal and capturing Thessalonika (Salonica), a significant Mediterranean trading port. Following Murat's death at the Battle of Kosovo in 1389, Bayezit extended Ottoman authority over the emirates in the east. Bayezit was captured and executed by the Mongols following a disastrous defeat in 1402, after which a prolonged period of civil war ensued. Mehmet I (1413–20) and Murat II (1420–51) oversaw the re-emergence of Ottomans as a regional power and set the stage for the imperial golden age under Mehmet II.

By the siege of Constantinople, Osman's descendants had gone from tribal chiefs to sultans, while the loosely organized principality that consisted of a warrior leader and his band of Turkic tribesmen had become a state with a fixed capital. This transformation from pastoral to sedentary state was the kind of metamorphosis that would happen time and again in Ottoman history. The *gaza* warrior principalities of Anatolia had been, by their nature, very unstable entities, partly because they maintained the Central Asian practice of polygeniture, whereby political power was distributed among male relatives rather than passed undivided to the eldest son. As a result, the emirates often collapsed in disarray during struggles for succession. The Ottomans jettisoned the pastoralist tradition of polygeniture and replaced it with a new system whereby the most able son, who was not necessarily the first-born, became the new sultan. Although it did not completely resolve the problem of succession, it contributed to a more stable transferral of power and produced a series of able rulers. It appears that the House of Osman survived also because it was more amenable to change in its search for a durable political order. Ottoman commitment to perennial holy war, for example, did not preclude alliances and intermarriage with Christian dynasties as a means of consolidating power in the region. Thus Orhan was linked to the Byzantine royal family, the Katakouzenoi, through his marriage to the princess Theodora in 1346, while Bayezit, whose mother was a Byzantine princess, became sultan with the support of Christian princes and a predominantly Christian army.

The versatility of the Ottomans may be attributable to the fact that they inhabited the frontier zone between the Christian and Islamic worlds, where civilizations not only clashed but, more commonly, interacted and blended.[3] Forms of religious syncretism, the melding of Christian, Muslim, shamanistic and animistic beliefs, for example, were commonplace throughout Anatolia and the Balkans.

CLASSICAL ERA, 1453–1566

When Mehmet II seized Constantinople, he rescued a dying city of a dead empire. The sultan repopulated it by transferring communities from other parts of his empire, and within a century it had again become the largest city in Europe. The Topkapi Palace was among the many new structures that reflected the glory of the empire: so grand that it took nearly a century to complete. Conquests by later sultans were commemorated with buildings, pavilions and other landmarks. Ottoman architectural and artistic styles drew much influence from Persian and Italian motifs, while the Italian artist Gentile Bellini was commissioned to paint portraits of Mehmet, who styled himself a new Caesar. The city was also made a fitting capital for a Muslim empire. The Hagia Sophia (Church of the Holy Wisdom), commissioned by the Emperor Justinian in the sixth century, the world's largest Christian basilica, was converted into the sultan's mosque. Mehmet also established eight *medreses* (colleges of Islamic law) and other religious institutions that made the city the new centre of Islamic

CONTROL OF THE BALKANS passed firmly into Ottoman hands after the Battle of Mohács, on the Danube in southern Hungary, in August 1526 (*above*). By now the Ottomans had surpassed their European rivals in military technology. Their modern artillery decimated the still-feudal Hungarian army. The Ottomans could now advance to the gates of Vienna, bringing fear into the heart of Europe.

THE JANISSARIES were an elite military corps guarding the Ottoman sultan, initially recruited from prisoners of war and Christian children brought up in the Muslim faith. The officer shown here (*opposite*) was portrayed by a French artist in the early 18th century.

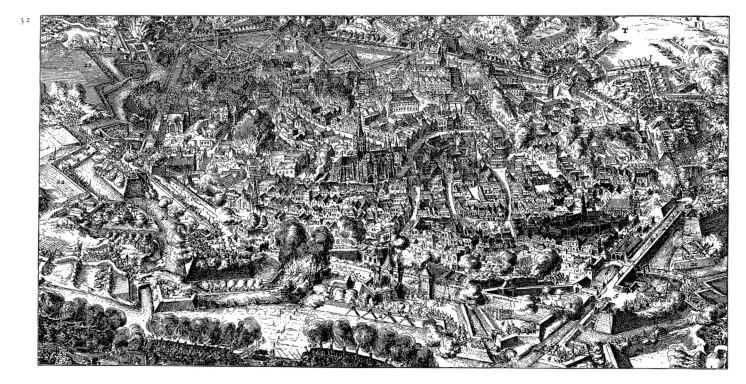

THE SIEGE OF VIENNA in 1653 marked the limit of Ottoman expansion (an earlier siege had failed in 1529). By mid-July the city was encircled and a continual bombardment was kept up against its walls (*above*, bottom left). During the next two months a large Austrian army with German and Polish allies reached Vienna and on 12 September the decisive battle was fought, ending in the defeat of the Turks.

THE CLASSICAL OTTOMAN EMPIRE faced its greatest challenges along its eastern border with Persia, while it also sought to extend its interests across the Caucasus. A miniature of 1582 (*opposite*) shows a cavalry encampment in Georgia.

learning. With Constantinople (or Istanbul) in hand, the House of Osman was bold enough to challenge the other great Muslim powers, including Safavid Persia and Mamluk Egypt. During the short reign of Selim I (1512–20), most of what is now the Middle East and North Africa as far as Algiers were incorporated into the empire. When Selim defeated the Mamluks in 1516 and 1517 and established his dominion over Mecca and Medina, he could convincingly claim leadership of the Muslim world. Süleyman, Selim's successor, took the next step and assumed the title of caliph.

Military historians have often assumed unfairly that the empire's military edge was based on numbers and sheer ferocity. Throughout the early modern period, field battles were not all that common, but where they did take place, superior Ottoman tactics and a highly disciplined, professional infantry, the legendary Janissaries, usually won the day. At the Battle of Mohaćs in 1526, for example, firearm-wielding Janissaries and field artillery decimated a Hungarian army of feudal knights. As one historian has put it, the battle saw 'the destruction of a medieval army by an early modern one'.[4] In terms of tactics and technology, the Ottomans kept abreast of changes chiefly by learning from their enemies. During a protracted struggle against the Kingdom of Hungary during the 1440s, the Ottomans were quick enough in adopting Hungarian military technology to blunt their opponents' military edge and emerge victorious: in this case it was cannons and mobile fortresses.[5] The Ottomans promptly became masters in the manufacture and use of large cannons, which gave them the means to breach the great walls of Constantinople in 1453. Fortresses dominated early modern warfare, and more often than not the Ottomans were tenaciously besieging towns and cities along their frontier lines using heavy artillery, siege towers, mangonels and tunnelling. During its classical phase the empire also demonstrated unmatched sophistication when it came to mobilization and provisioning. It created the most efficient fiscal mechanisms for funding imperial campaigns, while field manoeuvres, as one expert puts it, were a '*tour de force* of administrative precision and finesse'.[6]

Until recently, historians believed that the Ottoman political order assumed its classical form in the period between Mehmet II and Süleyman (1451–1566), but not unlike the feudal order in Europe, one is hard-pressed to find a precise moment when that system functioned in its ideal form. Discussion of some

THE IMPERIAL HAREM was an important institution in Ottoman political life, but as it was closed off to outsiders much about it remained a mystery. Ingres' *Turkish Bath*, however, belongs to the realm of pure fantasy, shedding no light on the harem but revealing much about the western European erotic imagination.

of these institutions in their designated 'classical' form, however, provides ample illustration of the characteristic resourcefulness that made the Ottomans so distinctive.

Perhaps the most striking feature of the classical Ottoman state was the immense concentration of power in the hands of the sultan. In contrast to states elsewhere in Europe and Asia, the classical Ottoman political system functioned without a landed aristocracy or nobility. Rather, ministers, bureaucrats, provincial administrators and the elite soldiery were recruited from a well-trained population of slaves. The highest officials, including the grand vizier, were essentially the sultan's possessions, or *kuls*. The main source of *kuls* was the *devshirme*, a child levy imposed on Christian families, whereby healthy males were recruited and raised to be Muslims and were trained in the arts of warfare or government service. Prisoners of war were another source of *kuls*, but it was the *devshirme* that provided the most reliable and eager recruits for the Janissaries, the most vital component of the classical Ottoman army. The *sipahis*, the sultan's elite cavalry force, were also totally beholden to the sultan, for they were recipients of land grants or *timars* that were conditional on service. *Timars* were not unlike feudal fiefdoms in that they gave *sipahis* the freedom to commit their energies to warfare, but *timars* remained the sultan's personal property and could not be inherited. As such, the system, which was an adaptation of Byzantine and Seljuk feudal traditions, worked against the formation of regional power bases.

The entire system was designed to give the ruler untrammelled authority, and no measure secured this more brutally than unigeniture. Upon the death of the sovereign, the male siblings, and therefore potential rivals, of the anointed successor were put to death. Unigeniture, however, was too callous to be a viable method of succession in a civilized society. This heart-rending and unpopular practice ended in 1595, after the execution of nineteen young princes appeared to cause a mass outcry in the capital.[7]

This system was quite novel in many respects, but it did not provide the basis for the empire's long-term viability. As imperial administration became increasingly complicated and required more specialized government and military expertise, the *devshirme* proved an increasingly inadequate source of talent. In Süleyman's later years, one begins to see much greater involvement in government affairs from members of the imperial household, namely mothers, sisters, daughters and their husbands. In the seventeenth century, elite families of independent means also became important pools of recruitment in government service, and as the *timar* system became unworkable provincial nobilities re-emerged. The *sipahis* and the *kuls* who were recruited for the Janissaries and the sultan's bureaucracy eventually found ways of circumventing a recruitment system that denied them a chance to bequeath wealth and status to their progeny. The *devshirme* was formally abolished by 1704, and although the Janissaries remained prominent in Istanbul's political life, they had long ceased to be the sultan's elite military force.

AN APPROACH TO DEMOCRACY came partly in response to pressure from Western Europe. The first Turkish parliament opened in 1876 with the express purpose of giving all citizens of the empire the same rights under the law. However, the very next year, Sultan Abdülhamit took a step backwards when he restored autocracy.

THE CHEEKY CHICK.

ALEXANDER THE LITTLE. "MY! WHAT A ROW I'M MAKING!!"

'THE CHEEKY CHICK' is Bulgaria and Romania emerging from an egg called 'Treaty of Berlin' laid by Turkey.

According to contemporaries and later historians, the death of Süleyman the Magnificent signalled the beginning of Ottoman decline, but the empire remained as formidable on the world stage throughout the seventeenth century as it had been in its classical era. Rather, as Daniel Goffman has argued: 'The secret to Ottoman longevity… was not its legendary military, its loyal bureaucracy, its series of competent rulers, or a particular system of land tenure. Rather, it was its flexibility in dealing with its diverse society.'[8] As the empire expanded and governance became more complicated, and as the costs of war became ever more exorbitant, state administration, revenue-raising and recruitment methods were transformed accordingly. Autocracy increasingly made way for a more differentiated and decentralized political order.

Such suppleness was vital when it came to governing a vast, heterogeneous society. The characteristic Ottoman approach was to accommodate the interests of the conquered without compromising the power of the state. The House of Osman wished to be seen as benevolent and just. As a rule, newly conquered subjects were left in possession of their lands, and non-Muslims (*dhimmi*) were free to observe their faith on condition that they paid a head tax. Despite its sustained commitment to *gaza*, the Ottoman state took it as given that it ruled a heterogeneous world. The spiritual heads of the various religious communities were accorded official status and required to take up residence in the capital. As for provincial administration, versatility was the key. Rather than impose a single, standard administrative and legal order across the empire, the Ottomans took into account indigenous traditions so that local interests and rights were made part of the new imperial order. The result was a complicated patchwork of administrative and legal systems, but the effect was to make the sultan appear the defender of sectional interests.

The first inklings of imperial decline were felt during the Battle of Vienna in 1683, the Ottomans' first major defeat on land since 1402. More portentous still was the Peace of Karlowitz in 1699, when the Ottomans were forced to sign a peace treaty and cede territory to Austria. The empire was no longer invincible on land, but it remained among the leading military powers until the 1770s. Wholesale reforms to the taxation system moderated the effects of mushrooming military costs, which meant the Ottomans survived a global military-fiscal crisis that precipitated the collapse of so many other states and empires.[9]

DECLINE AND RENEWAL, c.1770–1908

It was in the latter decades of the eighteenth century that the empire slipped dramatically behind its major European counterparts. An economic depression blighted the second half of the century, as fiscal reform and cheap Western goods devastated Ottoman commerce and manufacturing. Just as ruinous were the crushingly expensive and disruptive wars fought against Catherine the Great's Russia and Revolutionary France. Foreign armies were now capable of threatening Istanbul itself. In 1774, the Russians converged on the capital and forced the Ottoman government, described in official correspondence as 'the Sublime Porte', to sign the first of many humiliating treaties. The Treaty of Küçük-Kaynarca recognized Russia's patronage of Ottoman Christian communities, which was interpreted as a licence to interfere in internal Ottoman affairs.

After Küçük-Kaynarca, the very survival of the empire became a long-running issue within European diplomatic circles, where the main concern was how the division of its territories might affect inter-state power relations. The entire globe was now vulnerable to the machinations of Europe's 'Great Powers', which had developed the political, technological and economic means to completely alter the balance of global power. European economic interests had developed the means of tapping new and seemingly unlimited sources of energy to achieve unprecedented rates of economic growth and capital accumulation. European states were also applying scientific principles to rationalize political, social and fiscal systems in order to mobilize resources efficiently and effectively. Throughout the nineteenth century, European political and economic might was unassailable, and erstwhile major powers such as China, Persia and the Ottoman Empire found such strength overwhelming. The question is not why the Ottoman Empire declined, but how it survived into the twentieth century.

During the nineteenth century, only Meiji Japan managed to bridge the widening gap between the Western (European and North American) powers and the rest of the world. The Ottomans sought to do the same by modernizing its entire political order. With characteristic versatility, the Porte set about reforming government, military and legal institutions by drawing eclectically from various European models – by the century's end, Japan too had become an inspirational paradigm. During the nineteenth century and through to the eve of the First World War, the chief aim was to transform the empire into something akin to a modern nation-state, which involved developing a patriotic bond between state and society not unlike that which had mobilized Revolutionary France. By the beginning of the twentieth century, these attempts to modernize the empire appeared to be bearing fruit.

The impetus for reform was driven by the litany of defeats and territorial losses that followed Küçük-Kaynarca. By 1792, Russia had conquered the Crimea and Georgia, and it made further territorial gains in 1829. In 1830, Greece won its independence and the French occupied Algeria. In the meantime, the Porte had lost control over most of its provinces, including much of Anatolia and the Balkans, to regional power magnates. Egypt effectively functioned as an independent state from 1805 to 1882. In 1831, an Egyptian army under Muhammad Ali, an Ottoman governor who made himself the supreme authority in this rich province, defeated the Ottomans at the Battle of Konya. As the prestige of the empire diminished, regional, religious and ethnic groups began to question its legitimacy. One reaction came in the form of Islamic revivalist movements, most notably the Wahhabis in western Arabia, who did not recognize Ottoman authority and threatened its control over Mecca and Medina.

THE DISMEMBERMENT of the Ottoman Empire was made inevitable by the Congress of Berlin in 1878. Mehmet Ali, the Turkish representative, looks on powerlessly at the extreme right while the great powers settle his country's fate. From left to right: Karolyi of Austria, Gorchakov of Russia (seated), Disraeli of Great Britain (with cane), Andrássy of Hungary, and Bismarck of Germany and Shuvalov of Russia (shaking hands).

By the late 19th century, Istanbul was fast becoming a modern city. Much of its burgeoning population was seen increasingly in Western attire, reading newspapers, and subscribing to bourgeois leisure pursuits such as cycling, promenading and the cinema.

Another reaction came from educated Christian elites in the Balkans who, inspired by the Enlightenment and the example of the French Revolution, called for national self-determination and the removal of the Ottoman yoke. An alliance between such intellectuals and powerful Christian bandit chiefs led to the Greek War of Independence in 1821, the first successful secessionist rebellion in the Balkans.

Selim III (1789–1807), the first sultan not to imprison foreign diplomats if their monarchs misbehaved, was also the first to champion political reform.[10] Over the next century, Ottoman reformers waged a difficult campaign to create a modern state by streamlining the empire's vast and complex array of administrative and legal systems. The centralization of political power would also take generations of struggle to realize. Reforming central government was somewhat easier. The transition from the *ancien régime* to a modern system entailed a radically expanded government and public service. Between the 1790s and the beginning of the twentieth century Ottoman administration expanded: the number of bureaucrats rose from 2,000 to 35,000, and the number of public servants grew to half a million. Secular education rather than personal connections became the most vital qualifications for employment in state departments.

Under Selim III, who witnessed the power unleashed by such a comparatively modest-sized state as revolutionary France, the first attempts were made to reform the existing ruling order, but it was Mahmut II (1808–39) who started the process of creating modern institutions. Between 1835 and 1839, central government was divided into ministries and departments. Mahmut's reign set the stage for the so-called Tanzimat period (1839–76), an era defined by its 'beneficial reforms' (*Tanzimat-i Hayriye*). These included the promotion of legal equality for all the sultan's subjects, regardless of religious affiliation, and the introduction of constitutional government, including a parliamentary system. In the meantime, Mahmut succeeded in reasserting authority over most of the Ottoman provinces: Albania (1822), Iraq and Kurdistan (1831–38), Libya (1835), the Hijaz (1840).

Resistance to reform, however, proved formidable. In 1807 Selim III was overthrown by reactionary forces that included the Janissaries, but not before supporters of reform had been dragged into the capital's ancient hippodrome and slaughtered. The Janissaries in particular, who took a recalcitrant position on any reforms to the military, posed a constant threat to the sultanate. In 1826 Mahmut II suppressed yet another Janissary revolt and disbanded the entire corps.

Given that Ottoman society comprised a vast and heterogeneous collection of communities, each defined by particular rights and privileges, government reforms were often a source of deep resentment. For many Muslims, the most difficult reform to stomach was the granting of equal legal status to non-Muslims, which involved a transgression of Muslim sharia law. However, reformers were keen to win the loyalty of their large religious minorities, particularly in the Balkans where Christians in fact constituted a majority, and which were therefore susceptible to secessionist mobilization. By the Tanzimat period, the non-Muslim minorities were organized into confessional orders or *millets*, which functioned as states within the state, as each group held responsibility for organizing tax revenue, administering justice in accordance with their own laws, and overseeing such services as education. The reforms aimed to abolish this segregated system and create a comprehensive Ottoman citizenship. While Muslims resented the threat to their superior status, Greeks in particular feared the loss of particular rights and privileges, especially exemption from military service.

The constitutional agenda came unstuck in 1877, when Abdülhamit II (1876–1909), with the backing of most ministers, returned to a more autocratic political system. The loss of much of the Balkans to Christian separatist movements in 1878 saw 'Ottomanism' make way for 'Islamism' – the new regime focused on its Muslim subjects (e.g. ethnic Turks, Kurds, Arabs, Tartars, Circassians, Albanians) as the foundation of a rejuvenated state. In the meantime, state modernization and centralization continued. By the end of his reign, Abdülhamit had secured greater control of the empire's human and material resources than any of his predecessors. The army, local administration, public education, communications (steam shipping, and road, rail and telegraph networks) and palace administration had been significantly rationalized.

Ottoman society and its economy under Abdülhamit also began to display many of the hallmarks of modernization. By 1900, railways and steamships had eclipsed animal-driven transport and sailing craft. Between the 1830s and 1912, Istanbul had grown from 375,000 to 1,125,000 inhabitants, Izmir from 110,000 to 300,000, Salonica from 70,000 to 150,000, while Beirut began with 10,000 in 1800 and ended with 150,000 by 1914.[11] Urban expansion was largely a consequence of the commercialization of agriculture and the dramatic expansion of domestic and external trade. Having suffered heavily from cheap European imports in the period 1800–70, the Ottoman manufacturing sector enjoyed a significant revival. Factories proliferated in and around urban centres, especially Istanbul, Salonica, Izmir and Beirut, as did workers' organizations and labour protests. In 1908 Istanbul had 285 printing houses, a vibrant critical press that lampooned politicians and satirized modern life, including the effects of Western dress, automobile fatalities and the disorienting effects of Western clock-driven conceptions of time.[12] Prior to the First World War, youths in Salonica and other major centres had taken to Western-style dance, operettas, bicycles and the cinema.[13] Ottoman society remained overwhelmingly rural at the beginning of the twentieth century, but the habits of urban bourgeois society also showed unmistakeable patterns of change not unlike those found elsewhere in Europe.

SOURCES OF INSTABILITY

However one might interpret the pace of modernization over the nineteenth century, Ottoman standing in relation to the European powers continued to diminish. By the end of Abdülhamit's reign in 1909, its predicament seemed bleaker than ever. Whereas Japan had developed the wherewithal to become a predatory colonial power in its own right and to defeat Russia decisively in 1905, the Ottomans had in the meantime conceded most of their European and African territories. With Great Power support, the Serbs, Montenegrins and Romanians won formal independence in 1878. The Treaty of Berlin also granted Bulgaria autonomy, while Austria and Britain gained nominal control over Bosnia-Herzegovina and Cyprus, respectively. France established a protectorate over Tunisia in 1881, and Britain occupied Egypt the following year. The empire experienced this dramatic loss of territory even though it was a nominal member of the Concert of Europe, which was meant to maintain a balance of power on the continent but which effectively assumed that Ottoman interests were dispensable. After all, the Ottoman Empire was deemed Europe's 'Sick Man', whose death was only a matter of time.

Territorial contraction was not the only source of humiliation. In 1878, Abdülhamit complained bitterly that Britain 'appeared intent to use and administer the Sublime Porte as its own possession and colony'.[14] In 1881, Ottoman finances were placed under a Public Debt Administration overseen by Britain and France, and managed by Greek and Armenian intermediaries. Western capital investment increased significantly in the last two decades of the nineteenth century and, as happened with China, the empire was divided into spheres of economic influence. The same powers guaranteed economic and legal privileges (called 'capitulations') to Christian merchants, which caused much resentment among their Muslim counterparts.

To be sure, Great Power rivalries were such that no single European state was allowed to control the strategically sensitive Near East. For the time being at least, the region was best left in Ottoman hands. The empire therefore survived on European sufferance, not unlike Chakri Siam or Qing China. Russian ambitions to attain warm-water ports, particularly Istanbul, were constantly thwarted by British determination to keep the Near East, its gateway to India, out of rival hands. And yet, the same Concert of Europe was open to piecemeal dissection of Ottoman territories when it suited the interests of more powerful states. Moreover, the empire was vulnerable to European public opinion, which assumed that Muslims, and Turks in particular, were barbarians who persecuted Christians. Occasionally, public opinion influenced foreign policy against the empire, as happened when the Great Powers intervened to resuscitate the Greek War of Independence in 1827, or when British prime minister Gladstone exploited public outrage following the massacre of Bulgarian civilians in 1876 (the so-called 'Bulgarian Horrors') to win an election in 1880.

That the empire's welfare hinged on shifts in domestic and international politics in Europe inevitably engendered deep insecurities in Istanbul. So too did the loyalties of minority elites. Fears of nationalist awakenings among the Greeks, for example, were intensified by the rapid expansion in the latter half of the nineteenth century of Greek educational and cultural institutions, many sponsored by the Greek government. Abdülhamit's decision to promote Muslim interests and sanction the massacre of Armenian communities in 1894–96, in reprisal for the actions of Armenian nationalists, reflected a growing view among Muslim elites that Christian minorities were a security liability. Of particular concern was the propensity of nationalist secessionists to induce Great Power intervention by publicizing and, in Ottoman eyes at least, exaggerating

persecution of Christian minorities. In the first decade of the twentieth century, many advocates of reform became increasingly interested in an ethnically specific, namely Turkish, basis for reconstituting the empire. Renewed interest in Turkish heritage and culture, led by intellectuals such as Ziya Gökalp and Yusuf Akçura, led to the cultivation of Turkish, as opposed to Muslim, consciousness, and thus formed the seedbed of Turkish nationalism.

The extent to which ordinary Ottomans contributed to this nationalist awakening is a difficult question. Sectarian conflict certainly increased in the nineteenth century. National revolutions in the Balkans, which were explicitly anti-Turkish and anti-Muslim, and which involved the persecution and expulsion of Balkan Muslims, inevitably fuelled animosities towards Christians within other Ottoman territories. So too did the estimated 5–7 million Muslims who fled or emigrated from Russia during the nineteenth century through to 1913. In 1860, Lebanon was the scene of a major sectarian bloodbath, principally involving Druze and Maronite Christians. The Armenian Genocide (1915) was preceded by mass killings in 1894–96 and 1909, while violent exchanges between Christians and Muslims took place intermittently on Crete between 1841 and 1908. Yet it is important to note that the vast majority of Ottoman Muslims, Christians and Jews continued to coexist peacefully in this period. More characteristic of the period were the vibrant, cosmopolitan towns of the eastern Mediterranean littoral, where communities of all religions interacted and prospered. Across

A MASS DEMONSTRATION in Istanbul during the July Crisis, 1914. Although the demonstrators in this photograph are calling for intervention on the side of Germany, it is almost impossible to gage broader popular opinion on the matter. Needless to say, intervention proved to be fatal to the empire.

northern and western Anatolia, Muslims and Christians continued to celebrate many religious holidays together, venerated the same saints and sought miraculous cures from the same shrines. Nationalism had barely begun to seep into mass consciousness at the beginning of the twentieth century. Subjects within the Arab-speaking provinces continued to accept the legitimacy of the empire until at least the First World War. Most Greeks and Armenians in Anatolia, minorities living among an overwhelmingly Muslim majority, stood to lose a great deal if intercommunal relations deteriorated. Hence they were not particularly receptive to separatist nationalist ideas.[15] Relations, however, did deteriorate irretrievably during the empire's last, war-ravaged decade (1912–22), when millions of Muslims and Christians were persecuted and displaced by virtue of their religious identities.

END OF EMPIRE, 1908–22

Turkish nationalism emerged near the very end of Ottoman history. In 1908, the Young Turk movement, composed mainly of Western-educated military officers and bureaucrats, whose aim was to rescue the empire from imminent collapse by accelerating the political reform process, removed Abdülhamit from power and restored constitutional government, including the parliamentary system. Despite their name, the Young Turks did not constitute a nationalist movement as such, even if most of the leaders looked to ethnic Turks as their natural constituency. Rather, the Committee for Union and Progress (CUP), the movement's political arm, put Ottomanism back on the agenda. As an early Young Turk publication affirmed: 'We have tried… to defend the rights and the interests of all Ottomans. We have never treated Armenians and Greeks differently from Turks'.[16]

By aligning with Germany, the Ottoman Empire determined its fate. Kaiser and sultan are here shown to be sharing a carriage in Istanbul.

5400

By January 1913, however, the CUP had installed itself as a dictatorship and had abandoned Ottomanism. Political inexperience, an unstable parliamentary chamber and widespread resistance to its centralization policies frustrated their political agenda. Particularly disappointing was the reaction of minority elites, who, contrary to the spirit of Ottomanism, insisted on keeping their privileges. Bemused by such perceived ingratitude, the CUP leadership looked more and more to its ethnic Turkish core, though it was a series of disastrous military conflicts between 1910 and 1913 that set the Young Turks thinking seriously about an ethnically homogeneous state. Revolts in the Yemen (1910) and Albania (1910 and 1911) showed that not even all Muslim groups were reliable, but it was the loss of most of the empire's remaining European territories during the Balkan War of 1912 that proved the real turning point. Bulgarian troops came perilously close to Istanbul, while hundreds of thousands of Muslim refugees from Macedonia and Bulgaria poured into Anatolia. In Anatolia itself, Muslims began openly to resent the presence of Christian neighbours, as shown by mass participation in boycotts against Greek businesses. Most Anatolian Greeks saw the writing on the wall and began emigrating to Greece and Russia. By 1913, the Ottoman Empire no longer saw itself as a body combining many religions, and regarded the removal of significant Christian minorities, especially Greeks and Armenians, as vital to imperial security.

It is not altogether clear why the CUP committed the empire to war on the side of Germany and Austria in 1914. An alliance with Germany, the most powerful European state, must have seemed to promise the best chance of reclaiming lost territories and rebuilding the empire. It proved a fatal decision. The empire was attacked from all sides. A poorly conceived British invasion via the Gallipoli peninsula was successfully repulsed, but the Russians penetrated deep into northeastern Anatolia, and the British gradually seized control of the Arab provinces. The Ottoman Empire held on to the very end of the war, but the government had lost control of much of the countryside to bandit groups, whose ranks were swelled by deserters. Minority groups were removed from strategically sensitive areas, and many died in forced marches. The war provided the government, which was effectively run by a small coterie of military strongmen, with an excuse to remove the Armenian population from the vicinity of Russia and thus extinguish their territorial claims to eastern Anatolia. Over a million civilians died through forced marches, massacres and starvation.[17]

When Germany sought an armistice in the autumn of 1918, the Ottomans had no choice but to do the same. The peace imposed by the Allies was punitive in the extreme: the bulk of Anatolia, including Istanbul, was to be partitioned among the victorious powers. But remnants of the Ottoman army regrouped under the leadership of Kemal Mustafa, the hero of Gallipoli, and, with mass support, his Nationalist Army reclaimed Anatolia as an independent Turkish homeland. The Nationalists crushed a Greek expeditionary force in August 1922 and forced the British to forfeit their occupation of Istanbul in October. The Treaty of Lausanne of 1923 guaranteed the territorial boundaries that the Republic of Turkey possesses to this day, while it also stipulated a population exchange with Balkan states, especially Greece, in order to make Anatolia and Eastern Thrace more Turkish.

Ironically, it was the Turks themselves, not the Great Powers, who formally extinguished the Ottoman Empire. Kemal Mustafa, now known as 'Atatürk' (father of the Turks), who by this stage enjoyed incontestable authority, took that momentous step on 1 November 1922. In Atatürk's mind, and that of many Nationalists, modernization had by now assumed even greater importance than the empire itself. One of the more enduring and stable multi-ethnic states in world history, the Ottoman Empire, was extinguished at the stroke of a pen.

LED BY MUSTAFA KEMAL, the victor of Gallipoli, a revolution abolished the sultanate in 1918. Kemal, under the name Atatürk, became president and devoted himself to a programme of modernization. He replaced Arabic script with Latin, prohibited polygamy, championed Western dress and gave women equal rights with men.

Spain: The Genealogy of Modern Colonialism

JOSEP FRADERA

THE PROFIT MOTIVE has always been an ingredient in the foundation of empires. The Netherlandish artist Theodore de Bry never went to the New World, but his picture of the treatment endured by the natives at the hands of the conquistadors is not lacking in compassion (*opposite*).

UNDER CHARLES V (*below*), Spain became an empire. Between 1519 and 1533 he presided over the conquest of Mexico and Peru, which made Spain the richest country in the Western world.

THE MONARCHY OF THE KINGDOMS OF Castile, Navarre and Aragon became a genuine empire – in the terms of Roman and Carolingian imperial tradition – with the reign of King Carlos I of Spain (1516–56) – better known as Charles V after he had been elected Holy Roman Emperor.[1] The political entity that would constitute the backbone of Carlos' state, the kingdom of Castile, thereby committed itself to major expansion on the other side of the Atlantic, on the islands and mainland around the Caribbean Sea. The proclamation of Carlos as emperor coincided with and was inextricably linked with the formation of an enormous zone of expansion that would develop to an extraordinary extent in the Americas and Philippines during his reign and that of his son, Felipe II (1556–98), who did not succeed his father as Holy Roman Emperor. The discovery of America by Columbus in 1492 was soon followed by the successful campaigns of Cortes (1519–28) in Mexico and Pizarro (1532–33) in Peru. The Philippine Islands were acquired shortly afterwards (1564–71).

The conquest of new territories and the subjugation of their populations, in a world that had been totally unknown to Europeans, can be seen as the prolongation of the period of the Catholic Spanish rulers' expansion in the interior of the Iberian peninsula. This historical process of the destruction of the Muslim state of Al-Andalus in southern and eastern Spain is traditionally known as the *Reconquista*, a term that reflects an uncritical acceptance of the ideological assumptions and cultural justifications used by Castilian, Portuguese and Catalan-Aragonese rulers alike. The process in fact represented not so much a 'reconquest' as a conquest of territories and peoples by the social groups revolving around the Iberian monarchies, who had for centuries been pushing back the frontiers of their own territory at the expense of the Islamic caliphate of Cordoba.[2]

This conquest extended from the thirteenth century to the capture of the city of Granada in 1492 – the same year that Christopher Columbus set sail for the Americas. After centuries of neighbourliness between Catholics and Muslims in Iberia – albeit a cohabitation not exempt from marauding initiated by both sides

– the Christian kingdoms of the north set about systematically conquering new territories, thereby moving the frontier of their realm further and further south. At the heart of these military operations lay a desire to capture new land where they could set up their supporters as vassals, while they dominated and subordinated the local Muslim populations.[3] In most cases, the conquered population of Andalusia was inexorably wiped out, while the Muslim peasants of the glittering prizes of the Catalan-Aragonese monarchs – Majorca and the other Balearic Islands – also virtually disappeared within a generation of the Spanish conquest. Those who did survive were reduced in numbers, dispossessed of the lands that they had farmed for centuries, and forced to scrape by on the fringes of society. The area they had previously occupied was transferred to armed bands as part of a complex process of constructing large feudal estates, replacing old sorts of farming and land-holding and, at the same time, forming a new type of peasant society. The remaining population of Muslim Andalusia that survived in marginal enclaves tolerated by the Christian sovereigns was then brought to the verge of extinction by campaigns of extermination such as that in Granada's Alpujarra Mountains (1568–71), before the Muslims were finally expelled by Felipe III in 1609. The modern concept of 'ethnic cleansing' was thus created on the late-medieval stage in southern Spain – an indisputable fact that is very difficult to incorporate into the traditional narrative of Spanish history.

The Christian kingdoms' policy of advancing their frontiers in Iberia provides the immediate precedent for the conquest of the Americas. In this context, Patricia Seed has shown how the formula of *requerimiento* that sealed the submission of the conquered American peoples traced its origins to an earlier Arab-Muslim tradition.[4] As in so many other aspects of overseas expansion – the rush for the precious metals of silver and gold, the policy of massive

CULTURES IN COLLISION: Francisco Pizarro meets Atahualpa, the last Inca emperor, in Cajamarca, Peru in 1532. A convincingly realistic mosaic was made in the 19th century to commemorate the event on the same site.

enslavement of African peoples, the intensive deployment of military and maritime technology around the world – the Portuguese were the pioneers, and the Castilians and Aragonese followed in their footsteps. The military and social capacities of the group of Christian kingdoms centred on Castile, however, were greater than those of the Portuguese. It was indeed both the limits reached by the Portuguese in Africa, and the swift conquest and domination of the Canary Islands – along with the messianic impulse of the Genoese captain Christopher Columbus during Spain's 'Golden Age' – that led the Spanish to open up a new colonial frontier in the Atlantic, considered by some a short cut to Japan and China, and by others the road to possessions in hitherto unknown territories.[5] The first colonization of Hispaniola (the island now shared by the Dominican Republic and Haiti) opened the door to a new colonial frontier in an extraordinary intensification of a centuries-old impulse to Spanish expansion. This expansionism would be recast in the light of the ideas and innovations of the Renaissance, but its origins lay centuries in the past, in the conquest of the Iberian peninsula and the Mediterranean.

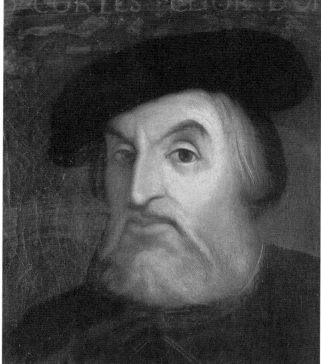

HERNAN CORTES, who, with a handful of Spanish soldiers, conquered and enslaved the mighty Aztec empire.

SPAIN IN THE AMERICAS

The foundations of the Spanish Empire were laid in the Americas and in the Atlantic world. This statement must nevertheless be qualified in two important respects. First, the Spanish monarchy of the sixteenth and seventeenth centuries boasted enormous possessions in Europe itself. Moreover, its commitment to the future of Roman Catholicism, in the face of the Protestant Reformation, as well as the crucial role of the Spanish Habsburgs in holding back the continuous expansion of the Turkish Empire in the Mediterranean, imposed a heavy military, political and financial burden on the 'Hispanic monarchy', with a subsequent dramatic impact on Castilian society.[6] The second caveat is equally important. Spain's imperial aspirations in the sixteenth century were not restricted to the vast American territories it had recently discovered and colonized, but were driven by a desire for world domination – which explains why the Spanish monarchy never renounced its expansionist intentions in North Africa or its plans to subjugate and Christianize Asia, including hopes for the conquest of China from its base in the Philippines.[7] The fact that such global pretensions were finally cut down to far more modest ambitions should not obscure the contemporary perspective concerning the scope of the Spanish Empire's self-appointed historic mission.

The empire's huge dimensions by the late sixteenth century – possessions in Europe ranging from the Low Countries to southern Italy, colonies covering most of Central and South America, some of the largest islands in the Caribbean, the Philippine Islands and toeholds in Africa – explain the characteristics of its internal organization. This motley collection of constitutional arrangements has been defined by John Elliott as a 'composite monarchy', i.e. a system in which the various components maintained their own constitutions, at least until the arrival on the throne of the Bourbons in early eighteenth-century Spain.[8] The decades of the 1640s and 1650s were particularly critical, as some of the minor possessions defied the authority of the monarchy in Madrid, creating a conflict that resulted in separation between Portugal and Spain, and serious altercations in the Castilian-ruled areas of Catalonia (in northeastern Iberia) and Naples (in southern Italy). Another surprising aspect of the Spanish Empire was the position of the American dominions and the Philippines within the framework of this global system, or more precisely their lack of any constitutional system or representative government, and their utter administrative dependence on the institutions of the Crown of Castile. This unique position can be explained by three significant factors. First, there were complex disputes within both the royal court and the Spanish church as to the very legality of the conquest of the American colonies.[9] This debate, far-reaching in doctrinal terms in accordance with the precepts firmly established by the late-medieval societies of Iberia, revolved around not only the legitimacy of the conquest and of the subjugation of the native American peoples but also the crucial question of whether the indigenous peoples could be enslaved. Moreover, a vital stage in the construction of the empire coincided with the internal conflict between the monarchy and the main Castilian cities. The Crown chose to govern the overseas territories of Castile from the metropole (a decision that led to the development of a wide-ranging body of legislation, the *Leyes de Indias*), and to set up a series of municipal and politico-judicial institutions (the *audiencias*) rooted in Castilian tradition. Finally, the critical circumstances surrounding the creation of the empire in the Americas made it advisable for the monarchy to opt for direct control over those vast and remote possessions, resulting in the design of a distinctive administrative structure without precedent in the Spanish Crown's European territories.

The creation of Spanish America never followed a predetermined plan. The Caribbean was conquered first (1492–96), then followed the Aztec Empire of Mexico and Central America (1519–29), and finally the Inca Empire of Quito, Peru and Chile then fell into Spanish hands (1531–34). The conquest was basically the initiative of the so-called *huestes*, small armed gangs financed by capitalists on the Iberian peninsula, who were attracted by the far from illusory prospect of rapid enrichment or, failing that, of domination of the local population and hopes for future wealth. The Crown and the administrative personnel – royal, civil and ecclesiastical – arrived only at a later stage of colonization, after the conquest of foreign territories by these *huestes*. The religious or cultural justifications advanced for the conquest were hastily improvised in the wake of this hurried expansion of territory.

This decentralized model of expansion, in which Crown rule followed in the wake of private parties' conquest, destruction and appropriation of Native American lands and peoples, was developed by means of limitless violence, as

CORTES ENTERS the Mexican capital in triumph – a near-contemporary European painting (*opposite*) that includes subjugated Aztecs on the left.

COLUMBUS NEVER REALIZED that he had discovered a new continent. The year after his return to Europe this woodcut (*below*) tried to illustrate his report. In the first picture his ship cruises past an imaginary castle; in the second (captioned *Insula hyspana*) the explorer is greeted by naked maidens; the third, with the same identification, shows a small town.

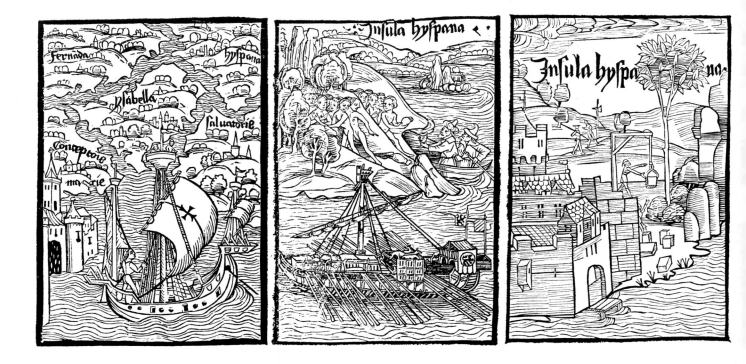

particularly exemplified by the Peruvian Civil War (1544–48).[10] The underlying dynamic behind these types of armed conflict was simply a struggle between the Crown and the various social, civil and religious participants in the initial conquest – via the system of the *encomienda* (or the surrender of Indians on condition that they converted to Christianity) for the appropriation of the greatest possible number of natives. Over time, and in the face of the news that came back of the rampant 'destruction of the Indies', the monarchy tried to introduce certain restrictions on the use of the *encomienda*, particularly to the financial obligations imposed on the subjugated Indians, enforced labour and the hereditary transfer of concessions.[11] In this crucial struggle, which ended with the defeat of the *encomenderos* in Peru and Mexico, the Crown's intention was to introduce a long-term plan for exploitation, rather than to end colonization itself. The possibility of freeing the native population from the burden of supporting the colonial structure was not envisaged even by a radical clergyman who supported the bishop of Chiapas, Bartolomé de las Casas, or by groups of the Catholic Church most committed to a kind of 'theocratic republic' in which the Indians would be placed under the protection of priests, out of the reach of the avaricious colonialists.

These crucial debates between different colonial actors were prompted by the demographic catastrophe unleashed by the American conquest. The Caribbean was dramatically emptied of its original inhabitants, who preserved only a marginal presence on some of the smaller islands. The West Indies would later be repopulated by contingents of Europeans and Africans – the latter victims of a massive enforced emigration that continued for centuries. This extermination of the Native American population on the islands was then implacably reproduced on the mainland, in a process of what the ethno-historian Alfred Crosby has defined as 'the Columbian exchange', a genocide of unprecedented proportions that, though unplanned, was nevertheless not at all accidental.[12] In little more than eighty years, the American populations plummeted. In Central America, the population declined in proportions of up to 20:1, while in the lands of the Inca Empire it resisted somewhat better, with differentials of 10:1 and 6:1 after the conquest, due to the greater difficulties in transmitting germs in the cold areas of the high plateau.[13] The collapse of the indigenous population, however, was not solely the result of contagion from epidemic diseases new to the Indians (such as influenza, measles, smallpox and whooping cough); social and psychological factors also played a role, along with sheer overwork under colonial coercion. The impact of this depopulation on the emergence and formation of colonial society was undoubtedly decisive to the future of the Americas.

The decimation of the Native American peoples marked the end of the pre-Columbian societies, as their economic, social and cultural structures were unable to withstand the catastrophe. A new colonial society was born from this massive destruction and the interlinking of the (now reconciled) objectives of the official imperial state and the early bands of private colonizers. It was also shaped by the capacity of indigenous society to resist and adapt to the demands of their new masters. Nothing would ever be the same again, as the societies that came into being were rooted in this dramatic fault-line of death, displacement and subordination. As Carlos Sempat Assadourian has explained, the most dynamic factor in the emerging colonial society was the booming mining economy of the two great Spanish viceroyalties of Peru and Mexico, in forms that accommodated the most rational alternative to the reduction in indigenous manpower.[14] Technical advances in silver mining were decisive, particularly the process known as 'amalgamation', which involved separating the mineral ore from the gangue using mercury. A dynamic business sector quickly took shape on this new technological base, allowing the objectives of local economic development and the needs of the empire to dovetail.[15] In a quarter of a century, a new society was thereby forged, in which the large mining districts (best exemplified by Potosí in Peru) and the administrative centres (where most

DISEASE WIPED OUT more American Indians than the conquistadors. The Spaniards brought with them infections such as smallpox previously unknown to the inhabitants of the New World and against which they had developed no immunity.

D. Fr. BARTOLOME DE LAS CASA
Nació en 1474.   *Murió en 1566.*

of the population of European origin lived) established new forms of agriculture and domestic industry very different in organization and commercial outlook from those of the pre-Hispanic societies. Precious metals – and their export to the metropole – fuelled these networks: 181 tonnes of gold and 17,000 of silver, for example, arrived in Seville between 1500 and 1650.[16] Gold and silver then went on to be the nexus of Spain's relationship with the final destinations of these South American exports – several of the northern European countries and the great Asian societies, especially China.

In order to satisfy the growing demands for cheap labour in the mines, the imperial power subordinated the Native American population to the needs of the new sector in multiple ways. The best-known example is the Peruvian *mita*, a system of large-scale forced labour devised by Viceroy Toledo at the beginning of the 1570s. Herein lies the explanation of the paradox of a depleted native population serving the demands of a thriving imperial economy. Thanks to these financial and labour policies, most of Spain's administrative, economic and social organization was firmly in place in the New World by the late sixteenth century.[17] Many of these structures would remain in place two centuries later.

WAS THE SPANISH EMPIRE 'COLONIAL'?

One of the most enduring distortions of the nature of the Spanish overseas empire is the confusion between its institutional manifestations and its social foundations. For centuries, the basis of this transatlantic world of Europeans, Africans and Native Americans was justified by strong Catholic messianism. Whatever doubts the Spanish theologians may have initially voiced about the legitimacy of the conquest of colonies, these were quickly put aside in favour of the accumulation of Spanish subjects and Christian souls. Furthermore, the papal imprimatur for conquest enshrined in the Treaty of Tordesilhas of 1494 – which divided the Atlantic arena between Castile and Portugal – provided an additional justification to the *fait accompli* of the Spanish conquest. The intense messianism invoked by the Crown, and also by the religious orders and the Spanish church, furnished certainty about a divine mission incarnated in the will of the Spanish monarchs, and further confirmed by the hostility of France and the Protestant powers to Spanish expansion.

As Spanish imperial expansion progressed, the challenge of building institutions for such a vast domain came to the fore. The process that led to the *Recopilación de las Leyes de Indias* (1681) – the gargantuan task of collating thousands of edicts pertaining to colonial rule – provides an excellent indicator of the enormous legislative commitments arising from this 'paper empire'. The empire's political organization was derived from earlier foundations, even from pacts made with some of the indigenous peoples at the time of the conquest, but it had to respond to new requirements. Viceroyalties, military districts and governorships were established, but they had no relationship with each other and were solely answerable to the central bodies of the monarchy – primarily the Consejo de Indias, which formed the centre of this institutional mosaic. Within this political framework the *audiencias* were convened as the highest juridical-political authority. One of their functions was to act as a counterweight to the administrators appointed by the Crown, whether viceroys or the last *corregidor* (magistrate) of the Indians in a remote corner of Chile or Guatemala. The institutional structure overlapped in many respects with the ecclesiastical administration, from the bishoprics to the parishes and missions – the tentacles of a Church that depended on the monarch himself, by means of so-called

SPANISH DREAMS of infinite riches came true in Peru, where they exploited the gold and silver deposits for all they were worth. The greatest production from silver mines took place at Potosí (*right*: an impression by Theodore de Bry), where thousands of Indians toiled without rest.

royal patronage. The Castilian model of a political body assembling cities' representatives that legislated alongside the king was ruled out in the colonial world. Also out of the question was the possibility of granting some form of representation to the American territories, along the lines followed in the first British Empire. This option would come into play only with the crisis triggered by the Napoleonic invasion of Spain, which made it advisable to extend liberal political representation to the overseas territories and to authorize them to send parliamentary delegates to Spain.

A far from impartial assessment of the empire's institutional elements and the absurd assimilationism of imperial politics has led Spanish historians, paradoxically, to deny the 'colonial' nature of New Spain and the Philippines – a position bespeaking ridiculous wordplay emanating from a confused overlapping of different fields of study. It is true that for a long time the Spanish did not employ the Portuguese, English or French concepts of *feitorias*, 'plantations' or 'colonies' – they only started to use the term 'colonies', coined by the English and French, late in the eighteenth century, and even then solely with reference to sugar-producing possessions in the Caribbean. These semantic discrepancies can be explained quite simply by the fact that the Spanish chose to wait longer than other Europeans before calling things by their true name. It is also the case, however, that the Spanish Empire was based on a very tight economic organization aimed at enhancing the status of the metropole and its subjects, both at home and in overseas territories. This organization of the productive economy can nevertheless safely be termed 'colonial'. Furthermore, this colonial situation was imposed without debate or restraint on the indigenous peoples, whose best land, water and assets unfailingly ended up in the hands of Spaniards.

THERE WERE SOME CULTURAL EFFECTS from Spanish rule. The Dominican missionaries taught their flock to read and write using picture-books, including this catechism (*above*) of 1525–28.

Overleaf
EXPLOITATION ON THE LARGEST SCALE was the guiding principle of imperial Spain. In 1545 rich deposits of silver were discovered at Potosí, then part of Peru. For the next hundred years they were mined with tremendous energy, producing vast wealth for the Spanish Crown. A populous town was laid out on a grid plan, containing a government house, town hall, cathedral and royal mint. The mine itself is in the hill in the background. By the end of Spanish rule it had been exhausted.

DESCRIPCION Ð ZERRO RICO Ê YMPERI
AL VILLA Ð POTOSI.

N.							
1	Zerro.	14	N. S. de la Concepcion.		Cas y Plaz principales.
2	Yglesia Matriz.	15	N. S. de Copacavana.	29	Casa de Cavildo.
	Conv Monast y Ospitales.	16	S. Pedro.	30	Casas R.s
3	S. Domingo.	17	S. Pablo.	31	Casa R. de Moneda.
4	S. Francisco.	18	Santiago.	32	Casa de Mercancia de P.ta
5	S. Agustin.	19	S. Juan.	33	Casa de pasto p. los Ynd. del Z.
6	N. S. de las Mercedes.	20	S. Benito.	34	Plaza mayor.
7	La Compañia de Jesus.	21	S. Bernardo.	35	Plaza del Baratillo.
8	S. Juan de Dios.	22	S. Francisco.	36	Lagunas.
9	S.ta Monica.	23	S. Martin.	37	Yngenios.
10	S.ta Theresa de Jesus.	24	S. Lorenzo.	38	Cam p.la Cal del Plata.
11	N. S. de la Misericordia.	25	S. Xptoval.	39	Cam p.la Cal. del Cerro.
12	N. S. de Jerusalen.	26	S. Sebastian.	40	Cam p.la Chc. de Buen Ayres.
13	N. S. de Bethelen.	27	S. Roque.	41	Cam p.la Costa.
	Parroquias de Yndios.	28	S.ta Barbara.		

Se pintò en la misma Villa à costa de D.n
Franc. Ant. Lopez Ortega, por el Mrô. Gaspar Miguel Berrío
Propiedad del D. S V Z T. En 24 de Sept.re 1758. Retocado por F de la C. T. 1872

There are very persuasive reasons for reasserting the 'colonial' nature of the Spanish overseas dominions. In the first place, the Indians were the only subjects obliged to pay the personal capitation tax, satisfy the demand for forced labour and buy the European goods sold by Spanish merchants in cahoots with local political leaders. These impositions were maintained until the end of the empire and even prolonged after its break-up. In short, it was the Spanish who demonstrated to the other Europeans the feasibility of annihilating, overpowering and subjugating enormous populations on a long-term basis. The fact that Adam Smith and his disciples did not consider the Spanish example appropriate for the British to emulate did not prevent their countrymen from zealously following the Spanish model of conquest, colonial governance and economic exploitation in Asia. Furthermore, the presence in Spanish America of slave populations from Africa – through experiments in large-scale exploitation in the sugar industry of Santo Domingo in the sixteenth century, on the Peruvian coast in the seventeenth century and along the entire Caribbean coastline in the eighteenth century – substantially contributed to making the Spanish world resemble that of the Portuguese in Brazil and of the north European nations in the West Indies.[18] The crucial role of slavery in all the economic sectors and in the subsequent large-scale production of sugar can only be suitably explained as part of a true colonial process on an immense scale.[19]

FOR THE MISSIONARIES the New World was an unprecedented opportunity to admit whole populations to the salvation promised by Christianity. Baptism was therefore the first priority of orders such as the Dominicans.

Once we have accepted the truly subordinate nature of Spanish America and the conquered Philippines, there is no doubt that they did enjoy great autonomy in their evolution vis-à-vis the central institutions of Spain. Once the monarchy had established rules that guaranteed the complementary status of its territories in Europe and abroad, the colonial societies were left with an enormous scope for defining their own development. The huge distance between the European centre and the colonial periphery, along with the crisis that wracked Spain in the seventeenth century, served to enhance colonial autonomy in the Americas. Comprehending the racial and social frontiers within the empire is extremely important for an understanding of certain aspects of the development of these colonial societies.

One starting point is the Spanish notion of organizing its American world in the form of two separate 'republics', that of the Indians and that of the Spanish. This aspiration reflected a society obsessed with 'purity of blood' – the purity of the Spanish race – and, at the same time, the desire of some sectors of the Church to keep the Indians out of the greedy clutches of Spanish colonizers. The impact of the demographic catastrophe that followed the conquest, and the disintegration of indigenous society as a result of the geographical relocation of the survivors and their mix into European and African populations – as well as the countless flights and subterfuges in which they engaged to avoid the excessive taxes – swelled the numbers of Native Americans separated from their own communities of origin. The maintenance of separate Indian communities and setting up of religious mission stations were still considered the ideal solution to the dilemma of how to keep the Indians under the control of the Spanish while avoiding the need for any large-scale contact between the two ethnic groups. The aftermath of colonial disruptions, however – the arrival of European and African emigrants, with an ensuing increase in interracial sexual relationships, and the emergence of large urban centres and new economic sectors, with their insatiable demand for labour, even in the domestic sphere – turned the ideal of a colonial society organized on the basis of two separate communities into a utopian dream.

Out of the failure of this idea of two racially separate 'republics' there slowly emerged what the Spanish called the society of 'castes' – a term borrowed from the Portuguese Jesuits to describe the divisions in India in the sixteenth century. In a society such as Castile – accustomed, after the virtual extermination of the Jews and Muslims on the Iberian Peninsula, to considering racial stigmas as hereditary – the idea of castes distinguishable by physical differences found fertile ground in America. Over time, the distinctions between castes became increasingly subtle, giving rise to a complex demarcation of racial categories and sub-categories. Despite this sophisticated system of classification – similar to those developed in contemporary slave societies – its value in determining the limits to social advancement and the formation of a social and cultural hierarchy needs to be closely scrutinized. Access to most social and economic activities was not overly preconditioned by supposed membership of a caste, and the same was true of access to property and specialized professions. Having said that, however, we still do not know the exact extent of the discrimination implied by caste membership, simply because the questions asked by historians on this point have been badly formulated. Full knowledge of caste and racial cleavages requires painstaking research into admission to and status in the trades and professions, the subtle rules of the marriage market, the behaviour of judges and magistrates, and the qualifications required for access to civil and ecclesiastical posts.

The fact that physical – racial – distinctions were not irrelevant seems to be borne out by the intensification of their use in the second half of the eighteenth century. The development of the modern state gave rise to new demands for law and order, some of which were very consciously accepted and manipulated by certain colonial social groups. Colonial and ecclesiastical administrators who ran

Overleaf

'PIGMENTOCRACY' is the name given to the rigid caste system based on colour introduced by the Spaniards. There were frequent marriages, or sexual unions, between Europeans, Indians and black Africans, but it was not until the 18th century that such liaisons were categorized according to a definitive, largely idealized, system in which each resulting offspring was given a descriptive name and allotted a place in the social hierarchy. Five examples out of sixteen: a *mestizo*, child of a Spaniard and an Indian woman (column one, top); a *castizo*, child of a *mestizo* and a Spaniard (column one, second); a Spaniard, child of a *castizo* and a Spanish woman (column one, third); a *mulata*, child of a Spaniard and a black woman (column one, bottom); a *movisio*, child of a Spaniard and a *mulata* (column two, top). And so on, through all the permutations and ending with pure Indian by both parents.

de Español, è Yndia
Mestizo

de Español i Mulata
Morisco.

de Mestiza, y Español
Castizo.

de Español, y Morisca
Albino.

de Castizo, y Española
Español.

de Español, y Albina
Negra Torna atras.

de Español y Negra
Mul...

De Yndio y Negra
L...

De Lobo⁹ y Negra
Chino.

13
de Arvarrasado è Yndia
Barsiño

de Chino¹⁰ è Yndia
Canbulo.

De Varsino¹⁴ è Yndia
Canpa mulato.

De Yndia¹¹ y Cambujo
Tenta en el Aire

De Yndio¹⁵ y Mestiza
Coyote.

12
De Tente en el Aire
y Mulata, Albarrasado

Frutas d la N.ᵉ Esp.ᵃ

16
Yndios Apachis.

A.. Sra Prinsipal con su negra,
Esclava
.Arbol de Granadillas, y su Fruta.
.Arbol del Nispero, y su Fruta.
.Fruta con nombre de Narangillas.
.Palma de Cocos grandes.
.Arbol de Coquitos de chile.

Vicente Alban, pintor en,
Quito, a. 1783.

2

SURROUNDED BY LUXURY, many Creole and Spanish families led lives that could equal or surpass those of the wealthiest aristocrats at home. Black slaves from Africa were brought over in large numbers. Their descendants are still a large part of the South American population.

the parishes and were responsible for the first labour censuses took an increasing interest in people's blood stock,[20] with significant racial correlations in the segregation of cities and marriage patterns.[21] This was undoubtedly the key factor in social advancement, rather than any impediment for individuals with a capacity to accumulate assets. It is not surprising, therefore, that the government forbade mixed marriages, thereby reasserting the unequal basis of the colonial relationship. As Verena Stolcke has demonstrated, when the 1776 *Pragmática Sanción* banning mixed marriages in the metropole reached the Americas, its effects were multiplied *ad infinitum*, as it was applied within a framework of a complex racial structure.[22] The effects were particularly intense and long-lasting in areas such as Cuba, where the existence of a substantial free black and mulatto social group turned the *Sanción* into an instrument for regulating the marriage market. The twilight years of the empire were therefore overshadowed by cultural issues focusing on hierarchical social structure and social exclusion. It is one of the ironies of history that the so-called 'coloured castes' – the descendants of slaves – were increasingly climbing the social ladder among the working classes, while in the urban professions, in the Army and in the Church, the empire's racial culture resisted any dismantlement of social structures based on skin colour or slave blood. The transformation of slavery itself, with the emergence of huge plantations, was not unconnected with the intensification of a racialist viewpoint.

THE ZENITH OF THE SPANISH EMPIRE – AND ITS FISCAL
AND POLITICAL CHALLENGES

Despite the supposed distance of the Spanish monarchy from the major currents of international affairs in the eighteenth century, the empire reached its apogee and greatest territorial extent during this period. Three factors explain this surprising and belated expansionist rush. First, the evident demographic recovery of indigenous populations must be taken into account, along with the relentless growth of mixed-race groups that were culturally open to the Europeans or people of African descent. Second, there occurred a continuous expansion of the frontiers both northwards and southwards in South America, as well as into the uncolonized 'empty' space around the Orinoco and Amazon rivers. Third, the peripheries of the empire were becoming increasingly integrated into its overall economic and social system – a metamorphosis true not only of the Americas but also of parts of Spain (such as Galicia and Catalonia) previously unabsorbed by the imperial system. The most noteworthy example of a development that both pushed back frontiers and integrated the peripheries was the successful organization of the viceroyalty of Río de la Plata in 1776.[23]

If any single reason explains the acceleration of the long-term trend towards expansion, it is the empire's definitive integration into the Atlantic economy, part of a process of the economic and social change of reformed mercantilism. The most visible aspect of such a change was the intensification of transatlantic economic exchanges.[24] Another aspect, less visible but ultimately more revealing, derives from the definitive integration of the two main sectors of the colonial economy – mining and the minting of coins, and commercial agriculture, increasingly aimed at the European markets for raw materials (cotton and dyes) and foodstuffs (sugar, tobacco, coffee). This growing integration of the two sectors – closely linked to the development of colonial economies geared towards foodstuffs for local consumption (including stimulants such as coca from the Andes), and to the production of textiles and utensils needed regionally – was subject to commercial and fiscal reform measures introduced in the 1760s and 1770s. Tariff reforms turned the system of a Spanish trade monopoly – first based in Seville from the late sixteenth century and in Cadiz from 1717 onwards – into an oligopoly involving various Spanish mainland ports, and were intended partially to deregulate trade and increase income from tariffs.[25] New economic policies of this type, geared towards taking fuller advantage of the empire, had been debated at length since the 1720s, but they were only implemented when the Seven Years' War (1756–63) made them inevitable.

The war had demonstrated the empire's military weakness, and showed an urgent need for Spain to reform armed forces and to raise money to pay for these reforms. Questions were also asked in Spain about the power-sharing within the American institutions (*audiencias* and *cabildos*) between Creoles (Europeans born in the Americas) and Spaniards.[26] The reforms considered vital by the Enlightenment monarchs and their ministers involved nothing less than a drastic reorganization of the empire's finances and power systems to align them more closely with their new priorities. As was the case with the French and British empires, however, payment for the war and subsequent reforms destabilized the internal equilibrium that had been so jealously guarded between metropole and colonies.[27] The sums collected in the Americas through indirect taxation, fiscal monopolies (especially on tobacco), 'compulsory loans' and higher tariffs, all aimed at counteracting the impulses of their economies, provided the state with the resources required to defend the empire as a whole, thus fulfilling the monarchy's main political objective.

The costs of this increase in fiscal pressure on the Americas were undoubtedly substantial, both in economic terms – it moved some sectors away from the informal economy into the hands of the state, while acting as a disincentive to others – and in political terms – it stirred up deep-rooted popular discontent, which exploded in the Andes in 1780 and in the Viceroyalty of New Spain in 1810.[28] The invasion of Spain by Napoleon in 1808, the erosion of the imperial system of governance and the ever-increasing contradictions of the American colonial world led the societies of the empire into a spiral of violence, in which the loyalties of the royalists or the supporters of the colonial insurgency were markedly different from one place to the other. In these circumstances, the only social group capable of formulating an alternative cultural and political discourse was the Creole bourgeoisie, the prime beneficiary of the economic expansion in the eighteenth century.

THE DECLINE OF IMPERIAL SPAIN

The empire forged in the Americas in the sixteenth century ceased to exist formally in the first half of the 1820s, as a result of Spain's military defeats by the American colonial separatists. The rebellion that broke out in 1810 and that after 1813 was led by Simon Bolivar resulted in the liberation of nearly all the former colonies and the creation of six independent countries – Venezuela, Colombia, Panama, Ecuador, Peru and Bolivia – though Bolivar himself had dreamed of a single united nation. This wholesale defeat occurred despite efforts by the Spanish rulers to co-opt the American settlers in new representative institutions after the Napoleonic Wars. This ambitious political project failed, most notably because of the implacable conflict between the nationalist and pro-independence forces in some parts of the Americas and the Spanish incapacity to accept the Americans' 'federalist' positions.

Despite the resounding failure of its attempts to keep the empire intact in Central and South America, Spain did manage to retain three very important colonies: Cuba, Puerto Rico and the Philippines. The first was one of the richest European possessions in the world, as Wellington never tired of reminding the

TOBACCO BECAME a major industry. This 18th-century illustration shows an elaborate machine for sifting leaves at the Royal Cigar Factory.

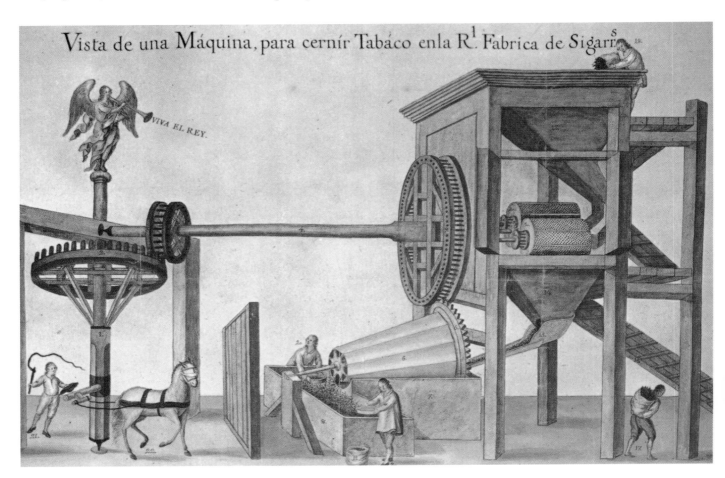

IIII.
Aqui se pone
la cochinilla
en las nuevas
plantas pasados
seis meses, y mas
que se plantaron.
La semilla se po-
ne por Marzo, y
Abril á los arbo-
les viejos, que
á los nuevos es
bien no poner-
sela, hasta que
tengan mas he-
dad de seis me-
ses, ó un año.

A SMALL INSECT that lived on a certain species of cactus was found, when crushed to a pulp, to yield a rich red dye called cochineal that could be used both for textiles and in food: one more unexpected bonus from the New World.

Spanish ambassadors in London. The fact that all three stayed in Spanish hands can be explained by their status as highly valuable enclaves, in both strategic and military terms, and by the successful implementation there of the reforms made between 1763 and 1782, in line with those applied throughout the empire. In contrast to the large continental viceroyalties, the island enclaves received immense resources for their military defence; these came from the rest of the empire and in the financial terms of the day they were known as *situados* (securities).[29]

Cuba thereby became the host for a vigorous sugar-based economy that reaped dazzling benefits from the sudden price rise triggered by the destruction of the neighbouring French colony of Saint-Domingue. Cuba's sugar boom was enhanced by the arrival of exiled sugar planters from this great colony and, above all, by the untrammelled importation of African slaves prior to the signing in 1820 of an Anglo-Spanish treaty to ban the slave trade. In Cuba, however, as in Brazil and the south of the United States, a great intensification of slavery occurred precisely when this trade had been prohibited internationally by abolitionist treaties that Britain signed with the majority of European states following the Napoleonic Wars – the Spanish authorities turned a blind eye to the smuggling of Africans. As a result of the sugar boom in Cuba, other crops were transferred to different parts of the island, making way for the development of the mechanized nineteenth-century plantations. This process of moving crops to the highly fertile central areas enabled Cuba to become the world's foremost producer of cane sugar and, consequently, an extraordinarily valuable colony for both the Spanish state (which financed its presence in the Caribbean with Cuban tariffs and had plenty of profits left over for use in Spain) and for Spanish capitalists.[30] In Puerto Rico, the parallel development of the sugar and coffee industries – which exported primarily to the North European markets, via the Danish West Indian *entrepôt* of St Thomas in the neighbouring Virgin Islands, and also to the United States – formed a base that was more than sufficient to justify the interest of the metropole. As in Cuba, the Puerto Rican sugar business ran on slavery, though coffee was mainly cultivated by peasants of European origin.

The Philippines always constituted a very special case in the Spanish Empire. This most remote of the Spanish possessions was sustained by a complex combination of taxes paid by the local population, financial aid that arrived from New Spain in the form of *situados* and customs duties yielded by the important

shipping link established in the late sixteenth century between Acapulco and Manila – that is, trade between the Spanish and Chinese empires, with the Philippines capital as staging post. For centuries, the export of South American silver to the Chinese market (where it was highly prized due to the demands of the Chinese monetary system, which did not use paper money) largely guaranteed the viability of such a remote and costly possession. For their return trip to Acapulco, the silver galleons loaded up with textiles, pottery and other coveted Chinese goods, as well as spices from the islands of southeast Asia. The Philippines also played a key role in the empire's rearguard defence against attacks from the Dutch and British in eastern Asia.

At the beginning of the nineteenth century, when the crisis in the Spanish Empire threatened to cast the Philippines to its fate, both politically and financially, the government in Manila managed to find a way to keep the archipelago in Spanish hands.[31] Within only a few years, they developed a formidable fiscal monopoly sector, along the lines previously established in the Americas. Tobacco would acquire a fundamental importance in this scheme; the state monopoly on tobacco quickly became the basis of the Philippines' official finances (and remained so until 1882), thereby guaranteeing a Spanish presence in the China Sea. Creating a tobacco monopoly meant turning the state into an economic agent: this required the imposition and control of tobacco-growing in some provinces, a system for transporting the leaves, the processing of the finished product in factories in Manila and a reliable distribution network. From 1840 onwards, the Philippine monopoly was also obliged to supply cut-price tobacco leaves to factories in the metropole. As the managers of the state monopoly had to strictly control both the illegal tobacco planting that was common practice among Philippine peasants and the ever-changing retail sector – in which the mixed-race (Chinese-Philippine) lower-middle class played an important role – the fiscal monopolies became a major instrument of colonization. While the tobacco monopoly played a decisive role in economic integration, military operations and steamships pushed the colonial frontier both inland (on the island of Luzón, in the Visayas) and into the territory of the Islamized populations of Mindanao and Sulu, in the southern part of the archipelago. In the last two decades of Spanish domination, fiscal monopolies were deregulated, the tax system was reformed and the investment of Spanish capital was encouraged. These moves were designed to create a new basis for Spanish domination and compete with emerging local capitalism, as well as with the European and American companies established in Philippine ports.

On these productive and fiscal foundations the new colonial model of liberal Spanish colonialism was built in the nineteenth century, once the neo-absolutist monarchy had definitively collapsed in Spain. Strangely, however, those liberals who had once rallied their American and Philippine counterparts to form part of a single system of representative institutions went on to separate them from this very system after securing power in the 1830s. Instead of a representative assembly and shared political rights, they hastily constructed a highly authoritarian and militarized system of government – the only way of filling

'THE LIBERATOR' (*opposite*). Simon Bolivar, born in Venezuela, became the leader of the revolt that broke out in 1812 against Spanish rule. Influenced by the European Enlightenment, he believed passionately in political freedom, and dreamed of uniting all the ex-Spanish colonies in one large republic. This never happened, but each state continues to revere him as its founder.

SUGAR CANE flourished in Cuba and soon became its most important export. Here (*below*), in the mid-19th century, it is being cut and loaded onto wagons.

the political vacuum in the colonies as a result of the suspension of the liberal constitutions approved in the metropole in 1837, 1845 and 1876. (Only much later, after a first Cuban War for Independence ended in stalemate and slavery had finally been abolished in 1886, did Spanish governments commit themselves to extending the benefits of representation to Cuba and Puerto Rico, although the Philippines unequivocally retained its status as a colony.)[32] Spanish assimilationist concepts arrived late on a scene of fratricidal conflict, mutual distrust and increasing interest in the Spanish Caribbean on the part of the United States. This is not to say that Spain acquiesced in the end of its four centuries in the Americas without a struggle. Its impressive show of strength – 250,000 Spanish soldiers were dispatched to Cuba in 1898 – proved insufficient to crush the Cuban insurgency, however, and President William McKinley's espousal of American imperialism definitively undermined Spain's capacity for resistance. Once its imperial grip on the Americas had been loosened, Spain finally ceased to be a nation straddling the Atlantic, with tentacles in Asia and North Africa.

THE SPANISH IMPERIAL MODEL

Cuba gained its independence in 1898 after a long war and several years of American military occupation. Puerto Rico shook off Spanish rule at the same time only to be occupied by US troops until 1900, when it became part of the USA, though with limited autonomy. The Philippines also ejected the Spanish with American help – but remained under US control until 1935.

It is a paradox of the Spanish Empire that, at the point when it came to an end it was readopting approaches highly reminiscent of the fifteenth and sixteenth centuries. Since the mid-nineteenth century, the demographic growth of the maritime regions of the Spanish mainland, coupled with a fall in long-distance shipping costs, encouraged tens of thousands of Spaniards to emigrate to the Americas, just as their forefathers had done centuries before. Up until around 1760–70, travel to the overseas territories was largely restricted to the southern regions of Spain closest to the main ports serving the Americas, and to groups such as the sailors, agents and merchants who maintained the commercial relationship between the two sides of the transoceanic empire. Emigration to the remaining colonies in the Caribbean, or to the former colonies on the American mainland, had been very selective and intermittent until the 1840s. From then on, however, it changed in character. A relentless flow of emigrants would 'Hispanicize', to a degree hitherto unknown, extensive parts of the old imperial realm, particularly in those areas still under Spanish control. Legislative changes of the 1850s, which put an end to the previous policies that restricted emigration, fomented the creation of significant Spanish communities on the other side of the Atlantic. This tendency continued in the early decades of the twentieth century – even in the newly proclaimed Republic of Cuba, where Spanish migrants continued to be warmly received. It is hardly surprising, therefore, that Havana and Buenos Aires at the beginning of the twentieth century were cities with major Spanish-born communities, well represented by political, cultural and leisure associations with a high social status.

After the defeat of Spain by the United States in 1898, the Spanish overseas empire was compared by one American commentator to a whale – an animal whose every part could be put to good use. Its dismemberment was carried out in the diplomatic salons of Paris, after Madrid and Washington signed a treaty

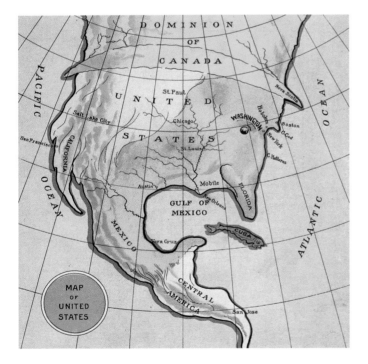

UNCLE SAM COVETS CUBA: 'I have had my eye on that morsel for a long time – guess I'll have to take it in.' Cuba remained under American protection until 1902 and even later.

that conceded to Spain certain commercial and financial concessions. The United States had strengthened its hold over the Caribbean island of Puerto Rico and Spain's Asian domain of the Philippines, as well as its capacity to intervene in Cuba, which had been the jewel in the Spanish crown throughout the nineteenth century. The agreement marked the end of four centuries of Spanish entrenchment in the Americas and the world outside Europe in general, and the very length of this imperial history should give us pause for thought.

The predictable end of a crisis-ridden empire should not deter us from re-evaluating its place in history and its significance in the shaping of the modern world, a story that has still not been fully written, despite its relevance to understanding the changes in world history that took place in the eighteenth and nineteenth centuries. The story of the latter years of the Spanish Empire is one of contraction in the face of the expansion of the emerging powers of the modern world, particularly Britain, but also France, Germany, the United States and Japan.[33] This essay has attempted to show how understanding the mechanisms of the decline of some empires and the rise of others throughout the development of the modern world is not strictly a question of geopolitics: the elimination of the Iberian empires provided a precondition for satisfying northern Europe's need to expand into the southern hemisphere. It should therefore be understood as something that had a fundamental effect on the transformation of the economic, social and cultural traits of modern imperialism.

It is not unreasonable to see the Spanish Empire as the hinge between the European Old World and developments of the modern world that are still in progress. The experience accumulated in those four centuries of history was a key element in the formation of the world as we know it today. For a long time, however, the justifications used by the Spanish themselves – Catholic messianism, monarchical imperialism, paternalistic feelings towards overseas territories and populations – found an easy echo and a self-interested confirmation in the ideas with which the Enlightenment and evangelical Protestantism formulated their own historical experience of expansion. However, just as we have moved away from a description of the nineteenth century based on technical changes in industry and transportation, complemented by the parallel dissemination of ideas of a genuinely European origin, the place occupied by the Spanish Empire in history is in need of re-evaluation. There is little doubt that the Spanish were the advance party, and the Spanish Empire was the first experiment on a large scale, in the European expansion that would later stretch into the first half of the twentieth century. In effect, the great enterprise of colonizing an entire continent – with unexpected branches in Asia – undertaken by emigrants, clergymen and court officials was the first major attempt to dominate and contain non-European peoples on a long-term basis. Its aim was nothing less than to create a new society that for generations could reproduce itself through its own momentum, and on those terms it was a success. Within this framework, the monarchical state marked out its objectives, the metropole was able to satisfy its thirst for wealth and domination, and the Catholic Church found an ideal setting for the massive conversion of culturally and psychologically exhausted populations. The script for subsequent developments had already been written in the sixteenth century.

3

Portugal: Empire-building in the Old World and the New

JILL DIAS

GOLD AND DIAMONDS FROM BRAZIL brought sudden wealth to Portugal, but did not contribute to the long-term health of the economy. A watercolour of 1762 (*opposite*) gives a powerful impression of diamond mines, worked by slaves under European supervision.

IT WAS IN THE SMALL DETAILS of daily life that the possession of an empire came home most vividly to the ordinary European. Chocolate was unknown before the colonization of America. By the reign of Portugal's João V (1707–50) it was sufficiently prestigious for the king to be shown drinking it (*above*).

PORTUGAL WAS THE FIRST European country to acquire an overseas empire, and the last to renounce it. By the 1540s, one of the smallest, most remote and poorest nations of Europe had created a merchant empire more than five times her size, stretching around the globe. The imperial centre of gravity shifted from Africa and Asia, to South America before 1600, and back again to Africa in the 1820s. While the orientation of Portuguese involvement overseas changed profoundly, the Portuguese remained omnipresent. Over five centuries, several million people embarked for Asia, Brazil and Africa. Webs of kinship maintained historical connections between different geographical regions, while the 'imagined community' of the empire was reinforced by chroniclers and poets, who elaborated a national ideology and mythology of Portuguese expansion. Like all empires, that of Portugal was marked by moments of extreme violence. It played a central role in the overseas slave trade that displaced between 10 and 20 million Africans, producing dynamic new cultural and social syntheses in America. The cultural legacy of Portuguese contacts also endures in identity, language and religion within post-colonial societies, from Japan, Macao, Indonesia, Malaysia and Timor, to Brazil, Angola, Mozambique, Guiné-Bissau, and the archipelagos of São Tomé and Cape Verde. Portugal herself was rarely the main economic beneficiary of the empire, remaining first and foremost a broker. National regeneration through empire was a persistent mirage, and Portugal remained as poor and backward at the end of empire as at its beginning.

AFRICAN BEGINNINGS: FROM CEUTA TO THE GULF OF GUINEA[1]
Portuguese expansion began with the invasion of North Africa and conquest of Ceuta by a crusading army in 1415. The campaign pleased the papacy, eager to recover Christian lands separated from the Church centuries earlier by Muslim political supremacy in the Mediterranean, and it put Portugal on the map internationally. The expedition's planner, the *Infante* Henrique, Prince Henry 'the Navigator',[2] in 1433 also became the architect of Portuguese colonization of Madeira and adjacent islands in the Atlantic. Chroniclers

PORTUGUESE GOA was a meeting place of peoples. A Dutch book of travels, published in 1614, provides a panorama of the various races to be found in its streets, from pure Portuguese to pure Indian and all the mixtures in between.

portray Henry as a pious and chivalrous warrior, but also as a shrewd businessman and active slave trader. For three decades, he used income from exploitation of Madeira, agriculture, trade and privateering to sponsor voyages down the West African coast, leading to the first European contacts with black African societies in Senegâmbia by the mid-1440s. If the major incentive was a search for gold and slaves, no less important was the desire to assess the southern limits of Islam and recruit African allies against the 'Moors'.

The first expeditions were intent on slave raiding, a costly and dangerous way to obtain a few captives; within a decade, this gave way to peaceful trade relations. The importance of a 'factory' established on Arguin Island by 1450 was rapidly surpassed by commercial relations with the more densely populated Senegâmbian societies, integrated into the trans-Saharan gold, ivory and slave trade. Political elites among the Wolof desired horses for prestige and warfare, and the Portuguese obliged. In exchange they received slaves, with the going rate seven slaves for one horse in the 1450s; 1,000–2,000 black slaves a year reached Portugal – a total of 15,000 to 20,000 between 1440 and 1460.[3]

Around 1470, the Lisbon merchant Fernão Gomes, under royal licence, sent ships to the shores beyond Sierra Leone. They developed the pepper trade from the Malagueta coast, revealed the rich potential of the Gold Coast, penetrated the Niger delta and discovered the archipelago of São Tomé. The exclusivity of Portuguese navigation and conquest in the Gulf of Guinea was assured when in 1455 Pope Nicholas V proclaimed the South Atlantic a Portuguese *mare clausum*. Rights were confirmed in 1479 when the Treaty of Alcaçovas-Toledo conceded the Canary Islands to Castile in exchange for Portuguese ownership of the Azores, Madeira, Cape Verde and 'lands discovered and to be discovered… and any other island which might be found and conquered beyond the Canary islands towards Guinea'.

Ratification of this treaty by the pope coincided with the 1481 accession to the Portuguese throne of João I. For the first time, the political objective

Missionaries followed the conquerors. Among the mixed motives that led to the foundation of empires, the saving of souls should not be forgotten – an enterprise that may not have brought much comfort to the native inhabitants but was fraught with danger for the priests. The Jesuit missionaries who accompanied military expeditions to Congo and Angola in the sixteenth century paradoxically condoned slave trading while working to establish Christianity.

Rio de Janeiro became the Brazilian capital in 1807 when King João VI set up his court there after the Napoleonic invasion of his homeland. This view (*below*) shows it in 1816.

of reaching India by sea was unequivocally assumed, both to further the Christian cause and to gain control of the highly lucrative pepper and spice trade from the East.[4] Such Jewish and Arabic-speaking emissaries as Alfonso de Paiva and Pero de Covilhã were sent on intelligence-gathering missions. In 1487, they journeyed from Cairo to Aden disguised as Muslim merchants. Covilhã sailed on into the Indian Ocean, visiting Calicut, Goa and Sofala, then made his way from Somalia inland to the court of the Coptic Christian ruler of Ethiopia, only to be retained there for the next thirty years. Meanwhile, in 1488, Bartolomeu Dias had rounded the Cape into the Indian Ocean.

Since conquests in Africa nevertheless remained more attractive than the risks of direct trade with Asia, in the early 1490s João dispatched emissaries to Mali and Timbuktu in his search for gold and Christian allies.[5] While occupation and settlement were not prime motives, João sought permanent bases from which to conduct trade and evangelization. The earliest, the fortress of São Jorge da Mina, was built in 1482 by stonemasons and carpenters shipped from Portugal, along with the necessary stones and timber. More than a dozen ships a year engaged in commerce, returning to Lisbon loaded with gold and other valuable goods.[6]

Portuguese traders infiltrated African commercial networks, transporting bark cloth and copper manilas from Congo, cola nuts from Sierra Leone and beads from Benin for exchange along the coast. The most important regional cargo, however, was slaves, destined to satisfy the porterage demands of African gold producers in the Mina hinterland. Many hundreds were obtained in the 'slave rivers' of the dense marsh and almost impenetrable forestland of the Niger delta.

By 1490, the archipelagos of Cape Verde, off the coast of Senegâmbia, and São Tomé – first sighted, respectively, in the 1450s and 1470s – were catalysts of commercial and social change in the Gulf of Guinea. The Crown integrated the islands into the Portuguese orbit by donating them as lordships or captaincies, with full juridical, institutional, military and economic powers, to individuals who undertook to settle and develop them at their own charge. The first settlers included Portuguese-Jewish converts ('New Christians'), gypsies and convicts deported from Portugal. In 1493, João ordered all children of Jewish parents who had taken refuge in Portugal following their expulsion from Castile to be separated, baptized and sent to colonize São Tomé;[7] six hundred survived there in 1506.[8]

The expansion of Christianity became a prime concern of the Crown. The standard bearer of Christian civilization, Dias raised stone pillars, incorporating a cross with the arms of the Portuguese kings, at prominent points of the

African coast. However, João II's repeated exhortations to African rulers to abandon 'idolatrous' practices fell on deaf ears. At Mina, the gold trade took precedence over Christian conversion, and while rulers in Senegâmbia and Benin displayed a fleeting interest in Christianity, friars who accompanied expeditions did not manage to convert any important African leaders in the fifteenth century, or later.

The greater receptivity of Congolese elites to European influence made the Congo the scene of the most ambitious and successful attempt to penetrate the African interior through Christianity and commerce between the 1490s and 1540s. Considerable acculturation of Congolese elites within Catholicism occurred as a result of intense missionary presence, although indigenous beliefs and practices persisted, and the Congo's Christianity remained strongly syncretic.[9] In the Congo, the overseas slave trade assumed its greatest proportions. Unlike the gold of Mina, the Congo's palm cloth, wood and copper represented relatively little value for the Portuguese. European merchandise was therefore exchanged for slaves – war captives, convicts, orphans and debtors provided by local rulers. The Congo quickly became a principal supplier of slaves to Portugal, São Tomé and, later, to Brazil.

Meanwhile private trading by colonists from São Tomé in Benin intensified. Unlike the Congo kings, Benin's rulers never became dependent on European commerce, as demonstrated by the embargo imposed on exports of male slaves before 1520. Yet traders and mercenaries from São Tomé had a profound cultural impact on Benin institutions and beliefs. They supported rulers in wars of expansion with sales of muskets. Enormous quantities of brass manilas were melted down for commemorative plaques, whose visual vocabulary and war narratives integrate images of Portuguese soldiers, courtiers and traders.[10]

Less than a century after arriving in West Africa, the Portuguese were making an impact from Senegâmbia to the Gulf of Guinea and the Congo out of all proportion to their numbers, which probably never exceeded 300 at any moment between 1450 and 1500. By this latter date, 150,000 Africans had been transported from Senegâmbia, Benin and the Congo to Mina, Cape Verde, São Tomé, Madeira or Portugal, and long-term patterns of interaction and trade were established.

The Crown's priorities were already shifting from Africa to India with the opening of the sea route to India. Following his accession to the throne in 1495, Manuel I recommended expeditions to India, ignoring advisers who questioned the utility of voyages beyond the Cape of Good Hope. Manuel notably commissioned ships under the command of Vasco da Gama,[11] his decision influenced by the messianic conviction that he had been 'chosen' by God to reconquer Jerusalem. Manuel's image as the new 'King David' harmonized with millenarian tendencies evident in the Iberian peninsula in the 1490s, following conquest of Granada, the last redoubt of Muslim power, and the expulsion of the Jews.[12]

THE EAST: A TRADING EMPIRE IN THE INDIAN OCEAN

The captain [Vasco da Gama] sent one of the convict-exiles to Calecute; and they took him to where there were two moors from Tunis, that could speak Castilian and Genoese. And the first greeting they gave him was the following:
The devil take thee; who brought thee here?
And they asked him what we had come to seek from so far. And he replied
– We come to seek Christians and spices.[13]

On 22 November 1497, after a five-month voyage from Lisbon, Vasco da Gama's four caravels rounded the Cape of Good Hope and sailed up the coast of eastern Africa. Suffering badly from scurvy, the crews reached Mozambique Island at the end of February 1498. Fearing treachery and desperate to take on fresh water, they bombarded the town before sailing northwards to Mombasa and Melindi. They eventually crossed the ocean, with the help of a Gujerati

By the mid-16th century the Portuguese were at home in their eastern possessions. Here (*right*), a group of merchants at Ormuz dine in a water-tank, *c*.1540. The first Jesuit missionary in Ormuz wrote: 'The country is so hot that the Portuguese go about naked and almost always in water-tanks.'

pilot, arriving at Calicut, in western India, on 21 May. Surprisingly, in view of João II's network of informants, Gama and his men knew next to nothing about the Indian Ocean world – they initially thought Calicut a Christian city, mistaking Hindu temples for churches. The sophistication of Indian Ocean societies came as a surprise; the Calicut ruler received Gama reclining on a couch covered with gold embroidered cloth, surrounded by gold and silver cups, basins and vases. Disconcerted, Gama boasted that the Portuguese king was the richest monarch in Europe, and had no need of gold and silver, words belied by the paltry gifts he offered: twelve belts, four cloaks and six hats, four branches of coral, six basins, a box of sugar, two barrels of olive oil and two of honey. Humiliatingly, his hosts refused the presents, saying that they were unworthy of the poorest merchant returned from Mecca. For the rest of their stay in Calicut, the Portuguese suffered official harassment, as well as the taunts and sneers of visiting Muslim traders. After three months, Gama abandoned attempts to cultivate the ruler's friendship, and abruptly set sail for home.[14]

Following the fleet's return in July 1499 Manuel triumphantly proclaimed Portugal's 'discovery' of India, and assumed the title of 'Lord of the Conquest, Navigation and Commerce of Ethiopia, Arabia, Persia and India'. Revelation of the vast commercial world of the Indian Ocean far exceeded the king's wildest dreams. The great coastal city-states – Aden, Ormuz, Kilwa, Cambay, Calicut, Malacca and Canton – that had long served commerce between Asia and Europe were the ports Manuel now intended to capture.

The Portuguese, realizing that the key was superior naval power, built fleets of large carracks (*naus*). Such floating fortresses and warehouses could withstand the firing of a row of cannon through opened portholes. Taken by surprise, the Muslim, Indian, Malay and Chinese merchants in the great port cities could not resist Portuguese firepower.[15]

Gama's first expedition was quickly followed by larger, highly successful, commercial voyages, comprising fleets of a dozen or more well-armed ships, some with over a thousand soldiers. They carried increasing numbers of Portuguese knights and noblemen willing to risk their lives on the extremely perilous voyage around the Cape for the economic and military opportunities opening up in the East.[16] For many, material profit gained through plunder of Muslim shipping and settlements beckoned more than peaceful commerce. For the rulers of Indian Ocean coastal societies, little distinguished the Portuguese fleets from ruthless pirates apart from superior naval strength.

Within a mere seven years of Gama's first landing at Calicut, the Portuguese were permanently established in India.[17] In 1505, the Crown created the *Estado da Índia* ('State of India'), appointing as first viceroy the aristocratic Francisco de Almeida. His mission was to impose Portuguese naval supremacy in the Indian Ocean and end the Muslim spice trade by blockading the Red Sea, and to capture and fortify the East African Swahili ports of Kilwa and Sofala, principal outlets of the African gold and ivory needed to buy spices in India. These aims were largely achieved by 1509. The king had also instructed Almeida to go to Sumatra, Malacca and the spice islands of the Indonesian archipelago beyond to 'subjugate and bring to our obedience the kings and lords of these islands'.[18] This task fell to Almeida's successor, Afonso de Albuquerque, an emblematic figure of expansion in the East. Albuquerque supplemented Portuguese naval control by a chain of militarized, land-based forts built to protect the commercial factories, notably at Mozambique Island (1507), Goa (1510), Malacca (1511), and Ormuz (1507).

By the 1520s, Portuguese ships were sailing, via the Coromandel coast, to East India, Bengal, Pegu (Burma) and the spice islands of the Moluccas, where cloves, nutmeg and mace were bartered for Indian textiles. The Crown moved quickly to control trade through the conquest or voluntary submission of rulers of islands and enclaves incorporated into the *Estado da Índia*.[19] A few spontaneous colonies of Portuguese merchants also emerged, the most important at Macao.[20]

POSSESSION OF BAHIA, one of the oldest towns in Brazil, was challenged by the Dutch in 1625. Their defeat was celebrated in this painted cloth by Juan Bautista Maino, made for the palace of Buen Retiro outside Madrid (Portugal was at this time united with Spain). General Don Fadrique de Toledo unveils a tapestry showing Philip IV and Count-Duke Olivares with a figure of Victory trampling on Heresy, Discord and War. In the centre wounded men are being tended, surrounded by women and children. Lope de Vega wrote a play about this called *El Brasil Restituido*.

SHAH JAHAN'S COURT at Agra was a
cosmopolitan meeting-place for visitors
from all over the known world (*right*). A
group of Portuguese offering gifts to
the Mughal emperor is seen bottom
left.

IN JAPAN the Portuguese were granted
valuable concessions, though their
mission was destined to end in disaster.
A screen attributed to the Japanese
artist Kano Domi of around 1600
(*below*) shows a group of Portuguese
recently disembarked from a ship
bearing gifts to the shogun of Nagasaki.

The dependence of widely scattered possessions on the viceregal government
in Goa was the most important unifying trait of the *Estado da Índia*. The viceroy,
to all intents, was an independent sovereign with virtually unlimited powers
during his three years of office. At Goa, he was assisted by an advisory council
consisting of the chief civil and judicial officials, the archbishop, the military
commander and the principal noblemen. Here, as in North Africa, there was
a strong Portuguese military presence, and members of the higher nobility
held prominence.

In reality, the Portuguese achieved a widespread, but shallow, political
presence in Asia. Those rulers who acknowledged Portuguese suzerainty
generally did so through payment of a symbolic tribute, which left indigenous
political and administrative systems mostly intact.[21] Indeed, the enormous
geographical extension, and cultural and political diversity, of the Crown's
'possessions' precluded integration within a unified administration imposed
from Goa. Furthermore, weak military presence in the Bay of Bengal, Southeast
Asia and the Far East decisively influenced patterns of Portuguese interaction.

Portuguese adventurers had made contact with China soon after Malacca was
captured in 1511. Though banned from Chinese shores in 1522, clandestine trade
continued privately and, in 1543, freelance traders also found their way to Japan.

Profiting from restrictions placed by the Chinese on their subjects trading with Japan, the Portuguese became brokers in the South China trade. Their introduction of Western firearms into Japan in the early 1540s had momentous political consequences. The new technology was rapidly adopted by local warlords, and in 1575 Oda Nobunaga employed 3,000 musketeers to devastating effect in the Battle of Nagashino, setting Japan on the road to political unification.[22]

By this date, new networks of intra-Asian Portuguese trade were assuming greater significance than direct trade with Portugal. Most of the intra-Asian Crown *carreiras* were replaced by 'concessionary-voyages', undertaken by nobles and other well-connected men in exchange for customs duties on cargoes and a percentage of the profits. The most lucrative was the Goa-Malacca-Macao-Nagasaki voyage, which as early as the 1560s provided pepper, spices, silk, copper, gold, silver and precious metals. Prosperity was greatly boosted by expansion of silver mining in Japan, and silver offered the main profits of the intra-Asia trade: between 1560 and 1600, the Portuguese annually carried between 22,500 and 37,500 kilos of silver from Japan, and over the next thirty years exports reached 187,000 kilos.[23] Most silver trading was organized from Macao, near Canton, which existed as a kind of mercantile republic, ruled by an elected municipal government from 1582.[24]

Portuguese presence in Asia was also characterized by intense missionary activity; by the 1630s, there were 1,800 missionaries in Portuguese Asia. They represented the major religious orders; most numerous were Jesuits,[25] followed closely by Franciscans. Over a third lived in Goa, with a further concentration in Cochin. The Jesuits also worked in East Asia, especially Japan, as well as in Ethiopia, the Mughal Empire and Tibet. There may have been as many as 1.5 million Christians in Asia by the early seventeenth century. The Christian population of Japan expanded rapidly in the first century of Jesuit activity. When Francisco Xavier sailed to Japan from Malacca in 1549, the Japanese saw the Jesuits as a means to attract trade. While Japanese warlords thus had an interest in allowing evangelization, the political unification of Japan produced a political and cultural climate less tolerant of Portuguese presence and the interference of missionaries in internal affairs. From the 1580s, Christian missionaries were brutally persecuted and then expelled from Japan in 1614.

THE FAR EAST was opened up by Portuguese traders but never became part of the empire. Shown here is Macao, near Canton, in the early 18th century, in a view by Pier van der Aa.

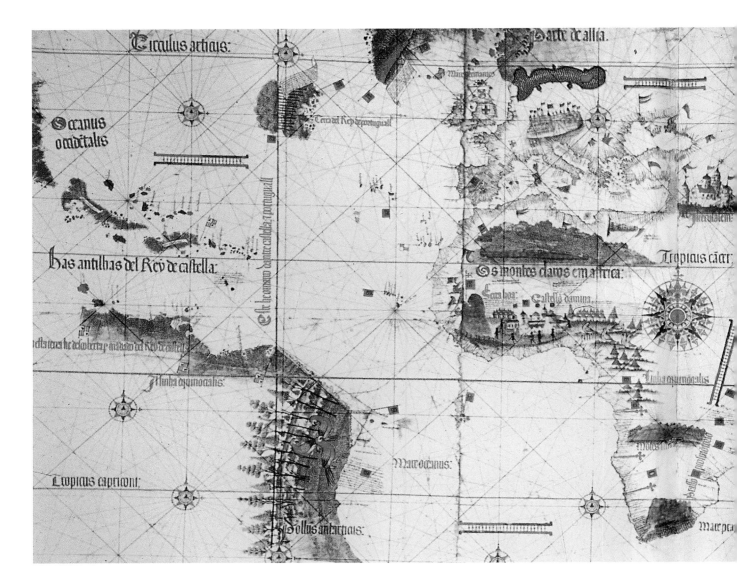

Twenty-five years later the Japanese emperor forbade trade by Macao merchants in Nagasaki; in 1640, sixty-one Portuguese members of an embassy of Macao were beheaded and their ship burnt.[26]

Within the settlements subject to the *Estado da Índia*, official Portuguese merchants, whose main business was intra-Asian trade, comprised a major social group. They were termed *casados* ('married men'), a concept originating in Albuquerque's desire to form permanent colonies at Goa and Malacca; the viceroy offered economic incentives to Portuguese willing to settle and take as wives local women who converted to Christianity. The colonists, like similar 'Creole' communities in Portuguese Africa or in Brazil, remained highly conscious of distinctions of race or birth that helped to determine social status. Those of mixed blood (*mestiços*) were regarded as inferior by those who claimed 'pure blood', whether they were born in Asia of European parentage or were migrants from Portugal.

While it is impossible to determine how many Portuguese lived in Asia, emigration to the East never occurred on the scale of emigration to Brazil. In 1540, Viceroy João de Castro estimated that there were 6,000–7,000 residents of the Portuguese possessions and factories between Sofala and China. Four hundred lived in Cochin, 250 in Malacca and 150 in Ormuz. By 1600, 'white' *casados* and soldiers numbered 5,000, with 2,000 in Goa alone. To the east of India, the largest settlement was Macao, with 500–600 people. In general, the Portuguese formed only a small minority even in the major settlements; in Malacca, they were clearly outnumbered by Javanese, Chinese,

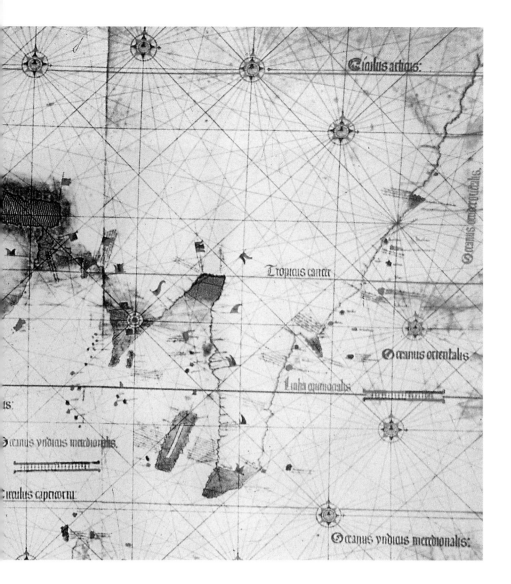

Kelings and Malays. In Goa, however, despite a substantial Hindu minority, Christians constituted a majority by the early 1600s. There were also considerable domestic slaves throughout the *Estado da Índia*, including female slave concubines – perhaps 8,000 in Goa.

A far greater number of Portuguese lived outside the cities, official settlements and garrisons of the *Estado da Índia*. During the first decades of the sixteenth century, commerce attracted many members of the lesser nobility and others seeking their fortune as petty coastal traders and mercenaries. They evaded the political control of the *Estado da Índia* and acted independently of Crown interests. By the 1630s, the total white and *mestiço* Portuguese population throughout Asia did not exceed 15,000, 5,000 of whom were apparently mercenaries in the service of Asian rulers.[27]

By the 1630s, the *Estado da Índia* was in retreat. Already in the last quarter of the sixteenth century, apart from Ottoman presence in the Red Sea, the Portuguese had to reckon with the rise of Iran (Persia) and the Mughal Empire. More important than Indian and Asian powers in the decline of formal Portuguese power, however, was the hostile action of English and (especially) Dutch military and naval forces. Between the 1620s and 1650s, Portugal lost most of its larger Asian possessions to Dutch assault, including Malacca and other key outposts in Indonesia, Sri Lanka and southwest India. When a peace was signed in 1663, the *Estado da Índia* had effectively shrunk to Goa, Damão, Bassein and Diu on the west coast of India, Macao, East Timor and a few settlements on the East African coast.

THE WEST: TRADE AND COLONIZATION IN THE SOUTH ATLANTIC, *c*.1570–1820

From the 1570s onwards, as foreign hostility and other difficulties threatened prosperity in the East, Portuguese attentions increasingly turned westwards to the profitable sugar economy of Brazil. In 1500, the India-bound fleet of Pedro Alvares de Cabral had unexpectedly made landfall on the Brazilian coast, which was immediately claimed by Portugal under the 1494 Treaty of Tordesilhas. This treaty, with the pope's blessing, had divided the world between Castile and Portugal; territories east of a meridian 370 leagues west of the Cape Verde Islands would belong to Portugal, while lands to the west would belong to Spain. The Tordesilhas Line cut through the easternmost part of the South American continent and constituted Brazil's first frontier. Colonial exploitation of the new land offered distinct advantages in comparison to Asia. The sea route from Portugal was shorter, less hazardous and less dependent on annual wind patterns. In contrast to the dense populations and complex political structures of Asia, the semi-sedentary Amerindian peoples dispersed along the Brazilian coast had no centralized political or commercial systems, and were less resistant to foreign intrusion. Even so, the Portuguese were at first too preoccupied with the riches of the Indian Ocean to give Brazilian dyewood, feathers, monkeys and parrots much attention.

By the mid-1530s, the urgency of occupying Brazilian territory, against the colonizing ambitions of France, led to the division of Brazil into fifteen captaincies, following the model adopted for Madeira and São Tomé. In 1549, a centralized administration, under a governor-general, was superimposed on the captaincies, and over the next twenty years authorities expanded control, stimulated economic development and drove the French out of southern Brazil. Centralization was aided by Jesuit missionaries who, though far fewer than in Asia, exercised disproportionate influence.

In the 1540s, the Portuguese population of Brazil was still less than a twentieth of that of Spanish America. However, the pace of colonization increased rapidly in response to rising European demand for sugar. The fertile soils and humid climate of the northeast coast were ideal for sugar, tobacco and cotton. Portuguese emigrants, attracted by easy access to land and opportunities for wealth and social mobility afforded by profits from sugar, developed *engenhos* – a term encompassing the whole complex of land, houses, slaves, animals, technical skills and capital that produced the sugar. The first generations were of relatively humble origins. By 1600, more than 50,000 Portuguese, including numerous women, were concentrated in Pernambuco and Bahia.[28] A hundred mills had an annual production of over 10,000 tons of sugar – 80 per cent of the colony's revenues. Soaring sugar prices kept pace with expanding production until the 1620s, and Brazil remained the world's leading sugar producer as late as 1640. Although fortunes were made from sugar, plantations provided a precarious living, dependent on credit and slaves, weather and the limitations of technology.

The initial growth of the sugar industry had been crucially dependent on cheap labour by the indigenous Tupian people.[29] The Crown, at the urging of the Jesuits, prohibited their enslavement, seeking instead to transform them into docile labourers through peaceful conversion. Thousands of Tupian families were relocated to mission villages under Jesuit protection and control. Such villages proved an easy target for slave raiders, particularly in the sugar areas. The flight of Tupian villagers away from colonized areas, combined with high mortality rates from smallpox and measles, led to a drastic shortfall in labour after 1560, just as the sugar industry was rapidly expanding. The planters looked to Africa to solve their problem. The slave trade to Portugal and the Atlantic islands was already more than a century old, and its extension to Brazil was a natural development. In the second half of the sixteenth century, the Atlantic slave trade delivered 50,000 Africans from Guinea, Mina, the Congo and Angola to the Brazilian plantations.[30]

As the sugar boom got under way, the Portuguese moved to secure the opposite shores of the Atlantic by reasserting authority in the Gulf of Guinea and moving south of the Congo to find new sources of slaves and mineral wealth, notably the silver rumoured to exist in the Angolan interior. Colonists from São Tomé, based on the island of Luanda, had long carried on a profitable contraband slave trade with the African kingdom of Angola, which extended south of the Kwanza river to the borderlands of the Congo. Failure to capture this trade and effect conversion through peaceful relations with Angola's ruler between the 1520s and 1560s led to the Crown's decision, backed by the Jesuits, to occupy and colonize the kingdom. In 1571, a minor noble, Paulo Dias de Novaes,[31] obtained the concession of a hundred miles of barren coastland and the governorship for life of a royal colony to be conquered between the Kwanza and Congo.[32] His invasion force of 300–700 men, accompanied by missionaries, arrived at Luanda on 22 February 1575. High mortality rates, inadequate rainfall for crop cultivation and militant African hostility all contributed to the rapid failure of the enterprise.

Novaes nevertheless managed to establish a foothold at Luanda. He also laid the basis of a future colony by rewarding his followers and Jesuit allies with grants of conquered land, alongside the right to collect tributes in slaves from subjugated African chiefs, in return for 'protecting' them and instructing them in the Catholic faith. By the late sixteenth century, almost half of the 3,000 slaves purchased annually by Brazil came from Angola.[33] In contrast to condemnation of the enslavement of indigenous Brazilians, the Jesuits showed no scruples in trading in black slaves, for which they won papal dispensation. With the aid of African allies and mercenaries, Novaes' successors vigorously completed the conquest of Angola by the 1670s. Continuous warfare and devastation lasting more than a century generated a steadily increasing number of slave captives, whose trade became the main occupation of the Portuguese in Luanda.

Imports of African slaves into Brazil, especially from Angola, eventually averaged 10,000 a year. After 1670, however, prices for sugar and tobacco fell sharply because of foreign competition and a general depression affecting the Atlantic economy. Economic ruin in Brazil was averted by the 1695 discovery of gold in Minas Gerais, which later also yielded diamonds. The discovery set off a gold rush among colonists from the depressed sugar regions to the north, soon outnumbered by emigrants from Portugal, at the rate of 4,000 a year, and the 5,000–6,000 African slaves imported annually into Minas Gerais by 1720. By 1775, Minas Gerais had 300,000 inhabitants – 20 per cent of the population of Brazil – half of them slaves.[34] The flood of immigrants created a volatile society that took more than a decade to bring under effective royal control. Gold production meanwhile grew rapidly, exceeding 15 tons by the 1750s. The southward shift in population, economic and military activity led to the replacement of Bahia by Rio de Janeiro as the colony's capital in 1765. The growth of sugar, indigo and rice plantations continued to stimulate slave imports, transforming the city into an important trade hub linking Brazil to Angola, Mozambique and India.

The upper ranks of colonial government, Church and commerce were filled with the Portuguese-born, and transatlantic kinship networks were maintained by the constant arrival of relatives seeking fortunes. The reward of offices, titles and

THE NATIVE BRAZILIANS did not always receive the Portuguese peacefully. A vivid scene by Theodore de Bry published in 1562, imagined from the descriptions of European eye-witnesses, shows a settlement attacked by a vast crowd of Indians attacking Portuguese boats and felling trees to prevent them escaping back to the sea.

military commissions closely aligned local oligarchies to the Crown. Identification with Portugal further strengthened after 1700 with the massive rush of migrants – half a million by the end of the century – in search of gold and diamonds.[35] There was little distinction between European and Brazilian-born Portuguese until the end of the eighteenth century, by which time a growing proportion were Brazilian-born, with no firsthand acquaintance with Portugal.

CREOLE OLIGARCHIES virtually independent of Lisbon held power in Angola and Mozambique. The estate of Sr Romão de Jesus Maria, an oasis of modern life in the jungle of the Zambesi, made its profits from a combination of agriculture and the slave trade.

BRAZIL: POPULATION, CULTURE AND TRADE

Social integration with Portugal was reinforced by cultural and intellectual dependence. No printing press was allowed in any of the Portuguese possessions before the 1840s. Moreover, any colonial subject who wished to study medicine or law did so at the University of Coimbra in the home country, which enrolled more than 3,000 Brazilians during the colonial era, strengthening a common sense, among colonial elites, of belonging to a wider, more inclusive Portuguese tradition.[36]

Despite the continuous flow of immigration from Portugal, Africans and their descendants formed the largest group in Brazil by 1800. While most were slaves, blacks and mulattoes also comprised a majority of the colony's free population in consequence of widespread miscegenation and manumission.[37] Outwardly European in its forms, Brazilian culture and society was overwhelmingly influenced by the African immigrants at its base. Most slaves learned Portuguese and adopted Catholicism, but the constant influx of blacks also kept alive African traditions.

As in North America, racial mixing resulted more often from necessity and abusive relationships between master and slave than from any unique Portuguese

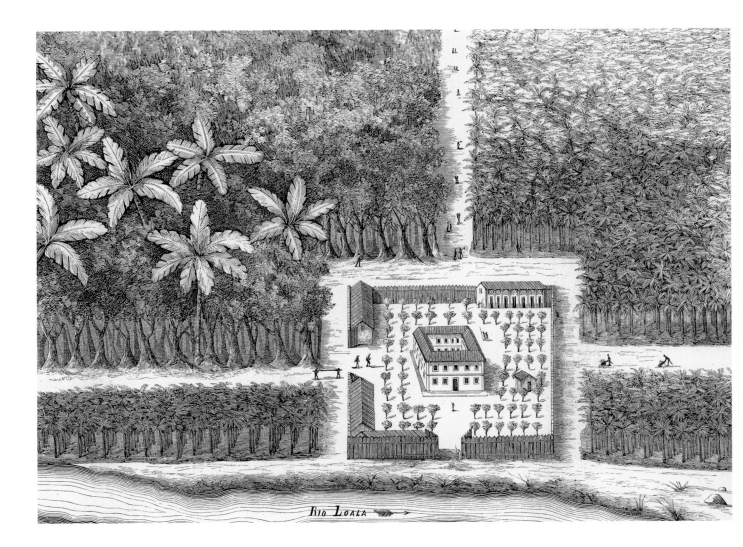

RIO LOALA

talent for racial tolerance, as later colonial apologists claimed.[38] In practice, Portuguese racial attitudes were often extremely prejudiced, especially where racial interaction was more intense. Free persons of mixed race were legally full members of colonial society, but in practice they suffered discrimination. Prejudices against open mixing with blacks did not apply to Amerindians, with whom the Portuguese had formed sexual and marital unions since their earliest encounters.

As Brazilian gold flowed into Portugal, the king observed, with satisfaction, that Brazil was his 'milch cow'.[39] But gold disguised the fact that metropolitan Portugal was only peripherally involved in generating the colonial revenues on which royal prosperity depended. The cloth and other trade goods used to acquire slaves from Africa were imported from northern Europe, mainly from Britain, against the sale of Brazilian sugar and other tropical products. As these fell in value after 1670, Portugal's national debt increased. Brazilian gold made it easy for Portugal to ignore the external trade imbalance. When gold production declined in the 1760s, and international prices of colonial commodities fell, Brazil entered a long period of depression.[40] Royal revenues plummeted, the government deficit increased, and it was apparent that the gold boom had left Portugal far weaker than before.

The crisis demanded vigorous measures. Not for the last time, the Portuguese prime minister, Sebastião José de Carvalho e Melo (later marquis of Pombal), looked to the empire – particularly Brazil – to effect Portugal's economic regeneration, and combat economic dependence on Britain. He launched a radical programme of reforms to make Brazil more responsive to metropolitan needs, reforming and centralizing fiscal procedures. When the Jesuits refused to comply, he confiscated the Order's property and expelled it from the empire. Colonial trade and development were nationalized through the use of monopoly companies, designed to allow Portuguese nationals to compete successfully with foreign merchants. Under Sebastião de Melo, the immense Amazon basin became a prime target for export of cotton, coffee, rare woods, spices and especially cacao. Nevertheless, Brazilian exports in 1776 were only 40 per cent of what they had been in 1760.

More favourable international markets stimulated a dramatic rise in Brazilian exports in the last two decades of the century. Slavery was intensified, and between 1780 and 1800 annual slave exports from Africa rose to 20,000 per annum, up from 16,000 in 1760; Angola supplied 70 per cent of the total.[41] Further escalation followed the Anglo-Portuguese Treaty of 1815, which effectively restricted legal slave exports to Portuguese possessions south of the equator, leaving Angola and, to a lesser extent, Mozambique as principal suppliers. Not surprisingly, the number of slaves transported reached unprecedented heights in the 1810s and 1820s.

In 1807, in the wake of the French invasion of Portugal, King João VI, his family, court, government and 10,000 subjects – among them the cultural elite – were transferred to Rio de Janeiro under British escort, and Rio became the financial and cultural capital of the empire.[42] Yet following a Liberal revolt in Portugal in 1820, the Portuguese parliament demanded the return of the king to Portugal. It also cancelled Brazil's recently acquired equal status as a kingdom within the empire, abolished the new institutions established during the court's sojourn in Rio, and insisted on the return of the royal heir, Pedro, who had meanwhile assumed the role of regent in Brazil. Urged by Brazilians to remain, and with British approval, Pedro declared Brazil's independence, with himself as monarch, in 1822.[43]

THE AFRICAN EMPIRE, 1822–1974

Brazilian independence heralded the dissolution of the empire,[44] which now consisted of a few widely separated enclaves on the coasts of Africa, Asia and the Far East – 'decadent fragments'[45] – over which the Crown exercised no more than formal sovereignty. The residents spoke some Portuguese, were nominally

Catholics and saw themselves loosely as subjects of the Crown. Of varying racial origins and widely distributed throughout the possessions, their role in sustaining the empire was nowhere more crucial than in Africa, where their wealth derived almost exclusively from the slave trade. Thus in Angola, Portuguese presence was sustained by Creole oligarchies, who had traditionally occupied the prestigious military, civil and ecclesiastical posts. They were nevertheless far from subservient to Lisbon. If they upheld Portuguese sovereignty, it was on their own terms.

The survival of the empire was further complicated by the changing international climate. Increasingly, Portuguese reassertion of colonial sovereignty had to be tempered with the need to secure support from rival European powers. The slave trade, in particular, became a central issue, profoundly influencing the way in which the Portuguese African empire was viewed, especially by Britain. By the 1820s, Portugal was the only European country that had not outlawed the 'odious' trade. Failure to suppress the slave trade or to enforce anti-slavery laws exposed Portugal's ineffective sovereignty over her African possessions, giving Britain – which, since the early 1800s, had unilaterally defined Portugal's colonial relations in the name of the Luso-British alliance – an easy moral pretext to intervene in Portuguese colonial affairs. In Portugal, the assertion of national sovereignty against British interference in the empire dominated political and public debate, becoming an important focus for nationalist sentiment.[46]

Nineteenth-century politicians and commentators increasingly looked to what remained of the empire to resolve the crisis of Portugal's identity and destiny. The link between nation and the empire was underlined by principles defined in the wake of the 1820 revolution, which invoked Enlightenment beliefs in universal values, laws, government and citizenship. The Constitutional Charter of 1826, which remained in force, with interruptions, until the proclamation of the republic in 1910, united Portugal and her possessions within one indivisible nation, transforming the African and Asian enclaves into 'provinces' of the mother country, with the right to representation in the parliament in Lisbon. This idea of a 'greater Portugal' remained dominant up to 1974. However, early attempts to assimilate the overseas 'provinces' within the metropolitan

PORTUGUESE OCCUPATION of African lands was achieved through military conquest. In 1895 a chief called Ngungunhana led a force of over ten thousand men in a fight for freedom, but they were defeated by an army a tenth of that size. Afterwards their leader was surprised and captured in a daring raid – an event commemorated by the Portuguese artist Morais Carvalho.

administrative structure were quickly reversed as impracticable in the 1830s. Likewise, the extension of citizenship and constitutional rights to Africans was only partially implemented in the absence of any effective 'civilizing mission' to spread Portuguese culture.

In parliamentary debates and the press, the colonial question became inseparable from that of national identity. Two overlapping discourses can be discerned. The first stressed the historical value of overseas territories, which bore witness to national greatness and past heroic deeds. This view was counterbalanced by an apparently more rational, yet equally mythical, notion that envisaged national salvation through the construction of a 'new Brazil' in the African territories. The idea built on the conviction, reiterated since the sixteenth century, that the African colonies, especially Angola, had unlimited mineral wealth and fertile soil which European colonization and capital could transform.

A CHANGING VISION OF EMPIRE

The first systematic efforts to implement this dream, in the 1850s, were, by and large, a failure. The meagre resources at the disposal of colonial governors were insufficient to overcome shortages of capital and manpower, and legislation designed to bring about the gradual abolition of slavery stayed mainly on paper. Audacious attempts to expand Portuguese sovereignty by military conquest of the hinterlands of Angola and Mozambique underestimated the strength of African resistance, leading to crushing defeats, while deadly tropical diseases decimated metropolitan troops.[47] By the late 1870s, according to one source, the Portuguese Empire in Angola was purely 'imaginary', the colonial outposts in the interior resembling 'islands lost in a boundless ocean of natives'.[48]

Yet, paradoxically, the industry of those 'natives' saved the colonies from bankruptcy. Between the 1840s and 1910s, the prosperity of the colonial enclaves depended overwhelmingly on trade with surrounding African societies.

A ROYAL COMMISSION was sent to Africa in 1891 to settle the frontier between Portuguese Mozambique and British Rhodesia.

The greater part of colonial exports came from independent initiatives by African farmers, hunters and foragers, responding to lower prices of imported European goods and rising prices of exports of palm products, wax, resin, groundnuts and ivory, and later coffee and rubber. To be sure, much of the trade escaped Portuguese fiscal control. Even so, the customs revenues of the Angolan colony doubled between the 1840s and 1870s. This commerce was the principal activity of backwoodsmen agents – whites as well as Creoles – of Portuguese firms at the coast. They extended the old slaving routes ever deeper into the interior of the continent in search of exports, disseminating Portuguese cultural and economic influences.

Longstanding claims to the Congo estuary, whose lucrative trade Portuguese politicians had tried to bring under fiscal control since the 1820s, were shattered by the Conference of Berlin in 1885, which gave international recognition to King Leopold of Belgium's Congo Free State. This loss was partially compensated by the Portuguese reoccupation of the capital of the old Congo kingdom, São Salvador, south of the river, with the consent of its octogenarian ruler who had reaffirmed his loyalty to the Portuguese Crown in 1881. There were also renewed attempts to realize the ancient dream, based on Portugal's presumed historical rights, of expanding the empire across the continent to join up Angola and Mozambique, and in 1886 Portugal formally claimed a huge swathe of central Africa. However, attempts to occupy it brought Lisbon into direct conflict with Cecil Rhodes and Britain. In February 1890, London delivered a formal ultimatum to Lisbon to halt all operations in the region. Portugal had no alternative but to back down and accept Britain's proposal of a negotiated settlement. Separate treaties signed with Britain and Germany in 1891 finally determined the modern frontiers of Angola and Mozambique. The loss of central Africa, with its potentially vast mining and agricultural wealth, dashed Portuguese fantasies of transforming the African empire into a 'new Brazil'. The British ultimatum engendered feelings of intense humiliation among the Portuguese, intensifying nationalistic fervour in defence of empire.

Portugal was also confronted by the urgent need to 'pacify' and occupy the three widely separated territories of Angola, Mozambique and Guiné-Bissau – an area approximately the size of western Europe. Most of the African societies there were still independent, although gradually being transformed through missionary activity and the cash economy. Many African rulers were still powerful enough to mobilize thousands of warriors, resisting colonial occupation with firearms obtained through external commerce. Only after introduction of the machine gun in the 1890s did the balance swing dramatically in favour of colonial forces. Even so, Portugal's military weakness prolonged local resistance, particularly in Angola and Guiné, where African insurgency continued well into the 1930s.[49]

Mozambique saw the largest deployment of white Portuguese soldiers; 1,000–2,000 took part in the campaigns which crushed the vast southern African 'empire' of Gaza, whose ruler, Ngungunhana, according to the Portuguese political commissar, could count on 100,000 supporters, 'not all warriors, but all of them fanatics'.[50] It took only a few months for Portuguese military columns to defeat Gaza in 1895. The decisive engagement came when 557 Portuguese and 500 African auxiliaries took just forty minutes to rout an estimated 10,000–15,000 of Ngungunhana's warriors, most of whom were slaughtered by machine-gun and rifle fire. Ngungunhana was captured in a daring raid; arriving as a captive in Lisbon three months later, the 'Lion of Gaza', his wives, son and advisers were imprisoned in an open cage mounted on a carriage, and paraded triumphantly through streets lined by thousands of curious spectators, before being deported to the Azores.[51]

The Gaza campaigns highlighted the emergence of an influential elite of administrators and military officers dedicated to the regeneration of Portugal and the empire. For the 'generation of 1895', the wars in Africa were not just about the patriotic mission of reviving Portugal's former glory in overseas military feats. They were an essential preliminary to the more systematic economic exploitation of the African territories. As Antonio Enes emphasized in 1898: 'The State must not have the least scruple in obliging and, if necessary, forcing those uncivilized African negroes… to work.' This sentiment was enshrined in the harsh 1899 colonial labour code, explicitly legalizing forced labour, which remained in force with little modification up to the late 1950s.

Between the 1890s and 1930s, Portugal suffered almost continuous economic, financial and political crisis. The republic which replaced the monarchy in 1910 tried to achieve more efficient and rational exploitation of the empire by decentralizing the administration, abolishing monopolies and reducing protectionism. The policies were frustrated by a slump in the prices of colonial raw materials, the outbreak of the First World War and political disintegration of the First Republic itself in the 1920s.

Portuguese political opinion was more or less unanimous as to the necessity of civilizing overseas territories through white colonization. Before the 1920s Portuguese rural and urban poor preferred to escape poverty by emigrating to Brazil, rather than to Africa, which was identified with penal sentence and death. Nevertheless, the white population in Angola and Mozambique increased gradually, due in part to settlement of soldiers from pacification campaigns, and to progressive substitution of commerce in the interior by mining and agriculture. Increases in white colonists brought about alienation of established Creole elites, whose members were thrust downwards into lower-paid jobs in the bureaucracy by raised educational standards and restricted promotions.

The financially feeble Portuguese state meanwhile faced the constant threat of alienation and repartition of its colonies by rival powers: in particular, Britain. A main bone of contention was the continuing slave trade, despite the official abolition of slavery and its replacement by a contract labour system in the 1870s. Perversely, before the 1910s, most African labourers contracted for colonial enterprises were 'ransomed' as slaves by Creole traders from the still autonomous African societies inland. The prosperity of coffee and cocoa plantations in São Tomé plunged the whole of Angola into a new upsurge of slave trading which reached a climax by 1910, when 3,000–4,000 labourers were annually contracted. As far back as 1877, the British consul in Luanda had

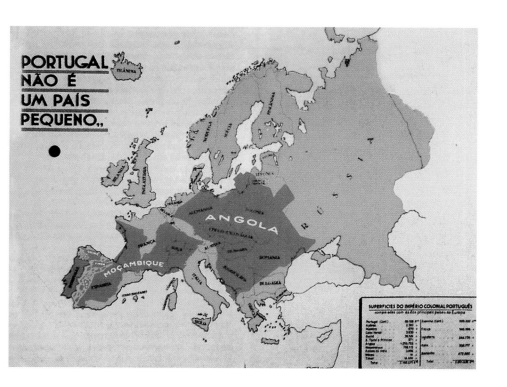

To BOOST IMPERIALIST PRIDE in 1931 an exhibition was held in Porto under President Salazar. It included this map, entitled 'Portugal Is Not a Small Country', which compares the relative sizes of the mother-country, Mozambique and Angola.

TALK OF ASSIMILATION was well intentioned but had little meaning for the 'natives' of Angola and Mozambique. A photograph of a plantation in the 1900s or 1910s tells its own story.

protested about the 'farce' of supposed free labour emigration between Angola and São Tomé, as well as the inhuman conditions in which labourers were transported in 'herds', 'like animals, without privacy or separation by sex, obliged to sleep together with pigs, goats and sheep'.[52] Denunciations culminated in the 1925 Ross Report, elaborated at the request of the League of Nations, which exposed the brutal conditions in Portuguese Africa.

THE 'NEW STATE' AND THE AFRICAN COLONIES, 1930–61

The First Republic was ended in 1926 by a military coup, which inaugurated the 'Dictatorship' and implantation of the authoritarian 'New State' led by António de Oliveira Salazar from 1933. Between the 1930s and 1960s, his regime focused, yet again, on using the empire to bolster nationalism and regenerate the weak home economy. In policy adopted in 1930, colonial economic activity was strictly subordinated to concepts of national unity, expressed through a renewed 'colonial pact'. Essentially, this involved a more systematic exploitation of colonies as suppliers of raw materials to metropolitan industries, and their establishment as protected markets for Portuguese manufactures. Measures nationalizing colonial economies, together with improvements in transport infrastructures, achieved the return of colonial prosperity in the 1940s. During the Second World War, the colonies registered an economic boom thanks to a general rise in international demand and in prices of colonial products. By 1950, the substantial surpluses generated from colonial trade and production were successfully subsidizing Portugal's chronic trade deficit. For the first time since the loss of Brazil, the empire brought relative prosperity to the Portuguese state.[53]

In parallel with the economic mobilization of the colonies, New State ideologues consciously used the empire, through rhetoric and imagery, to reinforce national pride and identity. Thus, for Armindo Monteiro, Minister for the Colonies between 1931 and 1935, the empire was 'above finances, economy and politics'. It was the 'consubstantiation of the Portuguese ideal itself', in communion with the past and with moral and national sentiments.[54]

Nowhere was the gap between rhetoric and colonial realities greater by the 1950s than in the Portuguese doctrine of 'assimilation'. Portuguese India, Macao and Cape Verde had long been considered culturally, as well as politically, assimilated with the metropole. In Portuguese Guinea, Angola and Mozambique, however, special policies were devised for the African majority. The separate legal status of 'natives', with particular legislation covering native affairs, had been established during the First Republic with the paternalist aim of protecting Africans from abuses of land and labour rights. The separation continued under the Dictatorship with the Native Statute (1926),[55] which institutionalized the distinction between '*civilizados*' and '*indigenas*', the latter governed by their own customs and not by metropolitan law. Assimilation or the right to the same juridical privileges as Portuguese-born citizens would be obtained through learning the Portuguese language, education and Christianity.[56] The philanthropic tone of the legislation belied the harsh reality of life for most Africans, since lack of educational provision and continuing labour abuses effectively maintained the status quo. By the 1950s, less than 0.5 per cent of Africans in Angola, Mozambique and Guiné were culturally assimilated into colonial society.[57]

From the Africans' point of view, the authoritarian and increasingly coercive colonial framework within which government and private agents operated between the 1920s and 1950s seems to have been more violent and oppressive even than that of neighbouring colonial regimes. Individual population mobility was denied, yet whole villages were relocated to places where inhabitants could be more easily controlled and taxed. Colonial labour demands for construction, porterage, mining, or work on plantations of sugar cane, sisal, tea, coffee or cotton often involved forced removal of African

PATRIOTIC SENTIMENTS underlay films of the 1930s, such as *The Enchantment of Empire*.

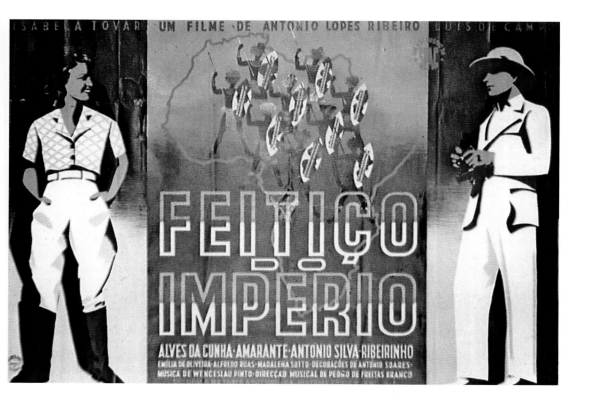

EDUCATION AND RELIGION were two of the benefits routinely quoted as the products of colonization. Teacher and pupils of the American Methodist Mission at Kisua.

workers. With the return of prosperity in the 1940s, forced cultivation of cotton intensified. Women and children in particular were pressed into agricultural labour and road-building. In Angola, the spread of white colonization and plantations led to alienation of the best arable land under African cultivation. Many Africans avoided direct confrontation or integration into the colonial world by migrating to inaccessible forests, bush or mountains, beyond the reach of colonial armies or labour recruiters.

Faced with renewed international pressures, in the context of the United Nations' Charter and Declaration of Human Rights, Portugal explicitly restated the underlying principle of assimilation which justified the empire. In 1951, a revised constitution explicitly defined Portugal as a 'pluricontinental nation' composed of European and overseas provinces integrated in an indivisible national unity.

In reality, the 1950s saw growing racial tension in colonial centres like Luanda. *Mestiços* and 'assimilated' Africans who occupied colonial administrative posts and skilled and semi-skilled jobs faced intense competition from white immigrants convinced of their racial superiority. Wage differentials based on skin colour were common.[58] The MPLA (*Movimento Popular para a Libertação de Angola* – 'Popular Movement for the Liberation of Angola') emerged in the late 1950s to defend *assimilado* interests,[59] gaining much support among the rapidly growing black urban working class in Luanda. By the late 1950s, Salazar's authoritarian regime was out of step with the social democratic governments in other European countries, which were rapidly decolonizing. Despite their best efforts, the New State's secret police, sent to the African colonies in 1957, proved unable to prevent incipient nationalist and liberation movements in Angola and Mozambique. The independence of the Belgian Congo in 1960 was the spark that ignited tensions in Angola. From 1961 onwards, the Portuguese regime was openly contested, in Portugal as well as in the colonies. In Angola, an attempt to liberate prisoners from Luanda gaols was followed by attacks on white coffee plantations and administrative posts.[60] Meanwhile, in December 1961, Goa, Damão and Diu were invaded and occupied by India. In Africa, colonial conflict spread to Guinea in 1963, and Mozambique in 1964, leading to a decade of armed struggle against the Portuguese in all three African territories.

In 1961, in the face of uprisings in Luanda, extensive measures were passed abolishing forced labour, forced cultivation and the Native Statute. With renewed emphasis on the formation of multiracial societies,[61] conditions for Africans finally improved through wider provisions for schooling and health care. Greater employment opportunities and freedom of movement resulted in an exodus of Africans from villages to colonial cities. This was favoured by high rates of economic growth as colonies were opened to foreign capital and the protectionist measures imposed in the 1930s were finally relaxed, attracting an unprecedented number of white colonists. The white populations of both Angola and Mozambique more than doubled between 1960 and 1973, when they totalled 324,000 and 190,000, respectively, giving substance to the vision of overseas provinces as a prolongation of Portugal. The Portuguese regime was thus able to resist the growing tide of African nationalism for well over a decade longer than other European powers, before decolonization was finally imposed by the revolution of 1974, and Portugal formally granted independence in 1975.

THE IMAGE of a new 'greater Portugal' persisted until the mid-century, but it was an ideal destined never to be realized. Shown *below* is the cover of a government magazine dedicated to primary school education, dated October 1960.

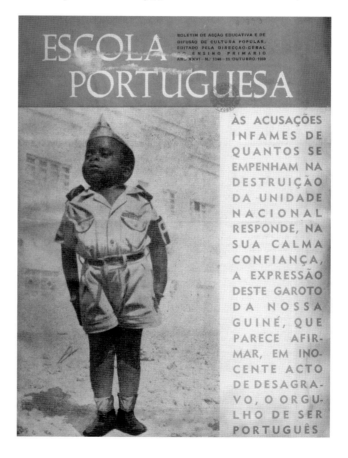

ESCOLA PORTUGUESA

BOLETIM DE ACÇÃO EDUCATIVA E DE DIFUSÃO DE CULTURA POPULAR, EDITADO PELA DIRECÇÃO-GERAL DO ENSINO PRIMARIO ANL XXVI - N. 1246 - 25 OUTUBRO 1960

ÀS ACUSAÇÕES INFAMES DE QUANTOS SE EMPENHAM NA DESTRUIÇÃO DA UNIDADE NACIONAL RESPONDE, NA SUA CALMA CONFIANÇA, A EXPRESSÃO DESTE GAROTO DA NOSSA GUINÉ, QUE PARECE AFIRMAR, EM INOCENTE ACTO DE DESAGRAVO, O ORGULHO DE SER PORTUGUÊS

4 The Netherlands: A Small Country with Imperial Ambitions

ESTHER CAPTAIN AND GUNO JONES

A FLOOD of scientific knowledge as well as material profit was among the rewards of empire. One result of the Dutch possession of Suriname, or Dutch Guiana, in South America was a lavish book of natural history, *Metamorphosis Insectorum Surinamensis* ('The Metamorphosis of Surinamese Insects') of 1705 by Maria Sibylla Merian (*opposite*). This plate shows the *Flos Pavonis* ('Peacock Flower'), which has a particular poignancy in the history of Suriname. It was used by slave women as an aid to abortion, so that their children should not become slaves themselves.

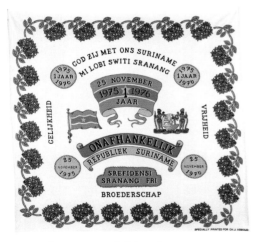

SURINAME GAINED its independence in 1975 and adopted this coat of arms (*above*), with mottoes in Creole and Dutch.

LIKE OTHER FORMER IMPERIALIST NATIONS, the Netherlands has recently heard strongly critical voices raised internally against colonialism and colonial institutions. It is important to pay attention to these voices, not only for the authors of this chapter, both of whom are post-colonial Dutch citizens of mixed ethnic descent with family linkages to the East (Captain) and West (Jones) as well as to the Netherlands, but for a more balanced historiography of Dutch colonial rule and decolonization in general.

The year 2002 proved to be unusually significant in this respect. First, the 400th anniversary of the Verenigde Oost-Indische Compagnie (VOC) was commemorated by a special government-funded committee set up for this occasion, and by other official institutions. These were contested by various private initiatives, varying from symposia featuring highly critical appraisals of Dutch colonialism by speakers of Eurasian, Dutch, Indonesian and Moluccan descent to a committee called 'Celebration of 400 Years of VOC? No!'. Second, a long-awaited monument commemorating the abolition of slavery in the West Indies was unveiled in Amsterdam by Queen Beatrix, in the presence of many distinguished Dutch and international guests, on 1 July 2002. This represented an important step in recognizing slavery as an integral part of Dutch history. Yet many visitors to the inaugural ceremony, mostly black, were kept out of sight of the dignitaries and away from the monument itself by fences, treatment that provoked tension and fierce protests.

At the same time, no one can deny the sheer magnitude of the historical Dutch presence overseas. The Netherlands is a small country. Yet, beginning in 1682 with the foundation of the West Indische Compagnie (WIC), Dutch trade, exploration and – when it came to colonization and slavery – exploitation stretched across the entire globe. In North America and the Caribbean, Dutch possessions ranged from New York, a city founded by the Dutch as New Amsterdam, to islands in the West Indies, including Aruba, Bonaire, Curaçao, Sint Maarten, Sint Eustacius and Saba, still part of the Kingdom of the Netherlands. In the Old World, in addition to the Indonesian archipelago,

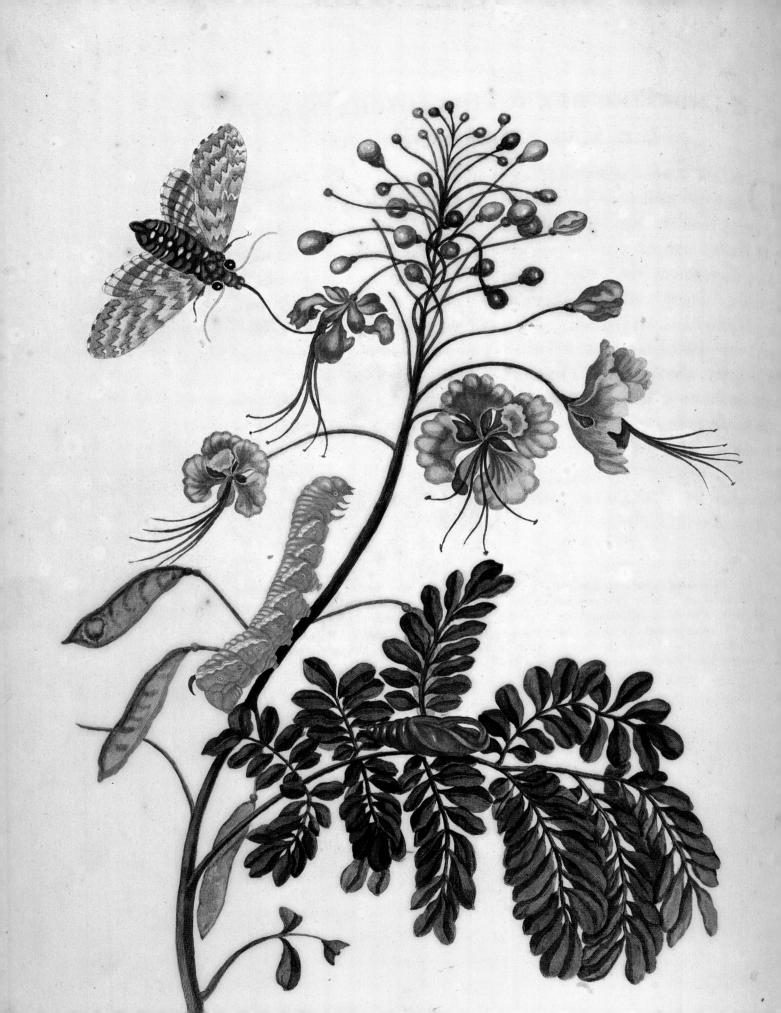

THE SENIOR MERCHANT of Batavia in 1665 was Pieter Cnoll, portrayed here with his Japanese wife, two daughters and Indonesian slave. The family display all the signs of wealth – costly jewelry, elegant fans and a golden *sirih*-box held by one of the daughters.

the Dutch claimed trading posts on the coasts of Africa, in India and in Ceylon (Sri Lanka), and Dutch Boers ('farmers') established major settler colonies near the Cape of Good Hope in southern Africa.[1]

Colonization enriched the Netherlands in many ways: from the fortunes made by private individuals and money earned for the national treasury, to the birth of new population groups of mixed ethnic descent and thus an increased demographic diversity in the country. The foreign relations of the Netherlands have been characterized as an intriguing mixture of peace, profits and principles.[2] Imperialism can be considered historically as an adjunct to the Netherlands' trading activities. Since decolonization, the Dutch have promoted human rights and development aid for other countries in global affairs. As a free-trade nation and an active member of international organizations, the Netherlands is often eager to set an example to other states, sometimes forgetting its own complex history of exploration as well as exploitation.[3]

AFRICA AND AMERICA: ACCIDENTAL EMPIRES

Before discussing Indonesia and Suriname, the main subjects of this chapter, two other areas of Dutch imperial enterprise deserve to be briefly mentioned. Neither counted seriously as empires, though both, in different circumstances, might have had lasting and far-reaching consequences: Africa and North America.

might have had lasting and far-reaching consequences: Africa and North America.

might have had lasting and far-reaching consequences: Africa and North America.

The settlement of South Africa was a consequence of the Dutch occupation of Indonesia. Dutch East India Company ships plying the spice trade formed the habit of putting in at the southern tip of Africa to replenish their food and water supplies. In 1652 a permanent station operated by company employees was established under Governor Jan van Riebeeck. The station, which soon expanded into a proto-colony with freehold farms worked by African slave labour, flourished to such an extent that by 1707 there were nearly 1,800 European settlers, including women and children. They were self-governing, though ultimately subject to the authority of Batavia, and beyond that to the European directors of the VOC in the Netherlands.

This arrangement, which amounted to virtual independence, continued until the late eighteenth century. The language spoken by the settlers, Afrikaans, in time deviated markedly from that spoken at home. The area under European occupation increased rapidly, the only opposition coming from Khoisan villagers. The colonists were rugged individualists, often living far from urban areas. Many had children with African women, giving birth to the population that came to be known as 'Cape Coloured'. All this formed a social milieu virtually beyond the control of the Dutch government, and very different from that of Indonesia and Suriname. No attempt was made to draw Dutch and Africans together.

From about 1780 relations between the Afrikaners and Africans deteriorated. As the Boers took over more territory, they found that northerly tribes such as the Xhosa proved more formidable enemies than the Khoisan. In 1795 the situation was further complicated by the arrival of two other European powers. First the French, who had conquered the Netherlands and now presumed to do the same with its colonies. Then the British, who captured Cape Town in the name of the prince of Orange, whom they supported as the legitimate ruler. In 1814 the Congress of Vienna decreed that South Africa should be British. After that, it becomes part of the story of the British Empire, though it retained, and still retains, crucial elements of its Dutch origin in areas such as law, commerce and land ownership. English became the official language. British immigrants flooded in, although they did not bond with the Boers. Tension increased until breaking point was reached when 12,000 Boers decided to leave the colony and found a new country of their own: this was the Great Trek, which lasted from 1835 to 1843. After years of mutual hostility and bloodshed a new republic, the Orange Free State, was recognized in 1852. There followed more years of a three-way conflict between British, Boers and Africans ending in the Anglo-Boer War of 1899–1902, which the British won. In 1910 South Africa became a self-governing dominion of the Commonwealth, characterized by a (not always happy) balance between British and Dutch: an unusual, if not unique, end to the story of an empire. In constitutional terms, to be more precise: the Dutch presence left as its legacy the enduring ideological and political legacy of 'apartheid', designed by (Amsterdam-born) Hendrik Verwoerd, which only came to an end after decades of persistent liberation struggle and continued pressure from the international community. After the release of Nelson Mandela in 1990, the oppressive apartheid system was finally dismantled and replaced by a non-racial democracy, based on the principle of 'one person one vote'.

Does North America perhaps offer a parallel? In 1609 the Dutch East Indies Company employed Henry Hudson to explore the coast of what is now New England and, encouraged by his report, claimed it for the Netherlands. In 1614 a company was formed by merchants from Amsterdam and Hoorn which promoted immigration, settlement and trade in the province they called New Netherlands, where they built Fort Orange (now Albany) and Fort Amsterdam (at the southern end of Manhattan Island). Immigrant farmers were encouraged to cross the Atlantic and settle there. The colony did well, though in 1641 the Dutch engaged in serious conflict with the Amerindians. By 1650, however, English settlers were building up another colony up the coast to the north and were claiming Manhattan as their own. In 1664, by which time the Dutch population numbered 10,000, the governor, Peter Stuyvesant, was forced to surrender New Amsterdam, which became New York. Apart from a brief period from 1673 to 1674 when the Dutch managed to recapture the outpost, that has been its name ever since, a few old family traditions and various street names now providing the major reminders of the Dutch colonial presence. Dutch colonialism in other parts of the world had a longer life.

EMPIRE AND EMPIRES: INDONESIA AND SURINAME

In 2005 the Dutch foreign minister, Ben Bot, journeyed to Jakarta for a ceremony commemorating the Indonesian Republic's sixty years of independence, a visit laden with symbolism even in the very choice of date. The Dutch Government, for the first time, implicitly recognized that the key date in contemporary Indonesian history was 17 August 1945, when Indonesia was declared independent by Sukarno, who became its first president, rather than 27 December 1949, when the Netherlands formally transferred sovereignty to Indonesia. In previous years no one from the Dutch Government had even attended the independence celebrations of its ex-colony.

In the western hemisphere, Suriname (often known in English as Dutch Guiana) also celebrated thirty years of *Srefidensi*, or independence, in 2005. In this case, the partition date of 25 November 1975 is undisputed by either Suriname or the Netherlands. Other parts of the Dutch Empire, the Netherlands Antilles and Aruba, autonomous territories in the West Indies, are still part of the Kingdom of the Netherlands; they will not be discussed in this chapter.

The remarkable difference in the timings of these acts of political decolonization shows that, for several reasons, it is impossible to talk about 'the Dutch empire' in the singular. The 'Kingdom of the Netherlands' covers very different economic, historical, political, constitutional and social situations. The two former colonies of Indonesia in the East and Suriname in the West were very different in size. The Netherlands established its rule in those countries with different administrative practices, and in the thirty-odd years between the two decolonization processes the historical context altered greatly. The mother country therefore left the two ex-colonies varying legacies.

All the same, there exist similarities and cross-connections between the two colonies. Racist views about the Indonesian and Surinamese peoples were used to justify the Dutch presence in both countries. Administrative methods that had been tested in the East were sometimes applied in the West. The populations of Indonesia and Suriname were alike in not submitting meekly to colonialism and its legacy. Neither in the East Indies nor in the West Indies, however, were colonizers and colonized totally divided into separate spheres, even though the distancing of the groups provided the basis of the colonial system and the ideology that underpinned it. To understand how Indonesia and Suriname were colonized and decolonized, it must be realized that the distinction between colonizers and colonized was flexible, and metamorphosed over time as circumstances themselves changed.

This chapter will address four main questions. First, how did the Netherlands establish its rule in Indonesia and Suriname and what were the administrative practices associated with that domination? Second, what was the legacy of Dutch colonialism in the countries that the Netherlands ruled? Third, how did their populations react to Dutch rule and its legacy? Fourth, how were the two countries decolonized? Paradoxically, perhaps, these questions are most easily answered by starting with the current situation and looking at Indonesia and Suriname from a contemporary perspective.

Indonesia is an enormous archipelago, covering an area of 1,919,440 sq km (741,096 sq miles), with a population of about 238 million,[4] and a GDP in 2005 of US$257 billion. This compares dramatically with Suriname, which covers an area of only 163,000 sq km (62,934 sq miles), and has a population of 500,000 and a GDP of US$1.5 billion.[5] This contrast explains why the national self-image

PILGRIMAGE was one of the duties of a Muslim. This man has just returned from Mecca, 1854.

of the Netherlands as an empire was related first and foremost to the East rather than the West, and also why the decolonization process was so different in the two countries.[6]

Both Indonesia and Suriname are culturally and ethnically very diverse, though in different ways. Indonesian society comprises 300 different ethnic groups speaking 250 languages.[7] Muslims form the overwhelming majority in religion; indeed, Indonesia is the largest Islamic country in the world. Suriname does not have a dominant religion. Besides the Amerindians, the original inhabitants who are now few in number, there are descendants of Dutch farmers, Jews, Chinese, Lebanese, Javanese (from the East Indies), Maroons (descendants of rebel enslaved Africans who settled in the interior of the country), Creoles (of African or mixed descent) and Hindus (from British India). Numerically, the last four groups in particular (in ascending order of size) define Suriname's ethnic 'mosaic', while the *métis* population is growing.[8] Christianity, Hinduism and Islam are all well represented. Since the ancestors of the current population came from all over the world, Suriname has been called 'the world in a nutshell'. That term reflects an important distinction between Indonesian and Surinamese diversity. The Dutch had virtually no impact on the make-up of the Indonesian population, because there the demographic diversity was already established when the Europeans arrived. In Suriname, on the other hand, the Netherlands created 'its own subjects' by taking people (or forcing them to come) there from all over the world.

DUTCH COLONIAL RULE IN INDONESIA AND SURINAME

Indonesia was originally a Dutch trading colony and remained so for several centuries; the Dutch presence in the East Indies was always based on economic interests. On 29 March 1602, the parliament of the Netherlands granted the VOC a charter giving it administrative powers, as well as an exclusive right to trade and sign treaties with indigenous rulers, in the Indonesian archipelago. The East Indies Company recognized the authority of these rulers and their legal systems, so long as this arrangement did not conflict with Dutch economic interests. Indonesia thus remained primarily a trading colony of the Netherlands until about 1830.[9]

As the years went by, the Dutch state's grip on the colony nevertheless became stronger. In 1796, property acquired by the Dutch in Indonesia was taken over by the state, and the VOC's administration of the country was

THE ESTABLISHED RELIGION of Indonesia was Islam. Dutch missionary efforts had practically no effect. In fact, it is still home to the largest Islamic population in the world. Javanese mosques constitute a distinctive type unlike any other.

DUTCH RULE in Indonesia was
administered by a governor-general
appointed from the mother country.
From 1617 to 1630 the post was
occupied by Jan Pieterszoon Coen
(*above*), who used his authority both to
defeat his English rivals and to 'ride the
natives with a sharp spur'. He founded
the capital, Batavia, and was largely
responsible for establishing the Dutch
Empire in the east, but left a reputation
for cruelty that has been a stain on its
memory.

THE DEEP HARBOUR of Batavia, in Java,
capable of taking great ocean-going
galleons, fronted a cosmopolitan city
with two long piers and a network of
canals like Amsterdam. In this painting
by Ivan Rynne of about 1780 (*right*) the
mighty Dutch ships loom over the frail
Chinese junks.

COFFEE BECAME a main export of Dutch Indonesia in the 18th century and continued to be so for nearly two centuries. This view of a plantation (*right*), the European owner standing in the centre, dates from about 1876.

SLAVES IMPORTED from West Africa provided the workforce of Suriname. In the first years of the 19th century they revolted and in a long campaign were ruthlessly suppressed and punished. John Gabriel Stedman expressed a widely shared horror in his 1806 book, which included this drawing of 'A negro hung alive by the ribs from a gallows' (*below*). There are skulls stuck on poles in the background.

dissolved.[10] The Netherlands henceforth ruled Indonesia directly, through a governor-general appointed by the Dutch parliament. Maintaining a hands-off policy in most of the East Indies, the Dutch concentrated their rule on specific parts of the archipelago, in particular Java and Ambon (the largest island in the Moluccas),[11] while exercising only limited authority over the other islands, which were known as the 'Outer Provinces'. The Dutch administration, it was officially stated, 'should refrain from expansion and seek to establish good relations with the Indonesian rulers',[12] a policy that continued until around 1870. Subsequently further territory was slowly but surely brought under Dutch rule. For instance the Sultanate of Aceh, whose independence the Netherlands had initially recognized, was taken over by the Dutch in a thirty-year war.[13]

The hands-off policy did not prevent the Netherlands from keeping a firm hold over the territories considered the core of its eastern empire. In 1830, for example, Governor-General Johannes van de Bosch introduced *cultuurstelsel*, or forced farming, to Java.[14] Under this system,[15] which reflected the transformation of Java from a trading colony to an agricultural colony, the Dutch administration forced the Javanese to grow crops such as sugar, indigo, pepper, tobacco, coffee, tea and cinnamon for the European market, paying labourers a pittance,[16] a form of exploitation reminiscent of slavery and indentured labour. The system underlined Indonesia's status as a conquered territory, which in fact the Dutch parliament proclaimed the East Indies colony to be in 1854.[17]

The forced farming system proved of relatively short duration and was abolished in 1891. From about 1900, the guiding principle of Dutch rule was the so-called 'ethical policy'. Open forms of exploitation of the Javanese population gave way to a phase in which the Dutch presence was legitimized as a *mission civilisatrice* for the people of the archipelago. Since 'strong state authority' was considered essential to the civilizing mission, the Dutch colonial administration, through military action, now established effective control over the Outer Provinces. From 1922, the Dutch East Indies was officially part – not simply a possession – of the Kingdom of the Netherlands. Even so, sovereignty was still vested in the central government, which long ignored Indonesian nationalism. Although the latter had first emerged around 1908, it was less tolerated in subsequent decades, widening the gulf between the Dutch and the Indonesians. Moderate nationalism did find expression in 1936 in the People's Council, a consultative body of the Dutch East Indies government, although the setting up of this 'Volksraad' did not signify the beginnings of self-government. The historian Elsbeth Locher-Scholten calls the 1930s, in which the Netherlands was hit by the world economic crisis, 'the most repressive decade in twentieth-century Dutch rule' in Indonesia. That rule lasted until 1942, when it was brought to an abrupt end by the Japanese occupation, which 'reversed the colonial hierarchy'.[18]

In Suriname, too, the pursuit of profit was the main factor in the genesis and establishment of Dutch colonial rule, which began in 1667 when Abraham Crijnsen captured Suriname from the British on behalf of the province of Zeeland. The West Indies Company administered Suriname in conjunction with the municipal government of Amsterdam and the Aerssens van Sommelsdijck family (proprietors of the 'Suriname Company').[19] In contrast to the East Indies, where the Dutch presence was linked to trade, the Dutch in Suriname established a plantation economy based on slavery – slavery certainly existed in Indonesia, but was not the basis of Dutch colonialism in Asia as it was in the Americas.[20]

Although the original slaves in Suriname were Amerindians, Africans were soon brought in as plantation labour. In the transatlantic slave trade, the British, French, Portuguese, Spanish and Dutch, among others, imported slaves from Africa and then sold them throughout the Americas and the Caribbean.[21] Dutch slave traders are estimated to have been responsible for 5 per cent of the total transatlantic slave trade, involving about 555,000 people.[22]

In 1791, when the West Indies Company collapsed, the Dutch parliament decided that administration of the colony would be transferred from the 'chartered company of Suriname', of which the West Indies Company had been part, to a 'council of state colonies and possessions'. The governor no longer represented the 'chartered company', but the state of the Netherlands. That change, however, did not end slavery, which was not officially abolished until 1863.[23]

From 1873 to the beginning of the twentieth century, indentured labourers recruited by the Netherlands from Java and from British India replaced slaves on the plantations, though the conditions in which Javanese and Indian contract labourers worked often differed very little from slavery.[24] The Surinamese thinker and activist Anton de Kom, born in Paramaribo in 1898, in *Wij slaven van Suriname* (1933) offered an analysis of the complex power relations between colonizer and colonized and an indictment of the practice of slavery and exploitation of the indentured labourers who took the place of the slaves.[25] De Kom added that as

HARVESTING SUGAR CANE in 1718 – then as now one of the main exports of Suriname.

THE ISLAND OF LOMBOK was the scene of the battle between the last Balinese ruler, Anak Agung Nengah, and Dutch troops under the command of General van der Vetter. This textile, printed in batik on cotton, was made about 1920.

long as famine, poverty, unemployment, infanticide and poor health care affected the lives of many Surinamese, they remained virtual slaves.

Suriname remained under direct colonial rule until the Second World War. The governor represented the Netherlands as head of the administration and could bypass the Surinamese people's council, which in any case was not representative; the first general elections were held only in 1949.[26] In 1954, Suriname was granted autonomous status within the Kingdom of the Netherlands, but only two decades later sovereignty was transferred.

CULTURAL PLURALISM VERSUS ASSIMILATION

What did Dutch policy mean for the people of Indonesia and Suriname? In general terms, Indonesia developed into a culturally pluralistic society with a dualistic political structure, whereas in Suriname, especially after the abolition of slavery, the guiding principle of Dutch overlordship was assimilation.

In the East Indies, Dutch rule was for long characterized by pluralistic legal and administrative systems. In particular, the colonial rulers rejected the idea of disseminating the Dutch language and Christianity to the Indonesian population, largely because of the size of the territory and population and the fact that Islam was an established faith. Dutch rule in Indonesia was closely associated with strict racial categories. In 1854 the colonial administration began dividing the population into three groups: Europeans (especially the white Dutch, but also those legally recognized Indo-Europeans of mixed Indonesian and European origin), 'Foreign Orientals' (especially Chinese and Arabs) and 'Natives' (i.e. the Indonesians). In 1892 that distinction served as the basis for the exclusion of the last group, on racial grounds, from full Dutch citizenship. Rules and regulations for the European colonial upper class, amounting to about 300,000 people, were different from those for the 60 million Indonesians who far outnumbered them. According to Dutch government criteria, the extent to which a person was Dutch was determined by whether he or she had gained access, through

education, training, employment, promotion, marriage, social contacts and status, to the European elite and its privileges. The boundaries between the racial groups could be crossed, but with no effect on the colonial structures and Dutch sovereignty over Indonesia. The colonial government thought that assimilation into Dutch culture and provision of equal rights for all inhabitants of the colony might jeopardize the Dutch hegemony. The colonial authorities justified this duality by citing 'respect for the difference between population groups' in the colony. The result was that influential positions in the colonial bureaucracy were mainly filled by the European elite class. Not until after the First World War was the 'dual system' based on racial categories even seriously debated.[27]

In Suriname, until the abolition of slavery in 1863, there were two 'legal communities', slaves and free citizens, to which different laws applied. The whole white population, the colonial socio-economic and political elite, as well as a sizeable section of the population regarded as 'coloured', the descendants of white men and black women, were classed as free citizens. In certain circumstances, black people, manumitted (freed) slaves and their children, could also be free citizens. The legal category of slaves was composed largely of black people and a smaller group who were coloured. Needless to say, there were no whites in this category. The whites were in charge, socially and politically,[28] and the European way of life, culture and religion were the norm. The black slaves remained subordinate, and until abolition the colonial government showed little interest in their language, culture or religion. But in contrast to Indonesia, after 1863 there occurred a radical change as the colonial government decided that the whole of the Surinamese population, regardless of race, should become a single linguistic and cultural community, with Dutch as its official language. This assimilation policy began as a mission to 'civilize' the blacks in order to transform them into 'good Dutch citizens'. Christianity, Western education and the Dutch language were actively propagated. The Afro-Surinamese language, culture and religion, on the other hand, were actively suppressed, for instance by making any use of the black language an offence.[29] In this cultural policy, what was European was presented as the successful norm, while the Afro-Surinamese culture was branded deficient.[30] From 1895 to 1933, the same policy of assimilation applied to the Indian and Javanese indentured labourers who had replaced slaves on the plantations. According to Governor Rutgers (1928–33), the aim of colonial policy in Suriname was for 'the whole population, white and brown, black and yellow, regardless of whether they were European or American, African or Asian, to merge together into a single linguistic and cultural community, with a single legal system comprehending both family and inheritance law. Suriname should thus become the Netherlands' twelfth province'. The Dutch colonial authorities were conscious of the differences between their approaches in West and East. Van Lier quotes the Dutch minister for the colonies, Koningsberger, who, speaking in 1928 to young Javanese in Suriname, said that the purpose of education was 'different from that in the Dutch East Indies, in that whereas for the latter the maintenance and development of its own language, manners and customs is an overriding principle of upbringing and education, in Suriname the consistent aim is the merging together of all races, including the Javanese, into a Dutch linguistic and cultural community'.[31]

SHARED POWERS in Indonesia: the Regent of Surakarta with the Dutch Resident.

In the 1930s, however, there occurred a radical change in colonial policy. Governor Kielstra, who took office in 1933, backed by Dutch Minister for the Colonies Welter, encouraged the preservation of Hindustani and Javanese culture through the establishment of village communities on the East Indies model, separate 'Asian family law' and separate schools. Kielstra ignored the fierce objections from the Creole elite that had emerged in Suriname and now protested in parliament. The colonial government believed that the new policy did justice to the Javanese and Hindustani indentured workers on whose labour the Surinamese economy depended. At the same time, however, the policy had a 'divide and rule' function. All the same, the Indians and Javanese in Suriname did not escape the legacy of the assimilationist policy even after its heyday was over. As the historian Hans Ramsoedh wrote in 1995: 'For the descendants of the indentured labourers, too, assimilation into the Dutch language and culture was a *sine qua non* for upward social mobility.'

Although, after the abolition of slavery, racial inequality in Suriname was no longer enshrined in law, Surinamese society long remained racially stratified. In the years immediately after the Second World War, the Javanese mainly worked on the plantations, the Indians were small farmers, the blacks did non-agricultural work, the coloureds were low-grade civil servants, and the Europeans occupied senior positions.[32]

THE IMPACT OF DUTCH COLONIALISM

The impact of Dutch colonialism differed between East and West. Whereas the Dutch influence on Indonesia is considered by some to have been only minor, Suriname is regarded as a wholly Dutch creation.[33] In Suriname, Dutch became the official language and Christianity still enjoys a prominent place. In the East Indies, the Netherlands found not an 'empty country', as in Suriname, but a sizeable population, made up of a large number of ethnic groups and polities with their own legal systems. The Dutch language and Christianity gained virtually no hold over most of the population, nor, after independence, did the language and religion of the colonizers retain a significant role in Indonesian society – the official language now is Bahasa Indonesia, not Dutch, and Islam remains the dominant religion. In 1998, Gert Oostindie summed up the contrasting experiences: 'In the West, and only in the West, the Dutch ruled over a large majority of colonized people whom they had brought there themselves, whereas in Asia... they were interlopers of whom it was later said that they only left behind "*krassen op een rots*" [scratches on a rock], [while] in the Caribbean they created their own subjects.'[34]

While this judgment is certainly true in some respects, it requires qualification. The response of the colonized people of Suriname was not simply accommodation of the Dutch colonial administration. There was also resistance

THE HEADQUARTERS of the Dutch East Indies Company in Indonesia were in the castle of Batavia, seen in the background of this painting of about 1656 by Adraes Beekman.

to and transformation of the Dutch influence. Amerindians and Maroons (escaped slaves and their descendants) waged a guerrilla war against slavery which was sometimes so successful that it seriously threatened the colonial system.[35] Javanese and Indian indentured labourers protested against their exploitation on plantations.[36] Surinamese Creole cultural nationalists rebelled against the assimilation policy.[37] The stigma attached to the Surinamese *lingua franca*, Sranan Tongo, regarded as an 'inferior' language in the colonial period, was removed only through its persistent use – Trefossa, pseudonym of the teacher and distinguished poet Henny de Ziel, brilliantly demonstrated that Sranan Tongo could express the most subtle and profound thoughts and emotions.

Dutch cultural influence in Suriname was also 'Creolized' over the years. A syncretic form of religion evolved, combining elements of Christianity and other faiths.[38] The official language[39] developed its own variant, Surinamese Dutch, which has recently been recognized by the Dutch Language Union (consisting of the Netherlands, Belgium, Suriname and South Africa) as a distinct dialect spoken in Suriname.

To see the Dutch influence on its colony in the East as simply one of 'minor impact' also pays too little attention to some aspects of the Dutch colonial experience there. The colonial hierarchy attached to skin colour obtained in the East Indies is still present in Indonesia, though now only as an unofficial categorization. 'Natives' had no access to the benefits that colonial society offered Europeans, such as a European education or senior positions in the colonial bureaucracy. As J.C. Baud, governor-general of the Dutch East

THE SLAVE REVOLT in Suriname referred to earlier was not the last. Between 1832 and 1834 another rising threatened to throw the colony into chaos. Here three ex-slaves come unexpectedly upon a body of government forces with fixed bayonets. Slavery was not abolished until 1863.

WHEN PRINCESS JULIANA visited Paramaribo, Suriname, in 1955 the children from the local orphanage were dressed in their best clothes to welcome her.

Indies and later minister for the colonies, baldly stated in the late nineteenth century: 'Language, colour, religion, customs, origin, historical memories: in all those respects the Dutch and the Javanese are different. We are the rulers, they the ruled!'[40]

The Eurasian intellectual Guus Cleintuar experienced such discrimination when, in 1952, the Dutch government withdrew his Dutch passport. An official explained that since Cleintuar's Dutch great-grandfather had failed to legally recognize his son before 1892, Cleintuar had never been a Dutch national. Thus, his Dutch citizenship, which had 'been experienced for generations', as Cleintuar put it, simply ceased to exist. In 1992, Cleintuar referred to this incident as representing the 'far-reaching legalism of the Dutch state, which tried to get rid of unfortunate legacies from its colonial past'.[41]

It is clear from Cleintuar's personal experience, however, that there was no strict dichotomy between colonizers and colonized. In both East and West, the two groups often crossed boundaries, although such transgression was in principle at odds with the colonial system. For the system to survive, a clear distinction had to be made between 'free citizens' and 'slaves' (in Suriname) or between Europeans and 'Natives' (in Indonesia). However, theory and practice were different, both in East and West.[42] The mixed-race offspring of European men and 'native' or 'black' women were called 'Indo-Europeans' in the East Indies and 'coloureds' in Suriname.[43] Over the years, many gained legal equality with the white colonials (as Europeans in the East Indies and as free citizens in Suriname), even though they still occupied an intermediate position in the social hierarchy. Around 1900, the colonial government explicitly termed interracial relations a threat to European supremacy, and the establishment of white 'Dutch' families in the colonies became the ideal.[44]

Another way in which boundaries were crossed was the 'vertical' social and legal mobility of individuals from groups at the bottom of the colonial hierarchy. In some circumstances, 'native' Indonesians could achieve equality with Europeans in the East Indies. 'Free blacks' who had managed to escape from slavery in Suriname during the slave period could occasionally rise to prominent positions in colonial society. One example is Elisabeth Samson, the daughter of a freed slave woman who worked her way up to become the wealthy owner of coffee plantations. Samson herself employed slave labour.[45] Another is Jan Ernst Matzeliger, born in Suriname in 1852 to a black enslaved woman and a white German engineer. Matzeliger, a freeman, travelled to the United States in

OIL TANKS belonging to the Dutch Shell Company are pulled by buffalo in Indonesia. The company is in fact Anglo-Dutch, a combination of (English) Shell and Royal Dutch.

1871, where eight years later he invented the shoe lasting machine, which revolutionized the shoemaking industry.[46]

FREEDOM, DECOLONIZATION AND EMIGRATION

After the Second World War, the decolonization processes were very different in Indonesia and Suriname. The handover of sovereignty to Indonesia in 1949 followed two bloody wars of independence, whereas in Suriname – where, ironically enough, the Dutch influence was to remain most evident – independence was won in 1975 without a struggle. The difference in the importance the Netherlands attached to the East Indies and Suriname, and changes in national and international attitudes to colonial relations over the period separating the two dates of independence, played a part in the varying trajectories.

In the East Indies, which had long been the Netherlands' most prized possession, Indonesian nationalism had a long history. Indo-European and Indonesian nationalists, sometimes with the same demands and sometimes with conflicting interests,[47] had been fighting for greater internal autonomy for the archipelago long before the handover of sovereignty in 1949.[48] In 1936 a motion for internal self-government was passed by the Volksraad but rejected by the Netherlands.

The Japanese invasion and occupation of the Dutch East Indies from 1942 to 1945 brought an end to European dominance. The wartime diaries and memoirs of Europeans show that for them the Japanese occupation meant a complete 'reversal of the colonial hierarchy'.[49] Meanwhile, however, radical Indonesian nationalism, ideologically overlapping with the Japanese bid to rid Asia of its Western occupiers, gained strength. In a radio address on 6 December 1942, Queen Wilhelmina held out the prospect of autonomy for the colonies in both the East and West Indies,[50] but the promise was considered meaningless by the Indonesian nationalists.[51] Two days after the Japanese surrender on 15 August 1945,[52] the nationalists, led by Sukarno and Hatto, declared Indonesia independent.[53]

The Netherlands then went to great lengths to hold on to its 'Gordel van Smaragd' ('Emerald Belt'), as the Indonesian archipelago was called. When the Dutch government and the nationalists were unable to agree on the content of post-war agreements that would give the country greater autonomy, armed warfare broke out. The fighting that took place in July 1947 and December 1948 are euphemistically referred to in the Netherlands as 'police action', while in Indonesian historiography they are called Dutch military aggression.[54] The Netherlands eventually handed over sovereignty to Indonesia on 27 December 1949, but only after lengthy debates in the Dutch parliament in which the transfer was presented as nothing less than a traumatic national event. Gerbrandy, a member of the Lower House, expressed the general feeling: 'We are shockingly abandoning the magnificent country of Insulinde [the East Indies], which winds along the equator like an emerald belt, since we can do nothing more there now to restore law and order.'[55]

Such emotional statements typified the politicians' attitude to Indonesian independence. Dutch rule there was seen as a natural state of affairs, and independence as an abrupt end to the civilizing mission. However, Dutch politicians saw the Indo-European and Moluccan migrants to the Netherlands (numbering 200,000 and 12,500, respectively) as a less 'natural' part of the Dutch nation. Initially political reaction to their arrival was defensive;[56] setting aside economic considerations linked to job and housing shortages in the 1950s, they were believed to be 'psychologically and physically' unsuited to life in the Netherlands.

The journalist and writer Jan Boon, better known by his pseudonyms Tjalie Robinson and Vincent Mahieu, as a Eurasian faced major difficulties in securing a loan for his passage to the Netherlands. It took him more than four years of writing requests and pleading with politicians before he and his family could leave Indonesia, even though he had actually been born in the Netherlands during a visit there by his parents. In 1955, a year after his arrival there, he wrote: 'I am a Dutch citizen because my father was one. If my father had been an Indonesian citizen, I would have been one too. But I have remained myself. The passport doesn't determine me as a person, but (sadly) determines some kind of power of control over me. But the state doesn't possess me.'[57]

Suriname's progress towards independence was quite different from that of Indonesia. Ironically, the radio address by Queen Wilhelmina about greater

A MUSICAL instrument works at Semarang, Java.

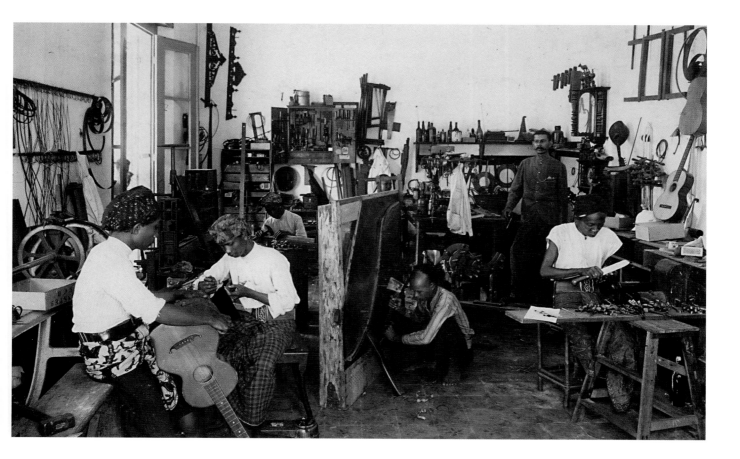

autonomy was made with a view to 'holding on to' the East Indies, but in fact it would turn out to be relevant to the relationship with the colonies in the West Indies, since in 1954 those colonies, including Suriname, won autonomy.[58] Under a statute of 9 September 1954 governing the new relationship between the Netherlands, Suriname and the Antilles, Suriname was granted home rule within the Kingdom of the Netherlands. The Netherlands had responded more favourably to moderate Surinamese nationalism[59] than to the Indonesian version in the 1930s. Circumstances had changed after the crisis in relations with the Indonesian nationalists and the subsequent transfer of sovereignty in 1949.[60] After the traumatic Indonesian decolonization process, the 1954 statute came as a relief.[61] Dutch members of parliament welcomed the successful visit to Suriname by Queen Wilhelmina's daughter, Queen Juliana, the following year,[62] which they saw as strengthening the 'idea of the kingdom': i.e. close relations between the Netherlands and its former possession in South America.[63]

Although under the new constitutional provisions Suriname and the Netherlands were, in formal terms, equal within the kingdom, economically and constitutionally the Netherlands was by far the stronger party. A radical Surinamese nationalist group, under the leadership of the lawyer Eddy Bruma, demanded an end to that disparity. His movement, begun as a cultural and nationalistic response to Dutch cultural dominance and its legacy in Suriname, would eventually lead to a plea for Surinamese independence, partly because Suriname wanted its own voice in international bodies. Under self-government this was not possible since foreign policy remained a 'national matter'; Suriname was thus particularly frustrated when the Netherlands abstained in a vote on a United Nations resolution condemning apartheid in 1959.[64]

In the 1970s, the struggle of the Surinamese nationalists coincided with moves towards decolonization by the Dutch political majority. The Nationalist Republican Party (the Surinamese nationalists) led by Bruma joined a coalition that came to power in 1973. Since most European colonies in Africa, Asia and

COLONIZATION IN REVERSE was experienced by the Netherlands, as by all the imperial powers. Here, in 1960, a Eurasian family strolls in a street in Arnhem near a Eurasian-Chinese restaurant.

the Caribbean had now become independent, the Netherlands appeared in danger of falling out of step with the rest of the world. In 1969 the Netherlands had provided military support for suppressing the biggest insurrection so far on Curaçao (Netherlands Antilles). Pictures in the international press of Dutch soldiers going into action 'overseas' had damaged the Netherlands' reputation as a progressive country, both nationally and internationally, and the Netherlands now wanted to cast off its colonial image. With readiness for 'full political independence' in Suriname and with a left-wing government in power in the Netherlands, the way ahead was clear. The increase in the numbers of Surinamese immigrants, whose presence in the Netherlands became a political question in the 1970s, made Dutch politicians even more willing to move towards independence for Suriname as quickly as possible. With independence, the Surinamese would formally become foreigners with restricted access to the Netherlands. Thus the progressive political agenda of decolonization went hand in hand with a desire to exclude Surinamese from the Dutch nation-state.[65] Ironically, the legacy of Surinamese independence was just what it had been designed to avoid: a large influx of (former) fellow citizens into the mother country. In the late 1960s and up to 1975, 'rumours' about the imminent declaration of independence led to an exodus to the Netherlands unequalled in the history of migration from the colony to the mother country.[66]

As it turned out, the political decolonization of Indonesia and Suriname did not put an end to the colonial mentality. The ideas about differences between white and coloured people that had been characteristic of colonial society were – in a weakened form – partly at the root of the defensive attitude to the immigrants coming to the Netherlands from the two colonies after independence. However, Dutch society seems to have come to terms with that legacy; Indo-Europeans and Surinamese in the Netherlands are now declared to be integrated, though the state of mind of these Dutch citizens from former colonies may remain that of travellers between 'there' and 'here', between 'now' and 'then', between 'black' and 'white', and between 'us' and 'them'.

EURASIAN WOMEN and a Dutch woman (middle) in traditional Dutch costume, c. 1960.

5

Scandinavia: An Outsider in European Imperialism

KNUD J.V. JESPERSEN

THE ATTEMPT to cash in on the slave trade had only limited success. In the 17th century the Danes gained a foothold in what is now Ghana which survived until 1850. This somewhat optimistic picture of a colonist in Africa with a black slave (*opposite*) is precisely dated to 17 September 1817, though the slave trade had been abolished by Denmark in 1803.

THE FAR NORTH was a part of the globe that aroused curiosity rather than imperial ambitions. Early attempts by the Danes to found settlements on Greenland came to nothing. This group of Inuit who visited Denmark in 1654 (*above*) was clearly seen as an object of exotic interest.

COMPARED WITH THE GREAT SEAFARING European nations which, in early modern times, built their vast colonial empires and so set a lasting mark on the history of the globe, Scandinavian overseas possessions remained small and insignificant in extent as well as historical importance. This was to some extent due to the region's rather backward economy, but must also be explained by its geographical position in the northernmost part of Europe. The long, cold winters often made the waters freeze over, thus hindering regular shipping for several months of the year. The Scandinavian contribution to the overall history of European overseas expansion is therefore bound to be a rather small one. On the other hand, the colonial experience of the Scandinavian nations is still part of the greater pattern and, at the same time, an exotic element in the history of Scandinavia. For these reasons the history deserves to be told.

Only in the mid-seventeenth century – two centuries after the Portuguese and Spanish discoveries had opened the overseas world to the Europeans – did the Scandinavians begin to show a serious interest in trying to acquire their own possessions on distant continents, where the Portuguese, the Spaniards, the Dutch and the English had already long established themselves. The Scandinavians were not driven by a wish to make new discoveries – as had been the case in the Viking age – but simply wanted to have their share of the large profits from the colonial trade. Another strong incentive was the prevailing economic doctrine of mercantilism, that the state ought to be self-sufficient and have a positive balance of trade. To achieve those goals in an increasingly competitive world economy, the possession of overseas colonies was vital. This made the question of direct access to the lucrative oriental markets an important issue in early modern Scandinavian politics.

Early modern Scandinavia was dominated by two large state formations: the kingdom of Sweden, which also included Finland, and the twin monarchy of Denmark-Norway, ruled by the Danish royal house of Oldenborg.[1]

In geographical terms Sweden covered the northern and eastern part of the Scandinavian peninsula and – owing to her possession of Finland – encircled the

ICELAND HAD BEEN settled by
Norwegians in the early Middle Ages
and followed Norway into the union
with Denmark in 1380. Icelandic sagas
are among the major items of Norse
literature. The capital Reykjavik is
traditionally said to have been founded
in 874. This 19th-century painting
(*right*) shows Danish merchant ships off
the coast.

SCANDINAVIA LEARNED WHALING and
seal hunting from the Inuit. This 18th-
century engraving (*below*) by an artist
who was perhaps not fully informed
tries to convey the scene.

Gulf of Bothnia down to the Gulf of Finland. Her only free access to the
international trade routes was the narrow area around the mouth of the Göta
River on the western coast of the Scandinavian peninsula where, eventually, the
large commercial city of Gothenburg emerged. Otherwise, all Swedish shipping
had to pass through the Sound – the narrow strait between Zealand and Scania –
which, until 1658, remained a Danish waterway under the close control of the
Danish navy.

Because of these geopolitical realities Sweden had no tradition of long-
distance trade by ocean-going ships. Instead she had succeeded in building
an economy mainly based on trade with eastern Europe across the Baltic Sea.
However, these basic conditions changed in the mid-seventeenth century when
Sweden, after a series of successful wars with Denmark and in Germany, came
into possession of the former Danish provinces on the Scandinavian peninsula –
whereby the Sound was changed from a Danish strait into an international
waterway – and, even more important, of the big commercial city of Bremen
in northwestern Germany, which opened up international trade routes to direct
Swedish access. Only now did it become realistic for the Swedish government
to contemplate the acquisition of overseas colonies.

The other large state, Denmark-Norway, covered the territory of present-day
Norway and Denmark proper, including the duchies of Schleswig and Holstein.
Unlike the Swedes, the Danes and the Norwegians thus had free access to an
open coastline stretching from the North Cape to the Elbe. Thanks to the warm
Gulf Stream, the many natural harbours along this coastline were ice-free for
most of the year, while the inner Danish waters and the Baltic Sea were often
frozen over during the winter months, thus paralysing Swedish shipping for
long periods. Denmark-Norway consequently had good natural conditions for
navigation over long distances and could boast a proud naval tradition going
back, indeed, to the Viking age.[2]

Back in the Middle Ages Denmark and Norway were separate kingdoms,
but in 1380 the two nations were united under the Danish king. This union
lasted until 1814, when Norway, as a consequence of the redrawing of the
map of Europe after the Napoleonic Wars, was forced to replace the union
with Denmark with a union with Sweden. This lasted until 1905, when

Norway finally achieved full independence after more than 500 years under foreign rulers.

THE NORTH ATLANTIC HERITAGE

When in 1380 Norway signed a treaty of union with Denmark, her far-flung possessions in the North Atlantic followed the motherland into the union and thus became part of the empire of the Danish king. These possessions included the Faeroe Islands, Iceland and Greenland, which back in the Viking age had been colonized mainly by Norwegian emigrants. The descendants of the original settlers continued to recognize Norway as their motherland and, eventually, also the Danish king as their sovereign lord. When, in 1814, Norway left the union with Denmark, the North Atlantic colonies remained under Danish sovereignty, and – with the exception of Iceland – are still part of the Danish commonwealth today.[3]

Iceland definitively cut its ties with Denmark during the Second World War, in 1944, when the island was occupied by the British, while the Danish motherland was occupied by the Germans, and it thus became an independent republic after having enjoyed a semi-independent status since 1918. The Faeroe Islands were given the formal status of a Danish county in 1821 and thereby became an integrated part of Denmark. For this reason the islands were also included in the Danish democratic constitution of 1849. During the Second World War the Faeroe Islands, like Iceland, were occupied by the British. This *de facto* separation for five years from the motherland gave rise to a growing separatist movement among the Faeroese and motivated, in 1948, the introduction of a Home Rule arrangement granting the Faeroese people extensive autonomy within the framework of the Danish constitution. This is still the status of the Faeroe Islands in the Danish North Atlantic commonwealth.

Unlike in Iceland and the Faeroe Islands, the Nordic colonization of Greenland was weak and erratic due to the inhospitable climate and the long distance separating it from the motherland. After a short growth in the Viking Age, where the Nordic colonists even reached as far as Newfoundland, the Norse colonies in Greenland faded away and disappeared for several centuries, leaving the Arctic to the original Inuit culture. However, in the early eighteenth century Danish and Norwegian colonists and missionaries returned to Greenland, where they founded a number of settlements on the west coast. At the same time, they ran a fairly regular trading route between Greenland and the motherland with support from the government in Copenhagen. Only from this point, therefore, is it meaningful to speak of a real colonization of Greenland.

Even if communications with Greenland were poor and irregular, Denmark endeavoured to maintain her sovereignty over the Arctic island. These efforts were crowned with definite success when, in 1917, the United States officially recognized Danish sovereignty over Greenland as part of the treaty by which the Danish islands in the West Indies were ceded to the United States. Notwithstanding its geographical position in the western hemisphere, Greenland thus remained a Danish colony in spite of growing public pressure to the opposite effect in America.

Danish sovereignty over the island became temporarily weakened, however, when Greenland during the Second World War came to host American military bases. This

THE BLEAK COAST of Greenland was the scene of several attempts at colonization, some of which ended tragically. One of the farthest outposts was Umanak.

THE NEW TESTAMENT was first translated into the Inuit language of Greenland by Poul Egede and printed in Copenhagen in 1766. This is the first page of the Gospel of St Matthew.

arrangement followed from a treaty in 1941 between the US government and the Danish ambassador to Washington, Henrik Kauffmann, who in this matter acted independently of the government in German-occupied Denmark. The treaty was subsequently confirmed in 1945 by the Danish liberation government, and since then Denmark has allowed American military bases in Greenland, while the United States has, in return, recognized Danish sovereignty over the island.

Greenland's ties to Denmark were further strengthened when, as a consequence of the revised Danish constitution of 1953, the island had its status as a colony changed to one where it was recognized as an integrated part of the Danish commonwealth in line with the Faeroe Islands. Since 1979 Greenland has enjoyed a Home Rule granting the population extensive autonomy: unlike Denmark proper and the Faeroe Islands, Greenland decided not to join the European Union. It is only fair to add, however, that Greenland's economy is still heavily dependent on the annual block grants from Denmark and on the revenue from the American military bases that are still active in the area.

SWEDEN GOES TO AMERICA

As early as the 1620s the Swedish government contemplated establishing a foothold overseas. However, Sweden's growing engagement in European conflicts put the plans on standby for a while. Only in the late 1630s were they resumed on a realistic basis – in the shape of an attempt to establish a Swedish colony on the western bank of the Delaware River not far from the present-day city of Philadelphia.[4]

The originator of this idea was a Dutch businessman by the name of Peter Minuit. He had formerly been a leading figure in the neighbouring Dutch colony, New Netherlands, and had great experience in trading with the local natives. Having fallen out with his Dutch colleagues, he approached the Swedish government and succeeded in interesting its leading figures in a plan to establish a Swedish trading station at the mouth of the Delaware River that could take some of the lucrative fur trade away from the Dutch.

Financed by Swedish and Dutch capital and equipped with detailed instructions from the Swedish government, Minuit's two ocean-going ships left Sweden in November 1637 in order to start a Swedish colony in the designated area. He reached his destination in March 1638 and at once founded a trading post, which he named Fort Christina after the reigning Swedish queen. The fort was built on the riverbank in the middle of an area bought from the locals. A Swedish colony – New Sweden – on the North American continent thus became a reality, and the Swedish government's dream of getting a foothold overseas had come true.

However, the Swedish enterprise never became a success: it lasted only seventeen years and ended abruptly when, in 1655, Peter Stuyvesant – the governor in the neighbouring New Netherlands – finally decided to put an end to the rivalry by occupying the defenceless Swedish colony and annexing it to the Dutch possessions. Shortly afterwards, however, the Dutch colony in North America was itself occupied by the British and made a part of the British colonial empire. At the same time New Amsterdam, the main city in the area, had its name changed to New York.

There are several explanations for the failure of this Swedish enterprise. First, Sweden was a latecomer in America compared with the Dutch and the British. When the Swedes arrived, British colonial communities had long been established in New England as well as in Maryland and Virginia to the south, and for several decades the Dutch had been operating in the intervening area southwest of Manhattan. For this reason it was difficult for the tiny Swedish colony to build up a permanent trading business with the Native Americans without finding itself at loggerheads with well-established British and Dutch interests. Second, the Swedish colony remained a small minority in the colonial environment. By 1650 nearly 44,000 British colonists were living on the eastern coast of America, while the Dutch population amounted to more than 4,000.

The number of Swedish colonists was only 185, and it was obvious that those few people were bound to live at the mercy of the British and Dutch majority – and this mercy ended, as mentioned, in 1655.

Third, communications with the Swedish motherland were severely limited. All in all only eleven ships arrived from Sweden during the years 1638–55 – that is, less than one per year. By the time they put in to port, many of the crew and passengers had died as a result of the unhealthy conditions on board. This modest traffic can be ascribed to the fact that Sweden was heavily engaged in the European wars, but the inevitable outcome was that the colonists for long periods felt that they had been deserted by the motherland. Alone they were not able to mount serious resistance when the final Dutch offensive was launched.

The history of New Sweden turned out to be only a brief intermezzo, but the Swedish presence in the area nevertheless left lasting traces. The area was long afterwards regarded as culturally Swedish. Even at the end of the eighteenth century more than 1,200 people there still had some knowledge of Swedish, and Swedish priests sent over from the motherland continued to serve in the six Swedish congregations right until the founding of the independent United States of America. Only in 1789 did the Swedish state Church reach the conclusion that

LIKE OTHER QUEENS, Sofie Amalie, wife of Frederick III of Denmark (reigned 1648–70), had to have a black slave. Here (hard to see in the shadow) he holds an exotic bird of prey in front of her. The portrait is by Abraham Wuchters.

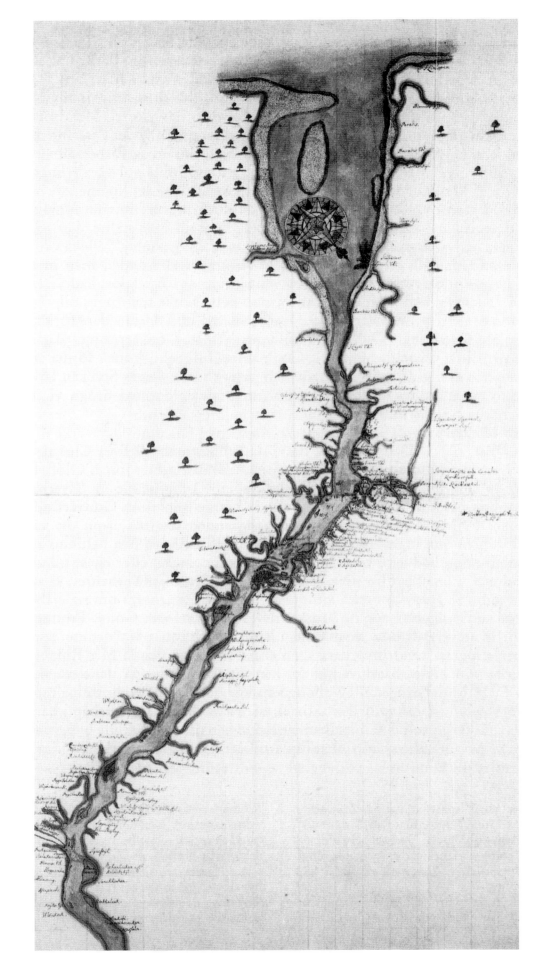

'NEW SWEDEN' was an ambitious enterprise in North America which began in 1638 but lasted only seventeen years, when it was conquered by the Dutch (who eventually had to surrender it to the British). It was centred on the Delaware River, near the present city of Philadelphia. Although its existence was only brief, it left traces of Swedish culture in the area into the 18th century. This map was sketched by Peter Lindström around 1650.

no more priests need be sent to America, and eventually the descendants of the New Sweden colonists therefore became fully integrated into the greater English-speaking community.

SWEDISH INTERMEZZO IN WEST AFRICA

The Swedish attempt to gain a permanent foothold in West Africa in order to get a share in the rapidly increasing slave trade to America also met with only qualified success. Initiatives to that effect were discussed in government circles in the 1620s, but they had to be postponed for two decades because of the Swedish engagement in the Thirty Years' War. Plans were not resumed until after the Peace of Westphalia of 1648, which gave Sweden control over Bremen-Verden and thus free access to the open seas.[5]

Resumption of the African project was due to Louis de Geer, a Dutch-born industrial tycoon who had become a naturalized Swedish citizen. At his own expense, but protected by a privilege granted by the Swedish government, in December 1648 he equipped two ships to be sent to West Africa in order to establish a permanent Swedish trading station in the name of the Swedish queen.

The expedition was a success, and in 1650 its leader, Henrik Carlof, as a representative of Louis de Geer, made a formal agreement with the local king of Fetu, according to which the Swedes bought a strip of land around a locality called Cape Coast and were allowed to establish a trading post there. Subsequently the Swedes built a number of other trading forts along the coast, both east and west of Cape Coast, in fierce competition with the already existing British and Dutch slave forts in the area. The Swedes prevailed until 1663 where, finally, they had to give up after a series of military raids alternately from the British and the Dutch, who were also fighting each other during the Navigation Wars. In this way Sweden had to pay the price for the warfare between the two leading sea powers in African waters. It was the end of Sweden's attempt at becoming a permanent player in the transatlantic slave trade.

AN ISLAND FOR A PRIVILEGE – SAINT BETHÉLEMY

Sweden's most long-lived overseas possession was the diminutive island of Saint Bethélemy near Guadeloupe in the French West Indies. However, it only came into Swedish hands late in the day in the history of European expansion. In 1784 the Swedish king, during a stay in Paris, signed a treaty according to which France handed over the uninhabited island to Sweden in return for trading privileges in Gothenburg.[6]

The following year a single Swedish man-of-war called at the small island, whose only attraction was a good natural harbour. During the stay, which lasted for several months, the crew constructed the first houses in what would later become a busy harbour-city and baptized it Gustavia in honour of the Swedish king, Gustav III. Over the following years the settlement grew steadily and eventually became a notable commercial town. It reached its peak during the Revolutionary and Napoleonic Wars, when it served as a neutral free harbour for the warring parties, and for a short period even became one of Sweden's biggest cities,

In the West Indies Sweden founded a colony on the island of Saint Bethélemy in 1785. Its major town was christened Gustavia after King Gustav III. It flourished during the Napoleonic Wars, when it maintained a position of neutrality – shown here in 1800 – but declined after 1831 and was abandoned in 1878.

temporarily prospering from the flourishing trade under the neutral Swedish flag.

However, Saint Bethélemy's time of greatness came to an abrupt end when the Napoleonic Wars terminated. The death-blow came in 1831 when Britain reopened her ports in the Caribbean to American shipping. This step made the Swedish harbour superfluous, and its key role as a port of transit was at an end. From having been an asset to Sweden for several golden decades around 1800, the island turned into a liability, and – to make things even worse – it was hit by a number of devastating hurricanes, which eradicated the last remnants of its commercial infrastructure. Taking the measure of these sad facts, the Swedish government decided in 1878 to return the island to its original owner, France. For Sweden the era of overseas enterprise was definitively concluded.

IN SEARCH OF THE NORTHWEST PASSAGE

Like many other European princes, the Danish king Christian IV (1588–1648) kept an eye on the overseas activities of the Dutch and the British, watching with envy the huge profits from the oriental trade that poured into commercial capitals like Amsterdam and London. In his heart the self-confident Danish king was convinced that he could emulate the success of the Western sea powers. The question was just which route the Danes should take to get direct access to the lucrative oriental market without falling into open conflict with the well-

To FIND the North-West Passage to India and the Far East was the dream of many European nations (*above*). In 1619 the Danish king Christian IV equipped an expedition under Jens Munk, which twice landed on Baffin Island to hunt but ultimately failed, with the loss of over sixty men.

THE CLOSEST DENMARK CAME TO founding an empire in India was the expedition that reached Ceylon in May 1620. A colony called Tranquebar on the mainland sheltered round a fort named Dansborg (*right*). It survived nearly thirty years of separation from the mother country (1640–69) and flourished throughout the 18th century, bringing enormous wealth to Copenhagen. It was finally sold to the British in 1868.

established trading nations. Of course, the optimal solution was to find an alternative route to India from the traditional one round the southern tip of Africa, and such considerations gave rise to the idea of trying to find a northern route round the American or the Asian continent. From a Danish point of view this would have the further advantage that such routes would cross the North Atlantic, where the Danish king claimed sovereignty. Earlier Dutch attempts, however, had clearly demonstrated that the northeast passage north of Russia was no option. Therefore, the Danish government instead decided to try to find out whether there existed a northwestern alternative north of the American continent.[7]

In order to answer this question an expedition was equipped in 1618–19 and put under the leadership of an experienced Norwegian sea captain, Jens Munk. He had at his disposal a frigate and a smaller vessel and commanded a crew of sixty-four men. In the summer of 1619 the expedition left Copenhagen, bound for the recently discovered Hudson Bay to explore its interior and perhaps find a route leading to Asia.

However, the mission proved impossible and ended in tragedy. Two hard winters in the ice-cold Arctic climate killed no fewer than sixty-one members of the crew, and after heroic efforts Jens Munk and his last two surviving fellow seamen managed to make the small vessel ready for a transatlantic navigation –

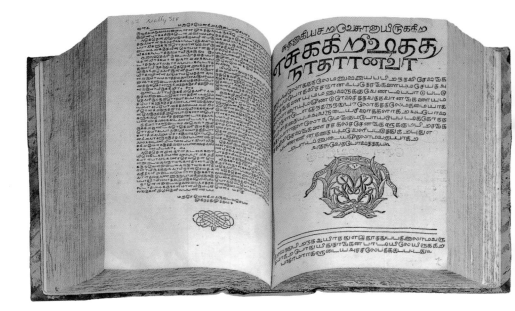

THE BIBLE IN TAMIL, published in 1715, was one of the cultural triumphs of Tranquebar – the first Bible in any language of the Indian subcontinent.

the frigate had to be left behind. Following two months of dangerous and exhausting navigation across the Atlantic they finally hit the Norwegian coast in the summer of 1621. In the light of this trial all further projects for opening a northwest passage were put on ice. The only remaining option was the well-tested route south of Africa and across the Indian Ocean.

THE KING'S INDIAN ENTERPRISE

The prelude to the Danish attempt at reaching India via the traditional route had a slight touch of comedy attached to it: it all began with a confidence trick by an enterprising Dutch businessman and – as it turned out – adventurer named Marcelis de Boshouwer.

The latter had for many years done business in India, and, during a visit to Copenhagen in the autumn in 1617, he asked for an audience with King Christian IV, claiming to represent the emperor of Ceylon, the Rajah Senarat of Kandy. Allegedly on behalf of this potentate he presented to the king a proposal for a formal treaty between Ceylon and Denmark, by which the Danes would be granted a monopoly for twelve years on all European trade with Ceylon and allowed a number of trading posts in the island.

Obviously captivated by the Dutchman's eloquence and fascinated by the staggering perspectives it opened, the king put his signature to the treaty and ordered the equipping of a naval force of four big ships to leave for Ceylon at short notice. The expedition was put under the command of the twenty-four-year-old admiral Ove Giedde, and money for the enterprise was provided by the newly established East India Company, which had the king as its greatest shareholder. The expedition left Copenhagen in November 1618 bound for Ceylon and, after a voyage of 535 days, it reached the island on 16 May 1620.

Here a surprise was waiting: the rajah of Kandy flatly denied knowing anything at all about the treaty, and the entire expedition threatened to end in total failure, the sad result of a Dutch adventurer's lively imagination. Admiral Giedde, however, was not that easy to knock out. Having failed with the rajah, he managed afterwards to make an agreement with another local prince, the nayak of Tanjore. On behalf of the Danish king he bought from him a strip of coastland on the southeastern coast of the Indian subcontinent with the right to build a fort, which he named Dansborg. This was the beginning of the Danish colony of Tranquebar.

At that time Tranquebar was only a small fishing village surrounded by a few square miles of hinterland. However, it was well situated to exploit the current conflicts between the Portuguese and Dutch tradesmen in the region which opened excellent opportunities for trading under the neutral Danish flag. Consequently, over the next twenty years Tranquebar developed into a busy commercial centre well protected by the guns of Fort Dansborg, and at regular intervals rich shiploads of oriental products were also sent back to Copenhagen to the great satisfaction of the shareholders in the East India Company.

However, owing to the almost permanent state of war between Denmark and Sweden in the mid-seventeenth century the Danish government was unable to provide ships to be sent to faraway Tranquebar. Indeed, the lines of communication were actually cut off for nearly thirty years. They were only re-established when, in 1669, a Danish fleet again cast anchor in the harbour. To his great relief the commanding officer found that the colony – under a brave and enterprising commandant at Fort Dansborg – had indeed survived the long separation and was even in better shape than thirty years before. The Danish foothold in India, in other words, remained intact and proved in the long run to be an important asset when, towards the end of the eighteenth century, thanks to Denmark's neutral position in the worldwide showdowns between the great powers, Danish oriental trade reached its peak.

In 1755 the original Danish stronghold in Tranquebar was supplemented by a second one in Bengal: a small locality called Serampore on the western bank of the Hughli River near British Calcutta. In 1756 also a small and isolated group of islands, the Nicobars, were added to the Danish possessions and renamed the Frederik Islands after the Danish king. The new trading post at Serampore rapidly developed into an important centre for the Danish oriental trade, while the Nicobars remained a disappointment: because of the malaria-infected climate they proved uninhabitable and never came to play a role in the Danish trading network.

From this far-flung Indian network of trading stations, enormous riches were brought back to Copenhagen. Huge new warehouses along the waterfront bore witness to the fact that oriental trade over a few decades at the end of the eighteenth century had turned the sleepy Danish capital into a city of the world and its staid merchant class into a rich, cosmopolitan elite.

This spectacular boom, however, was based on one fragile precondition: Denmark's ability to remain neutral in the great showdown between Britain

ON MAINLAND INDIA the Danes founded another trading post on the River Hughli near Calcutta, which became a centre for oriental trade. Like Tranquebar it was sold to the British East India Company in 1845.

and Napoleon Bonaparte's France. Thanks to the country's neutral status Danish merchant ships were chartered in great numbers by the warring parties to transport goods that would otherwise be in danger of getting arrested by the opposite side, and the payments for this risky business were very high. The neutral position of Denmark came to an abrupt end when, in 1807, the British – out of fear that the large Danish navy would fall into the hands of Napoleon – decided to act pre-emptively. In the late summer a British expeditionary force attacked Copenhagen, and after several days of shelling the Danish government surrendered its navy to the British and, at the same time, entered into a war with them which lasted until 1814. After this any further basis for maintaining even a small measure of Danish long-distance shipping was gone.[8]

During the war the Danish possessions in India were occupied by the British. They were returned at the end, but it soon became obvious that Denmark was no longer capable of maintaining regular shipping to the distant outposts. The Danish government lost interest in them and, after languishing in isolation, they were finally sold to the British East India Company in 1845 – except for the Nicobars, which the latter did not want to buy. Those islands were therefore ceded for free to Britain in 1868, after which British authorities for some years had tried to force the Danish government to intervene against the Malaysian pirates who operated from the islands. They were afterwards used as places of deportation for criminals from British India.

Such was the end of Danish colonial enterprise in India. The Danish presence there was never strong, but has nevertheless left a few permanent traces. The old Danish Fort Dansborg in Tranquebar has now been renovated with Danish funds, and the area still houses a number of Christian congregations founded back in the early eighteenth century by Danish Pietist missionaries. In Serampore – now an integrated part of metropolitan Calcutta – is situated the first Christian university of India. It was founded in 1793 by Baptist missionaries who found a haven for their activity in the small Danish enclave.

BLACK GOLD

Like many other European nations Denmark tried to win her share of the booming slave trade in the seventeenth and eighteenth centuries, and for that purpose, as we have seen, it was necessary to get a foothold in West Africa, where the black slaves were gathered before being shipped to the Americas.

In 1661 the Danish African Company succeeded for the first time in gaining a small foothold on the coast of Guinea, but only after many troubles and setbacks did representatives of the Danish government in 1694 obtain permission to establish themselves permanently with a slave fort, which they named Christiansborg after the Danish king. On the whole, however, the Danish presence was unsafe and heavily dependent on the ongoing political game between the local African tribes in the area and the bigger European agents in the slave business. Accordingly, for most of the time Danish profits were modest, but during the good years in the late eighteenth century the Danes actually succeeded in considerably expanding their sphere of influence and founding four additional forts on the coast west of the mouth of the Volta River.

In the wake of the French Revolution, with its new focus on

AFRICAN WARRIORS were enrolled into the Danish army to defend an outpost on the River Volta in West Africa. This engraving of 1784 by a Danish doctor, Paul Erdmann Isert, shows these troops under the command of Otho, king of the Accra tribe, taking part in a ceremonial event.

IT WAS IN THE CARIBBEAN that Danish colonial life reached its apogee, especially in the three islands of Saint Thomas, Saint John and Saint Croix. This lithograph by Johann Friedrich Fritz shows Christiansted on Saint Croix in about 1798.

human rights, popular opinion all over Europe turned increasingly against the slave trade. Against this background, in 1803 Denmark passed a law banning trade in slaves, and the forts in Africa became worthless overnight. They thus turned into an economic liability for the trading companies and the state finances. They went into decay and were largely ignored by the parties concerned, until, in 1850, they were handed over to the British for a symbolic payment. The British accepted the bargain only because they wanted to prevent the French from buying them. All in all, the slender Danish presence in West Africa thus remained an unimportant intermezzo, which left only a few traces in Denmark proper and only a few Danish place-names in present-day Ghana.

'THE FINEST JEWEL IN YOUR MAJESTY'S CROWN'

The Danish possessions in India and Africa were not colonies in the normal sense of the word, but rather trading posts always at the mercy of the local powers and the great seafaring nations. However, the three small tropical islands of Saint Thomas, Saint John and Saint Croix in the Caribbean, just east of Puerto Rico, were proper colonies and became, to some extent, also a settlement area for Danish emigrants.

The uninhabited rocky island of Saint Thomas was invaded by the Danish West India Company in 1672. The company was attracted by the fine natural harbour which gave a good refuge to its ships. Formally the island belonged to the king of Spain who, however, had his hands full with other matters and therefore silently accepted the Danish occupation. In 1718 the company laid hands on the neighbouring ownerless island of Saint John, and in 1733 it bought the larger island of Saint Croix from the French. The small Danish empire in the Caribbean was thus complete. Until 1755 the three islands remained the private property of the company, but after its bankruptcy the same year they officially became Danish state property under a royally appointed governor-general and with a permanent military garrison.

The economy of the islands was based on the production of cane sugar. The hard work on the plantations was done by a large number of black slaves imported from West Africa under the close surveillance of white managers and planters. It was a labour-intensive process and the slave population soon surpassed the number of whites several times over. In 1754 the proportion of whites to blacks was one to eight, and in the course of the economic boom in the late eighteenth century the black population increased further. The white population formed a small elite that generally led a comfortable life as colonial masters.

In good years – that is, years without devastating hurricanes and with adequate rainfall – the plantations produced a considerable surplus of raw sugar that was shipped back to Denmark for refining. In the late eighteenth century this traffic brought so much wealth to the motherland that the merchant Niels Ryberg in a letter to the king found it appropriate to describe the three islands as 'the finest jewel in Your Majesty's crown.'

However, as the new century dawned the sun was already setting on this adventure – for several reasons. First, the general ban on the import of black slaves in 1803 gave rise to a general scarcity of labour which caused wages to rise. Second, the war with Britain (1807–14) dramatically reduced Danish shipping capacity, causing a steep rise in freight rates. Finally, the introduction of beet sugar into the European market meant that cane sugar was no longer competitive.

In the course of the nineteenth century, therefore, the formerly busy sugar mills in the islands went into slow decay and the population decreased, while the Danish state's expenses were steadily increasing. In short, the basis for

'THE FINEST JEWEL in Your Majesty's crown' was how one merchant described the three islands of Saint Thomas, Saint John and Saint Croix. A later view of Christiansted by H.G.Beenfeldt in 1817 shows its continuing prosperity, but during the 19th century all three islands began to decline. In 1917 they were sold to the USA for $25 million.

maintaining the Danish tropical colonies no longer existed. Against this background Denmark started negotiations about a sale of the islands and, after a complicated diplomatic process and a referendum in Denmark, the three small islands were, by a military ceremony on 31 March 1917, handed over to the United States for a sum of US$25 million.

The Danish presence in the three islands in the Caribbean did indeed stretch over more than two centuries, but today the remnants of the Danish activities are visible only to very keen observers: a few houses in Danish architectural styles and a few place-names. That the Danish era actually left so few traces is mainly due to the fact that the Danish settler population never became particularly numerous. As already mentioned, the black population dominated in numbers from the very beginning, and even the smaller white community had a strong cosmopolitan character. The languages commonly spoken in this community were English and Dutch, seldom Danish. Only the military garrison and the officers in the civil administration were as a rule Danish, and they did not usually stay for long. The Danes who chose to remain in the islands after the transfer of the colonies to the United States rapidly became assimilated into the majority population and became an integrated part of the new American culture. Conversely, a small number of liberated slaves chose to move to Denmark, where, at first, they formed a small but very visible group in the native white population. After a few generations, however, this group, too, became a fully integrated part of the Danish population.

THE DANISH EMPIRE was virtually over by the early 20th century. Vilhelm Hammershøi's nostalgic painting of the Asiatic Company's offices in Copenhagen in 1902 seems to belong to the past.

SCANDINAVIAN OVERSEAS EXPANSION: A NICHE PHENOMENON

The colonial enterprise of the Scandinavian countries remained, from its beginnings in the seventeenth century to its end in the twentieth century, a marginal phenomenon in the sense that – compared with the great colonial powers – their overseas activities took place over a much shorter span of years and never resulted in making a permanent political or cultural imprint in the affected areas. It was, at the same time, a niche phenomenon in the sense that the Scandinavians had only the freedom of action that the great powers allowed them. Their initiatives succeeded only when the leading nations were restricted in their own activities by wars against each other. Significantly enough, the Scandinavian countries achieved their greatest overseas successes in the late seventeenth century, when Britain and the Netherlands were at war, and in the late eighteenth century, when Britain and France fought each other all over the world. When, in 1815, more peaceful conditions were re-established, they spelled doom for the colonial adventures of Scandinavia.

But, however much of a sideshow, the overseas experience of the Scandinavian countries has nevertheless added an exotic flavour to their long history – a history that might otherwise seem rather bound to the temperate North and the narrow Baltic region. Thus, the history of the Scandinavian overseas enterprise may be a reminder that Scandinavia, like all other places on the globe, has always been an integrated part of the greater world and heavily dependent on it – for good and for evil.

Britain: Ruling the Waves

KIRSTEN MCKENZIE

IN THE UNCHARACTERISTICALLY HOT Yorkshire spring of 1807, the British Empire was proving a mixed blessing for Tory electoral candidate Henry Lascelles. By the late eighteenth century, the wealth amassed over almost two hundred years of colonial expansion had transformed the social and geographical landscape of the British Isles. It was no accident that popular culture was obsessed by the *nouveau riche* upstart at this time, or that the term 'vulgar' had recently taken on the meaning we most commonly give it today.[1] In part under the influence of imperial riches, the British aristocracy expanded its ranks in unprecedented numbers between the 1780s and the 1820s.[2] The wealthy 'nabob' (whose fortune derived from India) and the West Indian planter became figures of public debate and popular satire. Comedies such as *The Nabob* (by Samuel Foote, 1778) and *The West Indian* (by Richard Cumberland, 1771) found a ready audience in London theatres. All over the English countryside, Palladian mansions were springing up, financed in many cases by the wealth obtained through British expansion into the Atlantic world and (increasingly) into India.

The Lascelles family of Yorkshire had used riches amassed in the West Indies to create one of the most prominent of these estates, a nerve centre of political power as much as it was a home. In Harewood House they built a vision of neoclassical Arcadia. It was a splendid example of what imperial money could buy, with interiors by Robert Adam and a landscaped park by Capability Brown. Any sense that the new edifice, built with such impeccable eighteenth-century taste, did not house an ancient aristocratic family – the house preceded the family's earldom by some decades – and any sense of the occupants' connections with the slave economies of the Caribbean were carefully excised in contemporary representations of the estate. A local guidebook written by a former estate employee said it all: 'The gods themselves might think Elysium here.'[3]

If empire, by this time, was central to the domestic world of Britain itself, this did not preclude the judicious turning of a host of blind eyes. Scandals of imperial brutality did surface in political machinations, such as the 1788 attempt

to impeach Warren Hastings, British governor of Bengal. For many, though, especially for those who were using imperial wealth to climb the British social ladder, it was perhaps better not to see, not to know, not to hear. Yet hooks of community knowledge could serve to snag the smooth surface of a *parvenu*'s silk attire. In 1807, the year in which the British slave trade was abolished, the Lascelles family suffered a defeat in bitterly contested elections for the county of Yorkshire. Described as 'a defender of the Slave Trade', and as a family that 'owed its consequence' to 'Bleeding Africa', the Lascelles were accused by disaffected Yorkshire cloth workers of trying to extend the labour practices of the West Indies to British working men.[4] After all, Britons never would be slaves.[5]

The political travails of Henry Lascelles took place approximately midway through almost four centuries of British imperial expansion and decline. I begin with his story because it encapsulates three of the themes that lie at the heart of my approach to this wider history. They arose most obviously in the eighteenth and nineteenth centuries (although they had precursors in the seventeenth) and they would do much to dictate the circumstances under which empire declined in the twentieth century.

In the first place, if Britain made the empire, so too did the empire make and remake Britain itself. If British imperial expansion, and subsequent collapse, changed the lives of millions around the globe, so too was Britain, and the British themselves (in their various manifestations), changed by this history. In the second place, this transformation took shape not just at a social level but at the level of personal identities. The Lascelles family might have refashioned themselves through imperial wealth, but at a broader level the imperial experience was crucial to the question of how concepts of race, gender, class and status were worked out in Britain and its colonies. These changing identities had concrete political implications with reference to individual rights and the practice of liberty. My third theme, then, lies in the way in which British wealth and freedoms were predicated upon the exploitation and unfreedoms of others. As the Yorkshire cloth workers of 1807 well knew, who was to be included and who excluded from those rights and freedoms would be a crucial ground for debate over the course of British imperial history.

Where to 'begin' this history is of course a matter of equal debate. Is Ireland, conquered during the Tudor period, the first instance of British imperial

THE GLORIES OF GEORGIAN ART and architecture owe a great deal to the profits of slavery. The Lascelles family were able to build Harewood House in Yorkshire because of their interests in the West Indies.

EAST INDIA HOUSE, in the City of
London, was one of the nerve-centres
of the global commercial enterprise
that lay at the heart of British imperial
expansion. It was adorned with
allegorical works such as 'The East
offering her riches to Britannia'.

domination? And if so, can Wales and Scotland really be situated with confidence
as part of the centre of imperial power? The Irish, Scots and Welsh were all
crucial players in Britain's global expansion, but there is no doubt that their lands
were under English economic and political dominance. While there might be
arguments for starting earlier, I begin my account of the British Empire in the
seventeenth century, when global economic and territorial expansion took off
at an unprecedented rate.

THE DIE IS CAST: *c.*1600–1780
In the first century of the British empire, neither of the terms comprising this
concept had much contemporary meaning among ordinary people. The Union
of the Crowns in 1603 incorporated the three kingdoms of England, Scotland
and Ireland. King James VI (of Scotland) and I (of England) used the term
Britain to refer to his domain,[6] but it would be another century before the notion
of 'Britons' took popular root.[7] Similarly, the idea of empire did not necessarily
carry with it overseas expansionist ambitions. By the end of the seventeenth
century, however, much of the pattern of imperial conquest had been set: wealth
was pouring into the British Isles by means of the extraction of raw materials
overseas, territory had been claimed (and defended from European rivals) to
safeguard that extraction, and the coerced labour necessary to sustain these
economies had led to a mass forced transportation of human beings on a
scale the world had never previously seen. By the early eighteenth century, the
success of these ventures meant that British identity could be predicated upon
the nation's status as a Protestant global power ranged against Catholic France
and Spain.

It was from fifteenth-century Ireland, some historians have argued, that
the extractive plantation settlements of North America and the Caribbean in
the sixteenth century took their model.[8] The first permanent settlement on the
North American continent was made at the James River in Virginia in 1607.
Others would follow to the north such as Plymouth in 1620 and the

THE PLANATION ECONOMIES of empires in the Americas created an insatiable demand for cheap labour. Both Africans and Europeans were involved in the mass capture and enslavement of an estimated eleven million men and women during the period of the Atlantic slave trade (*right*).

TOBACCO COULD be taken as snuff, smoked or chewed – see the three connoisseurs in the top picture (*below*), characterized as a Frenchman, a Dutchman and an Englishman. In London 'Best Virginia' was one of the attractions of coffee houses.

Massachusetts Bay colonies in 1630. St Christopher (St Kitts) became the first island in the Caribbean settled by the English in 1623, to be followed by other islands taken by occupation (for example, Barbados in 1625) or seized from rival powers such as Spain (the case of Jamaica in 1655). The early years showed some attempts at cultural accommodation between the newcomers and the native-born, but these were short-lived. For Europeans, the indigenous peoples of the Atlantic world showed an annoyingly persistent attachment to their own social organization and economies. Rapacious European demands for land and labour soon brought endemic violence. An organized uprising in 1622, for instance, nearly wiped out the Virginian colony entirely. As had already been the case with Ireland, a racialized language of 'civilizing' colonists domesticating the 'barbarous' prior inhabitants soon gained currency. The production of cash crops, first tobacco and later sugar, assured the commercial success of British ventures on continental North America and in the Caribbean. And if the protagonists were out for the main chance, the drama of imperial expansion in the Atlantic world could also be scripted as resistance against the global pre-eminence of Britain's Catholic rivals, Spain and later France.

White bonded servants, some transported criminals and some impoverished Britons who put themselves 'voluntarily' under indenture soon replaced the limited resources provided by indigenous labourers in North America and the Caribbean. From the 1640s black slaves began to be imported from Africa, and by the late seventeenth century they had become the preferred labour source, particularly in the southerly colonies of continental North America and in the West Indies. As economic and social divisions opened up between whites and blacks, the wealth and status of the free were increasingly predicated upon the bondage of the enslaved. Blacks were thus precluded from membership of the legislative assemblies that arose in the Atlantic world as white settlement became more entrenched.

If expansion into the Atlantic world was spurred by the production of staples like cotton, sugar and tobacco, the profit motive in the East was the extraction of local goods through trade. The English East India Company was granted a royal charter in 1600, prompted by the insatiable European demand for Asian crops, particularly pepper and spices, and manufactured goods such as silk and cotton textiles. By the end of the seventeenth century, the company was set to become the most successful of the European traders operating in Asia. It would also, over the course of the eighteenth century, acquire an empire of its own. Trade with Asia was extremely risky. Costs of transport were high, and local conditions for the permanent trading stations established in the Malay archipelago or on the coast of mainland India (known as factories) were unstable. European trading rivalries, especially with the French, were ever-present and could explode in violence. In the seventeenth century, trade in India was largely conducted by the British accommodating themselves to the pre-existing power structures of the subcontinent. By the eighteenth century, with the fall of the Mughal Empire destabilizing the region, circumstances were beginning to change, and the company began to exploit local alliances to gain political power and make territorial claims. The need to secure tax revenues to fund a growing trade system and finance the company armies that safeguarded British commercial interests made territorial expansion seem inescapable in some eyes. British conquests in India dwarfed all previous imperial expansions. The acquisition of Bengal alone – secured by Robert Clive in a victory at the Battle of Plassey in 1757 – brought the British twenty million new subjects and a revenue of £3 million from which a huge new army and civil service could be constructed.[9]

By the eighteenth century, tea imported from China by the East India Company, sweetened by sugar grown in the slave economies of the Atlantic world, were items that increasingly featured in the diet of Britons. Tea was equally popular in the North American colonies, which is why it ended up being dumped into Boston harbour in 1773. Tea's popularity made it a perfect

THE PRIVATE ARMIES of merchant bodies led to the growth of an 'empire' initially administered not by the state but by commercial companies. Robert Clive entered the service of the East India Company as a clerk, and later turned soldier. In 1757 at the Battle of Plassey (*below*) he defeated Siraj ud-Daula, nawab of Bengal, with the help of Mir Jafar, a local nobleman who was afterwards installed as a pro-British ruler. In 1765 Clive gained effective authority over Bengal for the British in the form of *diwani*, the right to collect tax revenue.

Overleaf
FORT SAINT GEORGE was built by the East India Company on the east coast of southern India, *c.*1639. This was the nucleus of the city of Madras. In the 18th century it withstood repeated attacks in the course of the struggle between British and rival European powers for ascendancy on the Indian subcontinent.

As a protest against the imposition of a British tax on tea in 1773 a group of outraged Americans in Boston disguised themselves as Indians and threw the tea into the harbour. Known as the 'Boston Tea Party', this was one of the first acts of the rebellion that culminated in the War of Independence.

commodity to tax when Britain was trying to recoup its financial losses in expensive wars against the French for control of the Atlantic world. Should not the colonists pay for their own protection? The response was an increasingly outraged negative, and the so-called Boston Tea Party was one of several protests against taxation in the lead-up to the American Revolutionary Wars (1775–83). As the British statesman Edmund Burke recognized, in communities where some are slaves and others are not, 'those who are free are by far the most proud and jealous of their freedom'.[10]

MAPPING THE HUMAN AND NATURAL WORLD: c.1780–1815

George III: But what of the colonies, Mr. Pitt?
Pitt: America is now a nation, sir.
George III: Is it? Well. We must try and get used to it.
I have known stranger things. I once saw a sheep with five legs.[11]

With hindsight, the 1783 loss of the American colonies was a far less permanent setback to British imperial expansion than it might have seemed to George III, at least as he is portrayed in Alan Bennett's film. There were similarities between the empire of the Atlantic world and developments after 1783,[12] but the late eighteenth century did indeed mark a watershed in the nature of the British Empire. One of the key differences between what historians have called the 'first' and 'second' British empires was geography. Since 1600, imperial expansion across the Atlantic had been westward – to the eastern shores of the North American continent and through the Caribbean. Now the focus increasingly turned East – to India and across the Pacific. The imperial centre of gravity moved from the Atlantic to the Indian Ocean.[13]

This shifting centre of gravity would have been impossible without the exploration of the Pacific that took place in the late eighteenth century. No name is more closely associated with this era of exploration than that of Captain James Cook. Cook led three expeditions to the Pacific between 1768 and 1779, before being killed by the islanders of Hawaii. Cook's voyages were instrumental in mapping the Pacific frontier for the British, a terrifyingly vast ocean without major land masses, dotted with small islands easily lost at a time in which navigators were still struggling to calculate longitude accurately. Cook's voyages were a navigational triumph, but they were also designed to map the world in other ways. Stuffed with newfangled and experimental scientific instruments, staffed by artists and scientific experts such as Joseph Banks and Daniel Solander, Cook's vessels were travelling laboratories, the heirs of a new kind of exploration born of the intellectual ferment of the Scientific Revolution and the Enlightenment.[14] They sought to map out a new world not just in geographical terms, but also by classifying its natural and human populations. Not for nothing was Solander a pupil of the greatest classifier of the age, Linnaeus. Cook's voyages were in part designed to collect information to be transmitted to the evolving branches of European science whose demand for raw data was insatiable. Thus it was that in the wake of these explorations came not only territorial expansion into the Pacific, especially Australasia, but new ways of thinking about humanity.

Enlightenment social theory about civilization in the late eighteenth century would reap a bitter harvest of racial classification in the nineteenth. It is perhaps because of this that James Cook continues to be a kind of lightning rod for popular feelings about empire. As early as the 1780s, Cook had been 'canonized' as an imperial martyr and hero. History paintings depicted his death at the hands of Hawaiian islanders, and engravings imagined his apotheosis, ascending into heaven accompanied by allegorical figures representing Universal Fame and Britannia. By the late nineteenth century, Cook was celebrated as a founding father by white Australian colonists who would far rather forget that their origins lay in penal settlements. A quite different role had emerged by the late twentieth century, in which Cook figured in anti-colonial narratives as harbinger of European oppression. 'Let me remind you that we killed Cook,' I heard a Hawaiian nationalist proclaim with pride at a conference in the 1990s. In the protean world of popular memory, the victim of an eighteenth-century squabble on a beach[15] became a nineteenth-century hero who in turn metamorphosed (in some eyes) into a late-twentieth-century villain.

From the middle of the nineteenth century, settlers in the colonies of Australia were eager to promote Cook as their 'founder' on the basis of the voyages which had begun to map their coastlines, and those of New Zealand. This conveniently sidestepped the fact that most of the Australian settlements had been established as, or expanded from, penal colonies. With the independence of the United States, the forcible movement of felons across the Atlantic was no longer possible. A solution to crime in Britain was to be the deterrence provided by transportation to the ends of the earth. The first fleet of convicts arrived at Botany Bay in 1788. Over the next seventy

EXPLORATION LED TO CONQUEST. It was thanks to the voyages of Captain Cook that Australia and New Zealand became part of the British Empire. A superb navigator and a man of wide intellectual interests, Cook was killed in a random skirmish with Hawaiian islanders in 1779.

years, more than 150,000 of them would be landed on Australian shores. The early years of the convict colonies in New South Wales and Van Diemen's Land (Tasmania) were precarious. The climate was far harsher, the indigenous peoples far more numerous (and hostile) than Cook's voyages had led the planners to suppose. Yet despite the very real horrors of 'the fatal shore',[16] the practical requirements to keep costs down and ensure the survival and prosperity of the settlement ameliorated the harshness of prison discipline. It was soon found that convicts worked far harder when their labour brought personal reward. Out of these ambiguities of prison rule emerged an entrepreneurial society which found wealth first in sealing and whaling, and later in pastoralism and wool production. As it did so, it destroyed the economic basis that sustained the lives of the Australian continent's indigenous inhabitants. The success of white settler society in Australia, as with North America before it, was predicated upon the violent dispossession and demographic devastation of the lands' prior inhabitants.

BRITAIN was the first European nation to abolish the slave trade and its navy subsequently reserved the right to capture foreign slave ships. Many of those 'liberated' ended up as indentured workers in British colonies. This photograph (above), taken in 1868, shows a group of Africans who have been recued by a naval vessel.

A PROCLAMATION to the indigenous peoples in Australia in 1816 (opposite) was intended to announce equality before British law. The ways in which its meaning was interpreted, however, remains open to question.

THE EMPIRE OF GOOD INTENTIONS:[17] c.1815–80

The nineteenth century would see unprecedented territorial expansion across Asia, Africa and the Pacific. This was matched by an 'informal empire' in China and Spanish America, in which countries not formally under British control would be pulled into the ambit of British trade, sometimes forcibly, as was the case with China in the Opium Wars of 1839–42 and 1856–60. Yet apart from Canada, southern Africa and Australasia, the new formal colonial possessions would not be settler colonies. A second change in the nature of the British Empire from the eighteenth to the nineteenth century had important implications for post-Enlightenment ways of classifying (and governing) the human world. A gap increasingly opened up between the administration of white settler colonies and the patterns of rule followed for colonies in Asia and Africa dominated by non-European populations. White settler colonies themselves were particularly keen to open this gap and to distinguish themselves from colonies like India. They needed to demonstrate that their communities were of equal status to those in Britain, and thus that they deserved the same political rights. As whiteness became an increasingly stable sign of power over the course of the nineteenth century, distinctions between white British colonial subjects who enjoyed the social and political 'rights of freeborn Englishmen', and brown and black British subjects who were to be ruled as dependent peoples became more marked.[18] 'Colonies of white settlement', writes Catherine Hall, 'were organized around the double need to dispossess indigenous peoples and build a settler population in their place.'[19] White settler obsession with British approval, sometimes stigmatized in a later century as 'the cultural cringe', needs to be understood in this light. The obsessive insistence on adhering to European standards of dress, hygiene and child-rearing in the colonies (to name but a few examples) grew out of these interlinked needs for personal, social and political status. In the political realm, these ambitions would come to fruition in the middle of the nineteenth century, when representative and later responsible legislatures were granted to white settler colonies.

When the Napoleonic Wars ended in 1815, Britain emerged with a global economic dominance born of its status as the world's most modern industrial nation. By the 1820s around 26 per cent of the world's population lived on soil defined as British.[20] A massively expanded territory now spanned the world, and control was sought over vast populations of peoples culturally and racially

COVERNOR DAVEY'S PROCLAMATION TO THE ABORIGINES 1816

"Why Massa Gubernor", said Black Jack— "You Proflamation all gammon.
"How blackfellow read him eh? He no learn him read book"
"Read that then", said the Governor, pointing to a Picture.

distinct from the British themselves. With these changes came increasing debate about the nature of empire. In the minds of many reformers this economic and political dominance needed to be matched by a moral and humanitarian high ground. At issue was a profound crisis about the *sort* of imperialists the British were to be – was this to be an empire of the godly, or of the godless? The concerns of humanitarian reformers were becoming increasingly powerful in the political realm by the first decades of the nineteenth century. They were as much about supporting the weak and dependent – women, children, slaves and the indigenous peoples of the empire – as about transforming Britain itself. They embodied a new vision of gendered political action in which white middle-class men, empowered by the economic changes following industrialization, had a profound duty to shape the world in a more humane image. The ideological energies of the humanitarians were initially channelled into debates over slavery. Arguments were mounted not only in moral terms, with the testimony of slaves themselves a powerful weapon,[21] but in a language that promoted the virtues of free labour and criticized the backwardness of slavery in a brave new industrialized world.

The campaigns against the slave trade, which had compromised the Lascelles family in 1807, and later against slavery itself, came to fruition in 1834. The rights of property were protected by means of government compensations to slave-holders. It was a triumph for a particular vision of empire, one that linked British nationality to humanitarian sentiment, making anti-slavery 'an emblem of national virtue'.[22] In its emphasis on free labour and on morality, it had wide appeal within the new moral climate of the nation. It provided a means by which the British could impress foreigners with their innate morality and love of liberty. In its emphasis on moral superiority in methods of colonization, it helped to change the way in which the British thought about their colonies. In the climate

AFTER LANDING at Botany Bay in 1788, the British settled in nearby Port Jackson where Sydney grew into the administrative centre of the colony of New South Wales. This watercolour by Thomas Worthing shows it as a mere village but with a superb natural harbour.

of moral reform and anti-slavery prevailing in Britain, new ideas about colonization gained a ready audience in the 1820s and 1830s. Arguments about moral depravity and the inefficiency of bonded labour, which had been used to discredit slavery, were also marshalled against convict labour. Slavery was abolished within the British Empire in 1834; just six years later the British parliament ended transportation to New South Wales. It would continue, dogged by scandals, in Van Diemen's Land for another decade, while in Western Australia, prompted by labour needs, transportation lasted until 1868.

From the campaign against slavery, it was but a short step to the belief that indigenous people should also be protected from exploitation. In 1836 the British and Foreign Aborigines Protection Society was founded in London. A parliamentary enquiry into the situation of indigenous people in the empire, in 1837, found that colonization in southern Africa, Australasia and northern America had had disastrous consequences. The full title of the Select Committee is instructive: 'The Select Committee to consider what measures ought to be adopted with regard to the Native Inhabitants of Countries where British Settlements are made, and to the neighbouring Tribes, in order to secure to them the due observance of Justice and the protection of their Rights; to promote the spread of Civilization among them, and to lead them to the peaceful and voluntary reception of the Christian Religion.' To put it baldly, then, the humanitarian argument of equality for whites and blacks depended on the belief that blacks should be Christianized and incorporated into white society on white terms.

Neither freed slaves nor colonized peoples proved tractable in this regard. Not surprisingly, they resisted attempts to convert them into an obedient and subservient free labour force, instead preferring self-sufficiency and the pursuit of their own cultural and economic goals. The resulting tension began to undercut the ideology of reform. Furthermore, humanitarians were perceived to pose a significant threat to their main opponents in the colonies – pastoralists and other white settlers seeking to occupy and develop the land masses of

ENCOUNTERS BETWEEN Europeans and the inhabitants of Australia have left a rich visual heritage from both Indigenous and non-Indigenous artists. *Above left*: image from the sketchbook of Tommy McRae of the Wahgunyah, Upper Murray, *c.*1880. *Above*: portrait of Bennelong by an unidentified European artist known as the Port Jackson Painter, *c.*1790. Bennelong, together with his compatriot Colbee, was captured in 1789 by order of Governor Phillip who hoped to learn the language and customs of his people.

A EUROPEAN VIEW of the benefits of
Christianity: a village in the Cook
Islands before and after conversion.

southern Africa, Australia, New Zealand and Canada without interference
and without regard for indigenous protection. An ideological battle was waged
between humanitarians and their enemies in both Britain and the colonies.
The view of colonization that the Select Committee on Aborigines projected
was bitterly contested by settlers who claimed that *they* were the true bringers
of civilization to the colonies, that they were engaged in a battle with savages.
Pastoralists and their allies set the language of capitalist progress and civilization
threatened by barbarism against the language of humanitarianism.[23] In our post-
imperial age, in which the racial hierarchies and economic exploitation of the
British Empire have rightly come under fire, it is important to realize the
inherent diversities of the colonial project. It was internally fractured and
marked by competing designs.

Ultimately, the promise of a greater regard for indigenous civil and land
rights that the humanitarian movement held out was short-lived. It failed in
large measure to halt the rapid dispossession of indigenous peoples under
the pressure of relentless white economic expansion. By the middle of the
nineteenth century, a profound disillusion had set in among reformers. The
stage was then set in large measure for the abandonment of moral ideals which
challenged the disregard for indigenous rights. Humanitarian sentiment which

emphasized the uniformity of human nature, while assuming that non-European cultures should be abandoned in favour of 'civilization', gave way to the ideas of Social Darwinism and scientific racism which prevailed in the second half of the nineteenth century. As a manifestation of these changes, Catherine Hall argues that the publication of Thomas Carlyle's 'Occasional Discourse on the Negro Question' (1849), later retitled 'Occasional Discourse on the Nigger Question' (1853), 'marked the moment when it became legitimate for public men to profess a belief in the essential inferiority of black people, and to claim that they were born to be mastered and could never attain the level of European civilization'.[24]

These ideological changes were underscored by events on the ground in which the colonized took matters firmly into their own hands. By the 1860s the British Empire had suffered a series of profound shocks which were widely interpreted as a rejection of British policies and values. Neither freed slaves nor conquered 'Native Inhabitants' had responded as they 'ought' to initiatives to transform them into a Christianized, tractable labouring force. Plantations in the West Indies were struggling, and full civil and political rights had not been conceded to former slaves. The resulting tensions in the Caribbean exploded in the Morant Bay Rebellion in Jamaica in 1865, which was repressed with extreme violence by Governor Edward Eyre. In its aftermath, the House of Assembly in Jamaica abolished itself in favour of direct rule from Britain, despite the protests of those few black members who had been admitted. Eyre's handling of the rising, after which 439 black Jamaicans were hanged, six hundred flogged and thousands of homes destroyed in reprisals, provoked heated debate among whites in Britain. It was a debate which became as much about the nature of freed black slaves as the behaviour of Eyre. Similar disillusionment with humanitarian reform was provoked by events in New Zealand. There, the Treaty of Waitangi, in 1840, intended to settle differences between Europeans and the indigenous Maori over the possession of land,

RESISTANCE AND REBELLION against British rule broke out across the empire at mid century: including India in 1857 and Jamaica in 1865. Both were suppressed with extreme savagery. The first, still popularly known in Britain by the question-begging name of the 'Indian Mutiny', spread from the army to the wider population. Reprisals included widespread hangings.

Picture Post, June 3, 1939

instead ushered in more than thirty years of armed conflict in which the Maori proved a formidable foe.

The most psychologically devastating of these mid-nineteenth-century traumas struck at the very heart of the new empire, India itself. What is remembered as the Great Rebellion in India (still sometimes referred to as the Indian Mutiny in Britain) broke out in 1857. By the middle of the nineteenth century, a series of annexations and wars pursued by the East India Company's private armies had established the boundaries of British rule to encompass most of the subcontinent. British interests were allied to a programme of reform and improvement of Indian society along British cultural lines. There were constant concerns about security, and the precarious hold that the British Raj (as the British government was referred to in India) had on the situation was exposed in 1857. The rebellion started among Indian soldiers in the Bengal army, protesting against the issue of cartridges apparently coated with ritually impure animal fat. It was a matter that might have been expressly designed to insult Hindus and Muslims alike, and the high-handed response of the British authorities to the grievance only made matters worse. The initial grievance, however, was only a spark that lit the powder of a far deeper resentment against white domination

PLANTERS used a variety of strategies to try and bind former slaves to plantation work after emancipation. This was painted about 1850.

of Indian politics, society and the economy. The uprising spread from the ranks of the army to both urban and rural populations – northern India exploded into violence. Reasons for rebellion were localized and various, and a significant proportion of the Indian population felt their interests were better served by supporting the British than by siding with the rebels. Ultimately the rebellion failed, yet the prophecy that was widely repeated while it raged – that Company rule would last only 100 years after the Battle of Plassey – was not completely without foundation. As a result of the rebellion, the rule of the East India Company was ended, and India was placed directly under the Crown and parliament. If the specific motivations for the Indian rebellion are complex, the bitterness of the fighting as the British clawed back control, and the often calculated atrocities committed on both sides, left an important legacy. While we should be extremely wary of sentimentalizing British rule in India in the late eighteenth and early nineteenth centuries,[25] any tentative hopes of cross-cultural accommodation between British and Indians held out by that world were ground into dust by 1857. The already existing gulf between colonial rulers and subjects was widened, and ideas about the possibility of reform and improvement in India and other non-settler colonies along British lines were irreparably damaged.

MASS BAPTISMS of slaves in Jamaica were ostensibly for the benefit of the baptized since it recognized them as individual souls to be saved. But they were not popular among the planters, and in 1791 the missionaries responsible were arrested. This picure shows a scene in 1842.

NEW IMPERIALISM: c.1880–1910

In the wake of these mid-nineteenth-century developments, a 'less benign view of empire' emerged.[26] It was this hard-edged vision of race, culture and power that would feed into the so-called 'scramble for Africa' and the 'New Imperialism' of the late nineteenth century. Britain had shown little interest in occupying territory in Africa before the late nineteenth century. As we have seen, its view was the reverse with regard to the inhabitants of Africa, whose mass abduction had powered the slave economies of the Atlantic world from the seventeenth century. Two hundred years later, although the continent had been profoundly destabilized by the demographic consequences of the transatlantic slave trade, its land remained relatively untouched. The British claimed toeholds in West Africa, which it had occupied in order to pursue the slave trade and other types of commerce. There was also the Cape Colony, annexed from the Dutch in the late eighteenth-century Napoleonic and Revolutionary Wars, primarily to protect the sea route to India from the French. Yet by 1900 the British had acquired huge territorial possessions across the African continent. Developments in Southeast Asia were perhaps less dramatic, but still resulted in the occupation of Burma and the Malay peninsula.

Britain's spectacular territorial gains in the late nineteenth century began with a trickle in the 1880s and ended with a flood a decade later. Both strategic and economic concerns make up the explanation. The need to stall expansion into areas by other rising European imperial powers, such as the old enemy, France, or a recently united Germany, was one factor. By the end of the nineteenth

century it had become abundantly clear that the unchallenged imperial position Britain had enjoyed since the Napoleonic Wars had come to an end. Equally significant was the economic importance of particular resources and markets, with raw materials such as palm oil, ivory and wild rubber figuring prominently. These strategic and economic factors also prompted the further expansion of 'informal empire'. Just as the Opium Wars had forced China to accept the dubious advantages of British free trade (or 'narco-imperialism' as Simon Schama has dubbed it),[27] so too was forced influence extended in Turkey and Egypt in the 1870s and 1880s. The construction of the Suez Canal in 1869 – built with French and Egyptian finance, the latter bought out by the British in 1875 – cut sailing time from Britain to India in half. This also intensified the strategic importance of British colonies acquired earlier: Singapore in 1819, outposts in the Malacca Straits taken over in 1826 and Hong Kong in 1842. Britain took the final step in its Egyptian interests by invading that country and placing it under 'occupation' in 1882.

The New Imperialism of the late nineteenth century was not just about strategic and economic interests, it also prompted new ways of thinking about British and colonial identities. The late nineteenth century was a world of heightened imperial competition with other European powers and increasing control over non-British peoples abroad. It was a time of popularized theories of evolution in which races evolved through competitive struggle. Imperial zeal was stimulated, in the historian Bill Nasson's words, by 'racial ideas of national superiority, an indulgent culture of glorification in wars of conquest and the relatively cheap costs of British expansion'.[28] This was not just about identity, then, but also about power. For Joseph Chamberlain, colonial secretary for the Conservatives between 1895 and 1903, it was essential that British public opinion be won over to the cause of empire. The imperial mission, conceived in terms of white racial vigour and a heightened militaristic masculinity, fed into popular music-hall entertainment, art, literature, education and youth movements such as the Boy Scouts.

Yet the New Imperialists were not to have it all their own way. Even as the sons of empire were reading Rudyard Kipling, or delighting in the stirring adventures of *The Boy's Own Paper* (founded in 1879), alternative visions were gaining force across the British imperial world. Anti-imperialist identities and political mobilizations were strengthening in both black and white communities. Radical nationalists in Australia used mass-circulation publications, which could be read by a newly literate generation benefiting from educational reform, to offer alternatives to imperial loyalty. National illustrated papers like *The Bulletin* (founded in 1880) drew on an appreciation of the Australian landscape and an idealized vision of pastoral life wedded to an aggressively anti-Asian concept of White Australia. As the paper proclaimed in 1887, 'No nigger, no Chinaman, no lascar, no kanaka, no purveyor of cheap coloured labour is an Australian.'[29] Britain was criticized in Australia for fostering cheap black labour and undermining the rights of white working men. Ultimately, however, the bonds of imperial loyalty held. It was otherwise for whites in South Africa. There the bitterness of the South African War (1899–1902) between Afrikaner republics and the powers of British imperialism sowed seeds of Afrikaner nationalism that bore tragic fruit in the policy of apartheid almost fifty years later.

Organized resistance to colonial oppression was nothing new, as the crises of imperial control in the middle of the nineteenth century described above indicate. By the late nineteenth century, however, mass education campaigns and rising literacy among all races in the colonies had produced effects that were perhaps unexpected. They helped to spur nationalist movements that worked within the language and institutions of the colonial state while rejecting the ideologies of European rule. In colonies like India, the British depended upon a local literate intelligentsia for rank-and-file administrators. Yet the education that provided such administrators simultaneously gave birth to a generation of critics who could use their new skills to pass judgment on the imperial regime

THE SAVAGE FIGHTING of the South African War prefigured the horrors of 1914–18, not least in the use of trench warfare. Here, British dead in Natal after the Battle of Spion Kop, January 1900.

in its own language.[30] The Indian National Congress was formed in 1885, calling for greater Indian involvement in the British administration. By 1906 it had committed itself to the self-government of India and was moving towards becoming a mass movement, with a wave of campaigns organized by Mahatma Gandhi between 1919 and 1922. The men who formed the South African Native National Congress in 1912 – it became the African National Congress in 1923 – similarly emerged from a mission-educated elite who could confront whites on their own parliamentary territory. Despite repeated petitions to British authorities to protect African rights, such organizations were marginalized in the negotiations between British and Afrikaners which effectively gave a free hand to white supremacy after the establishment of the Union of South Africa in 1910.

DECLINE AND LEGACY: THE TWENTIETH CENTURY

During the heights of late-nineteenth-century New Imperialism, J.R. Seeley famously pointed out in his *The Expansion of England,* published in 1883, that the British Empire had been acquired in 'a fit of absence of mind'. This assessment is not without its basis, as Bill Nasson has recently pointed out. This was an empire that lacked geographical contiguity, a uniform legal framework, or any single language or religion. Its possessions were acquired without any consistent pattern over a period of four hundred years in which sentiment about, and support for, empire was remarkably variable among Britons.[31] Yet given the massive global consequences of this supposed vagueness on the part of the British – consequences which include the economic exploitation and the mass forced migration of millions – the humour to be derived from Seeley's description now seems more than a trifle bleak.

The legacy of British imperialism continues to inspire heated debate, and to raise tempers. Part of the reason that evocations of empire still touch people on the raw (in both positive and negative ways) rests in how close the experience of decolonization still lies to our own generation. Britain went into the First World War to preserve its pre-eminence from the threat of European rivals, and marshalled the considerable human and natural resources of empire in order to

THE COLONIES were drawn into the conflicts of their rulers. Here General Kitchener, the British secretary for war, inspects Indian troops in 1914.

do so. The post-war division of the spoils of defeated empire saw the break-up of Turkish as well as German power, leading to expanded British control in the Middle East through mandates. There seemed little clear evidence that British imperial power was undermined. But the cost of the First World War had been high, and not only in human terms. The British emerged deeply in debt to creditors in the United States, a new world power with little stake in the maintenance of systems of direct colonial rule by Europeans.[32] Two decades later, the resources of empire needed to be assembled once more with the outbreak of the Second World War. Midway through that war, things were looking very black. The Japanese marched into Singapore in 1942, Australia seemed on the point of invasion, and India was convulsed by the mass civil disobedience of the Quit India movement.

As had happened in the First World War, the United States underlined its growing global supremacy, this time with atomic detonations in the Pacific. And so although the British Empire emerged from the Second World War pretty much intact territorially, the seeds of decolonization had already been sown. Reasons for the collapse can be found in both changing perceptions of national self-interest and in a variety of external pressures. British capital was shifting from imperial investment to a focus on the booming economies of the United States and western Europe. Global military, financial and economic pre-eminence had passed decisively from Britain to the United States. Colonial nationalist movements were also taking their toll on British power on the ground. In most cases this involved parliamentary lobbying and popular protest, which could meet with violent repression, but in some areas (for example, Kenya and Malaya) there was also armed resistance. In the wake of the defeat of the racist horror of Nazism and of the imperial ambitions of Japan, in a context of declarations of universal rights and the formation of the United Nations, international criticism of imperialism was mounting.

When decolonization came, it was swift. In the immediate aftermath of the Second World War, between 1947 and 1948, British rule ended in the Indian subcontinent and in Palestine. Between 1957 and the middle of the 1960s, a vast array of newly independent nations were created from colonies in Africa, the Caribbean and the Malay peninsula. Within twenty-five years after the Second World War, then, the entire world system of British imperial power was largely in collapse. As British prime minister Harold Macmillan was pleased to point out to the South African parliament in 1960, 'the wind of change is blowing through this continent.' The architects of apartheid might have responded by battening down the hatches, with tragic results, but they were in the minority. The anti-colonial nationalism that Macmillan was referring to was gaining ground not just in Africa, but across the empire.

It is often asserted that the British withdrew from empire in the period after the Second World War with greater grace and less violence than did their European counterparts. The rhetoric about 'preparation' for self-rule did perhaps make imperial withdrawal easier for the British, but this does not mean that the process was without violence. Left to themselves, the process of imperial withdrawal would have been far slower than it was. While nationalist leaders, such as Jomo Kenyatta in Kenya and Tunku Abdul Rahman in Malaya, for example, may not themselves have promoted violent uprisings, there is no doubt

THE END OF THE BRITISH EMPIRE took different forms in different areas, from armed conflict to peaceful persuasion. A leading advocate of the latter was Mahatma Gandhi, who used the tactic of civil disobedience first in South Africa and then in India. Here, in 1930, he is leading a 320-km (200-mile) march to the sea to manufacture salt in symbolic defiance of a salt tax imposed by the British.

that nationalist movements did benefit from unrest.[33] The British did not show a propensity to hold out for long against violence. Experiences were varied. Even where the British left or were removed with relative ease, others might be left to deal with an intractable situation – as was the case with Palestine in 1948, or with the partition of India the previous year. Those who lived and suffered through the violence of these debacles would find cold comfort in the contention that the British had no Algerian or Indochinese equivalent in decolonization. It is perhaps more profitable to situate British imperialism within the wider European imperial age than to construct some kind of historical balance sheet, comparing its record with that of other European powers.[34]

Empire has proved far more resilient, at least at the level of culture, imagination and identity, than this record of decolonization and imperial decline might suggest. Just as the British Empire seemed to be slipping into some kind of super-terrestrial twilight, the Falklands War with Argentina in 1982 exposed a still-existent imperial nerve and (said the cynical) distracted unwelcome attention from the Tory blues of Thatcherite Britain. In popular culture there were the diversions provided by the so-called 'Raj revival' films of the period, often made with American money. Decolonization seems to have inspired, among the white middle classes internationally, a strong element of post-imperial fantasy and nostalgia. With *A Passage to India* (directed by David Lean, 1984), *Out of Africa* (Sydney Pollack, 1985) and *White Mischief* (Michael Radford, 1987), among others, pith helmets entered high fashion, and clothing chains with names like 'British India' flourished. This was certainly a far cry from the actual experience of living in Britain in the 1980s, in the wake of the large numbers of immigrants who had been arriving from the Indian subcontinent and the West Indies since the 1950s. And if imperialism was implicitly criticized by these films – their protagonists were always somewhat eccentric, and contrasted, as such, with an exaggeratedly bigoted mainstream – they also glamorized the colonial experience and soft-pedalled the consequences of the paternalism of women like Karen Blixen, whose memoirs of her Kenyan farm inspired the film of *Out of Africa*. As Meryl Streep wafted elegantly across the African plains in a 1980s vision of colonial chic – for Francophiles there would be Catherine Deneuve in *Indochine* (Régis Wargnier, 1992) – audiences could be swept up in the rosy pleasures of imperial nostalgia, without probing the implications that these heroines' lives had for the oppression of minorities.[35] Once more we are faced with the paradoxical theme of freedom and unfreedom. The opportunities for independence and personal fulfilment which colonies like Kenya provided for women like Blixen were inseparable from the exploitation of 'her' Kikuyu. The gap between the images of benign paternalism represented by the Raj revival films, and the extraction of indigenous land and labour that sustained this life, is indicative of the complexities that lie at the heart of understanding the nature of the British Empire.

In current debates about empire there is often a mismatched conversation which takes place between scholars who generally try to provide complex,

THE MAU-MAU REBELLION in Kenya, a predominantly Kikuyu movement, led to a state of emergency being declared by the government in 1952. Victims of Mau-Mau violence included both European settlers and fellow Kikuyu. Some 80,000 people were detained and around 11,000 rebels were killed.

qualified answers to questions about historical change, and a public that seeks definitive (and often moral) judgment. An assessment of the British Empire, like one of all empires, *should* ask questions about moral responsibility, about consequences as well as causes. If the answers are inevitably hedged about with qualification, that is as it should be. Any history of four hundred years of global expansion and decline will inevitably be complex and contradictory. This is what History is. Perhaps more than any other fallen empire, British imperialism has had an immeasurable cultural, linguistic and structural impact on nations and communities in the early twenty-first century.

While anti-colonial movements promoted nationalistic unity during decolonization, the geographical boundaries of these new nations were often drawn as a result of imperial interference in previous centuries. At an even more profound level, British imperialism had huge consequences for world population patterns. It was Britain that carried the greatest majority of the eleven million enslaved Africans to the Americas, where they continue to form substantial populations including the vast majority in today's Caribbean. With the end of slavery, systems of indentured labour also took large numbers of Indians and Chinese from their homelands to countries such as Singapore, Malaysia, South Africa, Mauritius, Trinidad and Fiji. It was Britons and their descendants who dispossessed and largely displaced the indigenous peoples of North America and Australasia.[36] In terms of demography, Britain itself was transformed, particularly from the middle of the twentieth century, with mass migration from the former empire.

We need not think of the history of the British empire only in terms of the expansion of territory, the movement of armies, the extraction of raw materials or the lives of administrators, to name but four of the more 'traditional' possibilities. Empire can be understood in ways that illuminate how we live here and now; it is a cultural phenomenon with a profound legacy in our everyday lives. It is a way of thinking about identity, and about the divisions that still structure our society, whether we like it or not. The linguistic dominance of English in today's world focuses attention on the cultural impact that Britain brought to the globe. Yet Britain itself was equally remade. The empire lies at the heart of things we might conventionally see as uniquely 'British' in character: the class system (as the Lascelles well knew), sugar (where would all those sweet puddings be without it?) and, of course, afternoon tea.

IN 1948 Britain proclaimed a commitment to free entry by citizens of the colonial empire or Commonwealth. The arrival of significant numbers of immigrants in the 1950s, especially from the West Indies, India and Pakistan, prompted extensive debate. Restrictions were imposed in the Commonwealth Immigration Act of 1962.

7

France: Empire and the Mère-Patrie

JACQUES FRÉMEAUX

THAT BENEFITS were being bestowed by European imperialists on their subject peoples was for many the main justification of empire, and was not entirely wishful thinking. Here (*opposite*), a French colonist of about 1920 teaches African children to tell the time.

C'eſt à ce prix que vous mangez du ſucre en Europe.

Candide Chapitre 19.

'WHEN WE LABOUR IN THE SUGAR-WORKS, and the mill happens to snatch hold of a finger, they instantly chop off our hand. It is at this price that you eat sugar in Europe.' A brief conversation between Voltaire's Candide and a black slave. Voltaire was among those who campaigned to abolish the slave-trade. This engraving (*above*) appeared in 1787, the year before the foundation of the Société des Amis des Noires.

FROM THE END OF THE SIXTEENTH CENTURY onwards, French statesmen such as Cardinal Richelieu (Louis XIII's chief minister, 1624–42) and Colbert (Louis XIV's chief minister, 1665–83), started to give their support for colonial ventures to the merchants and ship-owners in the great ports – Nantes, Bordeaux and Marseille – in an effort to safeguard French markets and interests overseas. As a result, the French Empire began to expand in various directions. In North America, the French first colonized New France (in present-day Canada), starting from the St Lawrence Valley, where Quebec was founded in 1608 and Montreal in 1642, and stretching south to Louisiana, which at the time covered the entire Mississippi basin and where New Orleans was founded in 1718. In the Caribbean, they settled in Martinique, Guadeloupe, the eastern side of Hispaniola (Saint-Domingue, later to become Haiti), and then Grenada, St Lucia, Dominica and Tobago. More settlements were created in Guyana on the South American continent, where Cayenne was founded in 1635. The French were also interested in India and, after the formation of the French East India Company in 1664, they established bases in Pondicherry in 1674 and Chandernagore in 1684; the French took over islands in the Indian Ocean as well – the Île Bourbon (now Réunion) and Île de France (now Mauritius) in the Mascarene archipelago, which became important stopping places on voyages to Asia.

THE ROYAL EMPIRE

This expansion of the French Empire became a source of grave concern to the rulers of Britain. They were not prepared to see French possessions in North America thwarting the westward expansion of their own thirteen colonies along the Atlantic seaboard, while the ambitions of the French East India Company, under Dupleix, caused much alarm among the directors of its British counterpart. The threat was such that at the beginning of 1755 the British government declared war on France. The Seven Years' War that broke out in Europe the following year forced France to cut back on her overseas

commitments, and then, thanks to their superior naval power, the British were able to conquer French Canada and to occupy France's possessions in the Caribbean and India. In alliance with Prussia, Britain duly won the war, and under the terms of the peace treaty of 1763, France had to give up New France and all her territory on the east bank of the Mississippi; Louisiana was ceded to Spain as compensation for Florida, which went to the British. The treaty left France with just a few colonies: Martinique, Guadeloupe, half of Saint-Domingue, the Île Bourbon and the Île de France, as well as the tiny islands of Saint-Pierre and Miquelon off the coast of Newfoundland. As for India, the French were allowed to keep the five ports they already held but had to renounce any further expansion.

This setback, however, did not mark the end of French imperial ambitions. By taking part in the American War of Independence against Britain, France was able to regain Senegal and Tobago in 1782, but above all it was trade with the colonies that brought about a hitherto-unequalled prosperity. There was major growth, too, in contacts with Asia, which helped to bring great wealth to the Mascarene Islands, while the West Indies exported increasing quantities of sugar to France, as well as coffee and cotton. In 1788, French colonial trade surpassed that of Great Britain. The picture was not without its darker side. In the colonies themselves, the African slaves who formed the bulk of the labour force on plantations became more and more dissatisfied with their conditions, and there was constant fear of rebellion. In France, the philosophers of the Enlightenment, such as Montesquieu, Voltaire and Condorcet, condemned slavery as a fundamental violation of human rights, and the Société des Amis des Noirs, founded in 1788, advocated nothing less than the abolition of slavery. Meanwhile, colonists in the West Indies opposed the end to French slave-trading or the institution of slavery, and they criticized the system of the *exclusif*, which required the colonies to trade with the mother country and under the French flag. Some even demanded independence for the colonies from Paris.

REVOLUTION AND EMPIRE

The whole colonial edifice was profoundly shaken by the Revolution of 1789 and its aftermath. The revolutionary Constituent Assembly, which had adopted a Declaration of the Rights of Man and Citizen, nevertheless refused to abolish slavery, and the Legislative Assembly, which succeeded it in 1790, proved equally timid. Not until February 1794 did a new and more radical parliament, the Convention, with the backing of Robespierre, decide to abolish slavery, but by then it was too late to save the colonies. The British, at war with France since early 1793, had now occupied several of the French West Indian islands, and Saint-Domingue, racked by slave revolts, passed into the hands of Toussaint Louverture, a freed black revolutionary leader. The French were left only with Guadeloupe and Guyana in the Caribbean. They also lost their outposts in India. The Île Bourbon – renamed Réunion after the Revolution to discard the name of the discredited dynasty of the *ancien régime* – and Île de France became bases for French privateers, who attacked the convoys of the British East India Company. Under the Directory, the French government of the second half of the 1790s, a young general, Napoleon Bonaparte, mounted an expedition to Egypt in spring 1798, hoping to establish a toehold there and thus threaten the British in the Mediterranean and along the route to India. The expedition did a great deal to enhance Bonaparte's reputation, as this was the first time an Arab Muslim country had been occupied, but was nevertheless a failure. The expeditionary corps was left isolated by Nelson's destruction of the French fleet. Bonaparte returned to France in September 1799, and the expeditionary corps was attacked by the British and the Turks, and forced to surrender in August 1801.

Thanks to the Peace of Amiens, which he signed with Britain in March 1802, Bonaparte – who had now become First Consul, continuing his rise to power – did succeed, however, in recovering all of the possessions that France had held on the eve of the Revolution. His colonial policy, however, in no way conformed

to the principles of the Revolution, as he reintroduced slavery in the plantation colonies and reoccupied Saint-Domingue; Toussaint Louverture was arrested and deported to France, where he died in April 1803. Furthermore, the truce between France and its enemies did not last long, and war broke out again in May 1803. In March of that year, anticipating the renewed hostilities, Bonaparte had already sold Louisiana to the United States, under Thomas Jefferson's presidency, for the paltry sum of 80 million francs, hoping thereby to establish good relations with the Americans. Having crowned himself emperor in 1804, and finding himself all-powerful in Europe, Napoleon continued to pursue grandiose schemes: he considered joining up with the Russians to attack the British and drive them out of India, and he sent reconnaissance teams to Algeria, Syria and Persia. Without a strong navy, such plans were only dreams. After the Battle of Trafalgar, the superiority of the British navy was more pronounced than ever, and one by one France's colonies were occupied by the British. When Napoleon's empire finally fell, France did not have a single possession overseas.

RECONSTRUCTION

The Treaty of Paris of 1814 once more restored to France all the colonies she had held in 1789, apart from the Île de France (Mauritius), St Lucia and Tobago. Some of the leading figures of that time, such as the minister of the navy, Baron Portal, and the ship-builders in the great Atlantic ports of Bordeaux and Nantes and the Mediterranean port of Marseille, were determined to conquer the oceans with French ships and thus recapture the glory of former times. Their eagerness to reoccupy the lands that had been returned to France, however, led to a tragic event. The corvette *La Méduse*, carrying troops for the reoccupation of Senegal, ran aground; most of the crew boarded a raft but died of hunger or thirst, an

FOR ITS SUGAR France and the rest of Europe depended on West Indian plantations worked by slaves. These were a source of enormous wealth to their owners.

G·T·RAYNAL·

episode immortalized in the painter Géricault's *The Raft of the Medusa* of 1819. France nevertheless clung on to Senegal, Martinique, Guadeloupe, Réunion and the five Indian towns, henceforth referred to as the *vieilles colonies* ('old colonies') to distinguish them from territories acquired after 1830.

Each successive French government made its own contribution to the reconstruction of the overseas empire. The Restoration (1815–30) reoccupied the *vieilles colonies* and then turned its attention to North Africa. On 5 July 1830, after a French invasion, the *dey* of Algiers, who ruled under the nominal suzerainty of the Ottoman sultan, surrendered his city to the French. The conquest of the remainder of the huge country of Algeria was pursued under the July Monarchy (1830–48), the Second Republic (1848–52) and the Second Empire (1852–70). These regimes also opened up new territories in Oceania, where Tahiti was taken in 1842, and the Far East, where Saigon fell to the French in 1859. It was, however, the Third Republic (1870–1940) that brought about the greatest expansion of the colonial empire. It acquired the protectorates of Tunisia and Morocco, and territories in West and Equatorial Africa, Madagascar, Indochina and the South Pacific. Between 1871 and 1914, overseas possessions grew from approximately 700,000 sq km (270,270 sq miles), with a population of about seven million people, to more than 11 million sq km (4.25 million sq miles) and almost fifty million people. After the First World War, French domains increased still further through League of Nations mandates: Togo and Cameroon were taken away from vanquished Germany, and Syria and Lebanon from the defeated Ottoman Empire. Around 1930, French possessions covered just under 12 million sq km (4.63 million sq miles) containing 66 million people (as compared to 551,000 sq km [212,741 sq miles] and 42 million people in France itself). The French colonial empire was thus the second biggest in the world after that of Britain. More than 90 per cent of its area was in Africa, but with possessions in Asia, the Americas and Oceania, it was possible to speak of France being 'present in all five continents'.

FRANCE THE LIBERATOR

The highly reactionary court of Charles X (1824–30) regarded the conquest of Algiers as a triumph for Christianity, but any such vestige of the ideology of the medieval Crusades soon disappeared from official policies. Subsequent French governments from 1830 onwards, parading the Tricolour flag inherited from the Revolution, presented themselves as the heirs of the Enlightenment and the principles of the 1789 Declaration of the Rights of Man and Citizen. However, it was the two republican regimes that were best able to reconcile all-conquering imperialism with those precepts. The Second Republic finally abolished slavery in 1848, under the guiding influence of Victor Schoelcher (1804–93); during the Third Republic Pierre Savorgnan de Brazza (1852–1905) had the merit of freeing

THE REVOLUTION brought about an abrupt change in the status of the colonies. For decades Enlightenment figures such as Abbé Raynal had condemned slavery, but it was not until 1794 that the Convention, led by Robespierre, abolished it and agreed to representatives from the colonies attending the French parliament in Paris. The member for S. Dominique was Jean Baptiste Belley, portrayed (*opposite*) by Girodet, leaning against a bust of Raynal. Belley, unlike Toussaint Louverture, saw himself as a patriotic Frenchman, but was nevertheless later imprisoned under the Consulate and died in France in 1805.

'WHO SHALL HAVE MOROCCO?'
A satirical postcard of 1906 shows France, Germany, Spain and England chasing Morocco, who flees on the back of a camel.

a qui le Maroc?

It was to reoccupy Senegal, lost to the French during the Napoleonic Wars but restored to them in 1814, that the ill-fated *Medusa* set sail. The intention was to found a utopian community in Africa, with the native inhabitants as 'friends and allies' rather than slaves. This was one reason why its shipwreck and the terrible fate of its passengers made such an impact. But it was a flawed vision from the start. This drawing – closer to reality than Géricault's more famous symbol of France's corrupt society – shows the moment when the rescue ship was sighted.

the slaves captured by Arab traders in the Congo basin of Africa; while General Joseph Gallieni (1849–1916) ended slavery in Madagascar. In Muslim countries, there was also an end to discrimination against Jewish and Christian minorities.

The French also set out to take the basic institutions of their civilization overseas. They established primary schools and *lycées*, frequently introducing syllabuses from the mother country and propagating French language and culture among the so-called 'native' elite. On the other hand, they became interested in the study of local traditions: for instance, the École Française d'Extrême-Orient, established in Saigon in 1898, played an important part in rediscovering the great archaeological site of Angkor in Cambodia. The various governments in Paris also insisted on the need for improved sanitary and medical conditions overseas. A large number of doctors and scholars distinguished themselves in such activities: in 1880, Alphonse Laveran, studying malaria in Algeria, discovered the parasite that causes that debilitating disease; in 1894, Alexandre Yersin, based in Hong Kong, identified the bacillus that causes the plague. The Third Republic developed a network of Pasteur Institutes, whose task it was to develop and distribute the vaccines against epidemic diseases.

THE FRENCH COLONIAL LOBBY

The acquisition of an empire was not a project that involved the whole French nation. The French of the nineteenth century rarely emigrated, and those who did were often regarded as misfits who could not find a place for themselves at home. The climate in most of their colonies was tropical or equatorial, which made it difficult for Europeans to settle, and the only colonies that attracted settlers in any numbers were in North Africa, particularly Algeria. Just about half of the settlers there were actually French; the rest were mainly from Spain, Italy and Malta; the influx of new colonists from France and elsewhere in southern Europe, however, ceased almost completely after the start of the First World War. France was also represented overseas by specific groups – military officers, government officials, missionaries (mainly Catholics, but also some Protestants), planters and merchants. They were attracted by the lure of rapid social advancement or large profits, but on the debit side – particularly in the early days of imperialism – they led solitary lives in rough conditions, many meeting premature death from exhaustion or disease.

In the French ruling classes, the 'colonial adventure' was often regarded as an unattractive preoccupation. The ambition of patriotic Frenchmen was to make the Rhine their frontier with Prussia, and after 1870 with Germany. Left-wing sympathizers opposed the colonial conquests as being contrary to democratic principles. Republican leaders, especially Léon Gambetta (1838–82) and Jules Ferry (1832–93), were able to overcome this opposition with support from the *parti colonial* ('colonial party') – not a formally constituted political party as such, but a collection of people who lobbied for overseas expansion. They included army and navy officers, businessmen, ship-builders and also explorers. Settlers and others with French citizenship in Algeria elected representatives to the French parliament. Prior to 1914, the most notable was Eugène Étienne, who held the Algerian seat of Oran. He served as a government minister on several occasions and was even nicknamed 'Notre-Dame des Coloniaux'. Such people came together in a whole array of private organizations: geographical societies such as the Société de Géographie de Paris, associations like the Comité de l'Afrique Française, the Comité de l'Asie Française which promoted different areas of the empire, and the Union Coloniale, which centralized business interests. The Chambre des Députés and the Senate each had their own *groupe colonial* or colonial caucus.

WHY FRANCE WANTED COLONIES

'Colonial policy is the daughter of industrial policy,' declared Jules Ferry. There is no doubt that the Industrial Revolution played an important part in expansion,

ALGIERS FELL to the French in July 1830, a development dictated by national ambitions more than by the desire to eliminate Berber piracy. The rest of Algeria remained unconquered and resisted the French until 1857.

MEDICAL ADVANCES initiated by the French must certainly have improved the lives of their colonized subjects in Africa and the East. Alexandre Yersin, a director of the Institut Pasteur d'Indo-Chine, identified the plague bacillus and devised a serum to combat it. Alphonse Laveran, working in Algeria, discovered the parasite that caused malaria. His diagram of the various stages of its growth is shown here (*opposite*).

Overleaf
FRANCE OVERSEAS was made to be as like as possible to France at home. This photograph of Algiers makes the point vividly. The architecture is French. Most (but not all) of the clothes are French. But it is significant that no woman is to be seen.

in that it gave the French army and navy matchless technical superiority, as it did all European armies. Transport and the supply of military matériel were now much simpler for expeditionary forces, and firepower was massively increased with new types of weaponry. Greater national wealth gave the state the financial means to pursue its colonial policies without undue budgetary consequences. In industrial and business circles, expansion also fuelled the desire to find new sources of profit. In 1914, the empire accounted for slightly more than 10 per cent of France's foreign trade, occupying third place behind the United Kingdom and Germany. It also attracted investment, again taking third place in the league table of export capital, behind Russia and Latin America. The empire's commercial role became even more important with the Depression of the 1930s, when it served as a kind of financial refuge, attracting a third of France's foreign trade and between 40 and 50 per cent of its foreign investments.

A national desire for France to remain a major world power was undoubtedly another factor in the acquisition of colonial territories. The conquest of Algeria confirmed the renaissance of France's naval strength as well as her ambition to re-establish herself in the Mediterranean after being eclipsed during the Napoleonic Wars. Napoleon III – Bonaparte's nephew, who became prince-president in 1848 and crowned himself emperor several years later – dreamed of a grand Arab policy, with Algeria as a model for the 'regeneration' of the East through the introduction of modern science and technology. He also talked of founding 'a veritable empire' in the Far East. Napoleon III, however, suffered a humiliating defeat in the Franco-Prussian War of 1870, which cost France the provinces of Alsace and Lorraine, which it had to cede to Germany, and his regime came to an end. The leaders of the majority in the new Third Republic, Jules Ferry and Léon Gambetta, regarded the conquest of overseas territories as a means of safeguarding France's international position. In 1885, Ferry declared: 'Influence without action, without involvement in world affairs… is for a great nation – believe me – the same as abdication, and in a shorter time than you can imagine; it means descending from the first rank [of world powers] to the third or fourth.' He emphasized that the colonies would provide the French navy with bases and ports of call in all the world's oceans. The military later also underlined the fact that the colonies would provide soldiers for France, which had a considerably smaller population than Germany. In 1910, Charles Mangin, destined to become one of the great military leaders in the First World War, published a book entitled *La Force Noire*, in which he proposed the recruitment of large numbers of African soldiers for the French army.

HOW FRANCE ACQUIRED COLONIES
A number of different pretexts justified colonial conquests. Algiers, for instance, was occupied as an act of reprisal after the *dey*, Hussein, had publicly insulted the French consul and cannons had been fired by Algerians at a ship bearing French plenipotentiaries. The first expeditions to Cochin China and the capture of Saigon in 1859 aimed at avenging the murder of Catholic missionaries. Freedom and protection of trade formed part of the justification for the occupation of the Senegal and Niger basins, while the struggle against slavery served to legitimize expansion into the Congo basin and Chad. The invasion of Tunisia in 1881 was based on alleged unrest among tribes on the border with Algeria. There could also be an accumulation of motives for intervention, as was the case in Morocco. The indigenous government there was initially accused, in 1903, of being unable to secure its frontiers with Algeria; then an uprising against Europeans resident in Casablanca gave good reason for the French to take over that port city in 1907; and finally a rebellion against the sultan led the French army to take over the Moroccan capital of Fez in 1911.

The empire was acquired principally by military force. Algeria was beaten into submission only after a long-drawn-out conflict and almost inhuman violence from 1839 to 1857. Equally violent, though less protracted, was the conquest of French West Africa, between 1880 and 1897; that of Morocco, though less brutal,

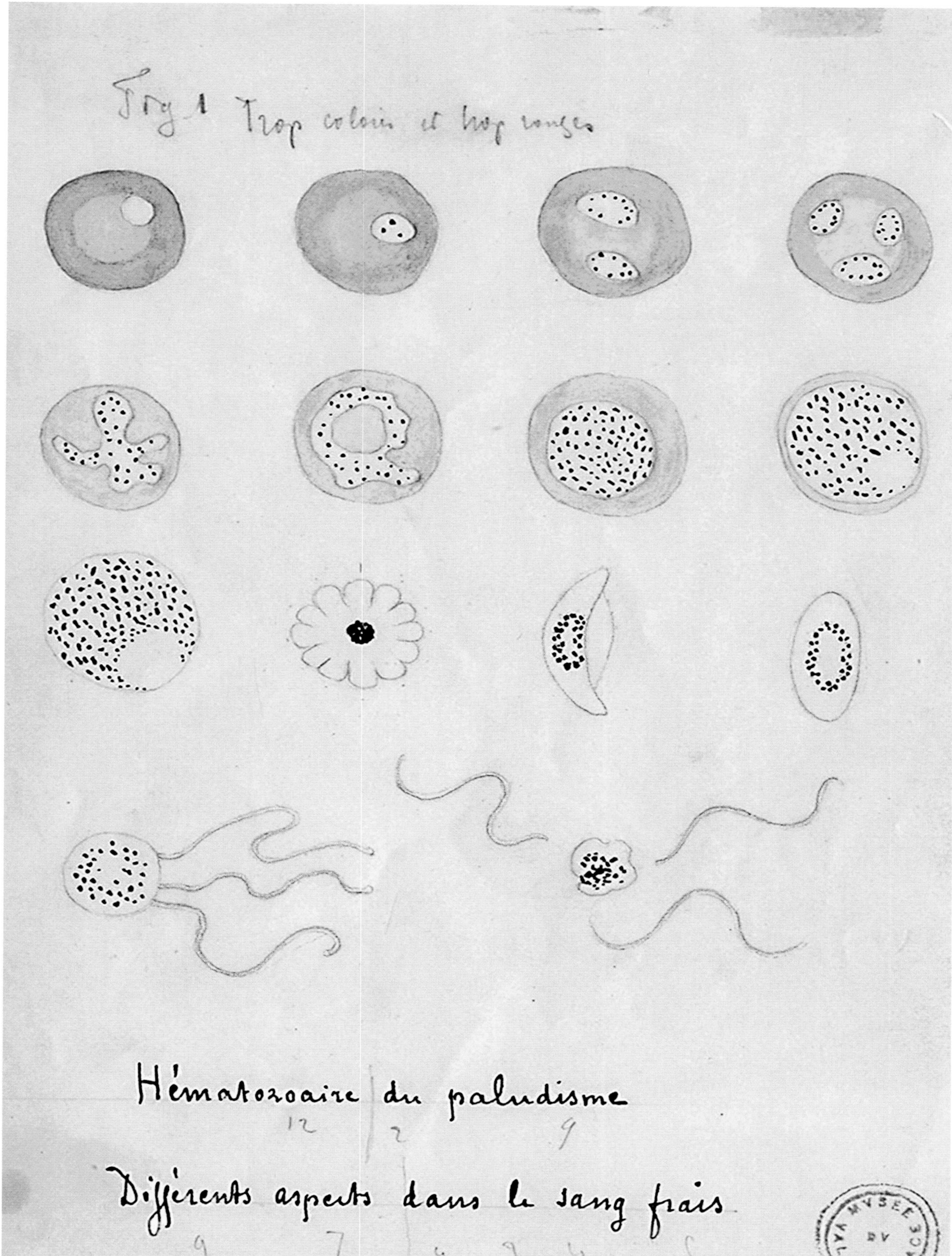

Fig 1 Trop colorés et trop rouges

Hématozoaire du paludisme

12 2 9

Différents aspects dans le sang frais

9 7 4 2 4 S

MATERIAL EXCHANGE was the
foundation of all empires. It was seen
as advantageous to both sides, though
inevitably the balance had to be in
favour of the colonizer. A French
school textbook of the 1920s (*right*)
illustrates the various products of
colonies across the world.

THE POLICY OF ASSIMILATION was as
much an ideal as a reality. Algerian
women might in theory be equal to
Frenchwomen, but nothing could
bridge the cultural gap between them
(*opposite*).

was also hard-fought from 1912 to 1934. In Indochina, the takeover of Annam
in central Vietnam and especially of Tonkin, further north, required a massive
military effort, most notably in order to secure control of the frontier with
China. The subjugation of Madagascar took several years as well, though by
contrast the ruler of Cambodia accepted the declaration of a French protectorate
in 1863 in order to save his realm from its ambitious neighbours, the king of
Siam and the emperor of Annam. The occupation of the French Congo, led by
Brazza, took place peacefully between 1875 and 1882, and from 1885 to 1887 the
explorer Auguste Pavie successfully used nothing but his powers of persuasion
to bring about the submission of the sovereigns of Laos. Subsequently, however,
even in countries that had submitted willingly to French rule, frequent rebellions
broke out. Some were on a very large scale, such as the Algerian revolt in Kabylia
in 1871, but none was major enough to threaten French domination until the
Communist insurrection exploded in Vietnam at the end of 1946.

Another major instrument used to acquire colonial territory was
international diplomacy. In the nineteenth century, agreement with the British
was essential to guarantee communications with overseas possessions. The 'first'
entente cordiale between Paris and London was established at mid-century between
Louis-Philippe's prime minister, François Guizot, and the British prime minister
Lord Aberdeen; the accord facilitated the conquest of Algeria as well as the
occupation of Tahiti. Relations between France and Britain remained friendly
under Napoleon III, but later turned sour, with the French government being
particularly upset over the British occupation of Egypt in 1882. In 1898, at
Fashoda on the Upper Nile, French forces under the command of Jean-Baptiste
Marchand, moving eastwards on their way from the French Congo, came up
against the army of Lord Kitchener, who had just taken Khartoum, leading to
a major international crisis. The French were forced to give up all claims to
Egypt, and the second *entente cordiale* of 1904 – negotiated by King Edward VII
and the French foreign minister Théophile Delcassé – finally settled the whole
'question of Egypt' to British advantage. In exchange, the British gave France
a free hand to impose a protectorate on Morocco. The French government
thus enjoyed the support of London in opposing the colonial ambitions of
Germany. In return for Germany renouncing its claims in Morocco, the French
ceded parcels of their possessions in equatorial Africa to the German colony
of Cameroon.

France's principal colonies, *c*.1939

1. Mauritania, Senegal, French Sudan (Mali), Niger, Guinea, Ivory Coast, Dahomey (Benin), Upper Volta (Burkina Faso).

2. Congo, Gabon, Ubangi (Central African Republic), Chad.

3. Guadeloupe, Martinique and dependencies.

4. Tonkin, Annam, Cochin China (Vietnam), Laos, Cambodia.

Name	*Status*	*Area (km²)*	*Total population*	*French citizens*	*Non-French Europeans*
ALGERIA	GROUP OF DEPARTMENTS	2,205,000	7,800,000	853,000	134,000
MOROCCO	PROTECTORATE	415,000	6,300,000	177,000	60,000
TUNISIA	PROTECTORATE	125,000	2,600,000	108,000	
SYRIA AND LEBANON	LEAGUE OF NATIONS MANDATE	200,000	3,200,000	3,000	
FRENCH WEST AFRICA	FEDERATION OF COLONIES[1]	4,702,000	14,700,000	97,000	7,000
CAMEROON	LEAGUE OF NATIONS MANDATE	431,000	2,100,000		
TOGO	LEAGUE OF NATIONS MANDATE	52,000	740,000		
FRENCH EQUATORIAL AFRICA	FEDERATION OF COLONIES[2]	2,200,000	3,000,000	3,800	900
MADAGASCAR	COLONY	616,000	3,800,000	25,000	14,000
WEST INDIES	COLONIES[3]				
GUYANA	COLONY	90,000	37,000	26,000	6,000
RÉUNION	COLONY	2,400	209,000	203,000	
DJIBOUTI	COLONY				
INDOCHINA	FEDERATION OF COLONIES[4]	740,000	23,000,000	30,000	
NEW CALEDONIA AND DEPENDENCIES	COLONY	30,000	113,000	15,000	2,000
FRENCH POLYNESIA	COLONY	4,000	40,000	22,000	

The empire was never administered by a single governing body, although some wished for it to be ruled centrally. The colonies came directly under the Ministry of the Navy until 1881, when an Under-Secretariat for the Colonies was created. This became a full-blown Colonial Ministry in 1894, but even then it did not cover all of France's overseas possessions. Algeria initially came under the Ministry for War, and then from 1870 was assigned to the Ministry of the Interior. Tunisia and Morocco were attached to the Foreign Ministry, later to be joined by Syria and Lebanon. These apparent anomalies resulted from the differing statuses of the overseas territories. Algeria was divided up into administrative units, *départements*, within a system theoretically identical to that of the metropole. Morocco and Tunisia were protectorates which retained their own sovereigns and, in principle, were subject only to general oversight by France. Syria and Lebanon were mandates under the guardianship of France in the name of the League of Nations; Paris's mission there was to guide these two countries as swiftly as possible towards independence – an eventuality not specified for the other two mandated territories, Togo and Cameroon.

There were, however, certain similarities among all the French outposts. Each colony was placed under the rule of a high-ranking official directly answerable to Paris and usually given the title of governor. Under his command came a centralized administration consisting of agents, called administrators or inspectors, who enjoyed very wide-ranging powers. They kept a close watch on the indigenous officials in local communities (such as the *caïds* in North Africa, chiefs of villages and cantons); they collected taxes, organized the police force and arbitrated disputes. They also held responsibility for public works, law enforcement and hygiene, and could impose prison sentences and fines. One governor, Robert Delavignette, wrote that they were 'the true chiefs of the empire'. Frequently they were criticized for a tendency to curb the powers of the native chiefs, and for preferring a harsher and more direct form of government than the 'indirect rule' practised by the British. On the other hand, supporters noted they were well educated at the École Coloniale, a training academy founded in Paris in 1889, and their integrity was rarely called into question.

In general, criticisms of the colonial system were limited. Most frequently they came from public figures or political parties that attacked abuses of power rather than the principle of colonization itself. The strongest pressure came from the Socialist Party, whose famous leader Jean Jaurès (1869–1914) denounced the violence used in the conquest of Morocco, and even refused to vote for the treaty making it a protectorate; he did not, however, demand independence for countries that had already been conquered. The only truly radical opposition came from the French Communists who, having founded a separate Communist Party in 1920 and taking their inspiration from Lenin, engaged in a systematic denunciation of all forms of imperialism. After the election of a Popular Front government in 1936, dominated by Socialists but with tacit support from Communists, the latter moderated their attacks and restricted themselves simply to a demand for colonial reform. As far as they and indeed the majority of French people were concerned, the overseas colonies had everything to gain by staying within the French system, which, they imagined, offered security, liberty and the chance to profit from the social advancement of the French proletariat.

THE SITUATION OF THE COLONIZED

There were also similarities in the way that native peoples were treated. More often than not, they were still subject to their own laws and customs in matters relating to marriage, inheritance and contracts drawn up among themselves. However, civil and criminal offences were dealt with under the French penal code. French civil law was generally applied only to property or land transactions involving Europeans, and though religious freedom was absolute, civil and political rights were limited. For the most part, the vote was either refused entirely to the natives or granted in a very restrictive manner, as was the right

CLASHES BETWEEN IMPERIALISTS were common. In 1898 both England and France hoped to establish routes across Africa (one north–south, the other east–west). They happened to meet at Fashoda, a village on the Nile. A French force under Captain Marchaud confronted an English one under General Kitchener. In March 1899 the French tactfully withdrew.

EXCUSES FOR CONQUEST were never hard to find. Several European powers coveted Morocco. Both Germany and France obtained substantial concessions there. French involvement intensified after an uprising against Europeans in Casablanca in 1907. Four years later they intervened to crush a rebellion against the sultan in Fez. A photograph of that time (*opposite*) shows Moroccan prisoners awaiting interrogation. Agreement with Germany was reached in 1911, and in 1912 a French protectorate was established. Morocco was never a French possession as Algeria was, but not until 1956 did it become fully independent.

to form associations and hold meetings. The press was placed under strict control, and natives could be imprisoned or fined by police officers or administrators without a trial. They could also be forced to work at any time on the maintenance of roads and public services, and after the First World War young men could be called up for compulsory military service. French citizenship was rarely granted, and then only to those who agreed to abide by the French civil code, which meant renouncing various traditional customs.

In everyday life, there was no official policy of ethnic segregation, and access to transport, public space, schools and hospitals was universal. The French were proud of this integration, which they contrasted with the attitudes of the British and the Americans. Even though Jules Ferry declared that the 'superior races' had a right and duty to civilize the 'inferior races', racism played no part in any official doctrine. When it came to the conduct of individuals, however, French colonists were by no means beyond reproach. There was a tendency to look down on the natives: attitudes varied from benign paternalism through indifference to brutality – the latter generally confined to verbal abuse, but sometimes also extending to physical violence. There were genuinely egalitarian relationships, but they were rare. Some of the prominent native figures who had studied in France found a distinct difference between the behaviour of the French colonists and that of the French in the *mère-patrie*, where they seemed to display a more open attitude to those from other backgrounds.

Some black people were able to receive the training that France reserved for outstanding scholars, going on to higher education and eventually holding important offices. Camille Mortenol, who came from Guadeloupe and was the son of a slave freed in 1847, passed the secondary school-leaving certificate, the *baccalauréat*, won a scholarship to the prestigious École Polytechnique in 1880, and became a ship's captain. In 1931, Blaise Diagne, a deputy from Senegal, became under-secretary of state for the colonies. In 1938, Félix Éboué, a black man from French Guyana, was appointed governor of Guadeloupe, and in 1940, after the defeat of France by Nazi Germany, was one of the first to rally to the Free French led by General de Gaulle, who made him governor-general of French Equatorial Africa. After the Second World War, the Guyanese senator Gaston Monnerville presided over the French Senate from 1947 until 1968. Félix Houphouët-Boigny, later president of the Ivory Coast from 1960 until 1993, and Léopold Sédar Senghor, president of Senegal from 1960 until 1980, were both at various times ministers in the governments of the Fourth Republic in the 1950s.

These glittering careers aroused the envy of many minority groups elsewhere in the world, for example black Americans such as the academic W.E.B. DuBois, but such advancement in the French colonies was confined to a privileged few. Widespread poverty prevented most blacks from entering higher education, which was reserved for the sons of prominent personalities or for a few particularly gifted students who had caught the attention of their French teachers. Even those who reached a level that might have put them on a par with their French counterparts were held back precisely because they were natives: in the army, for instance, there were very few indigenous officers, and they were seldom able to rise above the lower ranks. This situation did not really change until after 1945 – certainly too late to give the newly promoted officers the feeling that they could have a successful career within the French system. From this time onwards, the main consequence of social advancement was the formation of an elite for future independent countries.

THE EMPIRE AS A LIFELINE FOR FRANCE

The ordeals that the French endured after 1914 served to strengthen their ties to their overseas possessions. After the end of the First World War in 1918, the empire appeared to be the best means whereby the country, ravaged by the effects of the war, could maintain its demographic and economic status. The minister for the colonies, Albert Sarraut, spoke in 1920 of a 'greater France, no longer relying for its security on 40 million, but on 100 million people, and able to seek all its basic provisions from a unified domain twenty times bigger than the mother country'. The permanent presence in France of soldiers from the Maghreb and other African regions underlined their importance for the defence of the nation. Even primary schools lauded the achievements of great men like Pierre Savorgnan de Brazza, Marshal Joseph Gallieni (conqueror of Madagascar), and Marshal Hubert Lyautey (conqueror of Morocco). Advertisements for bananas, cocoa and rice were often adorned with exotic landscapes and characters dressed in traditional costumes. The most famous of all these pictures was probably that of the chocolate drink Banania, which featured a laughing Senegalese soldier; later, however, the image came to be regarded as offensive, and it disappeared during the 1970s. The international colonial exhibition held in Paris in 1931 attracted about eight million visitors over six months, and helped towards creating a better understanding of the colonies.

In the Second World War the empire became a vital issue. In 1940, when the French army was facing certain defeat, the question arose as to whether the government should abandon the metropole and continue the war overseas. The majority of those in power rejected this solution. Marshal Pétain's government prided itself on having saved the empire from occupation by signing an armistice with the Germans, thereby preserving the country's chances of reconstruction. By contrast, Pétain's opponents, General de Gaulle's Free French, insisted that the empire should enter the war. De Gaulle succeeded in rallying French Equatorial Africa and other colonies to the cause, then took control of Syria and Lebanon, and the Free French soldiers helped the British army to combat the Vichy forces. In November 1942, after British and American troops had landed in Morocco and Algeria, all of France's possessions came under his command, and a provisional Assembly was established in Algiers until the liberation of mainland France. North Africa was thus the base from which Europe was liberated, while New Caledonia was used by American forces in their Pacific operations against Japan.

The support of the colonies had indeed become more and more indispensable. During the First World War, they had supplied nearly 600,000 soldiers and about 200,000 workers to France. Subsequently, every effort was made to increase this contribution, and compulsory military service was introduced in all the colonies. In 1940, the French army sent 640,000 colonials and North Africans settlers into action, including 176,000 Algerians, 80,000 Tunisians, 80,000 Moroccans and 180,000 soldiers from black Africa and Madagascar – in all, about 10 per cent of the fighting force. These troops fought bravely, and many died in action or were taken prisoner. The call to arms did not end with the defeat of France, and colonials formed the majority of de Gaulle's freedom fighters. After 1943, when a French army was formed in North Africa, using American equipment, again the colonial contingent was the largest component. In 1944, out of 633,000 soldiers, about 60 per cent were 'natives'. Of the remaining 40 per cent, the majority were French Algerians (later known as the *pieds-noirs*), many of whom had never actually been to France. This army fought in Tunisia, France and Germany alongside troops from the British Commonwealth and the United States.

The shared wartime suffering seemed to strengthen the ties between France and its overseas possessions. General de Gaulle, in opening the 1944 Brazzaville conference of colonial governors and administrators, spoke of a 'definitive bond'. The constitution of the Fourth Republic, adopted in October 1946, replaced the term 'empire' with 'Union Française', which in itself suggested indissoluble ties. Having acquired such an empire, the French had accustomed themselves to seeing it as an integral part of the national heritage. A poll in 1949 showed that 81 per cent of the population considered it to be in the country's interests to have colonies. At the beginning of the 1950s, Prime Minister Pierre Mendès France declared that with its overseas possessions France remained a great power, comparable in population and area to the United States and the Soviet Union. In 1953, his minister of the interior, François Mitterrand, wrote

'EURAFRICA' was a concept that lasted from the 19th to the mid-20th century. A poster for the Colonial Exhibition of 1931 hails 'Greater France', many times larger than France itself.

that, thanks to its African dependencies, France was, 'from the Congo to the Rhine, the third nation-continent' – again a comparison of France with the US and the USSR. At the time, some even envisaged a link between the new Europe (the European Economic Community was formed in 1957) and the retention of African possessions within the framework of what they called 'Eurafrica'.

POLITICAL EVOLUTION

For a long time, there had been little change in the political structure of the empire. After 1870, the West Indies, Réunion, Senegal, the Indian trading posts and Algeria all sent elected representatives to Paris. But for more than seventy years there was never any question of extending these rights to all the colonies, or of envisaging a system of decentralized institutions for them, as was the case in the British colonies. At the end of the Second World War, the desire to grant a greater degree of liberty translated into even greater absorption by the *mère-patrie*: representatives from the colonies were summoned to sit in the new assembly charged with preparing a constitution for the Fourth Republic; a 1946 law, introduced by the Senegalese Lamine Gueye, conferred citizenship on all members of the Union Française. Yet no colony had the legal right to secede from the Union Française. With this proviso everything was directed towards the ultimate goal of making the citizens of the colonies as French as the citizens of France itself. This entire concept was based on a double illusion, or a double misunderstanding.

First, the peoples of the empire had no desire to remain perpetually under French dominion. The majority aspired to govern themselves, even if they did not want to break all ties with the old colonial power. They had been conquered only recently, and they were deeply conscious that they had been subjugated by force. This awareness was exacerbated by the humiliating treatment they had regularly suffered. Although there was often a very real attraction to French culture, this did not lessen their love for their own national cultures. The Arab and Indochinese countries were proud that they belonged to very ancient civilizations, as was indeed recognized by the West, while African cultures – which had for long been dismissed as 'primitive' – had gained new respect through the work of anthropologists and modern artists. After the First World

War, independence movements had begun to develop among the peoples of Indochina and the Maghreb, though for the most part these remained very moderate. After the Second World War, however, they gained strength from the support of the USA and the USSR, and they also received aid from international bodies such as the UN and the Arab League, as well as countries such as Egypt and India, which had recently gained their independence.

Second, the French themselves had never seriously envisaged a genuine union between metropolitan France and its overseas territories. Few believed that the indigenous peoples were ready for French-style institutions, and many thought that the granting of political rights would mean the end of colonization. They were afraid that the authorities, by relinquishing their overweening powers, would no longer be able to crush revolts. They also feared that power might pass to elected natives who would be hostile to French domination. Some even foresaw dire consequences for political life in France itself. As of the late 1950s, the overall population of the African countries that remained under French rule was more or less the same as that of the mother country (45 million), but their demographic growth was considerably faster. Equal rights, in the long term, would have resulted in a majority of elected deputies coming from overseas, and it would also have meant 'indigenous' administrators replacing French administrators, not only in the colonies but also within France itself. No one wanted the mother country to become a 'colony of the colonies'.

ECONOMIC EVOLUTION

The French authorities scarcely deviated from their original concept of economic relations between France and her colonies: the empire was meant to be an ever-expanding provider of raw materials and purchaser of manufactured goods. Every effort had to be made to increase local production, with a view to raising the standard of living and hence the purchasing power of the colonies. State expenditure overseas was long limited by the principle – which actually became law in 1900 – that the metropolitan budget should incorporate only the costs of so-called 'sovereignty', i.e. military expenses and the salaries of French officials in the overseas territories. Payment of indigenous officials and police, and the cost of building and maintaining administrative buildings, hospitals and schools must be met by the colonies themselves. They must also pay for their own infrastructure – roads, ports, railways, etc. The necessary funds were raised through taxes and loans, the interest on which came out of the colonies' own budgets.

THE BOND OF UNION between France and her colonial subjects exceeded that of any other imperial powers, manifested in the support given to the mother country in 1914. This was one reason why the eventual divorce was so painful. Shown here are Algerian infantry in the First World War – an important component of the French army.

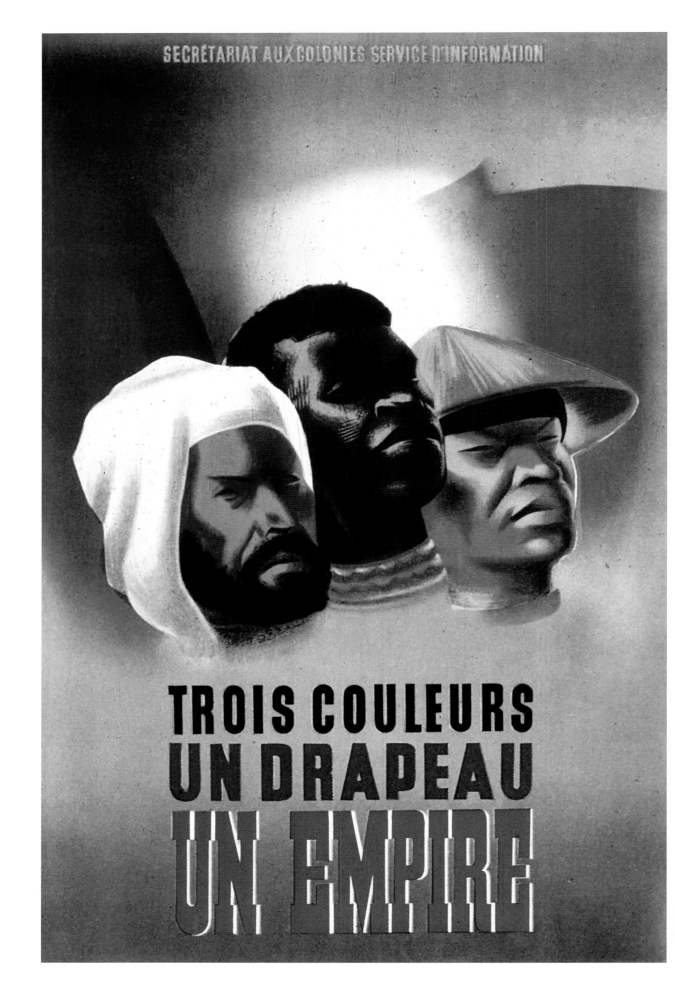

After the First World War, modifications to this fiscal system were proposed. In 1923, the minister for the colonies, Albert Sarraut, put forward 'a general plan for colonial development' that was designed to tighten the links between France and her colonies. In 1941, his successor, Admiral Platon, a member of the Vichy government, put forward a similar plan, aimed at 'the unification of production and exchange within the empire'. From 1946, the French budget was expected to contribute towards the economic and social development of the colonies. A special fund called FIDES (*Fonds de développement économique et social*), supplemented by state subsidies, was created specially for this purpose, but it was very soon felt that the cost was too high. After 1956, there was considerable support for a slogan coined by the journalist Raymond Cartier, who advocated financial aid for the development of French regions rather than overseas colonies – '*La Corrèze plutôt que la Zambèze*' ('The Corrèze region rather than the Zambezi colony'). In fact, the cost to the French budget was not excessive, but it was deemed unwise to ask the taxpayer to make sacrifices for the benefit of countries over which France's continued sovereignty was becoming less and less secure.

VIOLENT DECOLONIZATION

The post-war period underlined the gravity of the situation. In May 1945, a major uprising occurred in Algeria, and Madagascar rebelled in 1947. In both cases, the revolts were brutally suppressed. In Syria, however, intervention by British forces compelled the French government to back down in the face of riots that took place in Damascus in May 1945; the French had to withdraw troops from Syria and Lebanon, and grant both countries independence, as had been promised in 1941.

The war in Indochina resulted from the fact that the French authorities, who had been disempowered when the Japanese occupied the region, wished to retake control over these countries in 1945. The Vietnamese Communists had proclaimed independence, and attempts to reach agreement with them came to nothing. War broke out at the end of 1946. After seven years of fighting, with the loss of 90,000 French soldiers and many more Vietnamese Communist troops, as well as hundreds of thousands of civilians, the war ended with the military disaster of Dien Bien Phu. Within a few months, the Geneva Conference removed all traces of French political influence in Vietnam, Cambodia and Laos.

The Algerian War, which was unleashed in November 1954 by militants from the Algerian National Liberation Front, proved a similar catastrophe, with 25,000 French soldiers, 5,000 French civilians, and between 200,000 and 300,000 Algerians losing their lives. Even if this war was not lost militarily, it ended in an all-too-hurried independence which itself had disastrous consequences: in all, a million French Algerians were driven into exile, deprived of all their property and forcibly 'repatriated'; tens of thousands of Algerians who had worked closely with the French were massacred, especially the so-called *harkis* – former auxiliaries who had served in the French army – while similar numbers went into exile.

These two conflicts also had consequences for domestic politics. The war in Indochina was especially notable for violent campaigns by the powerful French Communist Party, which affirmed its solidarity with the Vietnamese Communists fighting against the French army. The French government, however, finally put an end to the effort to retain control of Indochina, much to the general public relief. The Algerian War, though, was much more divisive. In contrast to Indochina, in which only professional soldiers had been used, about a million young Frenchmen were called up for military service in North Africa – a move that aroused much public hostility. The anti-war opposition covered a wide spectrum: left-wing sympathizers, intellectuals and academics, the Catholic and Protestant Churches – all united in their disapproval of the government's refusal to grant independence to Algeria, and especially in condemnation of the inhumane methods employed by the army, which included torture. The conflict brought France to the verge of civil war. In May 1958, a rebellion by the army in

'THREE COLOURS, ONE FLAG': a First World War poster (*opposite*) appeals to a common patriotism throughout the empire. *Above*: white and black soldiers in the service of the same struggle are equally 'Algerian'.

THE END of the French presence in Indochina came when – following the defeat of the Japanese occupiers in 1945 – the Chinese Communist government backed a Vietnamese independence movement led by Ho Chi Minh. In 1950, as part of a worldwide anti-Communist campaign, the United States came to the aid of France. But in May 1954 the last French stronghold, Dien Bien Phu, fell, a bitter blow to French prestige (shown here: French soldiers being escorted to a prisoner-of-war camp). Vietnam was partitioned into North and South and the French lost control of both. In 1976, with the withdrawal of American support, the country was reunited.

Algiers helped to overthrow the Fourth Republic and to restore General de Gaulle to power. De Gaulle needed all his authority to put an end to the war by opposing the partisans of French Algeria. In April 1961, he succeeded in putting down an attempted military revolt, and then he suppressed a subversive plot by the OAS (*Organisation armée secrète* – a terrorist organization opposed to Algerian independence), which in a series of assassinations attempted to wreck de Gaulle's policy of negotiation with the Algerian nationalists. A referendum was finally held in France in March 1962, and 91 per cent voted in favour of the Évian Accords drawn up with the nationalists, which mandated independence for Algeria.

NEGOTIATED DECOLONIZATION

These tragic and bloody conflicts should not detract from the fact that Morocco and Tunisia achieved their independence through negotiation by their respective leaders. These two countries had also witnessed grave crises, but these had not degenerated into open conflict. The full independence of Morocco, under King Mohammed V, and of Tunisia, under President Habib Bourguiba, was recognized in 1956. Black African countries and Madagascar also achieved their independence by peaceful means. Having won French citizenship in 1946, the peoples of the Union Française saw a means of obtaining a greater degree of freedom, and hence of gaining a hearing for their demands. From 1956 onwards, the Fourth Republic granted internal autonomy to the African colonies and Madagascar, and the constitution of the Fifth Republic, in 1958, replaced the Union Française with the Communauté, making provision for all members to seek independence. This was granted in the case of the African colonies and Madagascar in 1960, as soon as the various local governments put in their requests.

Public opinion suffered no lasting damage from decolonization. Polls showed that from an early stage people were already convinced of the need for such a change. General de Gaulle was also able to endow this surrender with a gloss that satisfied national pride. He went to great lengths to prove that there was no point in holding on to possessions that were 'sterile, costly, and with no way out', and it was equally pointless to fight against a universal trend towards decolonization. He showed how much France would have to gain by replacing its outdated imperialism with economic and cultural co-operation that would bring goodwill from all the world's newly independent countries. He thus succeeded in formulating a whole range of diplomatic and military agreements that enabled France to establish solid foundations in post-colonial Africa.

Nevertheless, part of the empire survived even after 1962. Martinique, Guadeloupe, Réunion and French Guyana, the *vieilles colonies*, all of which had become French *départements* in 1946, remained outside the process of decolonization. Some overseas territories – Comoros, Djibouti, New Caledonia, French Polynesia and Wallis and Futuna – did not wish to join the states of the Communauté in 1958, and so remained tied to France. Subsequently, however, the independence of the Comoros Islands in the Indian Ocean (minus Mayotte, which remains under French administration) in 1975, and that of Djibouti, on the Horn of Africa, in 1977 took place quite smoothly and did not prevent France from maintaining its interests. New Caledonia, in the South Pacific, experienced a serious crisis in the 1980s, but since 1988 has been engaged on a more peaceful route to independence, and French Polynesia may possibly follow the same course.

What has sometimes been called the 'confetti' of the empire has not been without significance for successive French governments. The policy of co-operation has enabled France to maintain an important foothold in black Africa. Bases like Cape Verde, near Dakar, and Djibouti, at the entrance to the Red Sea, played an important role in the course of the Cold War and also in safeguarding supplies of petroleum. French Polynesia was used as an atomic testing centre until 1995, and French Guyana has become a base for launching spacecraft – in particular, the European Ariane programme. The countless islands and archipelagos in its possession have meant that, since 1994, France has enjoyed the benefits of an exclusive maritime economic zone extending up to 320 km (200 miles) offshore and covering an area of some 11 million sq km (4.25 million sq miles).

All the same, colonization has left indelible marks on the collective French memory. The effects of the Algerian War set the descendants of the *rapatriés* and the *harkis* who supported the French in Algeria against those who fought for Algerian independence. Large numbers of French people are in fact descended from Algerian immigrants. People from the French West Indies, the majority of whom are descendants of slaves, still demand declarations of 'repentance' for French participation in the institution of slavery. On a more international scale, there are contradictory assessments of the effects of colonization, and even among French authorities there are divergent views. A law passed by parliament on 23 February 2005 expressed the nation's gratitude to the men and women who took part in the work that France accomplished in her colonies. The city of Paris dedicated a memorial to the Algerians who were killed by the police on 17 October 1961 during a demonstration organized by nationalists, while authorities have recently refused to allow a memorial to be erected in Marignane, near Marseille, dedicated to members of the OAS. It will be a long time before French colonial history becomes a purely academic subject.

TO LOSE ALGERIA was even more painful to the French. An independence movement under Muslim leadership had begun immediately after the war. Hostility between the two sides became more and more vicious. Opinion in France was passionately divided. In 1958 General de Gaulle was elected president in the popular belief that he would keep Algeria French. But he had become convinced that independence was the only solution. This led to a revolt in Algeria supported by part of the army. Self-determination came in 1962.

8 Russia: The Two Empires

GRAEME GILL

SOVIET COMMUNISM was vehemently anti-imperialist (a tendency that it characterized as archetypally capitalist). In many cases, however, territories that had been incorporated into the Tsarist Empire were taken over by the Soviets and exploited in a comparable way. One such territory was Karelia, which was historically and ethnically Finnish. This rousing poster of 1926 – called 'Increased Production in Karelia' – identifies the region with revolutionary progress.

Τ HERE HAVE BEEN TWO RUSSIAN EMPIRES, the Tsarist Empire lasting from the 1550s until 1917 and, more controversially, the Soviet Empire, which was founded in 1917 and fell in 1991. While they shared a broadly common physical space (with some differences at the margins) and similar geostrategic outlooks, and the former provided a potent historical and cultural legacy for the latter, the two empires also had significant differences.

THE MATERIAL BASIS OF EMPIRE

The heartland of the Russian Empire was that part of the Eurasian plain around the city of Moscow. This had become the strongest of the Slavic principalities by the mid-sixteenth century, and it was the seat of a succession of monarchs (tsars) who all seem to have harboured expansionist designs. However, the economic basis upon which such designs rested was weak. Russia had a very short growing season, approximately half that of other major food producers, with large parts of the country not well suited to agriculture. Cultivation methods were primitive. As a result, Russia experienced approximately one bad harvest out of every three.[1] The consequent difficulty in generating consistent agricultural surpluses undercut the development of a powerful and independent nobility, thereby weakening a potential barrier to the emergence of absolutist monarchy. But the agricultural performance also made it difficult for the tsarist state to generate the sorts of revenues that would have facilitated the growth of a powerful state apparatus. This weak economic base, and the perceived need to supplement it from elsewhere, was one factor encouraging expansionist urges within elite circles.

The location of the heartland of the Russian state was important in explaining expansion in another respect. Moscow was situated in a vast plain lacking the sorts of physical barriers that could have accorded some security from outside enemies. To the south and southeast, the approaches to the Moscow region were wide open, and it was from this direction that the Russian state was incorporated into the Mongol Empire in the mid-thirteenth century.

It remained under Mongol suzerainty for nearly two and a half centuries. To the west and north, the land was devoid of major obstacles and from here too there were historically powerful foes, Lithuania/Poland and Sweden. The state that was developing around Moscow in the sixteenth century thus felt itself vulnerable to external foes, and one answer to this was to expand the territorial area of the state and thus push the border to a greater distance from the capital than had hitherto been possible.

THE GROWTH OF THE TSARIST EMPIRE

Under Tatar suzerainty, Moscow emerged as the leading Russian principality and was gradually able to expand the area of territory under its control. After throwing off the 'Tatar yoke', and especially under Ivan IV ('the Terrible'), the new Russian state expanded, so that by the middle of the sixteenth century much of the territory of the first Russian state, the former Kievan Rus, had been consolidated under Muscovite control. The Russian state now embarked on a process of imperial consolidation, gathering in lands never formerly part of Russia and, in some cases, occupied by hostile forces. In the second half of the sixteenth century, Ivan mounted a campaign against the Kazan, Astrakhan

VAST AREAS OF ASIA were opened up to Russian domination under the tsars. Vitus Bering was a Danish navigator who in 1724 was sent by Peter the Great to explore Siberia. Bering discovered the strait between Asia and America that now bears his name. One consequence was that Alaska was part of the Russian Empire from 1799 to 1867.

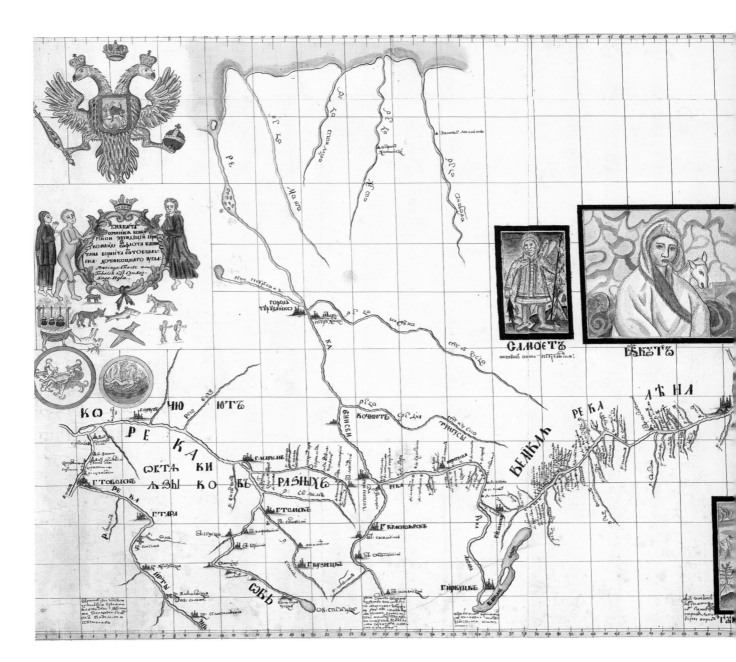

and Crimean khanates, which were subdued and the border pushed as far as the Caspian Sea. In the early 1580s a Cossack band led by Yermak crossed the Ural Mountains and took the Siberian khanate of Tiumen. In the seventeenth century, Siberia was conquered, with Russians reaching the Pacific shore by the mid-seventeenth century. Wooden forts established along the river routes formed the basis of towns resting on the fur trade, but it was not until the following two centuries that those areas suitable for agriculture were settled on a wide scale. And it was not until the completion of the Trans-Siberian railway in 1915 that a reliable line of communication was established in this region. Russian exploration and colonization, drawn principally by the fur trade, even extended to Alaska until the latter was sold to the US in 1867. In the eighteenth century, Russian control was pushed to the edge of Mongolia, into what is now southern Ukraine, virtually to the edge of the Caucasus Mountains, and in the west into the Baltic states, Poland, contemporary Belarus and western Ukraine. All of these gains were made on the back of military power. In the nineteenth century, the Amur region in the Far East, Kazakhstan, Turkestan and the Caucasus region in the south, and Finland, the remainder of Poland and contemporary Moldova in the west were all brought under Russian control. This was a massive expansion

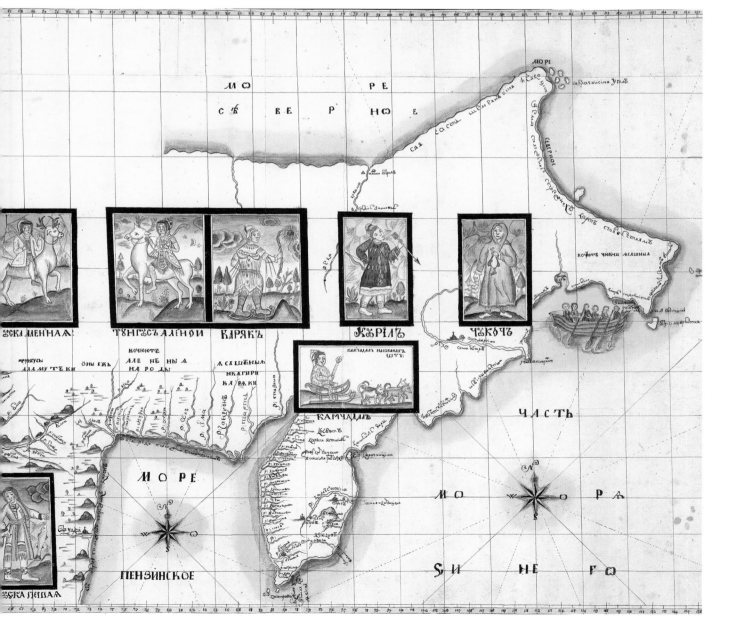

of territory, with the size of the Russian lands increasing from 24,000 sq km (9,000 sq miles) in 1462 to 13.5 million sq km (5.2 million sq miles) in 1914.[2]

This expansion was propelled by a combination of economic and strategic causes. The move into Siberia was almost purely economic, to gain control of the lucrative fur trade and to open up the natural resources of the region, especially cultivable land, minerals and timber. The southward move into 'New Russia' (mainly southern Ukraine and the middle-lower Volga region) was motivated by the desire to crush the remaining Mongol khanates in that region and to open up the fertile black soil lands of the western steppe. This area also gave control over major south-flowing rivers and therefore access to the Black Sea. The advances to the west were primarily strategic in intent as Russia sought to create a buffer of land between its heartland and hostile Western powers, with the takeover of Finland in particular prompted by the desire to move the international border further away from the capital (since 1709), St Petersburg; access to the sea was also significant in the case of the Baltic region. The assertion of Russian control over Kazakhstan and Turkestan was prompted in part by geostrategic considerations related to the British attempt to block Russia in the southwest, reflected in the Crimean War. The Russian counter was to press its control further in the direction of British India. This region soon became important economically through the production of cotton. The drive into the Caucasus region was stimulated by appeals for support from their fellow Orthodox Christian Georgians, and also by the perceived need to stabilize this region which was a crossroads of religions and cultures and was seen as potentially destabilizing to the southern part of the empire.

The expansion of Russian power and the creation of empire that this constituted brought under imperial control a large range of peoples with a significant diversity of languages, cultures, histories and levels of development. There were well over 100 different ethnic groups within the empire, possessing a vast range of languages, religions, cultures and economic styles of life. From formally illiterate reindeer herders in the north to nomadic Buddhist pastoralists around Lake Baikal, from enserfed peasants in central Russia to orthodox Jews beyond the pale of settlement, and from Muslim Chechen tribes to educated and cultured Russian elites in major cities, the Empire was a patchwork of ethnic, religious and cultural identities. Russians were the largest single ethnic group, comprising some 44 per cent of the population in 1897, although if the Slavic Ukrainians and Belorussians are included, the Slavic contingent constituted some two-thirds of the population of the empire.[3] As the Empire expanded, migration of many of these people occurred on a significant scale. Particularly important was the migration of Russians into what were traditionally non-Russian areas.

This sort of ethnic expansion was often driven largely by economic opportunities, but it was also administratively driven as a means of helping to tie the empire together.

Even though Russian imperialism was driven in part by economic motives, little attempt was made until the Soviet period to develop many of the newly absorbed territories. While there was some exploitation of the natural resources of Siberia, it was not until Soviet development of the vast mineral resources of this region that a major attempt was made to bring about economic development. Industrial development under the Tsarist Empire was characterized by a major spurt in the last decade of the nineteenth century and first decade of the twentieth century, but this was concentrated around Moscow (principally textiles) and the coal reserves of the Ural Mountains and Ukraine. Much of the rest of the empire remained relatively underdeveloped; a major role played by Siberia in the empire was to act as a home to political prisoners.

GOVERNMENT OF THE EMPIRE

In the Tsarist Empire, there was no strong sense of difference between metropole and colony, in part because Russia was a land-based empire lacking clear physical dividing features. This was reflected in the administrative structure. Although there needed to be some decentralization of authority from the capital, this was to administrative regions or provinces (*guberniia*) that were drawn on broadly administrative rather than ethnic lines. It was also reflected in the composition of the ruling elite. The Russian elite saw itself as the inheritor of European values, a stance which made it open to entry by non-ethnic Russians. This is reflected in the strong representation of Baltic Germans in Russia's ruling circles, especially in the eighteenth century.

Generally provinces were headed by a civil governor, while some frontier regions, the capital and some other provinces of special significance were headed by a governor-general who had direct access to the emperor.[4] Governors were directly responsible to the central government and were appointed by them; they were not accountable to those over whom they ruled. This system was generally maintained, with some strengthening of the governor's powers in 1837, until the 'great reforms' of the 1860s, which introduced an element of representative government into the running of local affairs. However, such representation was strictly limited, both in terms of the personnel involved and the matters over which this body (the *zemstvo*) had jurisdiction. Their most important role was as a forum for the expression of enlightened opinion. Finland and Poland were exceptions to this general rule of administration; both enjoyed significant autonomy in internal affairs.

The powers of the governor at the provincial level were more than matched by those of the emperor at the centre. Absolutist monarchy had been established in the sixteenth century, and despite a number of weak emperors and the breakdown of the centralized monarchy in the early seventeenth century,[5] this principle was maintained until 1905. The tsar, or emperor, was all-powerful, citing the principle of divine right and believing that he had no accountability

THE TSAR was an absolute monarch, beyond any constitutional restraint. Nicholas II, the last tsar, prompted by the 1905 revolution, here signs an edict introducing institutional reforms in the empire.

to those over whom he ruled. Government ministers were purely advisory, holding office at the emperor's pleasure. Although some ministers were able to exercise significant influence over government policy at different times – Speransky and Arakcheev in the early nineteenth century and Witte in the late nineteenth century are good examples – formally they always acted as the cipher of the emperor and the final decision always lay in the latter's hands. The reforms introduced following the 1905 revolution seemed to modify the absolutism of the imperial office by introducing an elected legislative organ, the Duma, but in practice this did little to curb the imperial prerogative.

The theoretically high levels of centralism were not always realized in practice. This is principally because the state bureaucracy was not a very efficient machine and could not easily cope with the vast distances that needed to be spanned if the empire was to be effectively governed. Not only were communications slow and clumsy, a fact reflecting the state of contemporary technology, the economic backwardness of much of Russia, and the distances involved, but many bureaucrats were corrupt and more interested in lining their pockets than administering efficiently. For much of this period many also lacked the educational levels to be able to perform satisfactorily.

The imperial system was underpinned by an ideology of Russian exceptionalism. Following the fall of Constantinople to the Turks in 1453 and the creation of a separate Moscow patriarchate in 1589 (which formally separated the Russian Church from that in Constantinople), the doctrine of the 'third Rome' appeared. This declared that both Rome and Constantinople had betrayed the true religion, and that Moscow was now the centre of that religion; it was the 'third Rome' and there would not be a fourth. This conception fed into the notion of 'holy Russia' often invoked by leading political and religious figures. This implied the unity of dynasty, Church and people, and was reflected in the trinity of concepts that for many symbolized the special status of Russia: 'orthodoxy, autocracy, nationality'. This ideological construct emphasized the unity of the people with the emperor and the Church, and underpinned the widespread popular belief in and commitment to the monarchy. This gained increased prominence during the nineteenth century when the upper ranks of the state administration became less cosmopolitan and more Russian than had been the case earlier. Russian exceptionalism also provided a basis for Russian expansionism.

THE FIRST DUMA, or elected parliament, met in May 1906, in the wake of the failed revolution of 1905. It held out the hope that Russia might become a constitutional democracy, but the tsar soon managed to reassert his authority and the whole initiative achieved little.

From the beginnings of imperial expansion, Russia always sought to play a role on the international stage befitting a major power. The chief arena in which it sought such a role was Europe. From the time of Peter I and his symbolic moving of the capital to the new city St Petersburg which was to give Russia its 'window on the West', most of Russia's efforts were directed at Europe. However, because of the weakness of its informal instruments of empire, financial and commercial power, Russia was forced to seek expanded influence in the international arena principally through state action, both diplomatic and military.

Russian aspirations were looked at nervously in the West. European leaders were all too aware of the history of Russian expansionism. In addition, the Russians were seen as being crude and rough, as lacking the refinement of the west Europeans; the metaphor of the 'Russian bear' had significant appeal. But there was also concern in Western chancelleries about Russian military power. The source of this was not the advanced technical level of Russian weaponry, but the imagined unlimited supply of peasant soldiers. Western leaders were concerned about the possibility of the enormous Russian military steamroller moving into central Europe, a fear that was strengthened by the entry of Russian troops into Paris after the defeat of Napoleon in 1814. Such concern meant that Russia was always confronted with an unsympathetic international environment in its Western theatre of interest.

Russia sought continually to overcome the geographical restrictions under which it laboured. To the north and east, there were no ports that were ice-free the year round. To the west and southwest, Russia's maritime access to the wider world was restricted through small choke points controlled by potentially hostile powers: access to and egress from the Baltic (and therefore from St Petersburg) was through the narrow channel between Sweden and Denmark, while movement from the Black Sea ports was through the Dardenelles. This situation made Russia's maritime activities, both military and commercial, vulnerable, and was behind continuing Russian attempts to break out of this straitjacket. The Crimean War (1853–56) was in part motivated by the Russian desire to gain control over the Dardenelles and thereby remove this constraint.

Ultimately the collapse of the first Russian Empire was precipitated by hostile action by competitors in Europe. With the outbreak of the First World War in 1914, the Russian Empire was cast into direct conflict with Germany and the Austro-Hungarian Empire, both located on her western borders. In military terms, the war was disastrous for Russia virtually from the outset. By 1917, with the Russian army demoralized by successive defeats and public opinion turned against the war, Tsar Nicholas II abdicated, bringing to an end the Russian monarchy and effectively marking the end of the empire. But this collapse was not solely due to the reverses in war. Also crucial had been the undermining of imperial authority by domestic developments.

THE FALL OF THE TSARIST EMPIRE

In the half-century following defeat in the Crimean War, Russian society experienced major strains as a result of government policy and economic development. The government's response to the Crimean defeat was to embark on a major programme of liberalization. The 'great reforms' that were introduced at that time involved the introduction of a measure of local and regional self-government (the *zemstvo*), the creation of a more regularized system of justice, the expansion, liberalization and restructuring of the education system, and the emancipation of the serfs. The first three of these helped to create the conditions for the emergence of a liberal, middle-class society that, by the end of the century, still represented only a small proportion of the empire's population but dominated educated and cultured life in the major cities. It was from this milieu that many of the revolutionary leaders were to come. The other aspect of the reforms, the emancipation of the serfs, was crucial. Although it gave the peasants what they had demanded for a long time, control over the land,

PETER THE GREAT had made Russia a functioning modern state and virtually introduced the idea of empire. He was an exceptional leader, combining political ruthlessness, a keen questing intellect and an obsession with practicality. In the background of this portrait (*opposite*) is a shipyard, where Peter himself had worked in the Netherlands. Like a woodworker, he holds an axe in his hand.

SYMBOLIC of Peter's determination to modernize his country was his decree of 1700 ordering the boyars to cut off their beards (*below*). At a stroke, Russia crossed over from the Middle Ages into the modern world.

UNDER ALEXANDER II the most far-
reaching reform in Russian history was
carried through: the emancipation of
the serfs in 1861. It was not an
unqualified success, and this painting,
intended to celebrate the event, conveys
(perhaps unintentionally) the prevailing
incomprehension of the serfs
themselves. In the east Alexander
vigorously promoted imperial
expansion but was responsible for
selling Alaska. Ironically, this most
liberal of tsars was assassinated in 1881.

the terms under which this was granted propelled the majority of peasants into
long-term and ever-increasing debt. The result was widespread peasant
dissatisfaction.

The emancipation of the serfs also facilitated another development that was
occurring at this time, the shifting of peasants off the land into the cities to work
in the newly emerging industries. In the last decades of the nineteenth century,
Russia experienced a dramatic industrial spurt, powered in part by state policies
championed by Minister of Finance and then Prime Minister Sergei Witte. This
industrial development transformed the economy and those areas of the country
(principally Moscow and St Petersburg, parts of the Urals and the mining areas
of Ukraine) where it was concentrated. It led to a huge influx of people into the
towns and the development of an urban working class. The conditions of life for
these people were very hard; housing was inadequate, with many men forced to
live in communal barracks and leave their families at home in the villages, there
was virtually no infrastructure or social facilities to cater for them, and there
was little legal protection for them against their employers. This created an
environment within which the emergent working class was susceptible to
revolutionary appeals.

Among the intelligentsia too there was growing disillusionment with the
tsarist system. Throughout the nineteenth century, many educated Russians
took their lead from the West, comparing the growth of more liberal societies
with representative political systems to their own experience in Russia where
the absolutism of tsarist rule continued to be asserted by successive tsars. By
the 1860s a revolutionary movement was already emerging. There was little
unity among the different strands of the revolutionary movement, with
differences occurring regarding the strategies and tactics to be used (for example,
the use of terror) as well as the type of system that should replace the existing
one. An important, but initially minor, strand was that infused with the views of
Karl Marx and his early Russian disciple, Georgii Plekhanov. Ultimately it was
this strand of the revolutionary movement that was to come to power on the
collapse of the empire.

Liberal circles were also becoming increasingly restive under the tsar's refusal
to limit his authority and, more specifically, to grant a constitution and political
representation. These strands, revolutionary and liberal, seemed to coalesce in
1905. Following Russian defeat in the Russo-Japanese War (1904–05), revolution
broke out. This was vigorously put down by force, but it also drove the tsar to
introduce a series of measures designed to stabilize the situation. A far-reaching
programme of land reform was introduced by interior minister and then prime

minister Petr Stolypin, designed to create a stable class of farmers in the countryside. Also significant was the introduction in 1906 of the Duma, a legislative body that was designed to give liberal society a role in government. However, the tsar retained the right to rule absolutely when the Duma was not sitting and to dissolve it at will. Over time, conservative manipulation of the franchise, added to exercise of the tsar's right of dissolution, robbed the Duma of any effective power. Nevertheless, the fourth Duma (1912–17) became increasingly critical of the tsar's war policy and of the imperial regime in general.

The strains imposed by the war in addition to the tensions created over the course of the preceding half-century were enough to topple the regime. When Tsar Nicholas II abdicated, his brother refused the throne, and there was insufficient support within Russian leading circles to restore the monarchy. The result was an interregnum of eight months, during which time public opinion was radicalized and one part of the Marxist revolutionary movement, the Bolsheviks, prepared to seize power. This they did in October 1917, and then set about reconstituting the empire.

THE GROWTH OF THE SOVIET EMPIRE

The use of the term 'empire' for the Soviet Union is contentious. The Soviet leaders themselves rejected its applicability; the ideology they espoused saw empire as stemming from capitalism and therefore the socialist USSR could not be an empire. Of course, this also meant that the term 'empire' had particularly negative connotations, and its use with regard to the Soviet Union within the context of the Cold War was seen as being ideologically laden; President Reagan's notion of 'the evil empire' is a good illustration of this. However, the Soviet Union covered much of the same territory as had the Tsarist Empire, included most of the same ethnic communities, and was largely run by Russians. While it was very different from its predecessor in many respects, it was also similar in many others, so the term 'empire' is justifiable.

RAILWAY-BUILDING UNDER THE TSARS was a major factor in the consolidation of the empire. It was Alexander III and his minister Count Witte who pressed ahead with the construction of the Trans-Siberian Railway.

When the Bolsheviks seized power in 1917, they were confronted with the immediate problem of armed conflict on their territory. The German front remained alive until the Treaty of Brest-Litovsk in March 1918 brought hostilities to an end, but three months later a civil war broke out which lasted into 1921. With the fall of tsarism, a number of parts of the old empire declared their independence. The new Soviet leaders accepted the independence of Finland, the Baltic states of Estonia, Latvia and Lithuania and, after an abortive attempt to carry the war into that country, Poland. These were the only parts of the former empire whose independence was recognized and, not coincidentally, these were the parts of the empire most accessible to the West and where any attempt to reassert Russian control might provoke expanded Western involvement. Poland also seized parts of contemporary Belarus and western Ukraine, while Romania occupied Bessarabia.

Other parts of the former empire also sought to break away from Russia. The Ukrainian declaration of independence in January 1918 was met with invasion by the new Red Army, but Communist control was not stabilized until the end of the civil war. Similar declarations in the Caucasian republics of Georgia, Azerbaijan and Armenia in May 1918 reflected the emergence of independence-minded governments, but these were overthrown by Soviet invasion in 1920–21. In other parts of the former empire, Soviet control was established, mainly through the extension of military power into these regions.

RUSSIAN'S DEFEAT in the war against Japan was one of the causes of the first revolution. The cavalry Battle of Mukden, in Manchuria in February 1905, depicted here by Nicolai Samokis, was a decisive turning point.

By the early 1920s, Soviet control had been established on most parts of the territory of the former empire. Further alterations to the boundaries occurred in the lead-up to the Great Patriotic War, as the Second World War was called. In September 1939, those White Russian (Belarus) and Ukrainian areas occupied by Poland were taken over, in March 1940 two parts of Finland were incorporated into the USSR, in June 1940 Romania ceded Bessarabia to the USSR, and in August 1940, the Baltic states were reincorporated. Although these gains were not secure until after the war (at which time Russia also gained part of East Prussia), with the exception of Poland and Finland, this re-established the extent of the Tsarist Empire under Soviet auspices.

THE SOVIET EMPIRE

From the time of its first constitution in 1918, the Soviet Union was formally a federation, consisting of nominally autonomous republics. The number of these changed over time, but the 1936 Constitution introduced the broad structure of fifteen republics that was still in existence at the time of the fall of the USSR. The republics were defined along ethnic lines, in the sense that the territory of each republic was meant to be the homeland of one particular ethnic community, although each republic was in fact multi-ethnic and had a substantial Russian population. The ethnic designation of each republic gave an appearance of self-government for the major ethnic groups; it was also to be a major factor in the break-up of the country in 1991.

Although the country was formally a federation, in practice it was run along highly centralized lines. Republican governments had little autonomy, with most important decisions being made in Moscow. An important factor in this was the Communist Party. This highly centralized and disciplined structure was the locus of effective power in the Soviet system. Its capacity to exercise administrative control over that system was an important factor in Soviet survival, and an important contrast with the Tsarist Empire.

The Soviet system was underpinned by a formal ideology, Marxism-Leninism. This was a doctrine based principally on the writings of Marx and the founder of the Soviet state, Vladimir Lenin (although during the period of Joseph Stalin's ascendancy, his writings too were part of it). All policy was justified on the basis of this ideology and, formally at least, this guided all decisions. Based on an extensive system of political education, all Soviet citizens were expected to have imbibed the values of the ideology and thereby to have become committed to what it stood for. The principal role of the ideology was to legitimize the existing Soviet system, and it did this by offering an interpretation of history and socio-economic development that culminated in the achievement of an ideal end-state, Communism. Those who followed Marxism-Leninism were able to build socialism and, through this, to achieve Communism. Formally, from 1936, socialism was said to have been attained in the USSR, so that the task was the building of Communism. Being guided by the ideology, the party was the institution best suited to lead the construction of communism and to rule in the country. The symbolism that was associated with this emphasized the common working man and woman, in stark contrast with the symbolism of other empires.

A key principle of the ideology was equality. This was to be achieved through a combination of the absence of the private ownership of productive capacity and the existence of substantial state-provided access to resources, like education, health care, housing, transport and employment. An important aspect of this was also the perceived equality between ethnic groups. At the outset, the Bolsheviks championed the development of indigenous national cultures. In the first decade of Soviet rule, significant resources were devoted to supporting the development and growth of national cultures in the non-Russian parts of the country. This process of 'nativization' led not only to the flowering of non-Russian cultures, but to the prominence in regional administrations of many non-Russians. However, with the push for industrialization and agricultural collectivization at the end of the 1920s, the policy of nativization was reversed and Slavs, especially Russians, were injected into leadership positions throughout the country. This was associated with the desire to 'modernize' the country and thereby to rely on those members of 'more advanced' nationalities. From 1936

LENIN'S BOLSHEVIK REVOLUTION of October 1917 snatched power from the more populist uprising of March. By 1921 he had succeeded in bringing the war to an end and is seen here reviewing the ranks of militia volunteers in Red Square, Moscow.

there was a full-blown policy of Russification in place, designed to eliminate the differences between national groups and make them all into Russians. This emphasis was reinforced during the Great Patriotic War when Russian nationalism was officially revived by Stalin as a device to encourage patriotism and stimulate the war effort. Following Stalin's death in 1953, the extremes of Russification were toned down, but the general principle remained, although from 1964 until the collapse of the USSR there was in practice much greater freedom for ethnic elites to exercise power at the republican and lower levels.[6] Nevertheless, throughout the Soviet period and notwithstanding Stalin's Georgian nationality, ethnic Russians dominated the political system, just as Russia dominated the federation.

One of the most important characteristics of the Soviet Empire is the massive economic development that it experienced. The rulers used a highly centralized economic system to direct that development in such a way as to turn what was a primarily agricultural country at the time of the Revolution into one of the post-war superpowers. This relied mainly on forced industrialization and the collectivization of agriculture. The issue of the economic relationship between metropole and colony remains disputed in the Soviet case.[7] There is no doubt that Moscow exploited the economic potential of the republics. For example, Central Asia was virtually turned into a cotton monoculture, Azeri oil and Ukrainian cereals and coal were extracted and their use determined by Moscow-based planners, and the development of all of the individual republics was made secondary to the development of the Soviet economy as a whole. But such exploitation was not the whole story. Many republics gained significantly as a result of the operation of the Soviet

A NEW IDEOLOGY was invented to rejuvenate the idea of empire. In reality the Soviet domination of its subject peoples was at least as oppressive as that of the tsars had been, but its propaganda image was unrelentingly optimistic and joyful. *Below left:* Yuri Ivanovitch Pimenov's *Heavy Industry*, 1928. *Below:* Happy, harvesting agricultural workers.

 БЬЕМ

ПО ЛЖЕУДАРНИКАМ

'WE SMITE THE LAZY WORKERS': heroes of Soviet labour toil like robots, while in the background 'bad elements' refuse to join them in the struggle (*above*).

THE EMPIRE AND STATE: a Bolshevik poster (*opposite*) celebrates the contribution of peoples outside Europe in supplying bread, meat and butter: 'Siberia welcomes the Red Army, Soviet Russia welcomes Siberia.'

federation. In economic terms, some republics were not self-sustaining, but survived on the basis of effective subsidies from the centre; many of these republics could not have developed economically to the extent that they did without the Soviet input. Many peoples gained not only education, but a written script and a codification of national culture through Soviet efforts. And clearly many individuals from non-Russian nationalities obtained positions of power and influence through the Soviet system. So the USSR was not simply an exploitative imperial structure; it was also a system that produced benefits for the constituent republics.

THE SOVIET GEOPOLITICAL ROLE

From its inauguration, the Soviet state faced almost unrelenting hostility from the countries of the West. In part this was because the USSR represented an ideological threat to the way in which the Western states were organized. The Soviet version of modernity rejected the capitalist principles upon which the West rested, offering an alternative that, for many, seemed much more attractive. But the USSR was also seen to pose a geopolitical threat, and one that was evident right from the start in the way the new state rejected many established international norms (e.g. cancelling the debts owed by its tsarist predecessor) and sought to support revolutionary groups seeking the overthrow of Western governments. From the outset, the USSR had a messianic quality to it as it sought to spread Communism across the globe. Accordingly, the international environment within which the new state sought to make its way was one characterized by a high level of hostility. Such external hostility was a major factor in encouraging the Stalin leadership at the end of the 1920s to opt for rapid industrialization and agricultural collectivization. These developments were seen as having two positive effects: weakening domestic enemies, and building up the military capacity of the state the better to be able to protect itself. The dimensions of this economic modernization were immense, with the country becoming a major industrial power within just over a decade. Indeed, this industrial development was of sufficient scope to enable the country to withstand the German invasion in the Great Patriotic War and, along with its new Western allies, to defeat the Nazi threat.

The Soviet Union emerged from the war as one of the two major powers on the globe. Its destroyed industry was rebuilt, its devastated cities reborn, and its military capacity vastly enhanced by the development of nuclear weapons. In the post-war period, the Soviet Union achieved the highest level of international political influence ever enjoyed by the Russian/Soviet Empire. It was a major player in virtually all parts of the globe. While the opposition to it on the part of the Western powers expressed in the Cold War meant that its will was not always supreme, the Soviet Union was clearly a player on the global stage with a much higher status than Russia had ever experienced before. Its ships sailed on all the seas, its diplomats and agents worked throughout the globe, and its influence was felt everywhere.[8]

The capacity to project its power was most marked in the region of strongest historical concern to it, central-eastern Europe. As a result of the war, the Soviet Union was able to establish an effective empire in this part of the world. This is sometimes referred to as the Soviet 'external empire', to distinguish it from the 'internal empire' of the Soviet Union itself. This 'external empire' comprised virtually all of central-eastern Europe and the Balkans, with the exception of Greece, Yugoslavia (which broke with the USSR in 1948), Albania (which broke in 1961), and possibly Romania (which distanced itself from Moscow in the second half of the 1960s). In the other countries – Poland, the German Democratic Republic, Czechoslovakia, Hungary, and Bulgaria – the Soviet Union had for the most part quiescent satellites. They were bound together through a variety of international organizations (chiefly the Warsaw Treaty Organisation and the Council for Mutual Economic Assistance), by tightly controlled economic connections, and by the dominance exercised over local Communist parties by the Soviet party. Leadership changes and major policy decisions were almost invariably approved in Moscow before they were adopted in the local countries. In effect, these states were ruled by people who were almost satraps of the Soviet leadership. While there was some variation in the degree of standardization Moscow imposed on the political and economic structures of the countries of the region, ultimately all were dependent upon Soviet goodwill.

THE END OF THE SOVIET EMPIRE came even more abruptly than that of the tsars, rescuing the satellite countries, Romania, Hungary, Bulgaria, Czechoslovakia and East Germany, from Russia's control. They threw off their chains in 1989. In Bucharest, as in the other capitals of Eastern Europe, statues of Lenin were thrown down from their pedestals.

When a country stepped too far out of line, as Hungary did in 1956 and Czechoslovakia in 1968, order could be restored through the use of troops. This 'external empire' constituted a geopolitical buffer between the USSR and the West, but it was also to prove an economic liability when the Soviet economy ran into difficulties in the 1970s.

The Soviet Union also had a unique instrument of informal empire, the international Communist movement. Non-ruling Communist parties throughout the world received often substantial funding and assistance from the Soviet Union and generally followed orders from Moscow; they acted largely as agents of the Soviet regime. This situation lasted until the split between the USSR and China, which came at the end of the 1950s and divided the international Communist movement. From that time on, the Soviet and Chinese parties competed for the allegiance of non-ruling Communist parties, a development that substantially curtailed this informal empire.

Soviet support for both ruling and non-ruling parties abroad was a constant drain on the Soviet budget. So too were the massive amounts of money that were directed into the military budget in an attempt to sustain the Soviet side of the Cold War and the arms race. When the economy ran into difficulties in the 1970s, such expenditures were a significant part of this. This was instrumental in the collapse of the Soviet Empire.

THE COLLAPSE OF THE SOVIET EMPIRE

In terms of its politico-administrative structure, the Soviet Empire was like no other. The high levels of integration between political and economic structures and the high degree of centralization characteristic of the structure as a whole created a system that was unique. This highly centralized system, labelled by some 'totalitarian', meant that the state's economy was directly controlled by the political leadership, and was used as a tool by that leadership to serve its political ends. This structure was useful in achieving the rapid industrialization of the 1930s and the post-war rebuilding, but once it came to the 1960s–70s and the need to shape a more consumer-oriented society (in line with popular desires), this structure was less satisfactory. However, instead of seeking to reform the system, Soviet elites simply muddled on. By the mid-1980s, the economy was in crisis.

In response, the Soviet leadership of Mikhail Gorbachev introduced a range of reform measures in the economic, political and cultural spheres, as well as in foreign policy.[9] However, these measures were neither well integrated into a coherent programme nor implemented efficiently, with the result that the economic situation did not improve, political opposition to the reforms mounted and popular discontent grew. Most important was the growth of nationalist sentiment in some of the non-Russian republics, and from the late 1980s this sentiment escalated and was used by republican elites to press for independence. At the same time popular pressures mounted in the external empire, and following Gorbachev's refusal to assist ruling elites to hold on to power, these countries broke free from Soviet control. Following a failed coup attempt against Gorbachev in August 1991, the Soviet Union broke up along the lines of the republics. The internal empire disintegrated, with the fifteen republics becoming independent states.

The collapse of the Soviet Empire thus resulted in the same sort of outcome as the fall of the European colonial empires: the independence of the colonies. Russia itself also gained independence. Despite the existence within its boundaries of more than 100 different ethnic groups (unlike in the USSR as a whole, where by 1989 Russians officially constituted only 50.8 per cent of the population), within Russia itself Russians were an overwhelming majority – some 83 per cent.[10] Russia had been reduced to an area that had been Soviet-defined, but which centred on the traditional principality of Muscovy and included those areas of north and south European Russia and Siberia colonized by the tsars. The Russian Empire was at an end.

9

Austria-Hungary: The Making of Central Europe

WALTER SAUER

THE DOUBLE-HEADED EAGLE, with its allusion to ancient Rome, became the insignia of the Holy Roman Empire (*above*). Although theoretically elective, its emperor was for many generations a member of the Habsburg family.

The Austro-Hungarian Empire, a large multi-national and multi-ethnic conglomeration of countries under the authoritarian rule of the Habsburg sovereigns, was one of Europe's great powers in the nineteenth century, though nationalist pressures and defeat in the First World War would bring about its demise. Although the Habsburgs did not amass an overseas empire, they carried out one notable expansionist undertaking inside Europe with the annexation of a Balkan region with a largely Muslim population, Bosnia and Herzegovina, in 1908. Lack of foreign colonies, moreover, did not prevent the Austro-Hungarians from becoming involved in many far-flung ventures, from the subjection of Egypt and the Sudan to Western imperialism to the quelling of the Boxer Rebellion in China. Traders from the port of Trieste, scientists, missionaries and adventures from Austria-Hungary made their presence felt in various parts of the colonial world, and the government in Vienna, openly harbouring international ambitions, willingly supported Europe's 'collective imperialism' in the late nineteenth century and the early years of the twentieth.

The Habsburg Empire itself – put together partly through conquest, centrally ruled from the imperial capital, marked by disparities in status, political rights and economic development between so-called 'historic nationalities' and subject peoples within its borders, battered by ethnically based rebellions and political movements during the nineteenth century – indeed bears, in some ways, marks of the other, and more geographically disparate, empires that were part of the international landscape in the modern age.

There is a particular interest today in the history of the Austro-Hungarian monarchy because of growing interest in the history of Central Europe. This trend shows little sign of abating. The reasons are fairly self-evident. Back in the early 1970s, there was already a lively discussion going on between the professional historians of the east and those of the west, but the political developments after 1989 presented a new challenge, with the disintegration of socialist systems in eastern and southeastern Europe, and the consequent

MAXIMILIANVS I IMP. PHILIPPVS HISP. REX I. MARIA DVCISSA
ARCHIDVX AVSTRIÆ ARCHIDVX AVSTRIÆ. BVRGVNDIÆ MAX:
DVX BVRGVNDIÆ

FERDINANDVS I IMP. CAROLVS V IMP.

ideological reorientation of their social elite. There was not only an increasing preoccupation with history, but also frequently a revision of earlier interpretations – 'reinventing Central Europe', in the words of Steven Beller.[1] Critical, modernistic detachment from the past has been replaced by analysis of (albeit ambivalent) cultural heritage, with 'Central Europe' as a reference point for current searches for identity.[2]

There is nothing new in the realization that Central Europe has for centuries been relatively homogeneous culturally, politically and economically, with the Habsburg monarchy very much at its heart as the form of state structure that existed until 1918.[3] What has changed is the perception of this empire. Nationalistic analysis of the Danube monarchy as a *Völkerkerker* (prison of nations), and enlightened criticism of the denial of democratic rights have given way to the often nostalgic image of a multi-ethnic community of civilizations – a 'caring empire'. Looking back at Austrian policy in Bosnia-Herzegovina, and drawing a distinction with the methods, for instance, of German imperialism, the American art historian Diana Reynolds even speaks of 'Mother Austria'.[4]

This view links post-modern studies of Central Europe at the end of the 'long twentieth century' (Eric Hobsbawm) to the new, more philosophically oriented assessment of the historical nature of the Austro-Hungarian Empire initiated many years ago by Claudio Magris.[5] However, it also takes up one of the pre-modern concepts which had been disseminated in the last decades of the Habsburg monarchy by its own leading lights: they saw it as an admittedly old-fashioned *empire*, subject to an uncertain destiny, but with a cultural diversity that spared it from the inhumane confusions of the approaching new age – in other words, an alternative to the modern *state*.

In the realm of literature, one might see this in terms of Joseph Roth's novel *The Radetzky March*, or Robert Musil's description of Kakania in *The Man Without Qualities*. There was a similar concept in the now-legendary *Kronprinzenwerk*, so called because its publication was suggested by Crown Prince Rudolf (who committed suicide in 1889) to make Austria great again. This encyclopaedic study, published simultaneously in German and Hungarian between 1885 and 1902, covered more than 1,200 pages with more than 4,500 illustrations and was intended to preserve the memory of all the fading social and cultural ways of life under the Habsburg Empire.[6] Against the background of two world wars and the various wars and interventions in the Balkan states during the 1990s, this idealized image of a relatively peaceful world clearly meets certain needs of today. Experts have therefore noted similarities between the view of the Habsburg monarchy in the *Kronprinzenwerk* and the Central European boom after the collapse of the Communist empire, and – not without a degree of irony – have deduced that 'Everyone looks there for something he cannot find, not being content with that which actually *is* there'.[7]

THE HABSBURG RISE TO POWER

It might be helpful at this point to sketch the history of the Habsburg monarchy. Not until 1526–27 were the three states in Central Europe – later to form the nucleus of the Austro-Hungarian monarchy – united under the rule of a single family, the Habsburgs. This turning point came after the death of the Hungarian-Bohemian King Ludwig II in the Battle of Mohács against the Ottomans (see p.31). As a result of a marriage and inheritance treaty of 1515, the young Habsburg Archduke Ferdinand[8] now had control of the following:

– The Archduchy of Austria, which had family links with several Alpine territories (Tirol, Steiermark, etc) and had been ruled since 1278 by the Habsburg dynasty. From the first half of the fifteenth century the Habsburgs had continously held the title of kings or emperors of the Holy Roman Empire.

– The rich Kingdom of Bohemia (linked with Moravia and various Silesian principalities), which was also part of the Holy Roman Empire and had been ruled by different royal houses since the twelfth century.

– The Kingdom of Hungary (roughly comprising the present Hungary, Slovakia, Croatia and northwest Romania), which had been occupied in the ninth century by immigrating Magyars and was a strategically and economically important bridge to eastern and southern Europe.

The Habsburgs' succession to the thrones previously occupied by the Jagiellons proved to be difficult. Throughout Europe there were social changes taking place rapidly: in the towns, the prosperous middle classes were demanding greater rights, and in rural areas the peasants were becoming increasingly vocal in their discontent; the teachings of religious reformers such as Martin Luther and Ulrich Zwingli, and also of revolutionaries like Thomas Müntzer, seemed to many to justify their demands for political change. Even in Austrian lands that had been ruled by the Habsburgs for about 250 years, the same political demands were now being heard, especially from the Viennese middle classes. They were quelled by the execution of some of the leading figures in 1522. King Ferdinand found himself confronted by even greater problems in Hungary and Bohemia, where the respective Assemblies representing the aristocracy, the ambitious middle classes and the priesthood were all pursuing their own interests.

In October 1526, Ferdinand was duly elected king of Bohemia, but twenty years later he had to face the first rebellion. Sympathy in many circles for the Reformation, while the Habsburgs were striving to promote the Catholic Counter-Reformation, led to more and more conflicts. In May 1618, these escalated into the so-called Defenestration of Prague, which sparked off the Thirty Years' War. Two years later, the army of the Catholic allies crushed the Bohemian revolt amid much bloodshed.

The situation in Hungary was even worse. Here, right from the start, there were divisions between social classes. The great landowners chose Archduke Ferdinand as their king, but the poorer nobles were in favour of the magnate Johann Szapolyai. When Ferdinand mounted a military assault on Hungary, Szapolyai turned for assistance to the Ottoman sultan Süleyman II. The latter advanced on Vienna in 1529, and although the attack was repulsed, Hungary remained divided into three: one region under the Habsburgs, one under the Ottomans (including the capital Buda), and Siebenbürgen (in present-day Romania) under Szapolyai's successors. The Habsburgs' rule over Hungary was not stabilized until the second Ottoman siege of Vienna failed in 1683 (see p.32),

JOSEPH II, emperor from 1765 to 1790, saw himself as the father of his people. His gesture of taking over the plough to show his respect for the peasants on one of his journeys through Moravia became a sort of icon of the Enlightenment (*below*).

Overleaf
THE MOST SERIOUS THREAT to the integrity of the empire came from the Thirty Years' War (1618–48), when many parts of Germany joined the Protestant Reformation and renounced allegiance to the Catholic Habsburgs. It began in Prague, when Ferdinand, king-elect, sent councillors to reimpose his authority. The rebellious Bohemians threw them out of the window of the castle (the 'defenestration' of Prague). The resulting confrontation soon involved almost all northern Europe.

and subsequently their army successfully reconquered Hungary, Croatia and part of Serbia under the command of Prince Eugene of Savoy;[9] in 1699, the Treaty of Karlowitz (*Sremski Karlovci*) and the brutal suppression of the Hungarian nobility cemented their dominance.

By the beginning of the eighteenth century, the Habsburgs and the noble families of different ethnic origins that were interlinked with them had claimed the rank of emperor, had secured their rule over a large part of Central Europe, and had also imposed the Catholic Counter-Reformation. On the other hand, when the Spanish line of the *Casa d'Austria* died out in 1700, Spain and its colonies together with southern Italy were lost, and only what was later to become Belgium came under Austrian rule. Relative political stability and a huge cultural upturn in the form of the Austrian Baroque allowed later historians to describe the empire of Charles VI as 'a great power'. They paid less attention, however, to the continuous social unrest manifested through various peasant uprisings and protests by the lower classes in the cities, and to the constant opposition of religious dissidents. It was only the political and military challenge to the monarchy posed by other European powers, once the male line of the Austrian Habsburgs had died out in 1740, that demonstrated both to contemporary decision-makers and later historians just how weak were the internal foundations of this great power.[10]

The wars waged by Charles VI's young daughter, Archduchess Maria Theresa (1740–80), in order to safeguard her throne gave a very practical reason for introducing reforms that would help the monarchy to survive. A gradual liberation of the peasants from exploitation by their aristocratic landlords was aimed not only at stimulating food production, but also in the long term at extending the state's basis for taxation; the expansion of central authority brought about greater uniformity and efficiency in state administration, as well as creating the necessary legal framework for the revival of the economy; structural and technical innovations helped to modernize the army, and the first steps were taken to restrict the excessive powers of the Catholic clergy. When the peace treaty of 1748 was signed in Aix-la-Chapelle (Aachen), even though Austria was forced to give up parts of northern Italy (to Bourbon Spain) and Silesia (to Prussia), the survival of the Habsburg-Lothringen dynasty was assured. In the 1770s, within the framework of the partition of Poland and the incipient decline of the Ottoman Empire, it was even able to make substantial territorial gains: southern Poland, Galicia (western Ukraine) and Bukovina (now part of Romania).

ENLIGHTENMENT, REVOLUTION AND NAPOLEON
In the last years of her life, Maria Theresa's relatively moderate reforms were replaced by the harsher measures of her son Joseph II (1780–90). At the same time there had been major advances in social and political conditions in Austria and throughout Europe. In the economic sphere, capitalist trade, colonial politics and the Industrial Revolution began to spread eastwards from the west of the continent, and the middle classes were becoming increasingly self-confident in their demand for political rights, at the expense of the absolute monarchy and the privileged aristocracy. The emperor and his advisors, influenced by the philosophy of the Enlightenment, tried to manipulate developments by means of limited reforms: feudal conditions of land ownership were modified, for instance by the abolition of serfdom, and there were reforms in the legal system, the granting of religious tolerance, further restrictions on the authority of the Catholic Church, and for a short time a relaxation of censorship.[11]

However, when the gallop to freedom began to overstep the marks acceptable to the authorities, the reins were tightened, especially under Joseph's next-but-one successor, Franz II (I) of Austria (1792–1835). On several occasions during the 1790s, so-called 'Jacobin' conspiracies – attributed to those sympathetic to the French Revolution – were thwarted.[12] This enabled the Habsburg monarchy to ward off the direct effects of the Revolution, but economic and political stability was only relative, and Napoleon's army met little opposition when it marched into Vienna in 1805.

When the alliance of the feudal monarchies of Austria, Russia and Prussia defeated the 'newcomer' Napoleon in 1813 and 1815, it opened the way for political restoration throughout Europe. The fact that the congress which assembled in 1814–15 to restructure Europe was held in Vienna was, to a certain degree, a recognition of the Habsburgs' stubborn resistance to Napoleon. In terms of territory, the Austrian Empire (Franz had declared himself emperor of Austria in 1804, and two years later had dissolved the now functionless Holy Roman Empire) profited mainly through the acquisition of Venetia and Salzburg. The importance of the Congress of Vienna lay in the redrawing of many borders (including those of a large number of overseas colonies), the political restoration of legitimate dynasties all over Europe, and multilateral agreements between the European powers. This 'Concert of Europe' provided a relatively stable structure for international relations which lasted until the First World War and might be viewed as a kind of informal precursor of the European Union.[13] One of the most prominent figures in this new system, who was to become Austria's most influential statesman in the next few decades, was Chancellor Clemens Wenzel Lothar von Metternich.[14]

Neither the 'Concert of Europe' nor the 'Holy Alliance' between the kings of Austria, Russia and Prussia could hold back the ever-strengthening trend towards liberalism, citizens' rights and democracy. Increasing social and national unrest, together with the effects of an economic crisis, led in March 1848 to political revolution, in Austria as in many other European countries. In Vienna and Prague and various other cities within the empire, the main demands were political and social, whereas in Budapest it was equal national rights that were at the forefront. After early concessions – the dismissal of Metternich and agreement to a new constitution – the representatives of the old order swiftly clamped down again. In late October 1848, the rebellious city of Vienna was besieged by the imperial army and captured, with excessive brutality towards the civilian population. Parliament was shifted to the remote Moravian town of Kremsier (Kroměříž), where it was to draw up the new constitution. Troops were also dispatched to crush the revolution in Hungary, with substantial

THE CONGRESS OF VIENNA (1814–15) returned most of the Habsburg lands to their pre-Napoleonic rulers. This painting by Engelbert Sieberts shows some of the leading statesmen who made those decisions. Within the curtain are Charles-Maurice de Talleyrand, the French foreign minister; Maximilian von Montgelas, first minister of Bavaria; Carl August Hardenberg of Prussia; Clemens von Metternich, chancellor of Austria; and Friedrich von Gentz, secretary to the conference.

support from the Russians. In October 1849, leading representatives of the independence movement were executed in Arad (now part of Romania).[15]

The subsequent period of 'neo-absolutism' – during the first years of the reign of Emperor Franz Joseph, who now ascended the throne at the age of eighteen – was characterized by a reactionary alliance between the Crown, the military and the Church, but there were also long-overdue reforms to the economy, administration and education.[16] However, in the face of mounting challenges from abroad – Italian unification and French and Prussian expansionism – the political basis of the aristocratic-cum-clerical regime proved to be too weak. After bloody wars against Sardinia, which was supported by the French, and then Prussia and Italy, most of Lombardy was lost in 1859. Venetia followed in 1866. This also marked the collapse of the counter-revolution that had prevailed since 1848. After a number of half-hearted constitutional experiments, the emperor and other leading figures finally agreed in December 1867 to a liberal constitution. This laid down essential democratic rights, established a two-chamber parliament on the basis of elections according to property qualifications, and granted autonomy to Hungary, apart from certain clearly defined 'common affairs'.[17] From then on, the Habsburg state was to be known as Austria-Hungary.

The establishment of these initial constitutional procedures and the *Ausgleich* (compromise) with Hungary seemed to offer a way out of the huge political crisis in which the monarchy found itself after the demise of the neo-absolutist experiment. The half-hearted nature of these measures, however, provided grounds for renewed political conflicts: Czech nationalists were dissatisfied; the *laissez-faire* liberalism of the upper classes ran counter to the social needs of the increasingly militant working class; there was only a superficial compromise between the economic interests of the liberal German industrialists and those of the feudal Hungarian landowners. After more than ten years of liberal government (marked abroad by the occupation in 1878–79 of Bosnia-Herzegovina, authorized by the 'Concert of Europe' at the Congress of Berlin, and carried out officially in the name of the Ottoman sultan) and fifteen years of conservative government, the conflicts between German, Slav and Hungarian nationalists escalated, and by the end of the century internal political stability was a thing of the past. Some governing bodies, and especially the

THE NEXT CRISIS came in 1848, the 'Year of Revolutions', when several nations of the Habsburg Empire demanded more liberal constitutions. Emperor Ferdinand I was forced to make concessions and then abdicate in favour of his nephew, the eighteen-year-old Franz Joseph. This lithograph urges fraternity between workers, students and citizen guards in the name of 'Right, Freedom and our Beloved Emperor'.

designated Crown Prince Archduke Franz Ferdinand, reacted with ever-increasing authoritarianism. At the same time, the rivalry between European states, the precariousness of the Ottoman Empire and unrest in Tsarist Russia all contributed to the growing danger of a war that would encompass not only Europe but all the colonies as well. The annexation, against international law, of Bosnia and Herzegovina in 1908, partly conceived as a diversion from the crisis at home, constituted one more step along the path that led to the assassination of Archduke Franz Ferdinand in Sarajevo on 28 June 1914. This precipitated the First World War and with it the end of the Austro-Hungarian monarchy.

BETWEEN FEUDAL EMPIRE AND MULTINATIONAL STATE

Two basic constants can be derived from this brief survey of the territorial and political history of the Austro-Hungarian monarchy. First, this was a process of *continental* expansion (we shall be looking later at the connection with European colonialism abroad); second, the stability of the resultant empire depended on alliances that the Habsburgs formed with the feudal elites in their respective territories and with the Catholic Church; later, it also required a centrally organized bureaucracy. The interests of the middle classes, of the rural peasants and of the non-Catholic population were generally taken into account only under duress, and with much reluctance.

THE UPRISINGS of 1848 spread rapidly across Europe – to Budapest, Prague and, most seriously, Vienna itself. This demonstration in front of a factory gate took place on 13 March (*above*).

Overleaf
MOST OF NORTHERN ITALY was assigned to Austria-Hungary by the Congress of Vienna, an arrangement deeply resented by all Italian patriots. Lombardy broke free in 1859 and Piedmont in 1861. The latter date was when the Kingdom of Italy was founded under Vittorio Emmanuele, joined by Venice in 1866. This monumental painting shows the Venetian delegation arriving at the royal palace of Turin.

On the surface, however, the figures were impressive: in 1910, shortly before the First World War, the Danube empire, including Bosnia and Herzegovina, covered some 677,000 sq km (261,000 sq miles) containing a population of 51.4 million. The total area of Austria-Hungary made it the second largest state in Europe (after Russia), and it had the third largest population (after Russia and the German Reich).[18] But one has to acknowledge an increasing decline in its political importance over the second half of the nineteenth century. By the beginning of the twentieth century, the impressive statistics concerning area and population had been dwarfed by inescapable internal conflicts and a massive reduction in its capacity to compete economically with western Europe. In 1913, measured by Gross National Product, Austria-Hungary was only in fifth place among European nations; in terms of GNP per person, it was in eleventh place.[19] Both factors contributed to the erosion of the monarchy's status as a major power and hence to its declining influence in the 'Concert of Europe'. It now found itself more and more often reduced to playing the role of the acquiescent observer, and when Europeans discussed foreign affairs, the 'sick man on the Bosphorus' began increasingly to be joined by 'the sick man on the Danube'.

We shall now look in detail at three key socio-political aspects of the Habsburg Empire.

A WEAK DEMOCRACY
Apart from the short-lived Kremsier constitution wrung out of the emperor, and the experiments of the early 1860s, it was not until late 1867 that agreement was reached on a constitution, although in fact there were two constitutions – one Austrian and one Hungarian – which worked together by means of complicated regulations. Of course there had been mechanisms of political participation in all the so-called crown-lands since the Middle Ages – the *Ständeversammlungen* (assemblies of representatives) – but representation had been restricted to the nobility, the Church and individual towns. Now, for both parts of the kingdom, parliamentary bodies were created – both bicameral – with a legal, constitutional basis, although their powers were limited by the strong position of the government and, especially, by extensive prerogatives granted to the emperor. Above all, the 1867 parliamentary system suffered from limitations on the right

AFTER INHERITING a divided and largely hostile empire, Franz Joseph (*above*) proved a strong but flexible constitutional monarch. The revolutionary movements were firmly suppressed. Liberal reforms were instituted and in 1867 a new constitution defined the rights and powers of Austria and Hungary under the name of 'Austria-Hungary'. The emperor's popularity increased, and as he grew older he became the symbol and almost the preserver of the Empire itself. He lived to be eighty-six, suffering many private sorrows but enjoying wide public admiration.

IT WAS THE MURDER of the heir to the Austro-Hungarian Empire by a Serbian patriot in June 1914 that detonated the First World War. Here (*right*), the bodies of the archduke and his wife lie in state. When the empire declared war on Serbia, it set in train a chain of alliances that drew in Germany, Russia, France and finally Britain.

to vote, which was linked to a relatively high payment of taxes and initially excluded more than 90 per cent of the population from any kind of representation. A relaxation of these restrictions in the 1880s allowed the foundation of major political parties, but it was not until 1906 that, after many years of campaigning by the workers' movement, a general and equal right to vote was achieved, though even then it was only for men.

When compared to other nations, the development of the constitution in Austria-Hungary seems somewhat ambivalent. By comparison with Tsarist Russia and the Ottoman Empire (the two other great multinational states), there was at least a degree of participation in the political process by some sections of the population, and basic human and civil rights were relatively assured. But next to western European states – even if their conditions were scarcely ideal – constitutional government came late and to the very end remained limited in its scope. Added to this was the historically conditioned lack of any emancipatory tradition. For centuries the Habsburg rulers had used every means of institutional force to crush all dissident movements, whether ideological or political. All attempts at revolution in the eighteenth and nineteenth centuries had failed, and any liberalizing trend had been nipped in the bud by censorship, surveillance and also a general lack of civic courage. Despite the emancipation of the peasants in 1848, conditions continued to be feudal in rural areas. Clearly, then, liberalism was weak, and there was little democratic awareness. After the agreement of 1867 which created Austria-Hungary, there was a great deal of public discussion by the media, associations and political parties in both halves of the kingdom, but it was generally confined to the urban centres and it excluded certain taboo subjects like military affairs or the escapades of the royal family. The political education of the rural masses continued, with a few exceptions, to be the province of the priests and the landowning aristocracy.

In view of the extremely restricted opportunities for political participation, identification by the masses with 'Austria-Hungary' was little more than superficial. There were strong patriotic feelings about the imperial city of Vienna and about the Emperor Franz Joseph himself, whose popularity – low at the

SARAJEVO IS NOT in Serbia but is the capital of Bosnia-Herzegovina, which was in 1914 part of the empire. There was, nevertheless, a strong popular movement in favour of union with Serbia and the city was a centre of Serbian nationalism. After the assassination, parties from both sides clashed violently, a foretaste of things to come.

beginning – actually increased with the failure of his policy to make his nation into a world power. As the internal crisis escalated, he stood as virtually the only symbol of a united state: 'For where right opposes right as unyieldingly as in Austria, where nation opposes nation, and tradition sets itself against tradition, only the sanctified sovereignty of the ruler can, in certain cases and to a certain degree, mediate, strike a compromise and deal justly – if the greatest right is not to degenerate into the greatest wrong and social peace disappear for ever.' These words come from a civic handbook published in connection with the electoral reforms of 1906.[20] Of course, there had been mechanisms of participation in most political entities under Habsburg domination since the Middle Ages, but populist agitators could easily, with the help of the burgeoning mass media and other means of large-scale organization, transmute them into nationalist ideologies.

NATIONALISM IN A MULTINATIONAL STATE

According to the language section of the final census, the nation was divided into 24 per cent German-speakers, 20 per cent Magyars, 16.4 per cent Czechs and Slovaks, 10.3 per cent Croats and Serbs, 10 per cent Poles, 8 per cent Ruthenians (Ukrainians), 6.4 per cent Romanians etc. Even in the two halves of the empire, the constitutionally privileged nationalities were still not an overall majority: German-speakers made up just 36 per cent of the people of Cisleithania (the Austrian half), while Hungary consisted of 48 per cent Magyars.[21]

The problem did not, however, lie in the multiplicity of languages. Since the eighteenth century, state institutions had developed a certain talent for communicating with the different groups in their own languages – although in Hungary only Magyar was permitted in the higher echelons. Indeed, the mixture of languages, cultures and religions in a single country might even have been seen as a potential enrichment for all concerned, had it not been for the constitutional and actual privileges enjoyed by some nationalities at the expense of others. It was especially the interests of the Czechs that were ignored by the compromise of 1867. During the 1870s attempts were made to change the dual monarchy into a triple monarchy (Austria-Hungary-Bohemia), but they foundered against the resistance of both German and Czech extremists. In the Hungarian half of the kingdom, the dominance of the Magyar population was laid down by law, while the Romanian-, Slovak- and Ukrainian-speaking groups were disadvantaged. Croats, however, enjoyed a degree of autonomy in Hungary, no doubt in gratitude for their military aid in 1848. Even the limited concessions granted in 1867 went too far for the already privileged German nationals: their inflammatory anti-Slav propaganda led to the infamous 'language riots' and the paralysis of parliament when in 1897 the Austrian government attempted to introduce bilingualism for Bohemia and Moravia. Increasingly vehement anti-Semitism from the 1880s onwards also stemmed from the German nationals, as well as Christian organizations, and was directed against Jewish members of the upper classes (e.g. in Vienna and Prague), but also against the already economically marginalized Jews in the east of the monarchy (e.g. Galicia).

IT WAS THE COEXISTENCE of so many nationalities and languages under a single government that made the empire so attractive to some and so hateful to others. This bucolic scene of 1900 shows the still almost feudal conditions in Transylvania, settled by the Magyars in the Middle Ages. A rich landowner, whip in hand, keeps a stern eye on his peasants.

LANGUAGE BECAME AN ISSUE in 1897, when the prime minister, Count Badeni, tried to introduce legislation that would make Czech one of the official languages of Bohemia. The attempt was defeated after angry scenes in the Viennese parliament.

This escalating conflict over – or against – the legal status of nationally defined *groups*, represented by a populist elite, may be viewed as merely a substitute for the missing or inadequate political rights of *individuals*. For instance, as there was no democratic right to vote for *common* political institutions, one of the preconditions for common political thought and action was missing. This enabled the politically dominant ethnic elites to use or even construct their 'national' languages, symbols and identities in order to reinforce or extend their power base at the expense of the state in general. The situation might be compared to that of the other nation-states of western Europe, in which the definition of 'nation' also excluded minorities, but in Austria-Hungary these developments took place in a multinational state that contained strong feudal elements and hence was already potentially separatist. The more radical the various nationalist factions became, the greater grew their hope that their aspirations might be fulfilled by joining their neighbouring 'nation-states' (such as a greater Germany or a Slav federation) or even by founding their own state (e.g. an independent Hungary, or a Jewish state which some dreamed of establishing in Palestine, and others as a settler colony in Africa).[22]

ECONOMIC BACKWARDNESS

Looking back, it can be said that at the end of the nineteenth century, the following features were characteristic of the Austria-Hungary monarchy: there was no widespread tradition of political participation; consequently there was political apathy, and a dwindling identification of the people with the state; there was increasing scope for rivalry between the different national elites; and finally, state institutions found it increasingly difficult to function. All of this was a result of the repressive policies the Habsburgs and their political allies were able to exercise. Later half-hearted reforms that were introduced under external pressure could not make up the lost ground. Herein lay the causes of what historians of the monarchy's economic development have called the breakdown of the state. During its last few decades, it proved incapable of using the new economic upturn to establish political stability. 'The dismemberment of the Empire may not have been inevitable, but apparently its political institutions had tremendous difficulties adapting to the pressures imposed by modern economic growth.'[23]

Especially between 1820 and 1870, the economic gap between western Europe and the Habsburg monarchy had widened. The after-effects of the Napoleonic and Italian wars (i.e. the costs of securing the monarchy's position as a great power), and social stagnation during the periods prior to the 1848 March Revolution and neo-absolutism (i.e. the costs of securing the dominance of the privileged elite) may be added to these causes. However, after the Hungarian compromise and in particular after the international economic crisis of 1873,

ECONOMICALLY Austria-Hungary fell behind Western Europe and socially conscious artists began to take the resulting problems as subjects for their works. A powerful painting that draws attention to industrial crises was Mihály Munkácsy's *Before the Strike* of 1895.

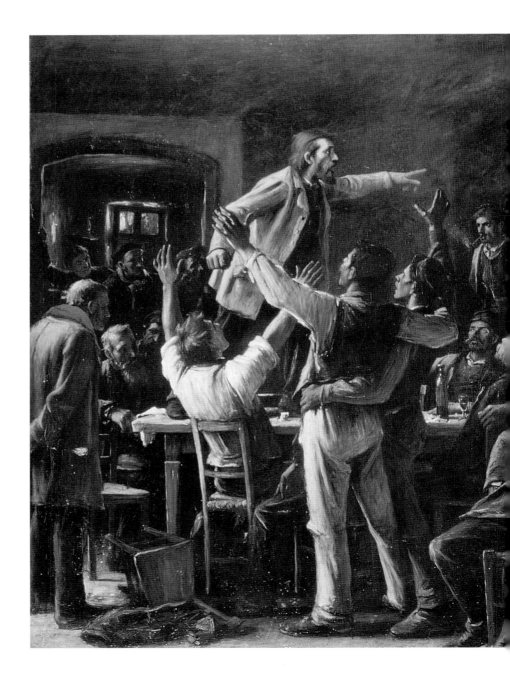

there was a comparatively fast growth rate, with a series of technological innovations, a substantial development of the infrastructure in some parts of the realm, and the founding of efficient banks and businesses. There were huge regional disparities, though, in the distribution of growth and economic productivity. The service and manufacturing industries were concentrated mainly in growth areas within the Austrian half of the monarchy (which included Galicia, whose oil production underwent rapid development), whereas the Hungarian half was dominated by agriculture. The consequence of this was a marginalization of remote rural areas, increased migration of workers – especially to the two capitals, Vienna and Budapest – and large-scale emigration, above all to the United States. There was no real improvement in the unfair distribution of wealth within the two halves, and this led to countless demonstrations by the workers in the towns and by the peasants in the country. Overall, however, it can be said that Gross National Product increased. The yearly growth rate per head between 1830 and 1870 was a mere 0.5 per cent, whereas between 1870 and 1913 it rose by 1.45 per cent, and although this still lagged far behind Sweden and Denmark and also a little way behind the German Reich, it was slightly better

than in Norway and Switzerland, and considerably higher than in Belgium, France and the United Kingdom.[24] The economic gap between Austria-Hungary and western Europe had therefore begun to narrow at this time.

Different areas continued to have different economic priorities. The prime object of industries in Lower Austria, Moravia and Bohemia – generally run by liberal, German-speaking entrepreneurs – was to sell their products inland and abroad. For this reason, the 1850–51 cancelling the customs borders with Hungary was of prime importance, as was free trading access to the German Reich and other western European states. This foreign free trade policy naturally met with resistance from the less competitive Hungarian farmers. Furthermore, the German Reich under Bismarck skilfully used its foreign trade and customs policy as a means of strengthening its position as a major political power in relation to the Habsburg monarchy. But in any case, after the international economic crisis of 1873, the tendency in Europe was towards protectionism, and so during the 1880s the two factions were able to agree on a policy of moderate customs tariffs. This took account of the needs of both sides, but discriminated against the smaller states of southern Europe. It was no coincidence that at this time there was heightened interest in the opening-up of new markets, and so yet again the monarchy's agenda included participation in an imperial division of the world through colonization both inland and overseas.

GLOBAL ASPIRATIONS?
In general, the Habsburg monarchy (along with the Scandinavian countries and Switzerland) has been presented as having largely abstained from colonialism – a view which since 1945 has been highlighted by Austrian historians and geographers.[25] It can be justified in that the Habsburg monarchy did not take any major part in the principal campaigns of European colonialism, such as the 'scramble for Africa', during the second half of the nineteenth century – for reasons which we shall be discussing later. The thinking behind its expansion was also more consistent with the acquisition of tribute-paying territories in a feudal Europe than with the interests of a bourgeois-dominated monopolistic capitalism typical of the early twentieth century. Nevertheless, there was one borderline case even here: the occupation of Bosnia-Herzegovina in 1878. It is clear from official sources that this was not only regarded by leading factions in the Viennese political establishment as an instant colony; they also had substantial, 'modern' economic interests in it – especially its raw materials and railways. The Austro-Hungarian regime's individual successes at modernizing Bosnia were even exaggeratedly held up as a model for the colonial 'civilization' of an Islamic society.

It is, however, only partially true to say that the Austrian (and Austro-Hungarian) foreign and foreign-trade policies – both in many ways imperialistic – were limited to colonialism in Europe. Seen from a wider perspective, the Habsburg monarchy was certainly involved in Europe's overseas colonialism, and indeed quite heavily and on various levels.[26] As a leading member state of the 'Concert of Europe', it was fully engaged in the overseas activities of this organization, for instance in military interventions such as the 1839–40 attack on the 'Founder of Modern Egypt', Muhammad Ali Pasha, or the 1900–01 campaign against the Boxer Rebellion in China. It played its full part in drawing up basic rules for the colonial expansion of individual European states, as at the Berlin Congo Conference of 1884–85, the Brussels Anti-Slavery Conference of 1889–90 and the international Morocco Conference of 1906 in Algeciras. In this context, one should also mention Austria-Hungary's active role in the Egyptian debt crisis – in April 1876, Khedive Ismail was obliged to declare the Egyptian state bankrupt – in which the monarchy, together with France, Britain and Italy, was involved as one of the main creditors.

None of these matters concerned the colonial expansion of a single state; they related to a kind of general, imperialistic co-ordination between the rival European nations, and also to the 'legal' justification for their colonial policies.[27]

Although the Danube monarchy was rarely involved directly in colonialism, it was politically and ideologically engaged in Europe's 'collective imperialism' – in other words, the establishment of an imperialist world order for the benefit of Europe's colonizing states.

Another area of activity that is frequently overlooked or dismissed by historians as insignificant is the many attempts made by the Habsburg monarchy or its official representatives to establish colonies. This is certainly a major omission. Although it may only have been a short episode in Austria's own history, in 1777–81 the Austrian East India Company had trading stations in Mozambique's Delagoa Bay and on the Nicobar Islands, and this was of profound significance in the early colonial history of Mozambique.[28] The very fact that such policies were also successfully put into operation around the middle of the nineteenth century, i.e. during the period of neo-absolutism, surely deserves more attention. The leading figure in this context was Archduke Ferdinand Maximilian, brother of the emperor and commander of the navy, which worked closely with maritime trading and industrial groups centred on the port of Trieste. One can also include Austrian support for the Suez Canal project within this framework. The main individual projects begun in the 1850s were as follows:[29] the Jesuit mission to southern Sudan (1850s–60s), which had substantial colonial implications and which, although it did not lead to the hoped-for establishment of an Austrian colony, nevertheless helped to undermine Egyptian dominance in the region, thereby opening the way for European ivory and slave traders; the 'secret' mission (which was in fact an open secret) of the young naval lieutenant Wilhelm von Tegetthof in March 1857 to acquire the island of Suqutra (Socotra) in the Gulf of Aden as a base for Austrian ships heading for Asia and as a penal colony; the second acquisition of the Nicobar Islands in the Indian Ocean, which was one task of the Novara fleet in 1857–59 on its spectacular round-the-world voyage, although this particular action was aborted at the last minute.

The failure of all these colonial ventures was due mainly to lack of money, military weakness and, especially, the mounting political crisis affecting the monarchy. Neo-absolutism was unable to integrate the liberal bourgeoisie, and this meant a lack of support for a colonial policy that was evidently based on the Habsburgs' desire to become a major world power; the only middle-class support for the policy came from the entrepreneurs of Trieste, who came from the Italian-speaking sector of the kingdom and for this very reason were frowned on by the German-speaking liberals. It fits perfectly into this picture that in 1864 Archduke Ferdinand Maximilian, who was evidently a fanatical supporter of colonial policy, put himself as a figurehead along with 6,000 Austrian mercenaries (recruited with the acquiescence of the authorities) at the disposal of French empire-building; he briefly became 'emperor' of Mexico, by the grace of Napoleon III, an adventure that led to his death.[30]

Even in later years, colonial dreams continued to haunt the minds of the aristocracy and the military, though generally not of the bourgeoisie. Quite apart from the Mexican disaster and ideological objections to power politics no longer sustainable by the state's budget, there was also the problem that there were

ATTEMPTS TO ESTABLISH overseas colonies came to nothing. The leading figure in these enterprises was the Emperor Franz Joseph's brother, the Archduke Ferdinand Maximilian. In 1864 he rashly accepted an invitation by Mexican exiles to become emperor of that country and with the support of Napoleon III of France enjoyed his troubled throne from 1864 to 1867. But in that year his supporters, deserted by the French, were defeated by republican forces and he was executed: the subject of one of Manet's most famous paintings.

relatively few businesses that could have profited from any state involvement in colonialism. And, last but not least, not even any settler colonies could be established – as was frequently discussed during the 1880s, when there was such a high rate of emigration – owing largely to the increasing intensity of national conflicts. 'What national traditions could be transplanted by those people into territories overseas?' asked the influential economist Franz Xaver Neumann-Spallart in 1885. 'German, Czech, Polish, Ruthenian, Slovenian, Serbo-Croat, Slovakian, Romanian, Magyar, Italian, or all of them together?... While the small numbers and the language divisions of Austro-Hungarian emigrants already banishes all thought of founding independent settlements, the quality of these emigrants also offers not the slightest hope that in a colony of their own they could swiftly develop into a flourishing force.'[31]

It was not until the end of the nineteenth century – when colonial hysteria had reached its zenith in Europe – that, with the rising imports of colonial goods contributing to an ever-increasing trade deficit in the monarchy, colonialism once again became a focus of interest even in Vienna. In view of the monarchy's limited economic resources, the political mainstream argued in favour of colonizing the Balkans rather than venturing overseas (as already mentioned, Bosnia was an important point of reference), but there was another faction, motivated by different economic interests, which advocated rapid exploitation of the few remaining opportunities to acquire overseas possessions – a lobby that enjoyed the support of the crown prince, Archduke Franz Ferdinand. In 1895–96, the naval commander Admiral Maximilian von Sterneck even placed a small fleet at the disposal of one of the most important firms in the Austrian steel and arms industries (Krupp), in order to take possession of an island in the Solomons that was particularly rich in raw materials. This venture, which was officially called 'private', failed when the local population resisted the invasion. No doubt the memory of this fiasco also contributed to the demise of a plan to buy the Spanish Western Sahara. Only the multilateral military intervention in China gave some symbolic satisfaction to the colonial ambitions of the monarchy: between 1901 and 1914, Austria-Hungary actually occupied a piece of land covering about 6 sq km (2⅓ sq miles) in Tianjin.[32] Even these very marginal overseas episodes, however, are a clear indication that neither the Austro-Hungarian decision-makers nor public opinion in general were opposed to colonialism in principle. Even if the monarchy was not a true colonial state, it was nevertheless far from being an anti-colonial force.

One final factor that should be mentioned is the participation of various people in what might be called 'informal' imperialism, i.e. the commonly used strategies of economic and/or cultural penetration of non-European societies and their political systems as a precursor to the establishment of a formal colonial rule ('flag follows trade'). Some of these enterprises took place in the name of the state, such as the above-mentioned Jesuit mission to Sudan, which was under the aegis of the emperor himself, and the use of Austrian tax experts and administrators during Egypt's debt crisis. The most prominent Austrian in this field was Rudolf Slatin, whose bizarre life and career have attracted considerable attention.[33] Having made a private trip to the region already at the age of seventeen, Slatin in late 1878 found his way into the Egyptian administration of the Sudan which stood under the nominal authority of the Khedive but in practical terms was tightly controlled by Egypt's European creditor nations, including the Austro-Hungarian monarchy; soon he became responsible for the Dara district in southern Sudan, then governor of the whole Darfur region. Increasingly, however, his term of office was overshadowed by the Mahdi rebellion. Slatin converted to Islam and married into the royal dynasty of the Fur, but he was forced to surrender in 1884 and held captive at the Mahdi's court where he served in various functions.

Clandestinely, British secret service agents prepared for his escape, which finally took place in early 1895. Slatin's narrative account of his imprisonment and flight, *Fire and Sword in the Sudan*, edited by the secret

RUDOLF SLATIN joined the Egyptian administration of the Sudan in 1878, at a time when Egypt's European creditors, which included Austria-Hungary, controlled the policies of the Khedive who was nominally in charge, and converted to Islam. In 1884 he was taken prisoner by the Mahdi (then in rebellion against Egypt) but ten years later was rescued by the British. After the Mahdi had been defeated by Kitchener in 1898 he served as inspector general of the Sudan until 1914.

IN CONTRAST to the relative economic and political decline of the empire, the intellectual life of Vienna flourished as never before. In art it produced the *Jugendstil* and the Secession with Otto Wagner and Adolf Loos, Anton Maria Olbrich, Egon Schiele and Oskar Kokoschka; in literature Robert Musil and Arthur Schnitzler; in psychology Sigmund Freud; in philosophy Oswald Spengler... This poster by Gustav Klimt advertises an exhibition by Secession artists in 1898.

service head, F.R. Wingate himself, became one of the most effective tools in preparing the British public for military intervention against the Mahdist Sudan; in February 1898, Omdurman and Khartoum were conquered. Slatin, highly honoured by Egypt and Britain as well as Austria-Hungary, and extremely popular all over Europe, was appointed inspector general, i.e. deputy head of the British colonial administration in Sudan in which he served until 1914.

Other 'informal' ventures, however, were undertaken for very specialized purposes. Even when these were connected with institutions that were state-run or closely connected with the state, one can scarcely speak of a co-ordinated colonial strategy on the part of the government or the state. These projects stemmed mainly from the military (especially the navy), science (the Austrian Akademie der Wissenschaften and various museums), the media, the church and missionary associations, and colonial organizations. Then there were also individuals who either on their own initiative or, more frequently, in the service of other European powers helped to prepare the way for a colonial takeover by way of economic, scientific or military actions.

THE ROUND-THE-WORLD VOYAGE of the frigate Novara (1857–59) was another initiative which might have led to overseas possessions, but attempts to colonize both the Nicobar Islands, in the Indian Ocean, and Stuart Island (*above*), in the Pacific, came to nothing.

Thus a large number of Austro-Hungarian soldiers and junior officers served as mercenaries in the Congo Free State of the Belgian king Leopold II, and in the *Schutztruppe* that 'protected' German East Africa. There were also civilians who dedicated themselves to specific areas of colonial research, e.g. in the framework of Portuguese rule in Angola (the biologist Friedrich Welwitsch), or that of the Germans in Tanganyika (the geographer Oscar Baumann). Still others undertook private initiatives which – possibly unwittingly – paved the way for colonial expansion, e.g. the Hungarian adventurer László Magyar, who in the 1850s set out to open up a west–east link between the Portuguese colonies of Angola and Mozambique, and the German-Bohemian 'idealist' Emil Holub, whose privately financed expeditions from British South Africa to the north anticipated the later Cape-to-Cairo strategy. Often described by earlier authors as 'innocently' scientific, these activities played an important part – though often overlooked – in the exploration of geographical structures and communications, soil fertility, and mineral and human resources. Anti-colonial actions were by comparison few and far between. As one of these critics of colonialism we should mention the Bohemian teacher Ferdinand Blumentritt, who – based on his intensive friendship with Filipino freedom fighter and author José Rizal – became an outstanding advocate of the independence struggle in the Philippines against Spanish colonial domination[34].

FIN-DE-SIÈCLE VIENNA

The different attempts to engage in colonial politics towards the end of the nineteenth century – already too late – were not the only area that reflected the economic upturn of the monarchy and the rising wealth of its upper middle classes (especially those from the German-speaking sector). Science, art and culture were another. Gifted and ambitious people from all parts of the 50 million-strong kingdom were drawn to the great cities – Budapest, Prague and above all Vienna. Finance from the state, through the universities and other public cultural institutions, as well as private patronage, helped to foster the creative environment. The intensity of this development during the final years, at least in Vienna itself, is reflected in terms like *Wiener Moderne* and *Wiener fin de siècle*, and it played no small part in the 'reinvention' of Central Europe.[35] 'Vienna in the *fin de siècle*, with its acutely felt tremors of social and political disintegration, proved one of the most fertile breeding grounds of our century's historical culture. Its great intellectual innovators – in music and philosophy, in economics and architecture, and, of course, in psychoanalysis – all broke, more or less deliberately, their ties to the historical outlook central to the nineteenth-century liberal culture in which they had been reared.'[36]

Indeed, the density and the richness of scientific and cultural achievements during the end phase of the monarchy are extraordinary – a remarkable contrast to its internal and external political weakness. There can be no disputing the fact that many of them, such as Sigmund Freud's psychoanalysis, had a profound influence on twentieth-century thinking which reached far beyond Europe, while artists like Gustav Klimt and the practitioners of *Jugendstil* (Art Nouveau) have stamped their mark on Vienna's cultural image right through to the present.

Basically, however, the 'creative milieus' which the rich bourgeoisie (mainly of Jewish origin) set up for artists and intellectuals – with their fascination with 'irrationalism, subjectivism and anxiety', according to Schorske – remained quite elitist (and so sometimes remain through the cliché pictures developed today). They barely took note of things like poverty, problems of everyday life, democracy and national identity. A huge gap therefore existed between the aestheticization of the outgoing empire and its ruling classes on the one hand and those future-oriented, modernizing forces in economics and politics which were about to dominate developments after 1918 on the other.[37] Indeed, *fin-de-siècle* Vienna was also the birthplace of a strong workers' movement deeply rooted in Marxist tradition (Viktor Adler), of a respected doctrine of Catholic social doctrine (Karl von Vogelsang), and of an Austrian school of liberal economics (Carl Menger, Eugen von Böhm-Bawerk).[38] In addition, the Anti-War Movement initiated by the aristocratic Lady Bertha von Suttner, who was awarded the Nobel Peace Prize in 1905 and who probably had a bigger impact in Czech lands than in Austria, should not be forgotten.

It was possibly one of the problems of the late monarchy, if not the biggest one, that in the end neither the social harmony image of the *Kronprinzenwerk* nor existing tendencies towards democracy, social justice and peace prevailed, but anti-modernism, anti-Semitism, intensified images of 'the enemy' and, finally, war. Frequently overlooked, the *fin de siècle* also had a martial character as the Austrian historian Roman Sandgruber rightly reminds us: 'A critical appraisal of attitudes within the aristocracy, the army and also the economic community towards violent solutions, power, war and authoritarian procedures is absolutely necessary if one is to give a critical judgment of what was unquestionably a decisive period of Austrian history.'[39] Not incidentally, the demise of the Habsburg Empire was related to one of the great catastrophes of the twentieth century: the outbreak of the First World War in 1914.

IO

Belgium: The Single-Colony Empire

JEAN-LUC VELLUT

FOR ALL ITS INTENTIONS, Europe's impact upon Central Africa was in many ways a tragic one, and Leopoldian Congo is often cited as the most tragic of all, its 'rubber system' having become a byword for colonial cruelty. At the time, forced collection of rubber and its accompanying atrocities were the object of widespread denunciation, in the world at large as well as in Belgium, at the risk of making of the Congo a scapegoat for atrocities occurring elsewhere in the colonial world. At the same time, the age of early colonization saw the battle against slavery, as exemplified here by the struggle waged by the White Fathers under Cardinal Charles Lavigerie (*opposite*).

Attitudes towards empire are divided. Traditionally the Roman, Chinese and Ottoman empires have been seen as marking progress in human history. Modern colonial empires have also been seen in the same light, but at the same time they have been condemned so strongly as, in retrospect, to have been denied any moral legitimacy.

This ambivalent assessment was shared by Marx. He saw the British in India as agents of inhuman oppression, guided by sordid interests. Yet equally he believed that such empires were necessary stages in world history. Like the bourgeoisie in industrial Europe, the British were helping humanity to accomplish a destiny which could be accomplished only by the destruction of old types of despotism.

The history of colonial Congo fits this pattern perfectly: it is an extreme example of both colonial failure and colonial success. On the international scene, and in particular in the English-speaking world, the Congo has become a paradigm of all that is most horrific about colonialism, associated with a 'heart of darkness', a humanitarian tragedy, an empire of barbarity. But from another perspective, in its own day, it was seen as a harbinger of an awakening Africa that would be shaped by a black industrial class. This represented a promising alternative at a time when South Africa, with its policy of reserving to white labour all skilled positions, was regarded as the only effective model of industrialization in Africa.

These contrasting assessments are historical constructs. They tend to ignore the complex interplay between local factors and wider imperial constraints. A generation after the end of colonial rule, differences between particular colonial policies in the past lose their relevance, while similarities between local situations have become overwhelming, transcending former colonial boundaries.

Beyond the bipolar connection between mother country and colony, the issue of Africa's future in the late 1880s also assumed an international dimension which tends to be forgotten or ignored. From the beginning, the Belgian Congo was the insecure member of an international community of empires in which

Central Africa was widely regarded as a weak link. Much of Belgian policy was directed at staving off the designs of other imperial powers on the Belgian colony. Taking account of all these local and international factors is necessary to understand the history of the Belgian Congo in the imperial system.

This chapter will first focus on the ongoing incorporation of Central Africa into the international order as perceived by contemporaries. In the face of major crises developing in the Sudan and the Great Lakes region, what were the possible outcomes? King Leopold's solution was only one of several that matured in this period.

It then follows the forceful pace of the Congo project and its derailment, first locally and then internationally. While not the first or the last human disaster in the history of the region, that of the Congo has acquired the status of an epitome of all that deserved to be condemned in imperialism.

Finally this chapter will explore the successive stages of the Belgian Congo project and how a new Congo exploded the old colonial order at a moment when it was reaching its economic climax.

THE AFRICAN AND EUROPEAN CONTEXTS: 1860–85

At the end of the nineteenth century, Europeans in Central Africa confronted decentralized societies that were militarily elusive – easy to penetrate but difficult to control. In the end, it was the non-egalitarian nature of the indigenous societies that provided the key to the rapid establishment of colonial empires across vast areas of land.

The challenge was not new. In central West Africa, from the sixteenth and seventeenth centuries onwards, links had already been set up between the Atlantic trading stations on the coast and some of the societies that lived inland. A long-term trend had been the development of new sorts of population and commercial centres that were new to the history of the region: trading centres, markets and small cosmopolitan communities composed of runaway slaves and refugees.

From the 1860s onwards, the rapid increase in inland trade accelerated the penetration process, which now also encompassed Zanzibar and the east coast. The commercial 'frontiers' both east and west deepened and broadened the split between, on the one hand, village societies and the traditional centres and, on the other, the new social classes that had access to imported goods – especially textiles and arms. This social division, accompanied by the violence of armed gangs and militias, conducive to the emergence of powerful new leaders, was reflected locally by a situation that was virtually one of civil war between tribal factions and the new social classes that were underpinned by one of the two coastal cultures – Christian and Portuguese in the west, Muslim and Swahili in the east. Such peripheral conflicts preceded the great European and Zanzibari commercial advance from the Upper Nile to the Uele-Ubangi, and from the Upper Congo to the Zambezi. In the latter case, it was Livingstone's final journeys that drew attention to the dramatic impact of Zanzibari traders and their local allies in the Tanganyika-Nyasa region. However, the Sudan was the focal point for a major crisis gathering momentum in the 1860s–80s in the wake of the gradual opening of the Upper Nile to commerce with the outside world. The decisive factor had been the attempts by Egypt to introduce a thin network of government stations in the Upper Nile basin, staffed by a cosmopolitan world of European and Turkish-Egyptian officers, commanding troops supplied by Egyptian and local levies. The aim was to impose some regulations on trade. By mid-century, under the influence of Austrian and Italian religious orders, missionary projects were also launched with the idea of reaching Central Africa through the southern Sudan, buttressing 'Nuba' populations against the encroachments of Islam. In its most sophisticated version, as conceived by Daniele Comboni, the Christian project aimed at converting 'pagan' Africans to Christianity through the agency of Africans themselves, backed by European material and spiritual support.[1] In its first stage, this ambitious project was placed under the protection of the Habsburg dynasty, but in the 1880s Cardinal Lavigerie imposed his own ambitions as part of a more general French geopolitical programme for Central Africa. There was a militant message from this great strategist of a Catholic mission that resumed the war against slavery: he too spoke of a crusade, and for that purpose went to Brussels to utter his battle cry.[2]

The late nineteenth century in general was also an era of religious fervour. Some Protestants – in Britain and Sweden, for example – were talking of Christ's Second Coming, for which the revivalist movements had the task of preparing people both in Europe and worldwide through their missions. Such messages found ready audiences in Africa.

In addition to these commercial and missionary designs there were other projects for incursions into the Sudan, but this time under Muslim auspices. A Muslim revivalist movement spread there in 1881, under the guidance of a Sufi prophet who proclaimed himself Mahdi (or Messiah) and set out to eradicate corruption and build a new world. This agenda was accompanied by prayers and invocations in mosques that spread from Sudan to Egypt and Turkey, and from Morocco to India.[3] In the face of all the different geopolitical projects that entangled Central Africa in the web of European strategies, the Mahdist movement was the only one that responded with a universal vision of its own. Leopold II's Congolese venture was one of many that would come into conflict with this formidable obstacle. Gordon, the officer in charge of the Egyptian garrison in Khartoum and a charismatic figure of the evangelical movement, had nearly accepted an offer from Leopold to join his service. But he was killed in 1885 and became an icon of Victorian imperialism. Later, the desire to revenge his death led to a major military expedition and ultimately to the incorporation of the Sudan in the British Empire.

These episodes gave credence to a simplified view of the stakes in Africa as seen from a European perspective. From that standpoint, it looked at the time as if two 'systems' were simultaneously embroiled in a major conflict for the control of Africa: on the one hand, the survival and further extension of slaving economies, contradicting the universal vision of human rights which had developed in the abolitionist movement; on the other, the prospect of rational development induced by legitimate commerce and civilization. At stake, there was the 'savage world'.

This reading of the situation led to a variety of opposing programmes for the takeover of Central Africa. Missionaries, among them some martyrs, side by side with crusaders and speculators, all consumed with ambition, had one aim in common – they wanted to remodel the world. They formed a new, all-conquering generation that trumpeted its arrival in Europe and Africa, determined to spread its different gospels, preaching in loud voices and sometimes abandoning the old rules of balanced diplomacy in favour of brute force. A whole gallery of portraits springs to mind: from Rhodes, ruthless financier and politician, to Stanley, constructing his image as an avenging angel, using steel and fire to crush the tribal nations that dared to stand in the way of the white man.[4]

As well as these ambitious designs by missionaries and traders, Catholics, Protestants and Muslims, other imperialists developed initiatives in Central Africa.

ENTER THE KING

It is in this immensely complex context that an unlikely newcomer began launching projects of his own. The name of the Belgian king, Leopold II, appeared first in Africa-minded circles when in 1876 he convened a geography conference in Brussels, dedicated to promoting the advancement of science and the elimination of the slave trade. Behind these noble declarations which assured Leopold a well-disposed audience in enlightened Europe, there lurked a readiness to put his finger into any project, to explore any strategy and to

HAS LEOPOLD II become a scapegoat for the misdeeds of all the imperialist powers? The atrocities committed in his name are impossible to justify, but they were not all his direct responsibility. There is evidence that when complaints reached him from the Congo he made efforts, usually in vain, to remedy them. In the end, he unfortunately convinced himself that 'his Congo' was the victim of prejudice and jealousy.

associate with every visionary scheme, always keeping alive his fascination for the Nile Valley, which he regarded as the key site for the opening up of African resources.

It is troubling to observe in Leopold a mixture of pre-1789 *ancien régime* colonialism, intent on securing benefits for the mother country and its ruling dynasty, coupled with a pioneering view of globalization. Active in the era of *Weltpolitik*, Leopold had understood that, in the future, the major sources of profit would be found outside Europe. For this rapacious man, the Congo was never anything other than a stepping stone towards something else: towards the Nile; towards major investments in China; towards the organization of a sustained flow of profit destined to make Brussels a world centre. As a ruthless believer in his own material ambitions, Leopold was definitely closer to Rhodes than he was to Livingstone. However, the two great practitioners of collusion between business and politics differed fundamentally in their perspectives. Rhodes had a colonial vision for southern Africa which left an imprint, extending even to the design of his own grandly conceived grave.

Leopold's legacy lasted longer economically than politically. His mobilization of the resources of state and capital in the service of a geopolitical dream survived only until the independence of the Congo in 1960. Yet his project eventually gave birth to a sense of Congolese identity.

It would, however, be a mistake to study Leopold's successes and failures as solely engineered by a European Moloch projecting its net onto Africa. The preceding pages have suggested that the complex historical contexts of Africa imposed their own resilience as well as their own social dynamics on the great designs coming from the outside. It is interesting to note that throughout his interventions in Central Africa Leopold was associated with two lasting fault lines in modern African history. The Sudan crisis, with its religious and ethnic overtones, in which Belgium also intervened, came to a head in the 1880s and has been revived in our day. In contemporary Congo too, the crisis has been revived through diverse episodes, culminating in the present-day rule of armed militias organically linked to a corrupt state apparatus. In both cases, weak states are striving to keep huge composite territories as coherent ensembles.

A GREAT DESIGN DERAILED: FROM UNBOUNDED AMBITIONS TO CRISIS, 1885–1908

Advancing under the banner of the International African Association which he had founded, Leopold II claimed initially that he was establishing a chain of trading stations lining the routes opened up in the east by Afro-Arab commerce in Zanzibar. But in 1877, while Belgian officers set up a post on the west bank of Lake Tanganyika, Stanley reached Boma, near the mouth of the Congo, at the end of an expedition that cost the lives of all his European companions and two-thirds of his African team. This crossing of the continent elicited one of those sudden changes of mind that were typical of Leopold: rather than opting for the penetration of Africa via an itinerary starting from the east, he now fixed his sights on the centre of Africa, starting from the west. The strategy was to be river- and not land-based. Before he could even return to England, Stanley was approached by emissaries from the king, and he quickly agreed to enter his service. Essentially financed by Leopold and several prominent bankers, Stanley's mission was to build stations that would link up by means of treaties with independent chiefs and would combine them into a 'negro confederation of free states'. This project was vaguely inspired by the precedent of African-American settlements in Liberia. It was hoped that it would serve as a partner in establishing an international company to finance the construction of a railway.

The international context led to this vision being abandoned. It was replaced by a string of bilateral agreements negotiated between Leopold and various powers, leading to the 'International Association of the Congo' – Leopold's new cover – being invited to join the declaration known as the Act of Berlin which, in February 1885, concluded the conference summoned by Bismarck. This gave an

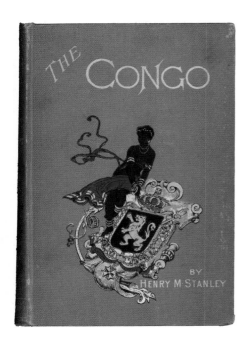

A RUTHLESS FIGURE in the gallery of 'explorers' of that time, H.M. Stanley nevertheless inspired a generation of adventurous young men, many of them English-speaking, who regarded themselves as 'Stanley's men', strong believers in the emancipation of Africa from slavery through the development of a 'free commercial State'. Stanley's account of his service under King Leopold was published in several languages in 1885 and it knew instant success throughout Europe and the United States. Its cover shows a half-clad African seeking the protection of the heraldic arms of Belgium.

How the Congolese saw the Belgians is expressed in this chair, built in the Pende area of the Kwilu in Western Congo. It is inspired by Tshokwe craftmanship, itself famous for its interpretations of 17th-century Portuguese furniture. Scenes on the side and on the back neatly summarize popular views on the working of the colonial economy in a palm oil-producing region of the Lever concession (Huileries du Congo belge). They show porters carrying oil palm fruits or palm oil-filled calabashes under the guard of armed soldiers escorting a European carried in a hammock. A European is riding a motorcycle. The chair rests on leopard's paws symbolizing the evil powers of the chief, accomplice of the system. The glass eyes on the back refer to his evil spirit.

international seal to Leopold as sovereign of 'the state founded in Africa by the International Association' with the reservation that there was no union between Belgium and the new state other than their sharing the same head of state. From now until 1908, the Congo – now called the Congo Free State – was thus not a colony in the same sense as applied to other European colonies.

The king's venture had become a recognized feature of the international scene, but the price to be paid was a set of conditions imposed throughout the Congo basin: a liberal policy to end slavery, protection of the indigenous population and free access to the internal market.

In the long run, under Leopold's rule, ruthless as it became, the state would bring huge profits to its sovereign. In the shorter term, however, the Berlin results were welcomed in Europe as a sign that Africa would be integrated into the developing world order. Even London, then the economic capital of the world, sent its lord mayor and his aldermen to 'thank the founder of the state of Congo for the enlightened and philanthropic endeavours which he had made and which had ended in a triumph more splendid than the finest conquests obtained through the sword'.[5]

'STANLEY'S MEN'

These were the days of triumph for the first colonial generation in the history of modern Congo. Seeing themselves as 'Stanley's men',[6] they were the first builders of public or missionary stations, the first surveyors, the first mechanics for a flotilla of small steamboats operating on the river system, the first military, the first European craftsmen. Theirs was a cosmopolitan world, both European and African. In addition to its Belgian agents, who became more and more numerous, the whole of Europe seemed to get involved: the Congo could not be navigated without Scandinavian pilots and engineers; there was no army without Belgian, Italian and Scandinavian units; there were no missions without Belgian, English, American and Swedish evangelists; there was no commerce without Dutch, French, Portuguese or Belgian traders. This cosmopolitanism also extended beyond Europe, for the king became obsessed with obtaining permits for recruitment – in East Africa from Zanzibar to Natal, in West Africa from Senegal to Sierra Leone and Nigeria, and even further afield, in Macao and Barbados.[7]

These men also represented the first colonial generation to engage with the African world in the interior of the Congo basin. There was a degree of exotic awe for the 'savage world', its industries such as the quality of metallurgical work in equatorial Congo, or its human qualities in the harsh context of the great forest. These sentiments were combined with the liberal conviction that this was a world which had to reform – and at the same time a rejection of it. There was the growing realization among reformers that it was a practical impossibility to separate the wheat from the chaff. The great Bobangi River commerce excited admiration but to prevent it from carrying slaves would doom it to extinction. The Yaka kingdom and the chain of Lunda principalities inspired respect but they too thrived on slave raids which were vital parts of their economy. To judge by the space that they occupied in the observations of this generation of Europeans, cannibals were an ever-present preoccupation and another incitation to reform. At the same time, they challenged the assumptions of Europeans surprised to find among them some of the 'most enlightened and enterprising of the Congo communities', as A. Herbert Ward wrote in his *Five Years among the Congo Cannibals*, published in 1890.

The notoriety still enjoyed by the Stanley generation may be attributed to the author of one of the great novellas of that period. In 1899, Joseph Conrad published *Heart of Darkness*, throwing a harsh light on an enterprise that claimed to be inspired by the Enlightenment whereas in fact it was motivated by sheer greed. 'Enlightened' civilization, it seemed, led to a nightmare of extermination. The victims were peoples whose origins could be traced back to prehistory and from whom there now emerged an unbearable cry of pain that was considered 'savage' but that was also profoundly human.

The evocative power of this account remains unabated, even though Conrad never knew the Congo of 'red rubber' and did not predict the course of its future history. Nor does his account contain even the smallest historical reflection on Africa's pre-colonial past. On the contrary, he presents an image of primitive Africa, outside time. *Heart of Darkness* transforms the 'Congolese question' into a symbol of the deep uncertainty that overcame the colonial world in its first confrontations with Africa. The novella circulated in Europe during a period in which, in many ways, Westerners became increasingly confronted with the 'primitive' – the *fin de siècle* and *Belle Époque* were a time when 'Fauve' artists such as Matisse and Derain introduced African art into Western aesthetics. The masks and statuettes, often originating from Central Africa, accompanied the Congo's entrance onto the world stage.

In fact, the tidy European fantasy, of 'Arab slaving' contrasting with liberal commerce and civilization, or of the 'savages' versus the 'civilized' world, could not account for a climate of confusion where realities were often blurred. Alliances with African powers were made and unmade in an international situation full of uncertainty. In 1892, the authorities of the Congo Free State

brought together all the African allies of the coastal traders, and the decision was taken locally – not in Brussels – to engage in a military confrontation with the traders of Zanzibar and their allies.[8] The successful outcome of this 'Arab campaign' in the eastern Congo earned the Free State the plaudits of the anti-slavery lobby, and helped to ensure the popularity of the king's exploits in Belgium itself. The impact of the formal eradication of slavery was distorted by various forms of compulsory labour which succeeded slavery, but it should nevertheless not been dismissed out of hand as mere window-dressing. Indeed, the reconstruction of the Kasai region in the 1890s owed much to the influx of refugees from the 'Arab zone' who at first accepted a servile status among the local population but soon benefited from the anti-slavery legislation, reclaimed their liberty and set up emancipated and progressive communities.

In the last decade of the nineteenth century, as seen from the outside the Congo was a hive of activity, demonstrating just what an industrial society could achieve in Africa. Progress and modernization were symbolized by the construction of a railway linking Matadi with Léopoldville, skirting the rapids of the river. Stanley had declared that when the railway reached Stanley Pool, the whole of Africa would stretch out ahead, and it would be from this moment on that it could be called civilized. Despite the difficulties caused by its 'murderous' location,[9] the line was opened at great expense in 1898. The achievement was in fact considerable when set against the extremely slow progress of other rail construction sites in colonial Africa. The white world of the Congo evoked 'the Africa of yesterday, primitive, barbarous and poor, bowing respectfully to the Africa of tomorrow'.[10]

Faith in the future imagined by the Westerners manifested itself through a flourishing scientific movement in which the various components of this

MODERN TECHNOLOGY came to the Congo through the efforts of a cosmopolitan body of European engineers and European, African and Chinese foremen and workers. The first Congo railway, from Matadi to Kinshasa/Léopoldville, covered 366 kilometres and was inaugurated in 1898. The first stages of its construction in the rugged hills surrounding Matadi were painstaking and were built at the expense of many lives, leading to a legend that each sleeper represented a human life. Fifty years later, the rail network of the country had a total length of 5,000 kilometres.

developing colonial world all took part. In a number of spheres, black and white teams on the spot recorded observations about nature and human society that provided raw material for scientific analysis. It was in this environment, particularly around the religious missions, that the first generations of Congolese intellectuals – *bona fide* interpreters of their culture – identified the basic forms of social structures and belief systems that advanced Western ethnographic understanding of Africa.

In the meantime, however, there were increasing signs of policies being marred by excess. The beginnings can be traced back to the early 1890s, when massive quantities of ivory and subsequently of rubber provided the Free State with a growing source of wealth, allowing the king to expand his geopolitical vision of the Congo's role in Central Africa.[11] By the late 1890s, a worldwide speculation on the world rubber market provided windfall benefits, changing the outlook for an enterprise that had been on the brink of financial failure. The Congo, or rather the king and some cosmopolitan companies based in Antwerp, garnered huge profits through a system of enforced trading and taxation ruthlessly imposed on villages in the rubber-rich areas. Free of financial constraints, Leopold could then proceed with his vision of uniting the Congo as a political and economic whole, which would extend to a 'natural frontier' in the east, following the Great Lakes from Nyasa to Albert, and continuing northwards to the Nile basin. The development of two mining basins would consolidate the political economy of this unified country – Katanga in the south and, in the north, the Hofrat copper mines in Nahas, southwest of Darfur.

The Free State army, the 'Force Publique', now increasingly recruited from the indigenous peoples, became the region's great war machine. It took part in the European campaigns against the Sudanese prophetic movement, but in 1898 it was a corps from the British imperial army, with troops provided by India and

AN EARLY OUTPOST in the Congo: Luluaburg station, dated from 1884, owed its name to its founder, H. Von Wissmann, a German officer long remembered locally for his harshness. It was for some time the most southerly outpost of the Free State, at the margins of the Afro-Arab zone in the East and of the Angolan trading area in the West.

the Dominions, that inflicted a decisive, and bloody, defeat on the army of the *khalifa*, the Mahdi's successor. Not long afterwards, both France and Leopold II were forced to reach a compromise with the British and relinquish their ambitious plans for the Nile. Nevertheless, the king continued to be fascinated by the Sudan. In 1908, once again he toyed with the idea of linking the Congo by way of the Nile to a future network of trans-Saharan railways. In the meantime, he had also turned his attention to the Chinese railways, in which he invested some of the capital that had come to him from the Congo.

By 1908, it was many years since the generation of 'Stanley's men' had left, losing its illusions as the cost of rapid development was becoming more and more apparent. Among the first warnings of the Congo enterprise going awry were rumours surrounding heavy human losses incurred during the construction of the Matadi-Kinshasa rail line. Some wildly exaggerated figures circulated, and up to this day they form part of the Congo legend, encapsulated in the image of 'one dead man per rail sleeper'.[12] The human cost of rail construction in the area came to the fore once again in the 1920s when independent enquiries denounced the death rate on the construction site of the French Congo-Ocean line from Pointe-Noire to Brazzaville and the brutal recruitment of labour sent to the reconstruction site of the Matadi line on the Belgian side.

CASEMENT'S REPORT

The great construction works, with their huge labour requirements, were limited in time. There were, however, recurring hardships linked to the communications infrastructure. In the early 1900s this appeared in a number of testimonies about the exploitation of the navigation system on the river and its affluents. Running steamer services required the construction of jetties, the establishment of woodcutters' camps to fuel the engines, the establishment of trading stations, the provision of food supplies for passengers and crew, and the clearing of shrub under the wire line running along the river. The first systematic study of these impositions was due in 1903 to Roger Casement, recently appointed British consul in Boma. Casement had served under Stanley in the pioneering phase of the Congo enterprise and the country was not unknown to him. His assignment in Boma had primarily been to follow from a good vantage point the evolution of the conflicts that were pitting English commerce against concessionary societies in the French Congo. Acting beyond his formal instructions, he decided to set out on a mission to investigate rumours reaching the coast about developments in the Upper Congo.[13]

During a seven-week journey, Casement painstakingly observed and described a colonial hierarchy that worked as a system, with each level putting extreme pressure on the one below in order to evade its own responsibilities to fill quotas, or simply to extract surplus from the weaker. At the top, demarcated by a colour line, were European station chiefs or factory managers, followed by assistants of West African or Zanzibari origin, or more rarely Congolese recruits, left in charge of an outpost. These were supported in turn by local assistants, buttressed sometimes by armed militias recruited among local allies. Casement's report denounced the arbitrary character of that organization which extracted labour and various other services from surrounding villages.

Casement praised the construction of the rail line and the impeccable naval yard in Kinshasa, which he contrasted with the miserable state of the local hospital. A typical man of his generation, he showed no awareness of the new, modern Congolese and cosmopolitan society that was developing along the communication lines. However, he showed himself at his most penetrating when going beyond the social cost of maintaining that infrastructure and addressing the economic requirements of navigation and rail companies which had to be supplied with cargo.

Collecting cargo on the river was another task entrusted to government bureaucrats. There again compulsion was generalized, leading to low prices and to the exploitation of African producers. Casement noted that a wage-earning

A BACKLASH IN BELGIUM against misgovernment in Leopoldian Congo as well as the impact of humanitarian campaigns abroad led to the annexation of the Free State of the Congo by the Belgian State in 1908. By and large and despite widespread ignorance, the country took pride in its colonial possession, a sentiment reinforced by the part taken by Belgian and Congolese troops in the campaign against German East Africa in the First World War. This photograph shows them entering Elizabethville in 1918.

labourer on a sternwheeler on the river made as much money in a few days as a local producer of copal (a coloured resin used in making varnishes and lacquers) earned in a year. Compounding the pressure on the victims of the system was the worldwide rush on rubber, feeding a speculative climate in all rubber-producing regions of the world.

Following the publication in England of Casement's report, Leopold was driven to send an independent commission of enquiry. The Belgian report and above all the depositions of numerous actors and victims by and large vindicated the accusations brought by Casement. They confirmed extensive atrocities, perpetrated with a large degree of impunity due to the absence of an efficient court system. The importance of the depositions made by a large number of African witnesses should be stressed. All the enquiries of the time which documented the rubber system in the Free State as well as in French Congo relied of course on private conversations with Africans as well as Europeans. There were also African plaintiffs summoned at occasional court sessions held in the main European centres. In such cases, a panel of judges formally collected evidence from whole communities and these give us the record of African voices, reaching us unadulterated by European interpreters and announcing the emergence of a 'native' civil society.[14]

The question of mutilations aroused the strongest emotions. They were generally inflicted on dead bodies in the course of the relentless guerrilla wars carried on in the rubber zone, but there were also some cases of living victims who laid their testimonies before the commission. Up until this time, it had been held that the other 'systems' mentioned above, those of slave trading and those of the 'savage world', had been responsible for mutilations and indeed there is abundant evidence for such practice in the sources of the late nineteenth century, not to mention earlier periods.[15] But it was a great shock to discover that the

EDUCATION was an undeniable benefit of Belgium's rule. This mission school dates from the post-Leopold era.

BAPTISM represented the entry into Christianity, a world religion which, at the time, was also equated with civilization. English, American and Swedish Baptist missions were among the first in the Congo field. They practised baptism by immersion, a ritual collectively shared by new converts. The christening rites, together with the Baptist expectation of revivals and reawakening, did strike a chord in local cultures, as was shown by the prophet movement of a Baptist faithful, Simon Kimbangu, who swept the Congo area in 1921.

Congo regime had nurtured a system where different layers of barbarity, European and African, had combined for the sake of profit.

Once again the question of hierarchy was the key. Crumbs of the profits of an exploitative system were distributed at a local level among African militias, purchasing or requisitioning wives as a form of accumulation. But, of course, incomparably larger profits were siphoned off to the European trading interests competing for the control of the expanding world rubber economy. The capitalist competition for control of raw material drew less attention than the accumulation of resources by the Fondation de la Couronne, a trust set up by King Leopold to fund various causes in Belgium. It was devised by Leopold to secure for himself and his descendants enough capital to sponsor urbanization works, scientific institutions and other activities in Belgium, beyond the reach of any political control. Concluding his observations on twenty-five years of Congo history, Herbert Ward, one of the few survivors of 'Stanley's men' and a subtle specialist on the Congo, referring to the contrast between pre-colonial and colonial times, noted with melancholy that the Central African natives 'never had a chance. First they persecuted one another, and then they were persecuted by others.'[16]

The denunciation of the Leopoldian regime inevitably took on political urgency in Belgium as it touched the constitutional foundation of the country. Two solidly documented indictments of the system were published in 1906. One emerged from the perspective of political economy; another came from a Christian reformist viewpoint informed by material from the Catholic missions that had previously kept silent about the labour atrocities.[17] The two still rank as classic analyses of a developing colonial economy and they were instrumental in the political decision to annex the Congo to Belgium, to dismantle the Leopoldian monopolies and to submit the colony to parliamentary control. Despite stubborn rearguard opposition by the king, the Congo indeed became a Belgian colony on 15 November 1908. To the end Leopold had remained faithful to his archaic understanding of colonies as sources of profit for their mother countries. In his final message as sovereign of the Free State, he attributed the attacks against the Congo to jealousy. In his view, when the Congo was in the midst of financial difficulties, it did not come under attack. This only occurred when it became prosperous, 'to the benefit of development in the world of Belgian commerce and industry'. His conclusion was that history would vindicate him.

The attacks mentioned by Leopold had indeed given a new twist to the history of the Free State. A campaign against colonial atrocities in the Congo had developed internationally. The first and better-known protest was organized

WIDELY POPULARIZED by local artists throughout Congo under the title of 'Colonie belge', the scene of flogging in a prison camp casts a cruel light on the operation of the colonial system as perceived by the Congolese population: immaculate white officers are supervising from a distance the dirty work of the *chicotte* (the hide whip) being administered by black military under the waving Belgian flag.

in England but soon attracted mass support throughout the English-speaking world. Heir to the abolitionist tradition, it also pioneered modern mass-campaign techniques. The moving spirit behind it was E.D. Morel who for a few years had been keenly following developments in Africa. Acting as attorney for English trading firms, Morel had earlier become interested in the concessionary system in the French Congo. The controversy there was above all commercial and political in character but it carried humanitarian undertones as well. In its wake, the Leopoldian Congo campaign changed in scope as it placed the humanitarian element in the forefront. Despite the secular convictions of Morel, his campaign enlisted the support of the congregationalist missionary movement, which was actively engaged in the Free State of the Congo.[18] Morel's Congo Reform Association translated local history into a discourse that made sense on the international scene. It was destined to become a milestone in the history of the liberal reform movement in imperial Britain.[19]

Another campaign developed in parallel in France. It centred on the humanitarian disaster brought about by the enforced collection of rubber in the two Congos, particularly the French part. Its main agents, such as F. Challaye and P. Mille, made their indictments public in the *Cahiers de la Quinzaine*, a collection of texts published in a militant spirit by Charles Péguy.[20] The French denunciations were more characteristic of an intellectual campaign than the mass movement directed by Morel.

Both campaigns represented a further step in the emergence of a world civil society, a movement already initiated in reaction to the sixteenth-century Spanish conquest of the Indies. The Congo reform campaign not only exposed extortions from indigenous people but also the fraud operated at their expense for the sake of dynastic grandeur in Europe. However, the simplification inherent in such a mass campaign carried a price, and aroused suspicions that the Congo was being made to serve as an expiatory victim for all the crimes of the period. Such good conscience was inherited from the abolitionist period and it helped the English-speaking world to control the official discourse on colonial ethics. Several direct witnesses of African conditions were aware of these ambiguities and, by the end of the war, Morel himself had broadened his denunciation of the Leopoldian Congo into a wider condemnation of European misdeeds in Africa, a recognition of which was a precondition for a new international order.[21]

The ghost of big-power agreements following the 'scramble for Africa' had haunted Belgian diplomats throughout the nineteenth century. It should thus come as no surprise that this fear acquired new urgency with the annexation of the Congo. The line was henceforth taken in Brussels that the Belgian Congo should become a 'model colony', offering no pretext for foreign criticism. As a corollary, a policy of denial was adopted towards the crimes of the past, a decision that ran counter to abundant evidence published in Belgium at the time. In the English-speaking world in the meantime, the Congo remained exotically associated with Conrad's *Heart of Darkness*, the land of cannibals, of cut-off hands and of enigmatic Kurtzes, straddling the uncertain boundary between civilization and savagery.[22]

ATTEMPT AT A NEW BEGINNING

The Congo as a colony of Belgium (rather than as a colony of the Belgian king) was born in a context of uncertainty extending over the international status of the whole Central African region. In 1908 Britain refused to recognize the annexation by Belgium. In 1911 France traded territories in the French Congo for a settlement of the Moroccan question; it conceded to Germany strips of territory that joined the Cameroon to the Congo and Ubangi rivers. In 1913 Anglo-German negotiations laid the ground for the future partition of the Portuguese colony of Angola into British and German 'spheres of influence'.

It was against this background that Belgian colonial policy concentrated on consolidating the economic and administrative occupation of the Congo.

COLLECTING IVORY in Central Africa often led to looting and the forcible capture of slaves to serve as porters. In the 1880s, ivory became the major source of income for the Free State, then deprived by international treaty of the right to levy duties on imports. During its first years, Antwerp came to rival Liverpool as a major entrepôt for the world trade in ivory.

Economically, by the turn of the century Leopold had realized that the cosmopolitan trading interests that had put the Congo and Antwerp on the map of the world rubber economy could not be sustained, and the policies that he initiated formed the basis for the reorganization carried out by the Belgian government.

This was also true on the religious side where Leopold took steps to forge links with the Catholic Church, leading to an agreement between the Congolese Free State and the Vatican guaranteeing preferential treatment for Catholic missions. This helped to give the Congo a Belgian identity based on family, mass elementary schooling and a close-knit network of associations.

The economic record has multiple strands, many to be traced to the last years of Leopold's rule. Production of gold had already begun in the northeast of the Congo, and it was clear that the country would soon be entering into an age of industrial mining. This led to an alliance between official colonial resources, major Belgian private businesses and international capitalism. A critical point was reached when control of the world's rubber market became the object of an offensive by the great American companies. From the Free State, the Belgian Congo inherited a guaranteed stake in several huge enterprises whose concessions covered two-thirds of Congo territory. The same pattern was followed when diamond reserves were discovered in Kasai and the Union Minière du Haut-Katanga came into being, eventually becoming a giant of the copper industry. Another company that similarly benefited was the Huileries du Congo Belge, a subsidiary of Lever, dealing in palm oil and expected to provide some goodwill on the British side. The 1920s saw a flood of private and public investment, chiefly in mining and transport. In the long run, however, profits were unequally divided between shareholders and reinvestment in the Congo.

A further drawback of the system was the complete absence of local involvement in decision-making. Authority always flowed from above and exercised insufficient control on the ground. Today, one of the major ills of contemporary Africa can be traced to the general failure of colonial states to develop a solid bureaucratic tradition at the grassroots level.

Lack of control at the local level was less true with regard to the administration of justice, thanks to the presence of a larger than usual number of professional magistrates. However, education suffered from the same handicap. Whereas the English and French colonial systems had reached a point where an (admittedly tiny) fraction of students could go on to university level, the Belgian system put a premium on preparing the young for the labour market through basic literacy, some practical training and respect for the work ethic. Teachers' pay was minimal, and education took up a mere 3 per cent of public expenditure. Up to the mid-1950s, higher education was available only in a few specialized centres, such as those preparing students as medical assistants, agricultural technicians, schoolteachers and local clergy.

A particular preoccupation of the colonial government in the interwar period was reversing the perceived trend towards depopulation. The reasons for the latter were the subject of wild speculation, ranging from epidemics to malnutrition and the harshness of labour recruitment dating back to the Leopoldian regime. Demographically, the fate of the Congo has unfortunately been in line with the massive losses inflicted on 'tribal people' worldwide. Ambitious measures were undertaken to remedy the situation. In 1930, Foréami (Fonds Reine Élisabeth d'Assistance Médicale aux Indigènes) was set up to offer preventative health care and, unusually for such initiatives – which were meant to be funded through local colonial budgets – it received financial support from the home country. Its scientific base was the Institut de Médecine Tropicale in Antwerp. The ultimate goal was no less than 'health for all' by the year 2000.

FROM THE HEIGHTS: THE HARDER THE FALL, 1940–60

When Belgium was occupied by Germany during the war, Governor-General Pierre Ryckmans in Léopoldville was instrumental in keeping the Congo in the

THE CATHOLIC MISSIONARY (*opposite*) remained an influential figure in the colonial imagination of Belgian Congo well into the 20th century. Exceeding that of public officials, the population of missionaries reached its peak in the 1950s.

war on the Allied side and negotiating access to export markets and essential supplies from abroad. The Congo was able to maintain deliveries of uranium required by atomic research, manganese, tin and rubber.

Beyond the economic and social horizons, however, there were signs of a new world emerging. In 1945, with the defeat of Germany, Brussels hoped to continue its policy of economic growth directed from the centre. There was the feeling, locally, that the Congolese had suffered economic deprivation for the sake of a foreign war while capitalist enterprises hoarded the profits. There were isolated signs that the Atlantic Charter with its promise of emancipation had met with some echoes among an admittedly small minority of the African population.

In fact, while the end of the Second World War was bringing a new assessment of the whole concept of colonization, the situation of Africa remained problematic: in 1943, Sumner Welles, the American under-secretary of state, still believed that the Congo needed another hundred years before independence.[23]

It was in this context that the Belgian government launched post-war Congo on a programme of accelerated economic development based on the Western industrial model. At the same time, within the colony itself there were signs of a new, modern Congolese identity taking shape among a progressive rising class.

By 1949, an ambitious ten-year development plan was launched, but results were mixed.[24] There is abundant statistical evidence that this was a period of material progress as all industrial and foreign trade indicators went upwards. A successful social programme was that of the Fonds du Bien-Être Indigène, financed by Brussels, which extended medical aid and the provision of drinking

INDEPENDENCE CAME on 30 June 1960, with the advent of the Republic of the Congo. The first prime minister, Patrice Lumumba, was educated in Protestant schools and later served as clerk in a post office. After being dismissed, he became agent for a brewery but above all, by 1958, he had taken the lead of the main nationalist party of the country. On 29 June 1960 King Baudouin, on the right, arrived at Léopoldville airport for the independence ceremony. In this photograph, in the forefront, from left to right: Joseph Ileo, President of the House, Joseph Kasavubu, President of the Republic, Patrice Lumumba, Prime Minister, Justin Bomboko, Minister of Foreign Affairs. After a few weeks of independence, as the country plunged into crisis, Lumumba was kept under house arrest but, after an adventurous escape and his recapture, he was eventually handed over to the secessionist State of Katanga where he was summarily executed in January 1961.

water to villages throughout the country. Yet the country still faced the unsolved challenge of a growing gap between capitalist sectors and the village economy. The difference in revenue between indigenous producers and wage-earners that had been exposed by Casement in 1903 remained unaltered fifty years later. This led to deep social discontent and was to prove a seriously destabilizing factor.

Some advances were mostly appreciated by the urban population. Such were progresses in the freedom of expression, as well as greater provisions for tertiary education in the colony – where no local college had previously prepared students for matriculation in the metropole – with the opening of a branch of the University of Louvain in 1954, and the establishment of a university in Elisabethville two years later. The church, too, seemed to provide greater avenues for Congolese participation with the ordination of the first 'native' bishop in 1956; by 1957, there were 298 Congolese priests in the colony.

The feeling was however widespread among the Congolese elite that they owed whatever timid steps towards liberalization to the new international climate rather than to Brussels' own volition. And, indeed, the political horizon remained clogged in the absence of any significant Congolese representation in government. Talk of the Congo as destined to become 'Belgium's tenth province' remained entirely limited to some white colonial circles.

The first signs of an impending change came from Belgium in the mid-1950s, when voices were heard in favour of a 'thirty-year emancipation plan', thus for the first time encouraging some to think in terms of an end to a colonial relationship. In the Congo itself, memoranda were drafted by local intellectuals, encouraged by the example of Ghana and by some openings to the wider world during the Brussels 1958 World Fair.[25]

As Congolese political parties began to emerge in the wake of the 1958 elections for local councils, confidence in the future of the Congo as a Belgian colony began to decline among European investors. From that time there were massive withdrawals of funds, and in the stock markets shares in colonial companies were heading downwards. However, the 1959 riots in Léopoldville came as a brutal awakening and led to an accelerated programme of constitutional reforms paving the way for independence. Much improvisation preceded the proclamation of Independence Day on 30 June 1960. A few days later, there was an uprising by the Force Publique. The European population began a dramatic exodus, and the country was plunged into the chaos of civil war. A new Congo had entered the world.

II Germany: The Latecomer

JOACHIM ZELLER

THE TITLE OF 'EMPEROR' was assumed by King Wilhelm I of Prussia after his victory in the Franco-Prussian War of 1870–71. At that time it referred only to his leadership of a united Germany. It was his son, Wilhelm II, who succeeded him in 1888, who nourished the ambition to turn it into a 'world empire'. A Russian cartoon of 1914 (*opposite*) represents him marching across the globe.

WILHELM'S CHANCELLOR, Otto von Bismarck, differed from his sovereign. He strongly opposed the idea of Germany acquiring overseas possessions. It was not the only source of friction between him and Wilhelm II, and Bismarck was forced to resign in 1890, the year of this portrait by Franz Lenbach (*above*).

'So LONG AS I AM IMPERIAL CHANCELLOR, we shall not pursue a policy of colonialism.'[1] Throughout his life, Bismarck – who made this statement in 1881 – was unequivocal in his objections to any formal colonization by the German Reich. And yet it was he who in 1884 gave way to massive pressure from colonial businesses and, with his famous telegram of 24 April, placed under the 'official protection of the German Empire' the 'acquisitions' that the Bremen tobacco merchant Adolf Lüderitz had made in the bay of Angra Pequena (now known as Lüderitz Bay) in Namibia.[2] Thus did Bismarck, albeit reluctantly, set the still new nation-state of Germany on the path to colonial power. During the years that followed, the Wilhelminian empire gathered up a whole series of colonies which, covering some 2.9 million sq km (1.12 million sq miles), comprised an area six times greater than that of the 'motherland'. Like Belgium and Italy, Germany was a latecomer to colonial power, but it was eager to catch up with its much-envied rivals, England and France. However, the race was to last barely thirty years before the straggler's imperial policy came to an involuntary end. The question of whether this 'historical experience' remained 'an imperial episode largely without consequence'[3] for Germany is one that we shall be discussing, along with such questions as whether the Federal Republic can be regarded as an 'unburdened' former colonial power, according to perceptions at home as well as abroad.[4]

A LATECOMER TO COLONIALISM

The totalitarian preconditions for founding a 'second empire' overseas did not come about until 1871, with the creation of the German Reich, which was characterized by rampant industrialization. Before the Imperial Reich entered the stage of European colonialism by hosting the West Africa Conference (also known as the Congo Conference)[5] in Berlin from November 1884 to February 1885, it had already played a major role a few months earlier in the 'scramble for Africa', acquiring various 'protectorates' from which were to emerge the colonies of German Southwest Africa (now Namibia), Togo and Cameroon. After 1885

AN INTERNATIONAL CONFERENCE was held in Berlin in 1884–85 (*right*). Its purpose was to agree on the partition of Africa, which had already begun, although Germany had so far had little to do with it. In the same year, however, Bismarck was obliged to abandon one of his principles and place part of Namibia under 'official protection'.

WHEN BERNHARD VON BÜLOW (*below*) became chancellor in 1900, German policy became more favourable to the idea of empire. In 1905 he did his best to frustrate France's claim to Morocco and initiated a coalition against England. The trading post of Kiaochow in China was one of his favourite projects.

there were further imperial declarations of 'protection' for German East Africa (now Tanzania, Rwanda, Burundi) and in the South Seas, with possessions scattered throughout the South Pacific: German New Guinea (Kaiser-Wilhelmsland, the Bismarck Archipelago, the northern Solomons, Nauru, and the Caroline, Mariana, Palau and Marshall islands) as well as German Samoa.[6] In China, the 'leasehold' occupation of Kiaochow (the German Hong Kong) in 1897 was regarded by the then chancellor Bernhard von Bülow as a particularly prestigious project. Through enormous investments in its infrastructure, Kiaochow was to be built up as a model colony, and it was the most expensive of all Germany's colonial enterprises. But there was no attempt to establish any formal sovereignty in this part of the world; the intention of the German Reich was to use Kiaochow – or the province of Shantung – as a springboard for German trade in East Asia, limiting its power to what was later to be called 'informal' imperialism.

German colonialism can only be understood in the context of European expansion in early modern times – i.e. within a general historical framework. This extends as far as the Portuguese exploration of the African coasts by Henry the Navigator, and the later, epoch-making 'discovery' of America by Christopher Columbus in 1492. The global process by which the European colonial powers sought political and territorial domination of the world, and their imposition of a Eurocentric, capitalist market system was closely linked, among other things, to the transatlantic expansion of the African slave trade, in which Brandenburg/Prussia also participated for a short time.

Earlier attempts at overseas expansion by the Germans had generally been unsuccessful or, at best, short-lived. Chronologically, the first notable instance followed on from the Spanish and Portuguese *conquista,* with the Welsers' governorship in 1528 of what is now Venezuela. The best known, however, was the Brandenburg/Prussian attempt to colonize the Gold Coast in West Africa (now Ghana). Founded in 1683, the colony of Großfriedrichsburg was finally lost in 1717, mainly as a result of financial problems.[7] Not until the 1840s was there a new wave of colonial projects, which entailed the creation of a fleet of ships that could conquer the high seas. The impetus for this nascent colonial movement came partly from long-established mercantile and economic factors, but also and especially from German emigration, which was to be steered in the direction of German-owned colonies. The list of targets was a long one: the Chatham Islands in New Zealand, California, Texas, Brazil and La Plata, and also the Far East: Siam, China, Japan and Formosa (Taiwan) all came under discussion as possible bases for Germany's colonial empire.

As far as Africa was concerned, German explorers such as Heinrich Barth, Gerhard Rohlfs, Eduard Vogel, Gustav Nachtigal, Hermann von Wissmann and later Leo Frobenius all played a significant role in opening up the Dark Continent, paving the way for it to be carved up by the great imperial powers. Although some of them were apologists for and servants of German colonialism, the majority of these explorers travelled to regions that did not belong to Germany. 'For all the imperial rivalry that was fought out for decades over the alternative scene of Africa, scientific and cultural colonialism was mainly a European project, while territorial colonialism was nationalistic.'[8]

'RIDICULOUSLY MODEST' ACQUISITIONS

The German colonies in Africa have so much in common that it is not unreasonable to describe them in general terms. They were all born around 1884 and expired in 1918. The Germans themselves had no illusions about the fact that, in their quest for colonial booty, most of the regions available to them were left over by the other European colonial powers when they carved up the southern hemisphere. Max Weber spoke of 'ridiculously modest colonial acquisitions'.[9]

In West Africa, Togo as a 'trading colony' was sandwiched uncomfortably between (British) Gold Coast and (French) Dahomey. Its main exports – to Germany – were palm oil and palm kernels. Occupation of Cameroon took place at the same time, though its extent was increased later by exploration. Cameroon – at least in its coastal regions and especially around the Cameroon Mountains – bore the features of a 'plantation colony'. In the west and in the southern forests, the land was expropriated from the Africans, who were put into reservations, and large areas were taken over by joint-stock companies that exported mainly

A PROTECTORATE OVER TOGO had been in place in 1884. The Germans introduced improvements in agriculture, trade and railways, but the number of Europeans was never more than 400. Here, shortly before 1914, German officers drill their African troops.

Marktscene in Kamerun.

Aus dem deutschen Colonial-Leben.

Th. Moskopf, FAHR (Rheinland)
liefert anerkannt besten
Rheinweinessig und feinsten Tafelsenf
mit der Traube.

GES. GESCH. N° 963
J. ABFRLE & C°. BERLIN

POPULAR IMAGES such as this
contemporary advertising postcard
from the firm Th. Moskopf,
Fahr/Rheinland, *c.*1914, portrayed an
idyllic view of the colonies that had
little in common with reality. In the
commercial world during the colonial
age, products of all kinds were sold
using exotic imagery – a marketing
strategy that is still used today.

rubber and cocoa, bringing about a system of crude exploitation which was
not confined to Cameroon.

Although mocked because of its arid climate as a 'sandbox', Southwest
Africa developed into a 'settlement colony' where more than half of all German
colonists lived. This was Adolf Lüderitz's acquisition, confirmed by Chancellor
Bismarck. The farms of these German 'southwesterners' (*Südwester-Deutschen*),
however, were all too often uneconomic. The colony suffered from serious
revolts in 1893–94, 1896–97, 1903 and 1904–08. In addition to large- and small-
scale cattle breeding, there were various ores and minerals, and the diamonds
discovered in the south of the country in 1908 eventually made up two-thirds
of the colony's income.

In terms of sheer size, German East Africa was the largest colony. It
was known as a 'mixed colony', since it was a combined trading centre and
settlement, with the traders and planters concentrated mainly on the coast and in
economic centres such as the region around Kilimanjaro. Its wealth was derived
mainly from sisal, cotton, coffee, groundnuts and copra. In order to solve labour
problems and to squeeze out growing competition from native producers, the
colonial masters forced the Africans into service by means of poll and property
taxes, tributes and socage – conditions that did not improve until the lengthy
governorship of Freiherr Albrecht von Rechenberg. From 1889 the country was
administered by the German government, which imposed its authority by force,
frequently brutal, leading to the Maji-Maji War in 1905–07. After the First World
War it became a British protectorate called Tanganyika, in 1961 an independent
state and in 1964 united with Zanzibar under the name of Tanzania.

Kiaochow was a geostrategic base and an outpost of the German economy,
while the main products from the remote islands in the South Pacific, handled
by Hamburg-based traders, were copra and phosphate.

Around 1913, the distribution of white settlers among the individual German
colonies was extremely varied: Togo (368), Cameroon (1,871), German
Southwest Africa (14,830), German East Africa (5,336), South Seas (1,984),

GERMANY'S POSSESSION of Cameroon, in West Africa, founded in 1884, was officially recognized in 1902. It flourished until 1919, when it was divided between France and Britain. In 1960, the southern part became the Federal Republic of Cameroon and the northern passed to Nigeria.

THE COLONIAL SOLDIER Richard von Bentivegni, instrumental in the acquisition of German East Africa (now Tanzania), prepares to cross Lake Nyassa in 1912.

Kiaochow (4,470). In total, up until the First World War, there were barely 29,000 white people (24,000 of them German) to be found living in the colonies of the Wilhelminian empire – an ever-decreasing figure when compared to the migration of Germans to the two Americas: from the 1840s onwards, some 4.5 million emigrated, four million of them to the USA.

As we have seen, Chancellor Bismarck had always resolutely opposed any policy of colonization by the state. In his view, the Reich was primarily a land power and territorially 'saturated', and he also feared conflict with Great Britain. He regarded colonialism as a form of foreign trade, and would only speak of 'protectorates' which must be financed, administered and exploited at their own risk by private, chartered companies with sovereign rights. However, Bismarck's concept of colonialism soon foundered, as the government was compelled to take over responsibility for these territories by sending its own administrators. The establishment of formal sovereignty under the aegis of the German Reich then led to the formation of a colonial army. The dispatch of imperial troops to the colonies came about as a result of a major crisis in 1888–89, when Germany failed to maintain its dominance in German East Africa, and saw its first attempts to establish authority in Southwest Africa and in Samoa brushed aside. Since the cost of the military, of administration and of infrastructure had to be borne by the Reich, approval had to be given by parliament. Yearly debates on the budget offered a public forum for the SPD and the Central Party to mount a sharp attack on this colonial policy.

German colonialism can be described as arbitrary rule by force – a definition equally applicable to European colonialism in general – and it was characterized

LOCALLY RECRUITED troops, the so-called Askaris, march with band playing through Dar es Salaam, the largest of Germany's colonies, c.1914.

by harsh discipline, forced labour and expropriation, even going as far as mass destruction and murder during the colonial wars.[10] Not infrequently, the violence stemmed from the 'sub-imperialism' of the men on the spot – the all-powerful officials and administrators or the radical settlers. A particularly blatant example of this racist *conquistador* attitude is associated with one Carl Peters, the so-called 'founder' of German East Africa. On account of his brutality – the Africans named him 'Mkono-wadamu' ('the man with the bloody hands') – he was finally dismissed from colonial service after the Reichstag scandal of 1896–97.[11] Christian Geulen wrote of this archetypal member of the 'master race': 'It was not because such people believed themselves to be the master race that they gave themselves the right to create a position of colonial power; they colonized in order to produce and to maintain the *feeling* that they were the master race.'[12] It was no coincidence that Peters was later declared a national hero by the Nazis and ranked as 'one of the great educators of the German Nation'.

There were, however, marked differences in German policy towards the indigenous peoples, as can be seen from a comparison between German South West Africa and German Samoa. In the former, especially after the colonial war of 1904–08, a 'racist society of privilege'[13] was set up with almost complete subjugation of the blacks, who were deprived of all rights, whereas in Samoa the governor, Wilhelm H. Solf, followed a relatively moderate line. He was one of the 'enlightened imperialists', and even if he was by no means exempt from the prevailing ideas of racial superiority, nevertheless his paternalistic approach demanded a 'fiduciary trusteeship with the native people'. He was convinced that the 'white man' had a cultural mission, and in his view colonized people were not to be oppressed or killed, but their cultural identity should in fact to a large extent be protected. Otherwise, German colonial ideology was virtually anchored in the basic principle that the 'natives must be taught to work'. There was greater uniformity when initial attempts from 1884 onwards to 'Germanize' them with a degree of European culture gave way after the turn of the century to a policy of segregation between white Germans and blacks.[14] People feared a levelling out of the 'racial hierarchy' and of the metropolitan and colonial claim to superiority. Being 'German' and being 'white' were synonymous in nineteenth-

'THE MASTER RACE': travelling in colonial style in Togo, carried in a hammock and protected from the sun by a canopy.

AFRICAN WORKERS on a tobacco plantation in Cameroon or Togo (*right*). This photograph was taken at the very end of Germany's occupation, in April 1918.

RESISTANCE to foreign influence in China culminated in the Boxer Rebellion of 1900–1901. It was suppressed by European troops, but in the accompanying violence the German minister, Baron von Ketteler, was killed (*below*).

century racial discourse, while 'German' and 'black' were seen as irreconcilable opposites. Colonial social policy aimed at preserving the racial purity of the German nation, and so there were separate legal systems in accordance with German and indigenous law, which included a ban on 'mixed marriages' passed in 1905 and imposed in German Southwest Africa and various other German colonies. Although there was no such formal ban in Germany itself, the authorities did everything in their power to prevent such 'immoral' alliances. If one of the few African men living in Germany wished to marry a German woman, he was refused the necessary papers, or was made to fulfil difficult conditions, such as acquiring various documents from the colonies.

A PLACE IN THE SUN: WILHELMINIAN WORLD POLITICS

Through its colonial possessions and its pursuit of naval prestige by way of an expanding fleet, the German Empire sought to become not just a major continental but also a world power. In his well-known quest for glory, Kaiser Wilhelm II proudly announced in 1896 that the German Empire had now become a 'world empire'.[15] And along precisely the same lines, the former governor of German East Africa, Eduard von Liebert, wrote that 'colonial possessions mean power and a share in world domination'.[16] While this sort of 'world empire' rhetoric also played its part in the self-presentation of other imperial states, only in Germany did 'the concept of "world politics" take on a provocative and aggressive tone'.[17] Within the colonial movement, the Deutsche Kolonialgesellschaft was the umbrella organization, and it played a major part in making colonial policy a central component of the empire's quest for world domination. Together with other nationalistic and imperialistic organizations such as the Pan-German League, the German Naval Association and the Association for Germans Abroad, it campaigned not least for an accelerated expansion of the navy as a necessary basis for Germany's ambitions in relation to colonialism and world power. There was no shortage of chauvinists to advance this campaign for further colonial acquisitions. However, the planned appropriation of Portuguese colonies and the attempted takeover of Morocco both failed, the latter bringing in its wake the two Moroccan crises of 1905 and 1911. Wilhelminian propaganda for new settlements even extended as far as Palestine, and the quest for expansion culminated in plans for a unified Central African colonial empire – 'German Central Africa'.

The most important prestige project set up by Wilhelminian world politics after 1900 – and viewed with great suspicion abroad – was the construction of the Baghdad Railway, which was meant to link Berlin with the Orient, extending the already existing line to Constantinople. This project, another prime example of imperialism unconnected with colonialism, fired the imagination of the speculators, while politicians dreamed of two million German settlers living along the route. The Prussian king Friedrich III, later Kaiser (Emperor) Friedrich, and after him Kaiser Wilhelm II, who was passionate about the East, had even taken the trouble to acquire permits for German archaeologists to excavate in the Ottoman Empire. Their discoveries in Asia Minor, of which the Pergamon Altar and the Market Gate of Miletus were the finest, are now prize exhibits in the Pergamon Museum in Berlin, evidence of the German cultural colonization of the Near East.

THE BATTLE FOR COLONIAL REVISION

After the First World War, Germany was forced to bow out as a colonial power. Article 119 of the Treaty of Versailles (28 June 1919) stipulated that Germany must surrender its overseas colonies, and these were then divided up among the allies as 'mandates' under the League of Nations. The allied and associated powers justified this thinly disguised annexation by talk of Germany's 'unworthiness in colonial matters' – a criticism that caused great resentment among the German people and was rejected as a 'lie of colonial guilt'.[18] There was also violent opposition to the occupation of the Rhineland and the Ruhr when the French occupying forces sent in troops of African origin. The presence of Africans was felt to be a reversal of the *situation coloniale* – with the colonial power now being colonized – and it provoked a storm of protest from the German public against the 'black disgrace on the Rhine'. Many Germans saw themselves as having been 'also conquered by the blacks in the world war.'[19]

After the loss of the colonies, the empire returned in the form of cultural memory, undergoing a process of nostalgic transformation. Burgeoning legends spread the image of a patriarchal regime that governed the 'natives' strictly but fairly, a successful German cultural mission, the loyal *Askari*, the Lettow-Vorbeck myth.[20] The precursor of this 'colonialism without colonies' was once again the Deutsche Kolonialgesellschaft, which led the campaign against the 'shameful dictates of Versailles' and for the restoration of Germany's colonial rights. With unprecedented unity, every party represented in parliament, apart from the Communists and the Independent Social Democrats, supported the demand for a revision of the colonial ban – even if most of them only did so verbally. Colonial affairs, however, were rarely part of the agenda in the Reichstag, although restoration of the colonies remained a firm component of Weimar foreign policy, and in spite of intensive propaganda by the various colonial associations, the issue was never given priority by the Weimar Republic. Of the four major fields covered by the Treaty of Versailles, the loss of the colonies came a poor fourth in German consciousness behind the financial, military and territorial conditions imposed in Europe. This is why, at the end of the 1920s, representatives of the colonial movement sought to join up with the National Socialists, because they hoped to gain new impetus from the radical right wing, even though the Nazi Party had so far done virtually nothing in this field.

In 1933, after Hitler had seized power, their propaganda became revitalized as many hoped to get involved once more in the power politics that had marked the period before 1914. But although the demand for colonies continued during the Third Reich, the majority of leading figures in the party – and especially Hitler himself – were thinking of establishing a new *Lebensraum* through conquests in eastern Europe, as opposed to Africa, which was the target of the colonialists. To their disappointment, out of all the different opinions concerning the colonial question, the one that prevailed was the unshakable quest for hegemony in Europe.[21] All other ideas were made secondary to that of continental

ONE OF THE KAISER'S INTERESTS was the ancient Mediterranean and it was a team of German archaeologists who excavated the Hellenistic site of Pergamon in Turkey. The frieze from its altar, with its passionate and contorted figures, is now in the Pergamon Museum in Berlin.

AFRICA UNDER the watchful eyes of
Berlin and Rome. This 1941 map does
not reveal the ongoing African
expansion plans of the German Reich.
As well as the intention of winning
back the former German colonies, a
plan that was already being mooted
during the First World War, the
National Socialist government planned
to build a 'united central African
colonial Reich', which would be created
after the 'final victory' by merging
together the Portuguese, Belgian,
French and British colonies in the
region.

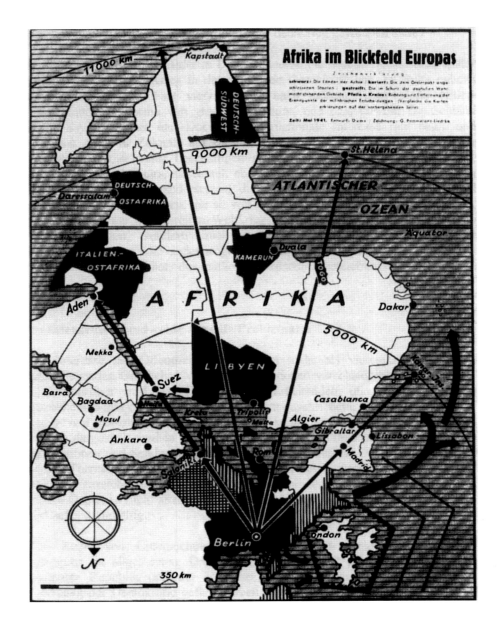

imperialism, although at no time was eastern Europe meant to constitute the
limit of German expansion. Ambitious plans for regaining the colonies and for
establishing a German empire in Central Africa fell through in the latter part of
the Second World War when, in February 1943, reversals on all fronts caused
Hitler to call a halt to colonial activities. In this context, it must be said that
conventional concepts of colonialism have long since been stretched to include
Germany's expansion to the east – discounting Central Europe – as a feature
of its colonial history. This view leads to the question of whether the fixation
with the east should not perhaps be regarded as the 'most important field of
colonial expansion'.[22]

A BALANCE SHEET

If one were to draw up a balance sheet with regard to the period of German
colonialism, it might well coincide with the view of the historian Klaus J. Bade:
'For Germany the visions of socio-economic, national and socio-ideological
crisis therapy through colonial expansion… remained almost completely
unfulfilled.'[23] The idea of sending off all the surplus population – which initially
did exist, though greatly exaggerated by the colonial propaganda of the time –
into the colonies proved to be unrealistic, while the exportation of the 'social
problem' was equally illusory. The vast majority of German emigrants headed

for North America, thanks not least to the fact that the African colonies – not to mention the South Seas and Kiaochow – were simply unsuitable for mass settlement. Furthermore, the significance of the colonial economy remained minor with regard both to imports and exports. The colonies played a very small role as markets and as providers of raw materials, and barely 2 per cent of Germany's foreign capital was invested there. However, through enormous expenditure on the infrastructure and, increasingly, on putting down 'native rebellions', German colonialism represented a large, state-subsidized loss, while only individual financiers and commercial enterprises stood to make a sizeable profit. In the long run, the Pan-German League and the naval movement offered a far greater potential for national, ideological integration than the colonial movement, which never developed any mass appeal. And so Germany's colonial policy, which frequently led to internal conflict, never overcame the contemporary perception of it as a dire disappointment. The consequence of this disillusionment – much lamented by the colonial movement itself – was the general 'colonial fatigue' of German society.

It is difficult to draw a general conclusion from the perspective of the subjugated peoples in the colonies. Conditions varied considerably according to place, time and the degree of constraint and repression imposed by the system. As colonialism by definition entails government by a foreign power – characterized by racism, paternalism and exploitation – the tendency was to argue theoretically in terms of dependence, i.e. to foreground the destructive effects brought about by the processes of colonization.[24] In more recent times, by comparison with the decades of decolonization, more emphasis has been laid on balancing out the good and the bad sides of German (and European) imperialism: quite apart from vague generalizations about its ambivalence, the racially motivated practices of repression and destruction in relation to native cultures have been set against the introduction of enlightened, pragmatic and constructive policies.[25] However, the imposition of such 'developments' by an outside dictatorship can only be viewed with a degree of scepticism, bearing in mind that it entails a purely Western concept of development and modernization.

The reactions of indigenous societies to their German colonial masters were extremely varied. They ranged from 'insubordination', resistance and refusal on the one hand, to co-operation in the role of middle man, and collaboration

RELATIONS WITH THE AFRICANS were far from ideal. A local king, Manga Bell from Cameroon (*above*, seated right) went to Germany in 1902 to protest against expropriation and corruption. In 1914 his son Rudolf Duala Manga Bell (standing behind him) was executed for 'treason'.

AN OFFICIAL 'HERO of German colonial science' was Robert Koch, who worked in the field of tropical medicine until his death in 1910. This painting (*left*) shows him giving injections in Africa.

UPRISINGS AGAINST German rule by
African tribesmen were savagely
punished. This photograph was first
published on 27 May 1926 in the
English-language newspaper *East
Africa*. It was taken in 1905 and shows
the execution of 'ringleaders' by the
German colonial army during the Maji-
Maji Rebellion in German East Africa
(now Tanzania).

whether voluntary or under compulsion on the other.[26] It would therefore be just as wrong to see the colonized people purely as victims of white imperialism as it would be to underestimate the range of actions open to the Africans and Oceanians, the dichotomous image of the omnipotent colonialist and the helpless subject having long since been discredited. A post-colonial history of colonial cultures must reach beyond the dichotomies of master and slave, centre and periphery, black and white.[27]

The whites certainly did not have a monopoly on matters of initiative. In total contrast to the strategy of the colonialists, to make indigenous peoples invisible as subjects of their own history, the Africans vigorously pursued their own interests, as can be seen for example in the context of missionary work. The tale is told of how local Nama chiefs in pre-colonial Namibia asked for missionaries to come to them, and then shared them out among themselves. Christianity was only one of the European achievements that the Nama wished to adopt. In particular they hoped that through it they might acquire firearms and increasingly important cultural assets such as colonial languages, agricultural techniques, new handicrafts and, not least, the ability to read and write.[28]

It is misleading, then, to claim that the 'modern' way of life was always forced on them, and furthermore one should not simplistically equate these processes of modernization with Westernization. Even if these new ways often were imposed on them, they nevertheless actively and even subversively adopted Western products and ideas to suit their own purposes. If we single out trade relations, the rapid expansion of the cocoa export industry in Cameroon will serve as a good example. Despite the obstructive economic policy of the German colonial government, the introduction of cocoa as a cash crop was an African initiative.

There is, however, a strong case to be made for the contrary point of view. Petitions from the Duala to the German Reichstag, protesting against its policy of expropriation and resettlement, offer an eloquent instance of African 'self-will'. King Rudolf Duala Manga Bell – who lived in South Germany from 1891 until 1896, and initially was far from anti-German – later paid for his resistance with his life: in 1914, he and some of his fellow countrymen were executed by the Germans for alleged high treason.[29] In 1904–08, rebellions in German Southwest Africa (Herero and Nama) and German East Africa (the Maji-Maji War), and unrest in northwest and southeast Cameroon (Mpawmanku wars) bore witness to the struggle of the 'natives' to protect their own identity and throw off the yoke of their oppressors. The Herero and Nama freedom-fighters were brutally crushed by German troops. There are serious historians who still maintain that the colonial war in German Southwest Africa was 'normal' and simply in keeping with the excessive violence that marked the imperial age.[30] The truth is very different. The general in charge, Lothar von Trotha – one of those soldiers who regarded this as a battle between the races – conducted the war as an exercise in genocide.[31] There is some debate as to whether and in what degree there are analogies between this colonial genocide and the Holocaust.[32] Hannah Arendt is always quoted as a witness for the prosecution, since her reading of Nazi tyranny also encompasses the historical roots of colonialism and imperialism.[33] In more recent times, Reinhart Kössler and Henning Melber argue emphatically that 'the uniqueness of the Holocaust [is relative to the extent] that its singularity is to be found in the synthesis of different forms of violence but absolutely not in a complete denial of any continuity with the exterminatory practices of colonialism'.[34] Modern research is at pains to provide empirical evidence for the analogies. If one focuses on such motivational concepts as 'race' and 'space', one can hardly ignore the structural affinities between colonialism and the Nazi policy of conquest and extermination, while reference to genocide and other colonial crimes also contradicts the traditional claim that Europeanization of the world was a progress-orientated enterprise.

NEW TRENDS IN RESEARCH

What is the current view of historians vis-à-vis German colonialism? Earlier empirical studies were mainly written from the perspective of the colonizers and their modes of governmental practice; more recent approaches also examine the role played by German women in the imperial process.[35] With the abandonment of these Eurocentric perspectives, interest for some years has focused increasingly on the colonized societies.[36] Here the subject matter of African, Asian and Oceanian history is no longer viewed solely in terms of colonization.[37] Innovative approaches also deal with the role of colonialism in the collective consciousness and memory of native societies,[38] or with the history of the African diaspora, which had been going on for centuries within the German-speaking world, not least as a result of Germany's colonial activities.[39] Related disciplines such as the history of literature, photography, film and art have also provided numerous studies analysing the image of the colonial 'other'.[40] Virtually unexplored sources are now being opened up, such as visual records of the mass culture of the colonial age, in order to track down the stereotypical image-building that went into the dichotomy of 'us and them'.[41] Most recently, there has been particular emphasis

THE GARRISON OF WINDHOEK, Southwest Africa, was besieged in 1904 by the Herero people. The retaliation, in which the whole people was virtually exterminated, was one of the worst atrocities committed by any colonial power.

on research into the home territory of the colonialists. The impetus here has come from the interdisciplinary work – especially discourse analysis – carried out in the field of post-colonial studies,[42] which tackles the subject in terms of a counter-process. With emphasis on exchange and interaction, this approach examines the effects of the colonial experience not only on the colonized people but also on the society of the colonizers. Currently, however, discussion tends to centre less on political, military and economic colonialism than on questions relating to the interdependence of identity and otherness, i.e. the manner in which colonial discourse has shaped the cultural and mental self-image of the former imperial powers.[43]

HERERO PRISONERS are guarded on the station platform of Karibib, in Namibia, in 1905.

There is a consensus insofar as Germany's attempt to catch up on overseas expansion – described by Russell A. Berman as secondary-epigonic[44] – had a significant impact on its history and culture. 'Colonial possessions are one thing, colonialism and colonial thinking are another… Germany [was] closely linked to this project, with or without its colonies.'[45] In other words, colonial discourse in the history of German culture and science goes far back into the eighteenth century, and did not even end with the decolonization that followed on from defeat in the First World War.[46] However, without wishing to deny that there are national characteristics, one must question the view still held by some today that Germany followed a unique colonial path of its own.[47]

Despite the fact that there are now so many individual studies that it is difficult to keep track of them all, German history has still treated the subject of colonialism as an almost peripheral matter. Some even talk of the 'historiographical exclusion of Germany's colonial experience'.[48] This also applies to the attitude of the public at large, which remains barely conscious of Germany's colonial history, except sporadically on commemorative occasions.[49] Even initiatives such as the renaming of colonial street names, the toppling or redesignation of the few surviving colonial monuments, and local efforts to shake the public out of its indifference towards the colonial past have, at best, had an extremely limited effect.[50] Entirely in keeping with this situation is the fact that the book *Deutsche Erinnerungsorte* ('German Places of Memory') by Étienne François and Hagen Schulze, which attempts to present a comprehensive survey of Germany's cultural memories, has no section under the heading of colonialism.[51] There are similar gaps in international research, for instance in the otherwise comprehensive collection of *Imperial Cities*,[52] which covers London, Paris, Marseille, Rome, Madrid and even Vienna, but fails to include either Berlin[53] or Hamburg.[54]

Clearly, then, colonial interaction has left no tangible presence in the historical memory of German society – in contrast to the British Empire, which made a substantial contribution to the British identity[55] – 'either in the form of imperial buildings or as the disposition of a colonially marked social group',[56] and until now it has played little part in the interpretation of Germany's own national history. Most literature attributes this to the following causes: the brevity of the German colonial age; the lack of any direct effects in the years of decolonization that followed 1945; the dominance of the Holocaust and of National Socialism in the political memory; the relatively small presence of a black diaspora, or Afro-German community;[57] and finally, the anti-imperialist movement that began at the end of the 1960s, for all its identification with the 'damned of this Earth' (Frantz Fanon), very rarely turned its attention to German colonialism and its long-term consequences.

One may conclude that German colonialism has still not been properly placed within the continuum of German history. Interpretations offered so far could scarcely be more varied: while some treat the colonies as a mere footnote in the history of the German Empire, others see them as a kind of laboratory preparing the way for Nazi policies of racism and expansion. The same applies to the former colonial countries themselves: no doubt the debate will continue for a long time yet over whether colonialism, despite its many far-reaching consequences, represented just an episode or a fundamental transformation. In any case, in addition to post-colonial studies, the concept of 'entangled histories'[58] offers another transnational approach that will shed new light on the age of colonialism as a global history of interconnections. What remains untenable is the view that Germany was 'unburdened' with colonial power and had a negligible tradition of imperialism. The year 2004 commemorated the centenary of the genocide inflicted on the Herero and the Nama, and provided a painful reminder of this fallacy.[59] And if there is truth in Charles S. Maier's contention that, in the context of globalization, the history of colonialism could catch on as the dominant tale, replacing other competing stories such as those of progress or of the Holocaust, then such a development will also leave its mark on Germany.[60]

COLONIAL WAR in German Southwest Africa (now Namibia), 1904–8: Herero prisoners in a concentration camp at Windhoek, c.1905–6. In the background stands the city's colonial fortress, which still survives today. This genocide has been compared to the Holocaust.

12

Italy: The Last Empire

IRMA TADDIA

IN THE FOOTSTEPS OF CAESAR.
Mussolini never forgot that Rome had
conquered the known world. The *fasces*
(axe and rods) were the symbol of the
Fascist Party, and the proud slogan of
the Roman Empire, SPQR (*Senatus
Populusque Romanus*, 'the Senate and the
People of Rome'), became the motto of
his own dominion.

The latest-comer to the European scramble for Africa, Italian colonialism
has long been dismissed by scholars with hasty and patronizing judgments
heavily influenced by Lenin's definition of 'beggar imperialism'. For that reason,
until the early 1980s Italian historiography dwelled mainly on the alleged anomaly
and peculiarity of Italian colonialism. This developed the old colonial stereotype
of good colonialism, better known as the stereotype of *italiani brava gente*
(Italians as 'nice people').[1] Only recently has a new generation of Italian scholars,
together with African and others foreign scholars, succeeded in overcoming the
conceptual and sometimes political barriers of previous writers and connected
Italian colonialism to the mainstream of colonial studies.[2]

What were the reasons behind Italy's decision to become involved in colonial
expansionism? In the second half of the nineteenth century she relied on the
overwhelming prevalence of agriculture as the main area of employment, with
a minimal industrial sector and a low level of urbanization. The rate of literacy
was also extremely low, and the situation of the public administration was quite
miserable as it was the product of a confused and clumsy mixture of different
systems. A major source of instability and social conflict was the great
discrepancy between the north and south of Italy, with the north deeply marked
by the experience of Napoleon's political and administrative unification and the
south still immersed in the relatively backward Bourbon tradition. All of these
features made the process of transition to statehood and nationhood particularly
uneasy, and dramatically emphasized the social, economic and cultural
differences within Italy that led to a highly unbalanced society.

One of the main results of this unbalanced situation, and a major source of
economic crisis and social unrest, was the high rate of unemployment among
rural labourers in these years, which fed a massive migratory movement
funnelled mainly towards the Americas and Australia. In the inflamed political
debate of the late nineteenth century, colonial expansion began to be discussed
as a possible solution to the economic and social crisis created by the protracted
drainage of the most productive segment of the population. Supporters of Italy's

involvement in the 'scramble for Africa' affirmed that the acquisition of overseas territories would offer an outlet for the unemployed peasantry that would prove beneficial to Italian economy instead of to foreign economies.[3]

This set of economic and social justifications for expansion was further developed by segments of the Italian intelligentsia and dressed up with an ideology of legitimacy similar to that developed during the Berlin Conference of 1884–85. Italy's Roman and Christian roots, it was argued, placed Italy at the forefront when it came to the European right and duty to spread civilization and progress among African populations – represented as ignorant, backward and plunged in intellectual and moral darkness. Nevertheless, it should not be assumed that such ideas met with the unconditional support of either its elites or masses. On the contrary, a lively debate emerged which reflected both ideological attitudes and the material interests of the parties involved.[4]

FIRST STEPS TOWARDS A COLONIAL EMPIRE: ERITREA
The first African territory to be occupied by Italy was Eritrea, a small region along the coast of the Red Sea, known in local sources as *Mareb Mellash* ('land beyond the Mareb River') or *medri bahri* ('land of the sea'). This small territory presented an assortment of languages, religions and economic practices: Semitic-speaking Christian farmers in the highlands, Kushitic language-speaking semi-nomadic Muslims in the eastern lowlands, Semitic language-speaking semi-nomadic Muslims in the western lowlands, and Nilo-Saharan language-speaking agro-pastoralists in the western lowlands.

The nineteenth century had been a particularly troubled period in Eritrea, marked by internecine conflicts reflecting both internal power struggles and the

THE LAND of Eritrea, on the Horn of Africa, was the first object of Italian imperialist ambitions. The port of Assab was acquired by purchase in 1869, with Massawa a later addition. Further expansion was blocked by Ethiopia. In 1890, the colony of Eritrea was officially recognized, but six years later Italian expansion was defeated for the second time by Ethiopia. The pace quickened with the rise of Mussolini, who regarded Ethiopia as within Italy's sphere of influence. Shown here: on the quayside of Messina, a crowd of troops embark for Africa Orientale Italiana in October 1935.

A MILITARY CAMP in Eritrea displays banners of the royal house of Savoy.

expansionistic pressure of neighbouring Ethiopia and the Sudan – a process aggravated by the droughts, famines and epidemics that ravaged the country, substantially weakening its economic capabilities and political cohesion.[5] This fragility is a crucial factor in understanding the relatively easy Italian colonial expansion in Eritrea. The earliest acquisition of colonial territory was the purchase of the small port of Assab on the Red Sea in 1869, through a middleman called Giuseppe Sapeto, a former Lazarist priest and missionary. To avoid contentious diplomatic issues with Britain and France, the purchase was formally made on behalf of the Rubattino Shipping Company, on the grounds that it needed a fuel depot and warehouse. Only in 1882 did the Italian government officially take possession of Assab and establish a small administrative presence there. Three years later came the first move towards further occupation of the region. After long diplomatic negotiations aimed at gaining British support, Rome was authorized by London to occupy the port of Massawa, then under Egyptian control. British endorsement was motivated by the calculation that a weak colonial presence on the Horn of Africa, such as that represented by Italy, was preferable to that of a stronger power, such as France.

The years between 1885 and 1889 saw the slow extension of the Italian presence to the inland area of Eritrea, and particularly towards the cooler and more salubrious highlands. This process was met with very little resistance and occurred mainly through negotiation with local peoples. The only serious opposition came from Ethiopia, which was undergoing a complex process of state-building consisting of territorial expansion and administrative reorganization. The most serious clash was the Battle of Dog'ali in 1887, which saw the signal defeat of the Italian army by troops led by *ras* Alula, who had been appointed by the Ethiopian emperor Yohannes IV as military and administrative governor of the region. The first of a series of Italian defeats, the Battle of Dog'ali shows how the Eritrean territory, by the end of the nineteenth century, had become a bone of contention between rival regional and foreign ambitions aiming for hegemony.

On 1 January 1890, Italy officially declared the establishment of a colony on the Red Sea called Eritrea, a word taken from the Greek name for the Red Sea. Its early years witnessed the establishment of a bureaucratic administration based in Massawa under the iron-fisted rule of military officers.[6] A very repressive policy towards the indigenous people was adopted, leading to the imprisonment or execution of a large number of local leaders charged with conspiracy or rebellion. At the same time, attempts were made to transform Eritrea into a settler colony. To this end, the best cultivable lands were confiscated, sparking episodes of resistance, the best known being a rebellion led by Bahta Hagos, a chief of the Akkala Guzay region.[7] This revolt, together with ill-advised Italian diplomatic strategy towards Ethiopia, led to the famous Battle of Adwa, on 1 March 1896, where Italy was defeated by an Ethiopian army led by Emperor Menelik II.[8]

The defeat at Adwa marked a watershed in Italy's colonial plans and also had a lasting impact on power relations in the region. On the one hand, Italy gave up (for the time being) its dreams of expansion into Ethiopia. On the other, Ethiopia officially acknowledged the existence of Eritrea as a separate political entity. Another important change was the replacement of the colonial military administration by a civilian one in 1897. Furthermore, a new attitude emerged about the use to which Eritrea could be put – it was now expected to become a source of raw materials for Italian industry. This led to a progressive suspension of land confiscation policies, which were finally ended in 1926. In the attempt to make Eritrea economically viable, the colonial administration tried to merge the traditional economic system with a capitalist colonial one.[9] However, such colonial economic policies were seriously hampered by the failure to attract investors in Eritrea and by the prevalent attitude of Italian concession holders, who preferred to speculate in the commercial sector rather than to invest in long-term productive plans.[10]

After crushing the resistance of traditional chiefs through imprisonment, assassination or exile, the Italian authorities introduced a new policy of co-opting local elites. This policy was based on a system of appointed and salaried chiefs who derived their legitimacy not from their constituency, but rather from the colonial administration. Another important means of co-opting Eritreans into the colonial system was the army. After an initial limited use of colonial troops, Italy radically changed its attitude and started to resort to the massive

THE PEOPLE'S LIBERATION FRONT of Eritrea did its best to resist the Italian takeover but ultimately succumbed.

A MODERN AIRFORCE was crucial to
Italy's tactics in the war against
Ethiopia. These biplanes are carrying
out exercises over Eritrea in 1935.

employment of colonial soldiers, known as *ascari*.[11] One of the consequences of
the large-scale recruitment of Eritrean *ascari* became clear during the prolonged
campaign for the conquest, occupation and 'pacification' of Libya in the early
twentieth century.

Italy's educational policies towards Eritreans highlights one of the anomalies
of Italian colonialism. She deliberately avoided the development of a Western-
educated Eritrean elite, which it was feared would be prejudicial to the stability
of the colonial system. For that reason, and also to save money, colonial
education was largely delegated to both Catholic and Protestant missionaries.[12]

These trends in colonial policy remained substantially unchanged until the
early 1930s, when Eritrea experienced a dramatic transformation mainly related
to the resurgence of expansionistic and bellicose attitudes towards Ethiopia.
Mussolini regarded Ethiopia as part of Italy's 'legitimate' sphere of influence
in the region and as its natural economic outlet. In order to conquer Ethiopia,
massive military preparations were undertaken in which Eritrea served as a main
logistical centre. At a demographic level the Italian population soared from 4,500
in 1934 to 75,000 by 1939.[13] A rapid process of urbanization was also set in
motion, creating a broad labour division between urban and rural sectors.

The 1930s also witnessed substantial changes in the Eritrean labour market, with an increased number of Eritreans involved in the colonial bureaucracy as clerks, interpreters, telephone and telegraph operators, drivers and also servants in Italian houses.[14] Yet another significant feature of colonial policies implemented in the late 1930s in Eritrea, as well in the rest of the Italian colonies, was the introduction of racial bars aimed at defending so-called 'racial prestige'.[15] According to this policy, urban spaces had to be rigidly divided along segregationist principles, and sexual intercourse between Italian citizens and indigenous people were forbidden.[16]

SOMALIA

Known to European travellers and explorers as the exotic 'land of aromas',[17] Somalia really came to the attention of Europe at the end of the nineteenth century, especially after the opening of the Suez Canal in 1869. Until that time, very little was known to Europeans about the country both because of geographical obstacles and the complex and elusive nature of Somali society. In fact, in spite of the alleged unity deriving from the existence of a common language and religion, the Somali region presented a very considerable degree of internal fragmentation along the lines of environmental variation, economic differences and clan loyalties. The predominantly pastoralist communities of the inland areas were forced into a pattern of permanent nomadism, their life controlled by the alternation of the *gu* (a season of heavy rains), the *jiilaal* (a harsh season without rain) and the *dayr* (a season of lighter rains). In this particularly inhospitable environment, mobility became a necessity for the majority of the population, and this also determined the way in which social alliances, political power and economic exchanges took shape. In the south, along the Jubba and Shabeelle rivers, a rather different climate and, particularly, regular access to water in form of rain or irrigation made possible the development of permanent cultivation. A third pattern of social and economic organization was offered by the coastal city-states stretching along the shore of the Indian Ocean, particularly in the region of Benadir, where the ports of Warsheikh, Muqdisho (Mogadishu), Marka, Baraawe and Kismayu were part of the broader Swahili civilization and played an active role in the long-distance trade crossing the Indian Ocean.[18]

Through the nineteenth century, this complex and highly articulated conglomeration of territories, traditionally involved in a fluid interaction among themselves, experienced a significant transformation. Starting from the early decades of the century, Somali coastal centres became the object of military and political pressure by the Omani rulers of Zanzibar, who managed to impose a shadowy sovereignty over the region of Benadir. Further along the coast, the Mijjertein region in the north suffered a period of internal strife with clashes in the town of Obbia among members of the ruling family. In this case, the main point of contention was control of the lucrative business of salvage operations for ships stranded in the insidious waters near Cape Gardafui.

Inland, meanwhile, the Ethiopian process of state-building under Emperor Menelik II led to a substantial expansion southwards, encroaching on the region of Ogaden, a territory traditionally inhabited by Somali people.[19] Pushed out of Ogaden, many Somali moved to the Jubaland, causing friction with local communities, igniting conflicts and creating a situation of instability. Further north, the Egyptians, after the opening of the Suez Canal, started looking with interest at the Somali coast from Tadjoura to Berbera, where they established military garrisons.[20] The Egyptians, who already had a foothold along the Eritrean coast of the Red Sea, saw Somalia as a base from which to start the penetration of Ethiopia in order to gain control of both the supposed wealth of its highlands and the sources of the Nile. Finally, the nineteenth century also witnessed the rise of European interest in the Somali territory. The French had already obtained the port of Obock in 1859. Britain, which since 1839 had held a base in Aden, on the opposite coast of the Red Sea, started looking towards the Somali coast, and by 1882 had taken the port of Zeila over from Egypt.

As with Eritrea, the occupation of Somalia was accidental and unplanned, yet with an even more marked British involvement. Indeed, as we have seen, Britain looked favourably on the Italian presence in Somalia, as it would neutralize the more dangerous ambitions of the Germans and French there. Already by 1886, France, Germany and Britain had decided on the limits of the territorial jurisdiction of the sultan of Zanzibar over the Swahili coast, including the Somali coast, making possible a *de facto* partition of the region among themselves. Italy, a latecomer starting only in 1885, also tried to find its place among the more powerful European rivals. Through Vincenzo Filonardi, the Italian consul in Zanzibar and a powerful businessman, Italy tried to obtain land concessions and protectorates over the Somali coast from the sultan. After protracted negotiations, from February to April 1889, Filonardi managed to procure local authorities' signatures on treaties acknowledging the Italian protectorate in exchange for monetary compensation. The next important step, on 12 August 1892, was an agreement between Gerard Portal, the British representative in Zanzibar, and Pierre Cottoni, the acting Italian consul, granting a concession over the Benadir coast to Italy for a payment of 200,000 rupees for customs concessions and an annual subsidy to the local sultan.

THE HUMILIATING DEFEAT of Italy at Adwa in 1896 still rankled in the national memory. Here, the Ethiopian emperor Menelik II, Haile Selassie's great-uncle, leads his troops into battle.

After Italy had obtained control over the whole Somali coast from the Juba River to Cape Guardafui, the main problem was how to administer this huge and complex territory. The Italian government opted to use a chartered company, and on 15 May 1893 granted a concession over the Benadir coast (temporarily leaving aside the northern protectorates of Obbia and Mijjertein) to the Filonardi Company.[21] Filonardi administered the Benadir coast from 1893 to 1896, trying to avoid clashes with the Somali people as far as possible. To this end, the company set up a highly personalized administration with only one European on its civilian staff. All uncultivated lands whose owners could not be found were declared the property of the Italian government, which also held a monopoly on exploiting or granting concessions for mineral resources. Slavery was prohibited and measures taken for its gradual abolition. However, in spite of a more or less complete freedom in establishing customs and regulating tariffs, the Filonardi Company ended up a financial failure due to its overwhelming administrative expenses.

The Italian government did not renew Filonardi's concession after its first three years, and on 15 April 1896 signed a new convention with the Società Anonima Commerciale del Benadir, known as the Benadir Company, controlled by Antonio Cecchi, a famous explorer and ardent supporter of Italian colonial expansion in the region. Cecchi's administration of Benadir did not substantially differ from the previous one, either in its management or in its financial results, and the adventure ended with his assassination in an ambush in Lafole on 26 November 1896.[22] The Italian government then decided to reorganize the Benadir Company, enlarging the civilian staff into a more articulated bureaucracy. Though the company managed to make substantial profits, discrepancies in staff

ITALIAN TROOPS mass in Eritrea in preparation for the invasion of Ethiopia.

remuneration, lack of success in attracting investors, and limited influence on the traditional patterns of the local economy made the new Benadir Company another failure, an outcome also exacerbated by charges of the persistence of slavery in the region with the alleged connivance of the Italian government. The scandal created by disclosures about these matters led to the establishment of a commission of inquiry which investigated the responsibilities of the company and called for a revision of the agreement between the Italian government and the company.

As a result, the Italian government purchased the Benadir ports on 13 January 1905 and set up direct administration over southern Somalia. Relations with the Somali people were regulated with a mix of paternalism and indirect rule based on co-opting salaried indigenous chiefs and religious authorities. Islamic Sharia law and Somali customary law were recognized as long as they did not contradict the fundamental principles of Italian law. A further institution was introduced, known as Tribunale dell'Indigenato, with a mandate to try Somalis charged with endangering the security, stability and prestige of the colonial authority. The enforcement of the Indigenato's decisions was mainly carried out through confiscation of goods, collective punishment and, in the most serious cases, deportation of offenders to Eritrea.

The first and most vigorous efforts of the new colonial administration were directed at making Somalia economically viable by revivifying its trade and developing a market-oriented agriculture. However, all such attempts were hampered by the absence of a unified currency, the failure of the colonial government to persuade Somali, Indian and Arab traders to accept Italian currency instead of the Maria Theresa thaler that was in circulation, a shortage of labour, a lack of investors and inadequate feasibility studies.

The most substantial problem facing the early Italian colonial administration of Somalia was the fact that real control of the territory did not extend far inland from the coast of the Indian Ocean, and even there it relied mainly on the acquiescence of local chiefs rather than on the exercise of full and undisputed authority. Furthermore, the northern protectorates of Obbia and Mijjertein for long remained only nominally under Italian authority. The fragility of this status quo appeared clearly in 1899, when Muhammad Abdilleh Hassan, the representative of the Salihiyya[23] Muslim brotherhood in British Somaliland, rebelled against British domination and started a *jihad* against the British, Italians and Ethiopians.[24] Resistance, a mix of anti-colonial nationalism and religious zealotry, spread very quickly in the north, Muhammad Abdilleh's homeland, and from there to a great part of Somalia, limiting the scope of the colonial authorities until he died of pneumonia on 10 February 1921. For the Italians, the situation grew even worse when in October 1905 the Bimal population rebelled and attacked Italian positions – a revolt mainly directed against the Italian anti-slavery policy. In fact, the very foundations of the Bimal economy were under threat since it was based on a clear division of labour between the elite, engaged

in the more prestigious activity of pastoralism, and agricultural work carried out by their slaves.[25]

After 1922, Fascist colonial rule tried to reorganize the Eritrean colony by addressing several key issues. The task of unifying its scattered and often unruly territories implied a greater military involvement and was achieved by creating a new force, the Zaptie Corps composed of Eritrean, Somali and Yemeni recruits. To provide the growing colonial budget with solider foundations, a system of direct taxation was introduced, in the form of an annual hut tax. *Qadis* and traditional chiefs were maintained as salaried personnel and the suspension of their salary, alongside other forms of punishment, was used as an instrument of political pressure. The area where Fascism introduced stronger measures than before was in agriculture. Great emphasis was placed on agricultural development and many concessions were given to Italian investors such as the Società Agricola Italo-Somala (SAIS) and the Azienda Agraria Governativa. However, these concessions, based on a mixture of subsistence and cash-crop agriculture, could barely survive without regular government subsidies. In the area of education, Italy made little investment for Somalis who, apart from the few missionary schools, were practically ignored until 1935; in that year, statistics showed ten government schools and five orphanages.[26]

The administration of Somalia after its incorporation into the administrative structure of Africa Orientale Italiana (AOI), to be examined below, changed slightly as the Fascists organized their colonial territories along ethnic lines.[27] The new Somalia therefore included also the whole Ogaden territory, largely inhabited by Somali people.[28]

LIBYA HAD BEEN OTTOMAN until the late 19th century, when, like other Turkish possessions, it became a temptation to the imperialist powers across the Mediterranean. In 1911, an Italian force occupied Tripoli and the coastal area. Italians were encouraged to settle there and it was seen as Italy's 'Fourth Shore'. The 'Ristorante Italia' in Tripoli in 1914 betrays its location only by the Islamic arcade at the back. But Muslim resistance continued in the south until 1932.

TRIPOLI AS AN ITALIAN PORT, 1911. The conquest of Libya proved more difficult than the Italians had anticipated. After 1922, under Mussolini, the campaign became more ruthless.

THE INVASION OF LIBYA

Unlike the history of Italy's other African colonies, that of Libya is primarily characterized by the prolonged Ottoman presence dating back to the sixteenth century. In the two regions of Tripolitania and Cyrenaica that form the territory of present-day Libya, that presence had lasting consequences both in developing a quite articulated and structured civil service and in determining its reactions to Italian colonialism.[29] Throughout the nineteenth century, in spite of an internal struggle for power between nomadic Bedouins and inhabitants of the coast, and notwithstanding a troubled international situation, the Ottomans succeeded in establishing a relatively efficient public administration and in providing services such as the telegraph (in 1861) and schools. Another important aspect of Libya's history is the unifying role played by Islam and particularly by the Sanusiyya brotherhood.[30] Originally based in Mecca, around 1854 the Sanusiyya had moved its headquarters to Djaraboub, on the border of Libya and Egypt, in order to be closer to one of the largest areas of its support, and also to control the important flow of wealth deriving from the caravan routes of Waddai. Throughout the century, the Sanusiyya played an important role in unifying local and tribal differences under the common flag of Islam. Through its dense network of religious and administrative centres (*zawiyas*), the brotherhood was also crucial in providing stability and peace in the Saharan hinterland, where the capacity of the Ottoman administration to exercise any real political and administrative control remained minimal.

In the second half of the nineteenth century, Libya became the object of increased attention from colonial powers, in particular Britain, France, Italy and the collapsing Ottoman state. Libya was relevant in two different contexts. In the Mediterranean, it provided one of the theatres for the European attempt to liquidate the increasingly weak Ottoman Empire, an attempt linked to a parallel development in the Balkans. At the same time, the hinterland of Libya offered an

DURING THE SECOND WORLD WAR the coast of Libya became one large battlefield as British and German armies swept to and fro across North Africa. Here, a British force prepares to occupy the burning city of Tobruk in 1941.

important domain in the broader scramble for Africa, as it controlled some of the most important trans-Saharan commercial routes.

Italy's interest in Libya increased after the declaration of a French protectorate over Tunisia in 1881. Italy, which, partly by virtue of the presence there of a significant Italian community, had always considered Tunisia as its own most natural outlet, was now looking frantically for territorial compensation in the southern Mediterranean. However, because of the volatility of the international situation and its reluctance to get involved in colonial adventures after the shock of Adwa, only on 3 October 1911 did the Italian government decided to dispatch troops to occupy Tripoli.

Contrary to Italian expectations, the occupation of Libya proved neither swift nor easy. In fact, the Libyans, instead of welcoming the Italians as their liberators from Ottoman oppression – as nationalist propaganda in Italy had depicted the campaign – created a joint anti-colonial front together with Young Turk officers.[31] The early phase of the Italian campaign can be divided into three. The first, which lasted only for a few months, led to Italian occupation of the main coastal urban centres such as Tripoli, Tobruk, Derna, Homs and Benghazi. This occupation was carried out with extreme caution, avoiding direct military confrontation as far as possible by resorting largely to naval bombardment and the first rudimentary use of an air force. Nevertheless, the Italian army met with resistance from the population and was repeatedly ambushed and severely beaten. This unexpected development led to the second phase, marked by the abandonment of tactics of attrition in favour of open confrontation. The deployment of troops in the barren desert far from the protective cover of the naval artillery and urban fortifications was made possible only by the massive use of Eritrean colonial troops. The Italians, however, did not succeed in suppressing the anti-colonial resistance led by Libyan and Turkish forces, which continued to inflict heavy losses on them. Only with the outbreak of the First World War did the Italian government avoid a political crisis because war censorship and the diversion of public opinion to the European front made it possible to ignore what was happening in Libya. Moreover, the involvement of Turkey in the war, as an ally of Germany and Austria, had further weakened its military potential and disrupted lines of communication with Libyan resistants. To weaken Libyan resistance further, the Italians in 1919 introduced the so-called *Statuto libico*, which sanctioned a separate status for Libyans – instead of being considered colonial subjects, they were accorded a sort of second-class citizenship which enabled them to work in Italy, to submit petitions to the Italian parliament and to have their own local parliament. Freedom of the press, the acknowledgment of Arabic as one of the official languages of Libya (together with Italian), and the election of Libyans to municipal councils also formed part of the package.[32]

However, the policy of the *Statuto libico* did not end confrontation between Libyans and Italians. The accession to power of Mussolini, in October 1922, marked a recrudescence of Italian belligerence and the beginning of a more aggressive foreign policy. No means were spared by the Italian government to suppress the Libyan resistance. Under the merciless leadership of Colonel Graziani, massive deployment of Eritrean *ascari*, the use of poison gas, the employment of the air force in bombing raids, the establishment of concentration camps and the deportation of entire communities were all adopted as part of Italian warfare in Libya.[33] The main object of the Italian repression was the Sanusiyya, rightly identified as the political and military leadership of the Libyan resistance. In an attempt to weaken the brotherhood, its *zawiyyas* were closed, all of its properties confiscated, and its main leader, Omar el-Mukhtar, ruthlessly pursued for years, until he was captured and

AN UNEQUAL STRUGGLE: Mussolini's brutal invasion of Ethiopia in October 1935 effectively allied Italy with Franco's Spain and Hitler's Germany, provoking condemnation from the liberal democracies. A cartoon in the German satirical magazine *Simplicissimus* shows poor rural Africa at the mercy of mighty industrial Europe.

executed in 1931.[34] His death marked the end of a decade of indiscriminate terror and violence, and by January 1932 Marshal Pietro Badoglio, who had been appointed governor of Tripolitania and Cyrenaica in 1929, could declare that the war was over and that Libya had been 'pacified'.[35]

The end of military operations opened a new chapter in the Italian occupation of Libya. Fascism launched a policy of 'demographic colonization' aimed at developing agriculture and at the same time providing investment possibilities to unemployed Italians. This large-scale scheme for settler colonization implied a system of state-sponsored and subsidized allocation of small plots of land to Italian peasant families. The scheme was launched in 1933; five years later, an ambitious and spectacular plan for the simultaneous settlement of 20,000 colonists was implemented, and a second wave of 12,000 migrants followed in 1939. In spite of the rodomontade rhetoric of Fascism, these schemes were extremely expensive for the meagre coffers of the Italian state, and they also came up against multiple structural problems, including the reluctance of many colonists to remain in Libya – which led to numerous attempts to return home – and a general lack of labour. The outbreak of the Second World War led to an increased labour shortage as more than a thousand colonists were enlisted in the Italian army. The war introduced other problems as well, such as a shortage of fuel and spare parts, further hampering settlement schemes.

ROYAL APPROVAL: King Victor Emmanuel and Queen Elena visit Tripoli to honour Mussolini's success (*above*).

MUSSOLINI THE CONQUERING warrior brandishes the sword of Islam: a propaganda image of 1937 (*opposite*).

Italian policies aimed at transforming Libya primarily into a settler colony for Italians, the so-called *Quarta sponda* ('fourth shore') of Italy in the Mediterranean. This meant that race relations were marked by clear subordination of Libyans to their colonial masters. Little room was left in Italy's vision for the development of a modern, Western-educated elite. Libyans were expected to provide a docile and cheap reservoir of labour for the developing market economy. Italy's involvement in the Second World War as an Axis power led to the sudden and relatively unexpected collapse of colonial rule everywhere. Tripoli fell under British control on 23 January 1943 – Libyan resistants recruited among the estimated 14,000 exiles living in Egypt played a role in the occupation.

THE LAST COLONIAL EMPIRE: ETHIOPIA

Ethiopia had represented one of the main objects of Italy's colonial ambitions since the very beginning of her involvement in the Horn of Africa. This attraction was fostered by belief in the huge economic potential of the country, which was supposed to be extremely promising both for agricultural production and the availability of precious minerals. A further factor was the bitter memory of the humiliating defeat suffered by the Italians in Adwa, which was exploited by Fascist rhetoric in the 1930s to legitimize Mussolini's invasion of Ethiopia.[36]

The coming to power of Fascism marked the beginning of a more aggressive and belligerent foreign policy, which in the case of Ethiopia meant the abandonment of the policy of good neighbour relations between that country and Italy's colonies of Eritrea and Somalia (which had been pursued more or less continuously since boundary agreements were reached in 1902), and heralded a very different attitude. An escalation of diplomatic and military provocations, along with an international campaign aimed at depicting Ethiopia as a backward, barbarous and primitive country, punctuated the years preceding Italy's invasion of Ethiopia. The themes of a struggle against slavery, detention of illegal weapons, and infringement of international conventions were utilized by the Fascist media for the consumption of both local and international public opinion.[37]

Parallel to its media and diplomatic campaign, Italy set up an impressive war machine with its main operational base in the Eritrean port of Massawa. The old infrastructure of Eritrea was modernized, particularly with the creation of new roads to facilitate the movement of troops and armaments towards Ethiopia. Somalia was also involved as a territory from which to launch the invasion of Ethiopia, though it experienced less economic and social transformation. Indeed, Somalia provided the *casus belli*: an incident that occurred at the oasis of Wal Wal in Ogaden was used as a pretext by the Italians, who accused the Ethiopians of deliberate aggression and unleashed against them the mighty military machine they had been carefully organizing since 1932. Foreshadowing the invasion, Mussolini on 15 January 1935 also declared the incorporation of Eritrea and Somalia into the newly created AOI.

THE WAR was prosecuted with every means available, including poison gas. Mussolini wanted a quick victory. It was depicted by the Ethiopian artist Haili Berhan Yemene from the point of view of the defeated.

By the summer of 1935, preparations for the invasion were complete. Apart from the military provisions, Mussolini had succeeded in obtaining a sort of informal French endorsement of Italy's plans for Ethiopia under the diplomatic formula of *désistement*. Relying as well on the disunion and ambiguities of the international community, Italy launched an offensive against Ethiopia on 2 October 1935 without any preliminary official declaration of war. Mussolini wanted a quick and impressive victory that would strengthen Italy's ambitions as an important international power and would also secure the support of Italian public opinion. However, military operations were slower than the sort of *Blitzkrieg* the Italians were expecting, and it was only on 5 May 1936, after fierce resistance, that Italian troops entered the capital, Addis Ababa, and declared the war won. A special role had been played by the combined use of aeroplanes and poison gas, which spread chaos and panic among Ethiopians troops. The Ethiopian emperor, Haile Selassie, had fled Addis Ababa on 1 May and went into exile in Britain, leaving the city in a state of confusion and anarchy.[38]

With the conquest of Addis Ababa, Mussolini proclaimed Ethiopia part of the so-called empire of the AOI, a state of affairs that in spite of repeated Ethiopian protests was met with little resistance by the League of Nations to which Ethiopia had belonged since 1923. By 1938, the main European powers acknowledged Italy's rule over the AOI, creating a dangerous precedent in international relations. In this regard, some historians have suggested that the invasion of Ethiopia, and Mussolini's open disregard of the symbolic and diplomatic status of the League of Nations, paved the way for the escalation of tense international relations that led to the outbreak of the Second World War.

However, the diplomatic success and the official declaration of the end of the Ethiopian war meant neither a real stabilization of the newly conquered territory nor the cessation of resistance. Resistance continued unabated through the whole period of the Italian presence in Ethiopia, to the point that some historians, particularly Ethiopians, reject the notion of an Italian *colonial* rule over Ethiopia, preferring the concept of military occupation. Italy's policy of ruthless repression alienated the majority of the Ethiopian (and other) elites. A key episode in this process was the Italian reaction to the attempted assassination of Marshal Graziani (the same figure who had earlier masterminded the cruel repression of Libyan resistance) on 19 February 1937. The retaliation unleashed by the Italian administration was appalling, and for three days Italian police, Italian civilians, and the Fascist militia had a completely free hand in taking revenge on all Ethiopians they encountered. Thousands were slaughtered in Addis Ababa during these days, often in the most cruel fashion, and a systematic policy of repression was also launched against the Ethiopian Church, intellectuals, students and even traditional storytellers.[39]

Immediately after the military occupation, Italy set about reorganizing its huge colonial possessions. To do so, a gigantic bureaucracy was established, in charge of implementing the Fascist vision of colonialism in the AOI, which was reorganized along ethnic lines into six major regional divisions. Fascist propaganda described this policy as aimed at establishing an 'empire of civilization and humanity for all peoples of Ethiopia' in opposition to the traditional hegemonic rule of the ethnic Amhara people. In reality, this divisive policy aimed at weakening resistance to colonial rule.

RESISTANCE WAS courageous but disorganized. Christians and Muslims came together against the common enemy.

The suggested development model for Ethiopia, as for other Italian colonies, was 'demographic colonization', which implied major settlement schemes for Italian peasant families.[40] However, this ambitious policy had to face many serious obstacles, such as the lack of security in the countryside, the lack of capital, and shortages of fuel, food and spare parts. Demographic colonization was thus never viable, and the AOI was not even able to feed itself from its own agricultural production.

Where the brief Italian occupation did leave a lasting mark was in urban and infrastructural development. To realize its dream of 'demographic colonization', which envisaged an AOI inhabited by millions of Italian settlers in the near future – and which explains the term 'Italian Africa' – Fascism embarked on an ambitious plan of urban development in Addis Ababa. All of the new gubernatorial capitals also experienced substantial architectural transformation, and monumental masterplans were designed for each of them. From the Fascist perspective, architecture was expected to become the visual expression of Italian and Fascist superiority and power.[41]

THE END OF THE EMPIRE AND ITS LEGACY

In spite of its claim that it would last for a millennium, the ambitious imperial dreams of Fascism collapsed at their earliest stage, owing to the Italian decision to get involved in the Second World War. By 25 February 1941 Allied troops had already occupied Muqadishu, and by 5 May 1941, only five years after the Italian conquest of Addis Ababa, Emperor Haile Selassie was back in power. On 11 June, British troops occupied Assab, and on 11 November the last pocket of Italian resistance was subdued in the Ethiopian town of Gondar. Finally, by mid-February 1943, the last Italian and German troops had been driven from Libya.

Apart from Germany, which lost its colonies at the end of the First World War, Italy represents the only case of a European colonial power that did not lead its colonies through the decolonization process. This anomaly determined

AFTER THEIR VICTORY – between 1936 and 1940 – the Italians poured vast resources into making Ethiopia into a modern Western state. Mussolini accorded himself semi-divine status.

a variety of enduring problems that afflicted these territories, particularly in the Horn of Africa. Broadly speaking, the history of contemporary Africa is characterized by the dilemma of former colonial states engaged in building national unities within the territorial and administrative framework of colonial borders. The nation itself can be considered and analysed merely as a result of a process initiated by the colonial political power. It is not the nation that makes states, but states that create nations; nationalism thus appears not as a cause of conflict, but rather as a consequence of it.

In the history of Italian colonialism, only some components of this pattern can be seen. In fact, though the main themes of decolonized societies are also the main features of the Horn of Africa, substantial differences appear in the decolonization process there. Italy, as a result of its military defeat in 1941, was not able to fulfil its colonial 'role' by providing a bridge for its former territories to independence. Nor, because of its obstinate policy of hampering the development of Western-educated elites, could Italy negotiate the transition with them.

The decolonization process in the case of the former Italian colonies was mainly determined by diplomatic factors and international relations. They developed through the intricate interaction of nationalism rooted in colonialism (Eritrea and Somalia), regional hegemonic ambitions (Ethiopia), and the pre-Cold War balance of power.[42] What in some way made this already complex picture even more unusual was the fact that Ethiopia, through the smart diplomacy of Emperor Haile Selassie, was able to exploit to its advantage the ambiguity of the situation, neutralizing both the confused and relatively disorganized Eritrean nationalism and Somali irredentism.[43]

THE MODEL CITY of Asmara, in Eritrea, was rebuilt by Italian architects in the 1930s to demonstrate their ideology and expertise. The Fascist Party Headquarters (Casa del Fascio) is one of the many buildings that make Asmara a political monument frozen in time. This particular building now houses the Ministry of Education.

Like that of the rest of colonial Africa, the complex and often troubled contemporary history of the Horn can be partially read as the uneasy legacy of colonial rule. The impact on local institutions, the emergence of new political identities and the reorganization of the territory are themes of relevance everywhere in colonial Africa. What makes the case of the Horn peculiar is the sudden and unpredictable end of Italian rule, which left no significant and active role for the former colonial authorities in the process of decolonization. This legacy, together with the intricate developments within local societies in the region, has extorted a heavy toll from the population, whose post-colonial history has been marked by repeated political crises, warfare, famines and instability.

THE DEPOSED EMPEROR Haile Selassie twice appealed to the League of Nations, in 1936 and 1938, for help against Italian aggression, but both times was met by apathy and indifference, an early example of the appeasement that the Western democracies soon came to regret. Haile Selassie was restored to his throne in 1941, but deposed again by an internal coup and murdered in 1975.

13

The United States:
Empire as a Way of Life?

FRANK SCHUMACHER

Is AMERICA NOW, or has it ever been, an imperialist power? Only in a special sense. There have been episodes when she has claimed power over foreign territories, but the manifestations of that power have been varied. Old-fashioned colonization is only one of them. Another is a world-wide network of military bases. Yet another, and one which comes closest to the present situation, is the assertion of cultural and commercial dominance – an ideological empire.

The early years of American expansion in the 19th century probably do approximate best to empire-building as Europe understood it. But in an allegory like 'American Progress' (*opposite*) the emphasis is not on conquest but on bringing railways and the telegraph – in other words, civilization – to a virtually empty land. Americans could thus see themselves not as imperialists or colonizers but as benefactors, and that is how they have tended to see themselves ever since.

'We go on creating what mankind calls an empire while we continue to believe quite sincerely that it is not an empire because it does not feel to us the way we imagine an empire ought to feel.'
Walter Lippmann, 1927[1]

'We don't seek empires, we're not imperialistic. We never have been. I can't imagine why you'd even ask the question.'
Donald Rumsfeld, 2003[2]

EMPIRE IS THE WORD OF THE HOUR in current debates about American foreign policy. In the United States and abroad the term is increasingly being used by proponents and opponents of America's current global strategy to debate the benefits and pitfalls of Washington's approach to international order. Many such arguments are enriched with historical references and locate American power within the wider context of the history of pre-modern and modern empires. They are used to explain the extent of American power, to predict the possible demise of American influence or to gain insights into the proper long-term defence and security of American interests.[3]

The application of the label *empire* to American foreign policy by liberal or conservative critics has a long tradition that dates back to the founding days of the republic. What is new is the inflationary, often metaphorical use of the terms empire, imperial and imperialism, which indicate not only a new assertiveness but also hint at the difficult and often contradictory profile of any description of the multiple dimensions and manifestations of American power and influence. It tends to generalize and categorize American influence as imperial beyond any recognition of temporal and spatial limits.

In the search for patterns in the American way of empire, this essay traces the evolution of the United States to world power from the late eighteenth century onwards. It argues that America throughout its history assumed successive and often overlapping formations of imperial and hegemonic power in continental, hemispheric and global contexts. Empire was never undisputed but proved a

durable approach as imperial aspiration was fused with a self-perception of America as universal nation.

From Jefferson's empire of liberty to Woodrow Wilson's liberal-democratic internationalism to Cold War containment, the creation of preponderant, sometimes clearly imperial, strength was thus often paradoxically described as a defensive and *anti*-imperial measure. Since the end of the First World War, American power has preferred hegemonic leadership on a global scale and mostly informal empire in the Western hemisphere. Formal colonial rule has assumed merely peripheral importance. This trend, however, did not preclude the possibility of quasi-colonial relationships and unambiguously imperial reactions (in specific historical circumstances and in specific regional contexts) to perceived regional instability.

'TO BEGIN THE WORLD ALL OVER AGAIN': AMERICA'S TRANSCONTINENTAL, COLONIAL AND INFORMAL EMPIRES (1780s–1914)

'We have it in our power to begin the world all over again.'
Thomas Paine, 1776[4]

'God has made us the master organizers of the world ... He has marked the American people as his chosen nation to finally lead in this regeneration of the world. This is the divine mission of America.'
Albert Beveridge, 1900[5]

Over the course of the nineteenth century the United States nearly quadrupled its national territory. This process of expansion encompassed the creation of three overlapping and intimately connected forms of empire: the imposition of United States rule across North America, informal empire in Latin America and Asia, and overseas colonial empire. The creation and maintenance of such positions of power was both driven by and simultaneously fostered the spectacular economic and demographic rise of the nation, the ability to fend off disintegrating tendencies through coercion, the creation of a unifying transportation and communication network, a coherent expansionist ideology, and a cultural setting conducive to imperial expansion.[6]

At the heart of the expansionist thrust lay the step-by-step acquisition and conquest of vast transcontinental spaces through diplomacy and war. Diplomatically, the strategy of acquisition was to take advantage of the inter-imperial rivalries or urgent financial needs of European powers, focusing on the purchase of vast stretches of land. Two prominent examples were the 1803 Louisiana Purchase from France, which doubled US territory for the price of $15 million, and the Alaska Purchase of 1867 for $7.2 million from Russia.

These territories were populated by a multitude of Native American cultures whose influence and demographic strength steadily decreased under the constant pressure of Euro-American expansion. The US government's control over those areas rested upon a threefold approach: negotiation, outright warfare, and assimilation policies.[7]

In hundreds of treaties Washington negotiated a continuous transfer of land from Native Americans to the central government. From the 1830s on, the federal government increasingly undermined the existence of the indigenous peoples as independent nations. The removal of the Cherokees and the ensuing Supreme Court legal battle over Indian status signalled the step-by-step degradation of Native Americans from sovereign nations to 'wards of the United States'.

If diplomacy failed, the next step was war. As the century proceeded Native Americans were militarily defeated and confined to reservations. The survivors of forced marches westwards were colonized on US territory. This consequent policy of internal colonialism was accompanied by widespread attempts to eradicate any traces of Indian culture as education was placed at the service of empire.[8]

Native Americans were not alone in experiencing the aggressive dynamic of the emerging transcontinental empire. In 1846 the United States went to war against Mexico. The victorious American troops conquered much of northern Mexico and occupied the nation's capital. By the summer of 1847 many expansionists were demanding the annexation of all of Mexico, which opponents rejected on racial grounds. They interpreted the inclusion of Mexicans as detrimental to the American body politic. The Treaty of Guadalupe-Hidalgo (1848) which ended the war allocated 1,300,000 sq km (500,000 sq miles) of territory (today's states of California, New Mexico, Arizona, Utah and Nevada, as well as parts of Colorado and Wyoming) to the United States and compensated the Mexican government for its loss with $15 million.

The expansionist dynamic of continental conquest was accompanied by the impressive rise of the United States to global economic preponderance. In the words of the historian Paul Kennedy: 'The United States seemed to have *all* the economic advantages which *some* of the other powers possessed *in part* but *none* of their disadvantages.'[9] Those advantages which would ultimately propel the United States to global hegemony were rich agricultural land, vast raw materials, technological innovations for the development of those resources (such as railways, the steam engine, mining equipment), lack of social and geographical constraints, absence of significant foreign threats, and flow of foreign and domestic investment capital. The incredible expansion of America's economic

THE MEXICAN WAR of 1846, which ended with the occupation of the capital, Mexico City (*below*), brought America vast areas in the Midwest, but the United States paid $15 million in compensation. Suggestions that the United States should take over Mexico itself were rejected.

Overleaf
THE FORCED MIGRATION of the Cherokee Indians from east of the Mississippi to what is now Oklahoma in 1838 has weighed heavily on the American conscience. A work such as William Lindneux's *Trail of Tears* is a vivid expression of a tragedy that continues to haunt white America today.

WESTWARD THE Course of Empire Takes its Way by Fanny Frances Palmer, 1868: a revealing use of the word 'empire' in connection with the expansion of the USA.

power was fostered and fuelled by impressive demographic increases from 3.9 million in 1790 to almost 76 million Americans by 1900.

The creation and expansion of a transcontinental empire also depended upon the nation's ability to fend off any challenges and disintegrating tendencies. The most serious threat was the attempted secession of the Confederacy – a threat defeated only by a long and bloody war. After 1865 the South was reintegrated into the nation as a formally and informally subordinated province, a condition that lasted for more than two decades.

The split between North and South was not the only dangerous division: the eastern seaboard and the American West were like two separate nations. The 'lawlessness' of the 'Wild West', immortalized in countless movies, was a challenge to the imperial centre as long as those territories were not constituted and integrated into the federal system. The capital's interests in trading routes, agricultural potential and strategic positions were frequently challenged and the US cavalry became the symbol of coercing locals into compliance, holding the territories in a state of quasi-colonial subjection.

The integration of those vast spaces into an emerging national transportation and communication network made these military expeditions more efficient. The evolution of the American railway system in this context is particularly instructive. By 1830 railroads extended for a mere 40 km (23 miles). By 1880 available railroad tracks had increased to 149,670 km (93,000 miles) and in the early years of the twentieth century had reached more than 321,870 km (200,000 miles). The construction of the first transcontinental railroad, referred to by one historian as 'Empire Express', was the ultimate symbol of western integration through transportation networks.[10]

Accelerating transportation opportunities were accompanied by equally revolutionary developments in communication technology.[11] At the beginning of the nineteenth century it took twenty-five days for news to travel from the eastern seaboard of the new republic to its western borders; by the end of the century news could be transmitted almost instantaneously through new media such as telephone, telegraph and wireless communication. By 1900 already more than 1.4 million telephones were in service, one for every sixty inhabitants. At the same time the experimental use of wireless, or radio, was just beginning to usher in a new era of communications technology.

The creation of a transcontinental empire with strong hemispheric interests and a global outlook was legitimized through a quasi-religious missionary ideology, the conviction of an exceptional national development and the idea of America as universal nation.[12] Those core convictions were destined to remain in place and made it possible to reconcile a belief in liberal democracy with the creation of an empire.

Since the early days of the Republic, Americans shared 'the notion that the United States was a sacred-secular *project*, a mission of world-historical significance in a designated continental setting of no determinate limits'.[13] The missionary myth drew on biblical ideas such as the millenarian concept of a coming kingdom and interpreted American history as the staging ground for a redemption and salvation, the United States as redeemer nation. This 'missionary' self-perception had two aspects: one saw the United States as beacon of hope for mankind, while another was not content with the 'city upon the hill' strategy but demanded an active role for the nation in the reshaping of world conditions.

Pride in the republican experiment and the messianic conviction of America's divine role resulted in the self-perception of America as universal nation. Even before the nation's independence, Thomas Paine offered one of the most powerful and enduring expositions of America's world role.[14] In *Common Sense* (1776), he emphasized the fundamental differences between Old and New Worlds, suggested a congruence of American and international aspirations, and emphasized the beneficial impact of mutual trade interdependence on the international system. Historian Serge Ricard, however, has suggested that this messianic universalism really disguised intervention and paternalism – first on the continent, then in the hemisphere, and ultimately the world – as altruism.[15]

But could a republic also be an empire? In contrast to Montesquieu and others who had warned that republics could not expand by conquest and expect to successfully reproduce their constitutional system, many founding 'fathers' of the United States, such as Alexander Hamilton, James Madison, Benjamin

UNINVITED, Commodore Matthew C. Perry arrived at Yokohoma in 1853 with the intention of opening Japan up to American trade. Until this point Japan had kept herself isolated from the rest of the world. Five years later a treaty was signed granting the USA access to five major ports. *Overleaf:* a Japanese print of Perry's paddle-steamer entering the bay bringing 300 sailors and armed marines.

THE CHINESE MARKET, with its 400 million potential customers, was opened up at the same time as the Japanese one by a mixture of force and persuasion (which included flooding the country with Christian missionaries).

Franklin, Thomas Jefferson, James Monroe and John Quincy Adams, argued in one way or another that extensive territory and a republican government were not merely compatible but a necessity. They countered apparent inconsistencies by the suggestion that a vast territory was a blessing for a republic with public sovereignty as it served as an insurance against the corruption of virtue and thus ultimate decline. A continuously expanding nation would prevent single interests from dominating the republic.

At the same time, the prescription for expansion was also interpreted as a defensive reflex against the potentialities of European imperial incursions in North America. Empire-building became an anti-colonial measure directed at the imperial influences of the Old World. Expansion and imperial control were deemed essential for the national security of the United States, an intellectual construct that would provide a long-lasting rationale for empire and hegemony throughout the history of the United States.

Throughout the nineteenth century Americans considered the Pacific Ocean, the Asian mainland and the Caribbean basin 'natural' spheres of commercial and strategic interest. But although some expansionists advocated the inclusion of much of the Caribbean, for example, in a greater American empire, this never dominated official foreign policy agenda. Instead Americans preferred methods of informal empire with instruments ranging from commercial penetration and punitive military expeditions to missionary reform and educational modernization.[16]

In Asia the United States conducted what Frank Ninkovich has described as 'hitchhiking imperialism',[17] following patterns set by British policies until its own position of power merited a more assertive policy. To 'open' Japan to American influence, the United States used a combination of military intimidation and offers at modernization. Commodore Matthew C. Perry's visits in 1853 and 1854 prepared the ground for a US-Japanese treaty (1858) which granted Washington access to five major ports for foreign trade and affirmed extraterritorial rights. In Korea, American attempts to repeat Perry's coup ended prematurely with the war of 1871.

The commercial potential of the Chinese market, with its imagined riches and the lure of 400 million Chinese eager to purchase American products, loomed large on the mental maps of American businessmen, politicians and strategic planners. Faced with surplus production resulting from the nation's rapid conversion to an industrial economy, Americans hoped to maintain social stability through access to overseas markets, which was also deemed beneficial to the rest of the world.[18]

To secure that access, the United States attempted to limit and direct great-power controversies and prevent China from being carved up into spheres of influence. The 'Open Door Notes' of 1899 and 1900 stood in the tradition of the 1844 Treaty of Wanghia which had granted the United States most-favoured-nation status and ensured that Washington automatically received all benefits extended by China to the European powers. Neither the other imperial powers, nor the Chinese themselves (as American participation in the western military intervention during the Boxer War in 1900 made amply clear) were to threaten the open access of the United States to China.

In China and other parts of Asia, American commercial penetration and the occasional use of expeditionary forces were accompanied by a powerful missionary and cultural reform movement. Between 1870 and 1900 American missionaries flooded China to promote the 'Evangelization of the World' and became a powerful foreign cultural presence. By 1925, their numbers had increased to about 5,000. Other secular institutions such as the YMCA and American social reformers and later philanthropic institutions also flocked to China. Their activities also looked increasingly for US government support and protection and their programmes of modernization produced demand which in turn had produced trade.

America's interest in Asia also led to an informal insular empire in the Pacific with Hawaii at its core. Since the 1820s American missionaries-turned-planters had helped to manoeuvre the country into the position of a culturally and commercially dependent satellite of the United States. Washington repeatedly warned European powers against annexation, granted Hawaiian products duty free entry to the United States and acquired naval rights in Pearl Harbor. In 1893, Washington even intervened to replace an indigenous government critical of the close association with America. Annexation was often debated but the prospect of inclusion of a substantial body of racially diverse Chinese, Japanese and native Hawaiians remained a main argument against it. Only a few years later, however,

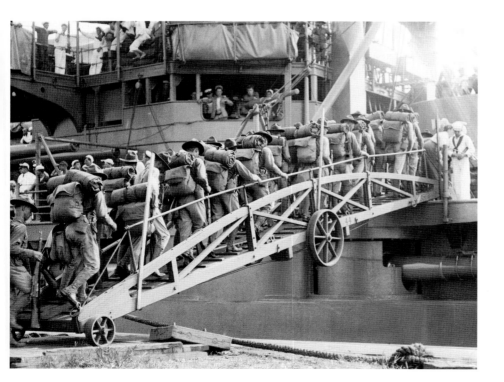

IF AMERICAN INTERESTS were threatened the USA did not hesitate to send military aid 'to disarm the unruly natives'. Here, in 1915, a force of 500 marines embarks for Haiti.

changing strategic considerations driven by colonial ambition and the fear of Japanese domination of the islands turned informal into formal empire and the archipelago was indeed annexed in 1898.[19]

In the Caribbean basin American power also shifted between informal and formal empire.[20] The United States contained European influence in the region and utilized commercial hegemony, cultural penetration and military intervention to secure virtual sovereignty in a number of countries such as Cuba, Haiti, the Dominican Republic, Panama, Nicaragua, Honduras and El Salvador. In many cases, Washington claimed indefinite intervention rights and frequently dispatched the US Marines Corps to take charge.[21]

The exemplum for a status between informal and formal empire was Cuba. Regarded as a natural and strategically important appendage to the United States, American business interests dominated the island. US firms almost monopolized the tobacco, sugar and fruit business, as well as the mining operations. The United Fruit Company alone controlled 200,000 acres (80,940 hectares) of land. By 1902 Americans had invested more than $100 million, a sum that would reach $1.5 billion by 1925.

After the defeat of Spain in the Spanish-American War of 1898, Cuba was placed under American military government. Although provisional plans for the annexation of Cuba dated back to the 1820s, a strong sense of racism inspired the Teller Amendment to the declaration of war against Spain which prohibited the incorporation of the island. But by the Platt Amendment to the Cuban constitution of 1903 Washington secured American intervention rights and a naval base at Guantanamo. In the following decades the United States (often prompted by warring factions of the local elite) repeatedly intervened, and even reinstalled military occupation between 1906 and 1909. Cuba's limited sovereignty thus securely locked the island into the American informal empire.

An even stronger quasi-colonial relationship was the result of America's unorthodox approach to 'nation-building' in Panama. After French failures to build a canal and British permission to assume sole responsibility, the United States selected Panama, Colombia's northernmost province, as the site for the monumental construction. The government in Bogotá rejected the terms, but a US-backed rebellion secured Panamanian independence. The new country gratefully acknowledged American intervention rights and provided Washington with a canal zone which constituted neither an incorporated nor unincorporated territory. It was a quasi-colony, sometimes referred to as a 'government-owned reservation'.

The Panama Canal, completed in August 1914, became the strategic centre of America's informal empire in the Caribbean basin. It provided commercial impetus, completed the network of inter-oceanic shipping links, and represented a strategic asset of utmost importance for American security. It also completed the integration of the transcontinental empire by linking two distant coasts together and simultaneously confirmed America's central position within a new set of global transportation and communication routes between East and West.[22]

By its victory in the Spanish-American War the United States thus acquired a colonial empire in the Caribbean and Pacific Ocean as the Philippines, Guam, Puerto Rico and Hawaii became colonies

RE-ENACTMENTS OF THE WILD WEST, America's heroic age, indicated pride in the past, and a certain confidence that problems had been solved.

and Cuba and Panama *de facto* protectorates.[23] Compared to the worldwide European possessions, America's colonial empire was relatively small but it was a springboard to conquer foreign markets and strategically secure American interests. This territorial limitation, however, by no means hampered the colonial fervour with which American policy set out to fundamentally transform the colonized societies.

In the Philippines the American project of colonial state-building was accompanied by one of the bloodiest and most costly colonial wars ever. Designed to crush an indigenous independence movement, the war turned much of the colony into a 'howling wilderness'. Five thousand out of nearly 130,000 American troops who had served in the islands and between 200,000 and 750,000 Filipinos were killed during the war.[24]

The fighting was accompanied by an extensive pacification programme based on social engineering. Despite a strong dosage of 'benevolent assimilation' policies, the imperial project created substantial opposition at home. A diverse group of businessmen, labour leaders, educators, clergy, social reformers, writers and politicians formed a powerful but ultimately ineffective alliance. Frequent reports about the brutal conduct of the war in the Philippines sustained the opposition. Mark Twain, a leading member of the Anti-Imperialist League, suggested changing the American flag: black stripes instead of white and a skull instead of the stars.[25]

Some of the powerful arguments against the colonial project reflected long-standing notions of racism and paternalism. They emphasized the perceived negative impact of tropical climate on the human condition and judged the entire justification of colonization as civilizational uplift to be nonsensical. Others stressed that the negative record of the United States in dealing with its

AMERICA'S SUPREMACY was signalled to the world in a series of great exhibitions, including the Saint Louis Exposition of 1904 marking the centenary of the Louisiana Purchase.

indigenous population as well as the enduring legacies of slavery hardly qualified the nation to provide for the educational improvement of colonized races. Most importantly, the anti-imperialist critique emphasized the fundamentally contradictory nature of an imperial republic.

The proponents of empire welcomed the colonial project as the nation's entrance ticket into the exclusive club of imperial powers. At the core was the conviction that the social efficiency of the Anglo-Saxon race was triumphant over all other races and that its two leading branches should co-operate for their mutual benefit.[26]

This set of ideas brought the USA and Great Britain into close comradeship.[27] Faced with the task of becoming a colonial state, Americans borrowed from the British experience on a wide range of issues from colonial administration and colonial urban planning to colonial medicine. At the same time they also re-examined their own national history for guidance. The inherent assumption in this process was, of course, that the colonial project was not an aberration but a logical progression from continental to overseas empire.[28]

So it followed that the construction of the insular empire could easily be built on accepted traditions, myths and practices which had characterized westward expansion as a formative factor in the rise of an exceptional nation. The cultural definition of the West entailed a strong dosage of racism and Social Darwinism as part of the frontier myth that permeated nineteenth-century American society. It was a myth that found its expression in a wide range of cultural artefacts ranging from dime novels and the artistic decoration of the US Capitol to ethnographic displays and Wild West re-enactments.[29]

The creation of overseas empire prompted an equally impressive outpouring of travelogues, poems and novels which not only introduced Americans to the conditions in the new possessions but integrated them into a conceptual framework to celebrate a national tradition of expansion. The World's Fairs and their suggestion of a 'symbolic universe' created the most attractive platform for imperial propaganda. Between 1853 and 1916 Americans hosted nineteen exhibitions with international participation of which five were major World's Fairs. In total those exhibits attracted about 100 million visitors and widely shaped the worldviews of contemporary Americans.[30]

The 1904 Louisiana Purchase Exposition at St Louis was the largest World's Fair ever held and the most impressive exhibit of American imperial mentalities. In particular the exposition's ethnographic displays of the 'exotic colonized' outlined America's overlapping imperial projects for a mass audience, provided imperial self-assurance and offered a synthesis of the driving forces, aspirations and manifestations of American history from its founding to the early twentieth century.

DOLLARS, MOVIES AND MARINES: AMERICA'S STRUGGLE FOR GLOBAL HEGEMONY (1914–45)

'The film is to America what the flag was once to Britain. By its means Uncle Sam may hope some day, if he be not checked in time, to Americanize the world.'
Morning Post (London), 1923[31]

'Once we cease to distract ourselves with lifeless arguments about isolationism, we shall be amazed to discover that there is already an immense American internationalism. American jazz, Hollywood movies, American slang, American machines and patented products, are in fact the only things that every community in the world, from Zanzibar to Hamburg, recognizes in common. Blindly, unintentionally, accidentally and really in spite of ourselves, we are already a world power in the all the trivial ways – in very human ways.'
Henry R. Luce, 'The American Century', 1941[32]

Any effort to come to terms with American power in the first half of the twentieth century is confronted with simultaneous and sometimes overlapping manifestations of influences of various kinds, such as the side-by-side existence of an American colonial empire in the Caribbean and the Pacific, an informal empire in Latin America and an emerging hegemonic status in Europe and Asia. Inspired by an irresistible vision of a stable international order conducive to American goals, the United States emerged as a power with global reach in the fields of commerce, communication, and cultural exports, but assumed a limited role in the construction and sustenance of durable international security. Only after the Second World War would America combine its strengths to uphold a network of institutional internationalism and security alliances, designed to forcefully transform the whole system along liberal-democratic lines.[33]

The conceptual basis for the rise of the United States to global hegemony was a combination of long-standing idealizing traditions of American exceptionalism, missionary ideology and commercial internationalism. But no set of ideas proved more enduring and powerful than the policy of liberal-democratic internationalism articulated by President Woodrow Wilson in the wake of the First World War.[34] At its core was the conviction that the peaceful interaction of democratic states, interdependent through free trade and a collective security system, would ensure international stability and security for the United States. American policy aimed at replacing the atavistic European balance of power system with what Joseph Nye has described as 'soft power'.[35]

Consequently, the United States assumed an increasingly ambivalent position towards the benefits of empire. Whereas Theodore Roosevelt's administration and the progressive imperialists had been optimistic about the ordering and civilizing influence of colonial empires, Wilsonianists diagnosed them as inherently destructive. This climatic change, however, did not necessarily translate into the dissolution of America's colonial empire or an end to the nation's often heavy-handed approach to informal empire in Latin America.

During the interwar years, the United States increased local participation in some colonial possessions and tightened control in others. By 1939, America's colonial empire encompassed more than 323,750 sq km (125,000 sq miles) with a total population of more than 15 million colonized subjects. Although Hawaii was an incorporated territory with citizenship extended to the population, it remained politically and economically in a state of colonial dependency. With regard to the Philippines, the United States repeatedly declared (i.e. in the Jones Act of 1916) that its colonial regime was only a temporary preparation for Filipino self-government. The Philippine Independence Act of 1934 (the Tydings-McDuffy Act) created a commonwealth status for the islands and projected independence by 1945. In Puerto Rico, which had the status of a territory, 'organized but not incorporated', inhabitants were granted US citizenship in 1917, and suffrage was extended in 1929. Throughout the 1930s, however, American colonial rule tightened in response to numerous strikes and an emergent independence movement on the island. In Guam and Samoa the US Navy continued colonial rule without local participation.

In Latin America the United States followed the established pattern of informal empire and regularly utilized the huge power differential between the USA and its southern neighbours to secure political control and advance

HENRY FORD'S INVENTION of the assembly line gave America the lead in the industrial production of automobiles. His 'Model T' was exported all over the world: shown here, finished cars ready for delivery, 1925.

economic and cultural penetration. Washington frequently intervened to restore order, protect investments or collect debts, following Theodore Roosevelt's 1904 rationale for informal empire: 'All that we desire is to see all neighboring countries stable, orderly, and prosperous. Any country whose people conduct themselves well can count upon our hearty friendliness... if it keeps order and pays its obligations, then it need fear no interference from the United States. Brutal wrongdoing, or an impotence which results in a general loosening of the ties of civilized society, may finally require intervention by some civilized nation, and... the United States cannot ignore this duty.'[36]

'Gunboat diplomacy' thus became an instrument of policing the 'American Mediterranean' and interventions targeted nations such as Mexico, Cuba, the Dominican Republic and Haiti. American Marines became a common sight in many nations of the Caribbean basin. In several cases, the short-term application of naval force turned into long-term military occupations, as in Haiti (1915–43) and Nicaragua (1912–33).[37]

By the mid-1930s, in response to increasing criticisms at home and abroad, accompanied by an infatuation with Latin American culture, as well as stiff commercial competition from the authoritarian power of Germany, the United States embarked on a new approach described as 'Good Neighbour Policy'. This tactical shift emphasized the co-operative spirit of Pan-Americanism and slowly replaced Washington's aggressive posture with more subtle methods of winning Latin American allegiance.

In the global arena, American power was the result first and foremost of the nation's dominant economic position. Although institutional internationalism and in particular membership of the League of Nations did not materialize as an option for the United States in the interwar years, liberal-democratic internationalism permeated all aspects of American foreign relations. Commercial internationalism became a core component of the conceptualization of America's relations with the world.

The dynamic of the American economy had surprised (and often scared) Europeans already before the war, as 'a lean and ambitious Uncle Sam challenged a rotund John Bull for titular leadership of the world economy' and surpassed Britain as the leading industrial power.[38] At the same time, however, the British still enjoyed a number of advantages over the United States, in particular control over international monetary policies and communication and transportation networks, which sustained the empire's claim to global economic primacy.

But the First World War fundamentally altered this power configuration. The United States became the world's greatest financial and creditor nation and supplanted Britain as the principal proponent of globalization. Throughout the war Washington had provided Britain with large quantities of foodstuffs, ammunition and weapons in part financed through American loans, which by 1917 reached $2.3 billion. The dependency of the economies of Britain and France on American goods and money set a pattern for the 1920s. Before the end of the decade international debts to the American public and private sector had risen to $20 billion.

The weakness of the Old World and the strength of America catapulted the United States to centre stage in the world economy. Washington pressed for open access to international trade, negotiated debt settlements, laid the foundations for international trade institutions and intensified its trade relations with every corner of the globe. On the eve of the stock market crash of 1929, the United States was the main engine of the global economy, accounting for two-fifths of its industrial production and 16 per cent of its commerce.[39]

Of equal importance and driven by America's rise to economic primacy was the nation's effort to secure 'an extensive communication empire'.[40] A strong government interest in securing a global information highway and ample business opportunity propelled the country from a marginal to a dominant international communication position within less than two decades after 1914.

Before the First World War, Great Britain was the undisputed leader in global communications. Close to 160,000 km (99,420 miles) of cables crossed the world's oceans and linked the imperial centre to India, Australia, Africa and Canada. An increase in America's share thus implied breaking the British monopoly on oceanic cable systems. Just as economic stability depended on open doors, Americans were convinced of the fundamental importance of communication power in international relations.

A practical outcome of this belief in the power of world opinion was the creation of the Committee on Public Information (CPI) under the leadership of journalist George Creel during the First World War. The CPI served as America's first government propaganda agency and conducted a massive campaign at home and abroad, creating the foundations for a global state-private network of information co-operation which would become the hallmark of America's leadership in the field of international communication.[41]

After Americans had broken the monopoly in cable networks as early as 1920, US corporations soon set out to link the Western hemisphere, the Caribbean and the outlying territories in the Pacific. But the United States went beyond a mere replacement of Great Britain in the field of cable communication: it promoted a new network with the technology of wireless or radio communication. Aided by extensive government support, the RCA Company quickly extended the emerging radio empire and by the 1930s American broadcasters reached steadily further into Latin America and developed markets in Africa and along the Pacific Rim.

Another dimension of 'soft power' was a massive increase in the export of popular culture. Cultural attractiveness paired with a prospering export

THE MILITARY MIGHT of America was decisive in both world wars. As the representatives of Japan were concluding the ceremony of surrender in September 1945 a dense formation of fighter planes flew over them – a somewhat unsubtle reminder of who had won.

economy had already before 1914 resulted in a widespread European awareness of both the benefits and the dark side of 'Americanization'. During the war, the CPI had ensured a worldwide communication offensive that utilized American products and cultural icons to sustain the Allied war spirit and American visions of a peaceful post-war international order. 'American books, movies, and press dispatches by 1920 were becoming as familiar around the world as Gillette razors and Heinz ketchup.'[42]

The wartime activities of the Creel Committee in particular fostered the rise of Hollywood and its quest for the global entertainment empire in the interwar years. Commercial power and cultural export went hand in hand, as by the end of the 1920s Kodak manufactured 75 per cent of all film worldwide, ITT monopolized the production of sound equipment and American companies owned over half of the world's leading movie houses.

In response to American insistence that cultural exports as much as trade fostered a peaceful international order, one French critic remarked that Americans assumed that 'the only way to assure peace is to Americanize the thoughts, the language, and the soul of foreigners'.[43] In 1923 a London newspaper followed a similar argument and warned of the enduring imaginative power of a virtual America, insisting that 'if the United States abolished its diplomatic and consular services, kept its ships in harbour and its tourists at home, and retired from the world's markets, its citizens, its problems, its towns and countryside, its roads, motor cars, counting houses and saloons would still be familiar in the uttermost corners of the world… The film is to America what the flag was once to Britain. By its means Uncle Sam may hope some day, if he be not checked in time, to Americanize the world.'[44]

NAGASAKI, AUGUST 1945: the explosion of the second atomic bomb, which ended the Second World War. For a while the USA was the only possessor of the bomb, the ultimate proof of world power.

And the journalist Edward G. Lowry commented in 1925: 'The sun, it now appears, never sets on the British empire and the American motion picture.'[45]

As new authoritarian power contenders rose to the fore in Europe and Asia, the United States was faced with the dire prospect of losing what its core foreign policy values deemed essential to a stable international order: a global system of free-flowing trade, communication and cultural exchange. As Henry Luce's recognition of American influence made clear, the United States had used the interwar period to increase its power position, but neither its stabilization policies, nor its disarmament policies nor its mediation efforts could eliminate regional challengers.

The United States intervened for a second time within a generation after the Japanese attack on Pearl Harbor in 1941. Unlike after the First World War, victory in 1945 completed the power shift from the *Pax Britannica* to global America. The United States was now determined to apply economic, military, political and cultural power in a framework of institutional internationalism to secure a worldwide liberal-democratic internationalist order.

FROM PARTIAL GLOBAL HEGEMONY TO 'EMPIRE *LIGHT*' (1945–2006)

'The ravaged old President, even as he was dying, continued the high business of reassembling the fragments of broken empires into a new pattern with himself at center, proud creator of the new imperium… The United States was master of the earth. No England, no France, no Germany, no Japan left to dispute the Republic's will. Only the mysterious Soviet would survive to act as other balance in the scale of power.'
Gore Vidal, 1967[46]

'Like a kaleidoscope, the pattern of world affairs shift with each spin of the world… In our era, moreover, neither the adversaries, nor the rules, nor even the location of the playing field are fully fixed… The challenges we face, compared to those confronted by previous generations are harder to categorize, more diverse, and quicker to change.'
Madeleine K. Albright, 1998[47]

In 1945, the United States enjoyed a moment of unsurpassed military and economic primacy. Germany and Japan were defeated, China engaged in civil war, and Britain and France reduced to secondary powers. More than seven million American soldiers were stationed overseas, the US Air Force controlled the world's air spaces, and America enjoyed a nuclear monopoly while its fleet of 1,200 major warships patrolled the oceans. In economic terms, the United States was the only great power to profit from the war while the Allies had exhausted their national economies. Washington controlled two-thirds of the world's gold reserves, produced 60 per cent of all industrial goods and was the globe's largest export nation. Finally, the United States was not only equipped with the means but also with the will to restructure the international system along the liberal-democratic-internationalist lines of its one-world vision.

And yet America's global visions were once again challenged, this time by Gore Vidal's 'mysterious Soviet'. The confrontation between two nations with mutually exclusive claims to universal leadership had simmered ever since America's military intervention in the Russian civil war after 1918 and had been submerged only temporarily by the wartime alliance.

At the core of America's Cold War foreign and security policy was the containment of the USSR through integration of the non-Communist world into an American-led system.[48] The blueprint for this strategy was the highly influential National Security Council paper NSC-68. In the binary logic of the East-West confrontation, the paper enshrined a sort of Manichean worldview of Good against Evil and emphasized the fundamental nature of the conflict. It was a challenge not only to American core values but to global civilization: 'The issues that face us are momentous, involving the fulfillment or destruction not only of this Republic but of civilization itself.'[49] Consequently NSC-68 enlarged the geostrategic boundaries of American engagement to encompass the entire globe: 'the assault on free institutions is worldwide now, and in the context of the present polarization of power a defeat of free institutions anywhere is a defeat everywhere.'[50] It also emphasized that while America's universal aspirations were considered congruent with those of other peoples, the United States could not contain the USSR without the help of allies: 'Strength at the center, in the United States, is only the first of two essential elements. The second is that our allies and potential allies do not as a result of a sense of frustration or of Soviet intimidation drift into a course of neutrality eventually leading to Soviet domination.'[51]

The United States did in fact realize those policy prescriptions, determined the contours of a capitalist international order, revived the economies of western Europe, spearheaded the democratization and the reintegration of Germany and Japan into the international system, created a global network of security alliances (such as NATO) and established a string of military bases around the world. As credibility was of central importance to American strategies, commitments mushroomed and the United States was soon engaged in even the remotest corners of the earth.

In western Europe, American policy naturally emphasized conviction rather than coercion. The United States, unlike other great powers in history, encouraged the creation of a potentially alternative power centre with its support for European integration, designed to contain the Soviet Union and prevent a resurgence of German expansionism. In the words of Jean Monnet: 'this was the first time in history that a great power, instead of basing its policy on ruling by dividing, has consistently and resolutely backed the creation of a larger Community uniting peoples previously apart.'[52] Despite frequent difficulties and disappointments in transatlantic relations (i.e. failure of the European Defence Community or France's retreat from NATO), America's hegemonic role in this process was welcomed by most Europeans, even if Washington envisioned an integrated Europe not as a 'third force' but a central component of a North Atlantic community of civilizations under American leadership. The Norwegian historian Geir Lundestad has described this process as 'empire by integration'.[53]

America's consistently strong anti-imperial and anti-colonial posture frequently influenced her judgment of other nations. But two factors contradicted her rhetorical support for decolonization: the continued existence of a quasi-colonial American empire in the Pacific and the Caribbean, and Washington's often ambivalent position vis-à-vis the decolonization efforts of its western European allies.[54] The fear of instability and the simultaneous interest in containment of the Soviet Union resulted in a limited US commitment to decolonization and the creation of an American empire in the developing world. In the eyes of American policymakers, colonialism became useful for controlling disorder.

As the European powers were no longer able to uphold their colonial rule, the United States frequently intervened to control or delay the process of decolonization, most prominently in Vietnam. It supported authoritarian regimes and covert and overt interventions became an important component of American policies in Asia, the Middle East and Latin America. Nationalist, neutralist or socialist regimes, or governments perceived as such, as well as public sentiment, became a target for clandestine intervention from the early 1950s until the end of the Cold War. This approach was on occasion applied to the industrial core of western Europe and northeast Asia as well, but took on an unparalleled intensity in the developing world. Covert operations were used to influence elections, change governments or secure a generally positive climate towards American hegemony.[55] American intervention in Vietnam for some ten years, from 1963 to 1973, was seen by many as another instance of American 'neo-imperialism'. The expenditure of almost $170 billion, and the deaths of 58,000 American soldiers in an unsuccessful attempt to prevent the unification of North and South Vietnam under a Marxist government – a further attempt to 'contain' Communism in Asia – provoked enormous protest both at home and overseas.

This arrogance of power produced results in the short run as such interventions reorganized nations and governments along American strategic parameters. In the long run, however, such actions provoked sustained international criticisms of Washington's heavy-handed quest for an integrated world community and undermined the nation's credibility in many parts of the southern hemisphere. In the industrial core, Americans were faced with a related but somewhat different dilemma: alliance management.

In contrast to the Soviets, who used force and intimidation to align their satellites with Moscow's foreign policy goals and reacted violently to any expression of discontent within their sphere of influence (i.e. East Germany in 1953, Hungary in 1956, Czechoslovakia in 1968), the United States emphasized the voluntary character of its alliance system. Washington's support for democratization (e.g. in Germany) and national self-determination provided ideological guidance but also created a dilemma: how could America lead a complicated system of alliances and client states, contain Soviet expansionism and ensure that other nations would comply with its wishes, and at the same time remain true to its core ideological convictions?

The United States chose a multi-layered approach which combined institutional internationalism and economic encouragement with the projection of America's cultural and ideological attractiveness. This aspect of American power and influence in the Cold War relied on the nation's leadership in international communication and the worldwide appeal of its popular culture. For more than four decades it provided the glue that helped to shore up and sustain an American-led system against the Soviet Union.

Cultural diplomacy and propaganda played important roles in the East-West confrontation, since the Cold War was in many respects a global competition for the hearts and minds of people everywhere. Through cultural export and propaganda, both sides attempted to isolate the respective opponent internationally, win the approval of world opinion and consolidate hegemonic order. Every opportunity from art exhibits to international sports events, and every medium from radio to satellite and computer technology was used in this symbolic confrontation between East and West.[56] For American policymakers, communication power and cultural exports served a dual purpose: they isolated Moscow internationally and simultaneously strengthened the morale, co-operation and sense of unified purpose of the non-Communist nations.

This 'Marshall Plan of Ideas' relied on close private-public co-operation, including extensive support for cover organizations such as the Congress for Cultural Freedom, and utilized a wide variety of media outlets to project the core ideas of America's Cold War strategy. Overseas libraries, exhibitions, concerts and ballets, magazines and newspapers, educational exchange and visitor programmes and support for the emerging discipline of American studies were all designed to achieve integration of the non-Communist world into the American system, to channel nationalism and neutralism in Europe and Asia into a desire for co-operation with the United States, and to neutralize the effects of similar Soviet offensives. The attractiveness of American entertainment, in particular film and music, coupled with the mass appeal of an 'American way of life', characterized by abundance and modernity, met a largely enthusiastic reception even behind the 'Iron Curtain'.

And yet there was also criticism of American cultural exports. After the 1960s, the global spread of the icons of the 'American Way of Life' was interpreted by critics as cultural imperialism. In industrialized and developing countries governments and critics feared, as they had in the interwar years, for

'SOMETHING FOR EVERYBODY': during and after the Second World War, the USA could afford to distribute charity to beleaguered Europe. Here, a box of groceries is opened by a family in England.

the future of their film industries and criticized the overpowering position of the United States with regard to access and control of international communication systems. In addition, the fear of losing identity once confronted with the power of 'McDonaldization' and 'Coca-Colonization' challenged the overall enthusiastic responses to American pop culture.

After the collapse of the Soviet Union the United States remained as the single most powerful nation. Unlike the post-war situation, no serious challenger to America's position was in sight. Although celebrated by some as the final victory of liberal-democratic-capitalist internationalism, in short 'the end of history', disorientation about a world without a visible containment of and challenge to American influence was widespread.[57] Dean Acheson's 1962 verdict that Britain had lost an empire and not yet found her role could also be applied to American relations with the world throughout the first post-cold war decade.[58] In the absence of a clear vision, all three administrations have to varying degrees continued the process of integration (for example, NAFTA) and have been concerned with securing America's dominant international position.

Their efforts have systematically widened the power gap between the United States and the rest of the world. Since the second half of the 1990s, the United States has steadily increased its defence budgets, a process that accelerated after the terrorist attacks of 11 September 2001. Today America spends more on defence than the next-largest fifteen to twenty of the world's nations combined, by expending only 3.5 per cent of its GDP. The country has overwhelming

THE ONLY CHALLENGE to US hegemony after the war came from Russia, which also possessed the bomb. Meetings between world leaders desperate for an entente sometimes solved problems and sometimes made them worse. Here US vice-president Richard Nixon pokes at the chest of Soviet premier Nikita Khrushchev in Moscow, July 1959.

nuclear superiority, the most powerful naval and air forces (including the unique ability to airlift troops and equipment to any part of the world), and large and highly trained ground forces. On military research and development alone, the United States expends more resources than the defence budgets of Germany and Great Britain combined.[59]

In addition, the United States also enjoys global economic power and holds a strong information advantage. After almost a decade of continuous growth since the end of the Cold War, America's economic dominance today 'surpasses that of any great power in modern history'.[60] The US economy is twice as large as that of Japan, its closest rival; California alone ranks as the fifth largest economy in the world. The United States produces 22 per cent of the global GNP, and 15 per cent of the worldwide trade. The dollar is as influential as ever, the global economy highly integrated, decisions by the Federal Reserve Bank and developments on Wall Street (the world's leading stock exchange) have global relevance. The country also holds the largest number of patents, hosts the highest number of Nobel laureates and provides 40 per cent of all internet use.[61]

The three post-cold war administrations have all contributed to the further extension of American power but wielded the nation's might in different ways.[62] The administration of George H.W. Bush (1989–93) projected American hegemony often within a multilateral framework. It operated through the United Nations to prepare for the liberation of Kuwait and containment of Iraq. Washington could have fought the Gulf War alone but preferred the creation of an impressive alliance. In Panama, however, America's military intervention resembled long-standing behavioural patterns of informal empire.

The administration of Bill Clinton (1993–2001) initially subscribed to a form of 'assertive multilateralism' but proved no less willing to increase the already considerable power gap between the United States and the rest of the world. The Clinton administration continued its predecessor's struggle for the North American Free Trade Area (NAFTA) and placed great emphasis on aligning American power with the demands of a rapidly integrating world. Clinton and his advisers were infatuated with the stabilizing impact of commercial interdependence, or as Thomas Friedman enthusiastically proclaimed: 'No two countries that both have a McDonald's have ever fought as war against each other'.[63] US foreign relations thus placed greater emphasis on an economically grounded definition of national security and international stability. Its strategy acted multi- or unilaterally to strengthen market democracies, to foster the spread of democratization and market economies, and to counter the aggression of so-called 'backlash states' (Libya, North Korea, Iran, Iraq and Cuba) as well as terror organizations, extreme nationalists and organized crime.

In contrast to the first two post-Cold War administrations, the current White House under President George W. Bush (inaugurated in 2001) has little to no interest in framing American hegemony in a multilateral framework. In fields ranging from environmental diplomacy to the International Court of Justice, the Bush administration followed a path of unilateralism. While the current government continues a tradition of military planning based on the containment of worldwide challenges to America's leadership, its willingness to apply military force is by far less restrained than that of previous administrations. The terrorist attacks of 11 September 2001 have refocused and accelerated this trend. Its clearest conceptual exposition with a pronounced claim to unrivalled global leadership was the National Security Strategy of the United States (NSS) released on 20 September 2002.[64]

The Bush administration's foreign policy blueprint emphasized Washington's desire to continue the quest for global democratization and foster the stabilization of the international system through intensified trade and commerce. Most importantly, NSS emphasized America's claim to pre-emptive strikes, preferably within a multilateral framework, but when deemed necessary also carried out alone: 'we will not hesitate to act alone, if necessary, to exercise our

DID SPREADING the 'American way of life' count as 'cultural imperialism'? Many outsiders thought so. McDonald's invented a witty way of marketing its burgers on Lenin's 124th birthday in 1994.

right of self-defense by acting preemptively against such terrorists, to prevent them from doing harm against our people and our country.'[65]

During the cold war, the containment doctrine had provided the symbolic integration of an American-led system of hegemonic relationships and justified informal empire. In the post-11 September world, the Bush administration expected that the 'war on terror' would prove equally integrative. This assumption has so far turned out to be misguided. Washington underestimated the interests, positions, and worldviews of alternative power centres, as illustrated by the rift in transatlantic relations over the Iraq War. Preponderant power neither automatically equated empire nor did it enable Washington to convince a number of allies to follow its militarized foreign policy objectives.

EPILOGUE: 'EMPIRE AS A WAY OF LIFE'?

'The Empires of the Future are the Empires of the Mind.'
Winston Churchill, at Harvard University, 1943[66]

'Empire became so intrinsically our American way of life that we rationalized and suppressed the nature of our means in the euphoria of our enjoyments of the ends.'

William Appleman Williams, 1980[67]

Throughout the last three centuries the American record on empire has been highly ambivalent. It has been characterized by the nation's shifting shape of power, its close and multiple connections to processes of globalization, and its global ideational appeal.

Since its founding days America has been equipped with a powerful anti-imperial rhetoric and yet that same rhetoric fused the concept of a Jeffersonian

WHEN SADDAM HUSSEIN invaded Kuwait in 1990, the USA immediately intervened to protect her oil interests. The American forces triumphed, though Iraq tried to destroy the oil wells by setting them on fire.

'empire of liberty' with racially charged notions of Manifest Destiny and provided a universalist framework whose application to nation-building in many parts of the world was nothing less than imperial. The United States extended control to varying degrees, configurations and often overlapping spatial manifestations, whether as transcontinental empire, colonial empire, informal empire, 'empire by invitation' or global hegemon.

Like other modern empires, America legitimized expansion in universalist terms. But no other empire decoupled its claim to rule from spatial demarcations in as consequent a manner as the United States. To be sure, geostrategic and geopolitical considerations have always played their part but America's position as both Atlantic and Pacific power, its moving frontier and the explicit claim to global applicability of the American experience are evidence that territorial considerations were seen as only intermediate manifestations. In the long term a mental predisposition towards the universal, culturally even the inter-planetary projection of republican empire was constant. From the early twentieth century on, America has been less concerned with control over space than over the arteries of modernity such as trade, transportation, communication and cultural exchange. The internet is only the latest manifestation of this trend by which the United States uniquely positioned itself to prosper from and simultaneously limit potentially harmful side effects of globalization.

Finally, the outside world's imagination and idea of America have been powerful factors that preceded and anticipated the actual global reach of the United States. At least since the late nineteenth century Americans have utilized this mental predisposition in combination with its ever-increasing power base to project visions of America into the epicentre of global discourses. This has, does and is likely also in the future to continue to produce admiration, adaptation, emulation, rejection and hatred. Any effort to counterbalance or even contain the spread of the imaginary appeal of America has so far failed. In response to the terrorist attacks on the United States on 11 September 2001, many abroad responded with a manifestation of solidarity nicely captured by the slogan 'We are all Americans now'. America as image and idea might well be an indication of the most successful empire of all. Protest against, as well as admiration for, it defines itself through America itself. Winston Churchill after all was correct when in 1943 he described the empires of the future as 'Empires of the Mind'.

THE BITTER BLOW of September 11th 2001 has had a traumatic impact on American consciousness, producing a climate of insecurity for which there was little precedent in the past. For the first time since Pearl Harbor the country felt under attack and responded with the assertion and projections of preponderant military might. In many American deliberations on national security and international stability, the idea of empire has assumed a positive/*defensive* meaning, a tendency which has alienated many nations hitherto sympathetic to the current foreign and security policies of the Bush administration.

Notes and Bibliographies

Introduction

1 The literature on colonial history is vast; the chapters here provide key bibliographical references, so in this introduction only a very few specific sources are cited.

2 See Barbara Goff (ed.), *Classics and Colonialism* (London, 2005).

3 John Hobson, *Imperialism: A Study* (London, 1902); for recent reassessments, see John Pheby (ed.), *J.A. Hobson after Fifty Years: Freethinker of the Social Sciences* (London, 1994).

4 Edward Said, *Orientalism* (London, 1978), followed by *Culture and Imperialism* (London, 1993); John M. MacKenzie, *Orientalism: History, Theory and the Arts* (Manchester, 1995) provides a critique.

5 Kwame Nkrumah, *Neo-Colonialism, the Last Stage of Imperialism* (London, 1965); Michael Hechter, *Internal Colonialism: The Celtic Fringe in British National Development, 1536–1966* (London, 1975).

6 Angela Woollacott, *Gender and Empire* (London, 2006) and Philippa Levine (ed.), *Gender and Empire* (Oxford, 2004).

7 See e.g. Richard H. Grove, *Green Imperialism: Colonial Expansion, Tropical Island Edens and the Origins of Environmentalism, 1600–1860* (Cambridge, 1995); Tom Griffiths and Libby Robin (eds), *Ecology and Empire: Environmental History of Settler Societies* (Melbourne, 1997); Tim Bonyhady, *The Colonial Earth* (Melbourne, 2000).

8 Gérald-George Lemaires, *The Orient in Western Art* (Cologne, 2001) is an overview; on the French example, Darcy Grimaldo Grisby, *Extremities: Painting Empire in Post-Revolutionary France* (New Haven, 2002) and Roger Benjamin, *Orientalist Aesthetics: Art, Colonialism and French North Africa* (Berkeley, 2003) are recent studies.

9 Alison Bashford, *Imperial Hygiene: A Critical History of Colonialism, Nationalism and Public Hygiene* (London, 2004).

10 See, notably, Catherine Hall, *Civilizing Subjects: Metropole and Colony in the English Imagination, 1830–1917* (London, 2002). Cf. Herman Lebovics, *Bringing the Empire Back Home: France in the Global Age* (Durham, NC, 2004).

11 Roy Moxhan, *The Great Hedge of India: The Search for the Living Barrier That Divided a People* (London, 2002); Charles Corn, *The Scents of Eden: A History of the Spice Trade* (London, 1999).

12 Claudio G. Segrè, *Fourth Shore: The Italian Colonization of Libya* (Chicago, 1974).

13 Petrine Archer Straw, *Negrophilia: Avant-Garde Paris and Black Culture in the 1920s* (New York, 2000).

14 Robert Aldrich and John Connell, *The Last Colonies* (Cambridge, 1998).

15 Jean-Claude Guillebaud, *Les Confettis de l'empire* (Paris, 1976).

16 William Roger Louis and Ronald Robinson, 'The Imperialism of Decolonization', *Journal of Imperial and Commonwealth History*, Vol. 22, No. 3 (1994), pp. 462–511, and Bernard Porter, *Empire and Superempire: Britain, America and the World* (New Haven, Conn., 2006).

17 James Walvin, *Fruits of Empire: Exotic Produce and British Taste, 1660–1800* (London, 1997).

18 Dawn Jacobson, *Chinoiserie* (London, 1993).

19 Dominique Taffin (ed.), *Du Musée colonial au musée des cultures du monde* (Paris, 2000).

20 Nadine Beauthéac and François-Xavier Bouchart, *L'Europe exotique* (Paris, 1985).

21 Robert Aldrich, *Vestiges of the Overseas Empire in France: Monuments, Museums and Colonial Memories* (London, 2005); Ulrich van der Heyden and Joachim Zeller, *Kolonialmetropole Berlin: Eine Spurensuche* (Berlin, 2002); Evald Vanvugt, *De maagd en de soldaat: Koloniale monumenten in Amsterdam en elders* (Amsterdam, 1998).

Chapter 1 The Ottoman Empire

BIBLIOGRAPHY

On Central Asia and Turkoman peoples:

David Christian, *A History of Russia, Central Asia and Mongolia*, Vol. 1, *Inner Eurasia from Prehistory to the Mongol Empire* (Oxford, 1998).

Carter Vaugh Findley, *The Turks in World History* (New York, 2004).

On the early Ottomans:

Claude Cahen, *The Formation of Turkey: History of the Near East* (London, 2001).

Cemal Kafadar, *Between Two Worlds: The Construction of the Ottoman State* (Berkeley, 1995).

Rudi Paul Lindner, *Nomads and Ottomans in Medieval Anatolia* (Bloomington, 1983).

Heath Lowry, *The Nature of the Early Ottoman State* (New York, 2003).

The classical empire:

Suraiya Faroqhi, *Subjects of the Sultan: Culture and Daily Life in the Ottoman Empire* (London, 2000).

Daniel Goffman, *The Ottoman Empire and Early Modern Europe* (Cambridge, 2002).

Colin Imber, *The Ottoman Empire 1300–1650: The Structure of power* (London, 2002).

Halil Inalcik, *The Ottoman Empire: The Classical Age, 1300–1600* (London, 1973).

Halil Inalcik with Donald Quataert (eds), *An Economic and Social History of the Ottoman Empire, 1300–1914* (Cambridge, 1994).

Karen Barkey, *Bandits and Bureaucrats: The Ottoman Route to State Centralization* (Ithaca, NY, 1997).

Leslie P. Peirce, *The Imperial Harem: Women and Sovereignty in the Ottoman Empire* (New York, 1993).

On the late empire:

Benjamin Braude and Bernard Lewis (eds), *Christians and Jews in the Ottoman Empire: The Central Lands / The Arabic-Speaking Lands* (New York, 1982).

Selim Deringil, *Well-Protected Domains: Ideology and the Legitimation of Power in the Ottoman Empire, 1876–1909* (London, 1999).

Fatma Müge Göçek, *Rise of the Bourgeoisie, Demise of Empire: Ottoman Westernization and Social Change* (New York, 1996).

Donald Quataert, *The Ottoman Empire, 1700–1922*, 2nd edn (Cambridge, 2005).

Kemal H. Karpat, *Ottoman Population, 1830–1914: Demographic and Social Characteristics* (Madison, Wisconsin, 1985).

Ussama Makdisi, *The Culture of Sectarianism: Community, History, and Violence in Nineteenth-Century Ottoman Lebanon* (Berkeley, 2000).

On the end of the empire and Turkey:

Karen Barkey and Mark von Hagen (eds), *After Empire: Multiethnic Societies and Nation-Building* (Boulder, Colorado, 1997).

Donald Bloxham, *The Great Game of Genocide: Imperialism, Nationalism, and the Destruction of the Ottoman Armenians* (Oxford, 2005).

A.L. Macfie, *The End of the Ottoman Empire, 1908–1923* (London, 1998).

Erik J. Zürcher, *Turkey: A Modern History* (London, 2004).

NOTES

1 Quoted in Halil Inalcik, 'The Rise of the Ottoman Empire', in M.A. Cook (ed.), *A History of the Ottoman Empire to 1730* (Cambridge, 1976), pp. 41–42.

2 Quoted in David Christian, p. 87.

3 The main proponent of this line of argument is Cemal Kafadar, *Between Two Worlds*.

4 Andrew Ayton, 'Arms, Armour and Horses', in Maurice Keen, (ed.), *Medieval Warfare: A History* (Oxford, 1999), p. 208.

5 Imber, *The Ottoman Empire*, pp. 269–71.

6 Rhoads Murphey, *Ottoman Warfare 1500–1700* (London, 1999), p. 63.

7 Imber, *The Ottoman Empire*, p. 108.

8 Daniel Goffman, *Ottoman Empire and Early Modern Europe* (Cambridge, 2002), pp. 91–92.

9 Christopher A. Bayly, *The Birth of the Modern World, 1780–1914* (Oxford, 2003), p. 91.

10 Donald Quataert, *The Ottoman Empire, 1700–1922*, 2nd edn (Cambridge, 2005), p. 77.

11 Donald Quataert, 'The Age of Reforms, 1812–1914', in Inalcik and Quataert (eds), *Economic and Social History of the Ottoman Empire*, p. 781.

12 See Palmira Brummett, *Image and Imperialism in the Ottoman Revolutionary Press, 1908–1911* (New York, 2000).

13 Mark Mazower, *Salonica: City of Ghosts* (London, 2004), p. 209.

14 Quoted in Kemal H. Karpat, *The Politicization of Islam: Reconstructing Identity, State, Faith and Community in the Late Ottoman Empire* (New York, 2001). p. 179.

15 Bloxham, p. 50.

16 Quoted in Sükrü Hanioglu, 'Turkish Nationalism and the Young Turks 1889–1908', in Fatma Müge Göçek (ed.), *Social Construction of Nationalism in the Middle East* (New York, 2002), p. 87.

17 Bloxham, *The Great Game of Genocide*.

Chapter 2 Spain

1 J.H. Elliott, *Imperial Spain, 1469–1716* (Harmondsworth, 1963).

2 P. Guichard, *Al-Andalus frente a la conquista cristiana de los musulmanes de Valencia, siglos XI–XIII* (Madrid, 2001).

3 J. Torró, *El naixement d'una colònia. Dominació i resistència a la frontera valenciana* (València, 1999).

4 P. Seed, *Ceremonies of Possession in Europe's Conquest of the New World, 1492–1640* (Cambridge, 1995).

5 J. Gil, *Mitos y utopías del descubrimiento* (Madrid, 1989).

6 B. Yun, *Marte contra Minerva. El precio del Imperio español, c. 1450–1600* (Barcelona, 2004).

7 M. Ollé, *La empresa de China* (Barcelona, 2002).

8 J. Elliott, 'A Europe of Composite Monarchies', *Past and Present*, No. 137 (1992), pp. 48–71.

9 A. Pagden, *The Fall of Natural Man: The American Indian and the Origins of Comparative Ethnology* (Cambridge, 1982).

10 S.J. Stern, *Peru's Indian Peoples and the Challenge of Spanish Conquest. Huamanga to 1640* (Madison, WI, 1982); see also Peter Bakewell, 'La maduración del gobierno del Perú en la década de 1560', *Historia Mexicana*, Vol. 39, No. 1 (1989), pp. 41–70.

11 S. Zavala, *La encomienda indiana* (Mexico City, 1973); see also *El servicio personal de los indios en Nueva España* (Mexico City, 1978).

12 A. Crosby, *The Columbian Exchange: Biological and Cultural Consequences of 1492* (Westport, CT, 1973).

13 W.W. Borah and S.F. Cook, *The Aboriginal Population in Central Mexico on the Eve of Spanish Conquest* (Berkeley, CA, 1963); see also, by the same authors, *Essays in Population History. Mexico and the Caribbean*, 3 vols (Berkeley, CA, 1971); N.D. Cook, *Demographic Collapse. Indian Peru, 1520–1620* (Cambridge, 1981).

14 C. Sempat Assadourian, 'La despoblación indígena de Perú y Nueva España durante el siglo XVI y la formación de la economía colonial', *Historia Mexicana*, Vol. 38, No. 3 (1989), pp. 419–54.

15 P. Bakewell, *Silver Mining and Society in Colonial Mexico Zacatecas, 1546–1700* (Cambridge, 1971); see also *Miners of the Red Mountain. Indian Labor in Potosí, 1545–1650* (Albuquerque, NM, 1984).

16 E.J. Hamilton, *El tesoro americano y la revolución de los precios, 1501–1650* (Barcelona, 1975).

17 J.M. Ots Capdequí, *El Estado español en las Indias* (Mexico City, 1941).

18 F. Moya Pons, *La Española en el siglo XVI. Trabajo, sociedad y política en la economía del oro* (Santiago de los Caballeros, 1973); see also D. Watts, *The West Indies. Patterns: Development, Culture and Environmental Change since 1492* (Cambridge, 1987).

19 H.S. Klein, *African Slavery in Latin America and the Caribbean* (New York, 1986).

20 P. Seed, 'Social Dimensions of Race: Mexico City, 1753', *Hispanic American Historical Review*, Vol. 62, No. 4 (1982), pp. 569–606.

21 W.B. Taylor, *Magistrates of the Sacred: Priests and Parishioners in Eighteenth-Century Mexico* (Stanford, 1996).

22 V. Stolcke, *Marriage, Class and Colour in Nineteenth-Century Cuba. A Study of Racial Attitudes and Sexual Values in a Slave Society* (Cambridge, 1974).

23 J. Lynch, *Spanish Colonial Administration, 1782–1810: The Intendant System in the Viceroyalty of the Río de la Plata* (Westport, CT, 1969 [1958]).

24 The proportions, however, are still largely unknown, as the tariff reforms of 1720, 1765 and 1778 are extraordinarily difficult to assess. See A. García Baquero, *Cádiz y el Atlántico, 1717–1778. El comercio colonial español bajo el monopolio gaditano* (Seville, 1976); J. Fisher, *Commercial Relations between Spain and Spanish America in the Era of Free Trade, 1778–1796* (Liverpool, 1985).

25 S.J. Stein and B.H. Stein, *Silver, Trade and War. Spain and America in the Making of Early Modern Europe* (Baltimore, 2000); by the same authors, *Apogee of Empire. Spain and New Spain in the Age of Charles III, 1759–1789* (Baltimore, 2003).

26 M.A. Burkholder and D.S. Chandler, *From Impotence to Authority: The Spanish Crown and the American Audiencias, 1687–1808* (Columbia, Miss., 1977).

27 The impact of this package of legislative modifications is still subject to debate, although it no longer seems necessary to justify the inevitable interlinking of the economic reforms and the fiscal imperatives that determined their purpose. The most obvious result of these reforms was the increase in the tax-raising capacity of the state – one of the few in the 1790s that had still not entered the spiral of debt experienced by its rivals in the Atlantic. H.S. Klein, *The American Finances of the Spanish Empire: Royal Income and Expenditure in Colonial Mexico, Peru and Bolivia, 1680–1809* (Albuquerque, NM, 1998).

28 S. Thomson, *We Alone Will Rule: Native Andean Politics in the Age of Insurgency* (Madison, WI, 2002); E. Van Young, *The Other Rebellion: Popular Violence, Ideology, and the Struggle for Mexican Independence, 1810–1821* (Stanford, 2001).

29 A.J. Kuethe, *Cuba, 1753–1815: Crown, Military, and Society* (Knoxville, TN, 1986).

30 M. Moreno Fraginals, *El Ingenio. Complejo económico-social cubano del azúcar*, 3 vols (Havana, 1973).

31 J.M. Fradera, *Colonias para después de un imperio* (Barcelona, 2005).

32 R.J. Scott, *Slave Emancipation in Cuba: The Transition to Free Labor, 1860–1899* (Princeton, NJ, 1985).

33 The best book about this phase of shifting imperialisms is C.A. Bayly, *The Birth of the Modern World, 1780–1914* (London, 2004), a contribution to world history that points up the scant attention given to the history of the Iberian empires of the Spanish and Portuguese monarchies in the social sciences.

Chapter 3 Portugal

1 The classic history of the early period is Charles R. Boxer, *The Portuguese Seaborne Empire* (London, 1969). The most recent overview is Malyn Newitt, *A History of Portuguese Overseas Expansion, 1400–1668* (London, 2005). Other stimulating historical introductions are A.J.R. Russell-Wood, *A World on the Move* (Manchester, 1992), and Bailey W. Diffie and Goerge D. Winnius, *Foundations of the Portuguese Empire* (Minneapolis, 1977). The following offer important complementary perspectives: Luis Filipe Thomaz, *De Ceuta a Timor* (Lisbon, 1994); Vitorino Magalhães Godinho, *Os Descobrimentos e a Economia Mundial*, 4 vols, 2nd edn (Lisbon, 1981–83). Jorge Flores, 'Expansão portuguesa, expansões europeias e mundoa não-europeu na época moderna: o estado da questão', in *Ler História*, 50 (2006), pp. 23–43, offers a valuable critical overview and guide to the historiography of Portuguese expansion.

2 The most recent biography is Peter Russell, *Prince Henry 'the Navigator'. A Life* (New Haven and London, 2001).

3 Magalhães Godinho, *Os Descobrimentos e a Economia Mundial*, Vol. IV, p. 157.

4 João de Barros, *Ásia, 1º Década, Livro terceiro*.

5 *Ibid.*

6 Magalhães Godinho, *Os Descobrimentos e a Economia Mundial*, Vol. IV. See also John Vogt, *Portuguese Rule on the Gold Coast* (Athens, GA, 1979).

7 Rui de Pina, *Crónicas de Rui de Pina*, ed. M. Lopes de Almeida (Porto, 1977), cáp. LXVIII.

8 Magalhães Godinho, *Os Descobrimentos e a Economia Mundial*, Vol. IV.

9 On the history of the Congo kingdom, see Anne Hilton, *The Kingdom of Kongo* (Oxford, 1985) and John Thornton, *The Kingdom of Kongo* (Madison, 1983).

10 Paula Ben-Amos, *The Art of Benin* (London, 1980). For the history of Benin, see Alan Ryder, *Benin and the Europeans* (London, 1969).

11 On Vasco da Gama, see, particularly, Sanjay Subrahmanyam, *The Career and Legend of Vasco da Gama* (Cambridge, 1997).

12 See Luís Filipe Thomaz, 'Factions, Interests and Messianism: The Politics of Portuguese Expansion in the East, 1500–1521', *The Indian Economic and Social History Review*, Vol. 28, No. 1 (1991), pp. 97–109.

13 Anonymous (?Álvaro Velho), *Relação da Primeira Viagem à Índia pela Armada Chefiada por Vasco da Gama*, in José Manuel Garcia (ed.), *As Viagens dos Descobrimentos* (Lisbon, 1983), p. 183.

14 *Ibid.*

15 The most important recent study of the Portuguese in Asia in this period is Sanjay Subrahmanyam, *The Portuguese Empire in Asia 1500–1700: A Political and Economic History* (London, 1993), from which this chapter borrows freely.

16 See Charles Boxer, *The Tragic History of the Sea* (London, 1968).

17 Gujerati reactions to the Portuguese are examined in Michael N. Pearson, *Merchants and Rulers in Gujarat. The Response to the Portuguese in the Sixteenth Century* (Berkeley/Los Angeles, 1976). See also *The Portuguese in India* (The New Cambridge History of India, Vol. I, chapter 1), (Cambridge, 1987).

18 Luís Filipe F.R. Thomaz, 'Estrutura política e administrativa do Estado da Índia no século XVI', in Luis de Albuquerque and Inácio Guerreiro (eds), *Actas do II Seminário Internacional de História Indo-Portuguesa* (Lisbon, 1985).

19 John Villiers, 'The Estado da India in Southeast Asia', in M. Newitt (ed.), *The First Portuguese Colonial Empire* (Exeter, 1986), p. 37.

20 Thomaz, 'Estrutura política e administrativa do Estado da Índia no século XVI'. See also Artur Teodoro de Matos, *O Estado da Índia nos anos de 1581–1588, estrutura administrtiva e económica. Alguns elementos para o seu estudo* (Ponta Delgada, 1982).

21 See Villiers, 'The Estado da India in Southeast Asia', p. 37.

22 Subrahmanyam, *The Portuguese Empire in Asia, 1500–1700*, pp. 75–78, 258–61.

23 *Ibid.*, p. 150.

24 See C.R. Boxer, *Portuguese Society in the Tropics: The Municipal Councils of Goa, Macao, Bahia and Luanda 1510–1800* (Madison, 1965), pp. 42–71.

25 For a detailed history of the Jesuits in the Portuguese Empire, see, especially, Dauril Alden, *The Making of an Enterprise: The Society of Jesus in Portugal, its Empire, and Beyond, 1540–1750* (Stanford, 1996).

26 Subrahmanyam, *The Portuguese Empire in Asia*, pp. 102–03, 151. See also Charles R. Boxer, *The Christian Century in Japan, 1549–1650* (Manchester, 1993 [1951]). For the history of later Portuguese trade relations with China, see George B. Souza, *The Survival of Empire. Portuguese Trade and Society in China and the South China Sea 1630–1754* (Cambridge, 1986).

27 Anthony R. Disney, *Twilight of the Pepper Empire: Portuguese Trade in Southwest India in the Early Seventeenth Century* (Cambridge, Mass., 1978), p. 21.

28 See James Lockhart and Stuart B. Schwartz, *Early Latin America: A History of Colonial Spanish America and Brazil* (Cambridge, 1983), p. 202. The present chapter borrows freely from data included in the chapters on Brazil.

29 An important re-evaluation of the historical role of Amerindians in the economic development of Brazil between the sixteenth and eighteenth centuries is John Manuel Monteiro, *Negros da Terra: Índios e Bandeirantes nas Origens de São Paulo* (São Paulo, 1994).

30 David Birmingham, *Trade and Empire in the Atlantic, 1400–1600* (London and New York, 2000), p. 80.

31 He was the grandson of Bartolomeu Dias, who had first made landfall on the Angolan coast on his way to the Cape in 1488.

32 David Birmingham, *Trade and Conflict in Angola* (Oxford, 1966), pp. 46–47.

33 Birmingham, *Trade and Empire in the Atlantic, 1400–1600*, p. 86.

34 Lockhart and Schwartz, *Early Latin America*, pp. 374–79.

35 T.W. Merrick and Douglas H. Graham, *Population and Economic Development in Brazil, 1800 to the Present* (Baltimore, MD, 1979), p. 29.

36 Lockhart and Schwartz, *Early Latin America*, pp. 392–93.

37 *Ibid.*, p. 238.

38 On this, see Charles Boxer, *Race Relations in the Portuguese Empire, 1415–1825* (Oxford, 1963). Stuart B. Schwartz, 'The Formation of Identity in Brazil', in Nicholas Canny and Anthony Pagden (eds), *Colonial Identity in the Atlantic World* (Princeton, 1987), pp. 15–50.

39 Charles R. Boxer, *The Golden Age of Brazil, 1695–1750* (Berkeley and Los Angeles, 1962), p. 324.

40 Carla Rahn Phillips, 'The Growth and Composition of Trade in the Iberian Empires, 1450–1750', in James D. Tracey (ed.), *The Rise of Merchant Empires* (Cambridge, 1990), p. 65.

41 Herbert S. Klein, *The Middle Passage: Comparative Studies of the Atlantic Slave Trade* (Princeton, NJ, 1978), p. 25.

42 On the Portuguese court in Rio, see Patrick Wilcken, *Empire Adrift* (London, 2004). Kirsten Schultz, *Tropical Versailles: Empire, Monarchy, and the Portuguese Royal Court in Rio de Janeiro, 1808–1821* (London, 2001). Jeffrey D. Needell, *A Tropical Belle Époque* (Cambridge, 1987).

43 *Ibid.*, p. 418.

44 An important analysis of the crisis caused by the loss of Brazil is Valentim Alexandre, *Os Sentidos do Império: Questão Nacional e Questão Colonial na crise do Antigo Regime Português* (Lisbon, 1993).

45 Sá da Bandeira, minister for the navy, in a report presented to the Portuguese *Cortes* in February 1836.

46 An important recent study of the politics of Portuguese abolitionism is João Pedro Marques, *The Sounds of Silence: Nineteenth-Century Portugal and the Abolition of the Slave Trade* (Oxford, 2006).

47 See Malyn Newitt, *Portuguese Settlement on the Zambesi*, chapter 15. The campaigns are described in detail in René Pélissier, *Naissance du Mozambique. Résistances et révoltes anticoloniales (1854–1918)*, 2 vols (Orgeval, 1984); and *Les Guerres grises. Résistances et révoltes en Angola, 1845–1941*, 2 vols (Orgeval, 1977).

48 Cited in Jill Dias, 'Angola', in Valentim Alexandre and Jill Dias (eds), *O Império Africano 1825–1890*, p. 435.

49 Details of military campaigns are in Réne Pélissier, *Les Guerres grises* and *Naissance de la Guiné. Portugais et Africains en Sénégambie (1841–1936)* (Orgeval, 1988).

50 António Enes, *A Guerra de África em 1895*, 2nd edn (Porto, 1945 [1898]), p. 166.

51 A detailed account of Ngungunhane's reception in Lisbon appeared in *Diario de Notícias*, 14 March 1896.

52 Cited in Jill Dias, 'Angola', p. 461.

53 Gervase Clarence-Smith, 'Capital Accumulation and Class Formation in Angola', p. 188.

54 *Boletim Geral as Colonias* Ano 9, No. 100 (1933), p. 5.

55 *Estatuto politico, civil e criminal dos indigenas de Angola e Moçambique*.

56 J.M. da Silva Cunha, *O sistema português de política indígena* (Coimbra, 1953), pp. 143–44.

57 James Duffy, *Portuguese Africa* (Cambridge, Mass., 1961), p. 295.

58 Clarence-Smith, 'Capital Accumulation and Class Formation in Angola', p. 192.

59 See John Marcum, *The Angolan Revolution, Vol. I, 1950–1962* (Cambridge, Mass., 1969).

60 'União Popular Angolana/Frente Nacional para a Libertação de Angola'.

61 António de Oliveira Salazar, *Entrevistas: 1960–1966* (Coimbra, 1967), p. 53.

Chapter 4 Netherlands

1 Ena Jansen and Wilfred Jonckheere (eds), *Boer en Brit. Ooggetuigen en schrijvers over de Anglo-Boerenoorlog in Zuid-Afrika* (Amsterdam, 2001).

2 Joris Voorhoeve, *Peace, Profits and Principles: A Study of Dutch Foreign Policy* (Leiden, 1985).

3 Wim van Noort and Rob Wiche, *Nederland als voorbeeldige natie* (Hilversum, 2006).

4 Esther Captain, Marieke Hellevoort and Marian van der Klein (eds), *Vertrouwd en vreemd. Ontmoetingen tussen Nederland, Indië en Indonesië* (Hilversum, 2000), p. 20.

5 Pitou van Dijck, 'Continuity and Change in a Small Open Economy: External Dependency and Policy Inconsistencies', in Rosemarijn Hoefte and Peter Meel (eds), *20th Century Suriname: Continuities and Discontinuities in a New World Society* (Leiden, 2001). p. 48. According to a national census by the Algemeen Bureau voor de Statistiek in Suriname, the population in August 2004 was 492,892. See Algemeen bureau voor de statistiek (censuskantoor), *Zevende algemene volks- en woningtelling in Suriname, landelijke resultaten volume 1, demografische en sociale karakteristieken* (Paramaribo, 2005).

6 Gert Oostindie, *Het paradijs overzee, de 'Nederlands' Caraïben en Nederland* (Amsterdam, 1998), p. 27 ff.

7 J. Van Goor, *De Nederlandse Koloniën. Geschiedenis van de Nederlandse expansie, 1600–1975* (Den Haag, 1994), p. 76.

8 Algemeen Bureau voor de Statistiek (Censuskantoor), *Zevende algemene volks– en woningtelling in Suriname, landelijke resultaten volume 1.*

9 Jan A. Somers, *Nederlandsch-Indië. Staatkundige ontwikkelingen binnen een koloniale relatie* (Zutphen, 2005), p. 101.

10 Van Goor 1994: 177, Somers: 81.

11 Somers 2005: 99 Van Goor 1994: 231.

12 Van Goor 1994: 232.

13 Somers 2005: pp. 114–119, Van Goor 1994: 234.

14 Somers 2005: 101, Amy Wassing, 'Roodkapje in Batik', in *Vertrouwd en vreemd*, p. 95.

15 This form of forced labour was ended in 1870, except in the case of the sugar crop, which was grown compulsorily until 1891. Wassing: 95.

16 *Ibid.*

17 Somers: 14.

18 Dutch imperial policy is discussed in depth by Amy Wassing, 'Roodkapje in batik. Van batik Belanda tot batik Hokokai (1870–1945)', in Esther Captain, etc., *op. cit* Note 4, pp. 87–96; and Elsbeth Locker-Scholten, *op. cit*, pp. 15–21; and by Somers (see Note 14).

19 Rudolf van Lier, *Samenleving in een grensgebied. Een sociaal-historische studie van Suriname* (Deventer, 1971), p. 15.

20 Somers 2005: 98, Oostindie 1998: 29.

21 Guno Jones, 'Het belang van een gedenkteken', *Kleio. Tijdschrift van de vereniging van docenten in geschiedenis en staatsinrichting in Nederland*, vol. 52 (no. 5): 2001, pp. 9–10.

22 E. van Vugt, *Een gedenkteken voor de slavernij*, Vrij Nederland, 1 July 2000, p. 55.

23 For these constitutional moves, see Goor, Van Lier and Jones.

24 Cynthia Mcleod, *Slavernij en de memorie* (Schoorl, 2002), pp. 70–71.

25 Anton de Kom, *Wij slaven van Suriname* (Bussum, 1981).

26 Michael Sharpe, 'Globalization and Migration: Post-Colonial Dutch Antillean and Aruban Immigrant Political Incorporation in the Netherlands', *Dialectical Anthropology*, vol. 29 (nrs. 3–4): 2005, p. 299.

27 K. Groeneboer (ed.), *Koloniale taalpolitiek in Oost en West: Nederlands-Indië, Suriname, Nederlandse Antillen en Aruba* (Amsterdam, 1977); J. van Goor, see Note 7; and Esther Captain, see Note 49.

28 See Van Lier (1971).

29 For the dominance of Europe in culture and religion, see Hans Ramsoedh ('De Nederlandse assimilatiepolitiek in Suriname tussen 1863 en 1945', in Gobardhan-Rambocus, et. al., *De Erfenis van de Slavernij* (Paramaribo, 1995)), Van Lier (see Note 19), Groeneboer (See Note 27), Marshall (see Note 37) and Jones (see Note 38).

30 This created a situation that has been researched extensively by the black psychiatrist Fanon in other Caribbean contexts (Marshall 2003: 27).

31 For the policy of assimilation see Ramsoedh, Van Lier and Marshall.

32 This change in colonial policy is covered by Van Lier, Mcleod, Wekker and Ramsoedh.

33 Van Goor 1994: 365, Oostindie 1998: 28, Somers 2005: 11.

34 Oostindie 1998: 28.

35 Wim Hoogbergen, *De bosnegers zijn gekomen: slavernij en rebellie in Suriname* (Amsterdam, 1992), Frank Dragtenstein, *De ondraaglijke stoutheid der weglopers: marronage en koloniaal beleid in Suriname, 1667–1778* (Utrecht, 2002), Sandew Hira, *Van Priary tot en met De Kom: de geschiedenis van het verzet in Suriname, 1630–1940* (Rotterdam, 1982).

36 See Hira (1982).

37 Edwin Marshall, *Ontstaan en ontwikkeling van het Surinaams Nationalisme. Natievorming als opgave* (Delft, 2003).

38 Johan Jones, *Kwakoe en christus. Een beschouwing over de ontmoeting van de Afro-Amerikaanse cultuur en religie met de Hernhutter zending in Suriname* (Brussels, 1981), Sam Jones, *Met vlag en rimpel: Surinamers over Nederland* (Utrecht, 2004), pp. 40–49.

39 Hein Eersel, 'De Surinaamse taalpolitiek: een historisch overzicht', in Kees Groeneboer (red.), *Koloniale taalpolitiek in Oost en West: Nederlands-Indië, Suriname, Nederlandse Antillen en Aruba* (Amsterdam, 1997), p. 215.

40 Quoted in Fasseur, *Tijdschrift voor geschiedenis* 1992 (2), p. 220.

41 Guus Cleintuar, 'Hoe vreemd mijn Holland was' in: Wim Willems en Leo Lucassen (red.) *Het onbekende vaderland* ('s-Gravenhage 1994).

42 According to McLeod, cohabitation by black men and coloured women was tolerated in the mid-18th century, but they were not approved of by the colonial power. Governors and clergymen regularly expressed their disapproval of these unlawful alliances. Cynthia Mcleod, *Elisabeth Samson, een vrije zwarte vrouw in het 18ᵉ – eeuwse Suriname* (Schoorl, 1996), p. 22.

43 Ann Stoler, *Race and the education of desire. Foucault's history of sexuality and the colonial order of things* (London, 1995), pp. 40–41.

44 Gloria Wekker, 'Of Mimic Men and Unruly Women: Family, Sexuality and Gender in Twentieth-Century Suriname', in *20th Century Suriname: Continuities and Discontinuities in a New World Society*, pp. 181, 195.

45 McLeod 1996: pp. 60–66, 106–114.

46 www.landsarchief.sr/geschiedenis/plantages/cotticarivier/twijfelachtig

47 Both were in competition with the white European upper class and with each other. The Indo-Europeans thought that, because they were legally part of the European and Dutch group, they should have equal status (to white Europeans) in the colonial bureaucracy, whilst the up-and-coming Indonesian group was also demanding a place.

48 Hans Meijer, *In Indië geworteld* (Amsterdam, 2004), pp. 154–171.

49 Esther Captain, *Achter het kawat was Nederland* (Kampen, 2002), pp. 75–96.

50 'I imagine, without anticipating the opinion of the National Conference, that they will focus on a National Alliance of which the Netherlands, Indonesia, Suriname and Curaçao will be part, whilst each of them will look after their own internal affairs independently, relying on their own efforts, but with the will to support each other', in John Schuster, *Poortwachters over immigranten. Het debat over de immigratie in het naoorlogse Groot-Brittannië en Nederland* (Amsterdam, 1999), p. 82.

51 Oostindie 1998: 156–157, Somers 2005: 210.

52 Captain 2002: 123, Meijer 2004: 236. According to Meijer (2004: 236), the Japanese did not officially surrender in the Dutch East Indies until 23 August 1945.

53 Meijer 2004: 237.

54 Captain 2002: 124.

55 *Handelingen Tweede Kamer*, 1949–1950, pp. 799–931.

56 The politicians seemed to regard these groups, which had traditionally always been close to the colonial power and had become dependent on it (for instance by working as civil servants, teachers and soldiers for the KNIL, the Dutch army) as belonging more naturally to Indonesia than to the Netherlands. These minorities loyal to the Dutch authority, who were largely excluded by Indonesian society after independence, were initially not welcomed in the home country. The government at first discouraged the Indo-Europeans from emigrating to the Netherlands. That meant that, although they were Dutch nationals, they were not eligible for the *rijksvoorshot*, the government loan, and so could not actually travel to the Netherlands. Eventually (in 1956), the Dutch Government scrapped that disincentive policy. In all about 300,000 Dutch citizens, including 200,000 Indo-Europeans, came to the Netherlands between 1949 and 1964. The 12,500 Ambonese soldiers (with their families), who had fought for the restoration of the Dutch system and, unlike the Indo-Europeans, had become Indonesian citizens (against their will), were only admitted to the Netherlands after court proceedings. See also Schuster 1998: *Poortwachters over immigranten. Het debat over immigratie in het naoorlogse Groot-Brittannië en Nederland*, pp. 81–116.

57 Tjalie Robinson, 'Wie is Tjalie Robinson?' in: *Moesson*, 15 augustus 1982.

58 Marshall 2003: 57–58, Sharpe 2005: 291, Oostindie 1998: 157.

59 Marshall 2003: 57–58.

60 Apart from that, the signature of the statute did not happen without a struggle. Suriname thought it should provide for the right to secede, to separate politically from the kingdom, whereas initially the Netherlands did not want to go that far. Eventually Suriname agreed to withdraw its demand for the right to secede. Source: TK 1953–1954, 3200, chapter XIII, *Rijksbegroting overzeese rijksdeling over 1954, memorie van antwoord (no 9)*, 9 November 1953, p. 1, Oostindie 1998: 157.

61 Oostindie (1998: 158) says: 'After the Indonesian fiasco a friendly decolonization arranged in joint consultation was worth a great deal. And in the West, unlike the East Indies, there was not a lot to lose from the transfer of power ratified in the statute'.

62 TK 1955–1956, *Rijksbegroting voor 1956, Hoofdstuk XIII, overzeese rijksdeling, voorlopig verslag (no 8)*, p. 1.

63 TK 1955–1956, *Plenaire vergadering op 7 December 1955, Hoofdstuk XIII (4100), vaststelling van de rijksbegroting over 1956*, pp. 438–457.

64 See Marshall, 2003 and Oostindie, 1998.

65 Public justifications quite often came down to the argument that it was 'in the interests of Suriname's development' to prevent a brain drain.

66 Oostindie 1998: 165, Marshall 2003: 193.

Chapter 5 Scandinavia

1 For a general introduction to the political geography of seventeenth-century Scandinavia and to the economic life of the region, see David Kirby, *Northern Europe in the Early Modern Period: The Baltic World 1492–1772* (London, 1990) and John P. Maarbjerg, *Scandinavia in the European World-Economy, ca.1570–1625* (New York, 1995).

2 A general introduction to Danish history 1500–2000 is found in Knud J.V. Jespersen, *A History of Denmark* (London, 2004).

3 There is no up-to-date general survey of the Danish North Atlantic empire in English. The most recent relevant work in Danish is Michael Bregnsbo and Kurt Villads Jensen, *Det danske imperium. Storhed og fald* (Copenhagen, 2004). On Greenland, see also Finn Gad, *Grønlands historie*, Vols I–III (Copenhagen, 1967–76).

4 The fate of the Swedish colonial enterprise in North America is given a lively description in Stellan Dahlgren and Hans Norman, *The Rise and Fall of New Sweden: Governor Johan Risingh's Journal 1654–1655 in its Historical Context* (Uppsala, 1988).

5 The Swedish activities in West Africa are discussed by Ole Justesen in Ole Feldbæk and Ole Justesen, *Kolonierne i Asien og Afrika* (Copenhagen, 1980), pp. 301 ff.; see also K.Y. Daaku, *Trade and Politics on the Gold Coast 1600–1720: A Study of African Reaction to European Trade* (London, 1970).

6 The history of the Swedish rule over Saint Bethélemy is treated in Gösta Franzén, *Svenskstad i Västindien* (Stockholm, 1974). The book is provided with an English summary.

7 The following description of the Danish overseas enterprise is, unless otherwise stated, based upon Feldbæk and Justesen, *Kolonierne i Asien og Afrika* and Ove Hornby, *Kolonierne i Vestindien* (Copenhagen, 1980). The Danish India trade is thoroughly discussed in Ole Feldbæk, *India Trade under the Danish Flag 1772–1808* (Copenhagen, 1969).

8 The British raid on Copenhagen is briefly described in Knud J.V. Jespersen, *The Besieging of Copenhagen in 1807 and the Map in the Governor's Library in Odense* (Odense, 1974).

Chapter 6 Britain

1 James Raven, *Judging New Wealth: Popular Publishing and Responses to Commerce in England, 1750–1800* (Oxford, 1992), p. 138.

2 David Cannadine, 'The Making of the British Upper Classes', in *Aristocracy: Grandeur and Decline in Modern Britain* (New Haven and London, 1994).

3 John Jewell, *The Tourist's Companion, or, The History and Antiquities of Harewood* (Leeds, 1819), pp. 7–8.

4 *Yorkshire Election: A Collection of the Speeches, Addresses and Squibs Produced by All Parties during the Late Contested Election* (Leeds, 1807).

5 *Rule Britannia*, words by James Thompson, music by Thomas Arne (*c*.1740).

6 Nicholas Canny, 'The Origins of Empire: An Introduction', in *The Oxford History of the British Empire, Vol. 1* (Oxford, 1998).

7 Linda Colley, *Britons: Forging the Nation* (New Haven, 1992).

8 Canny, 'The Origins of Empire', p. 7.

9 P.J. Marshall, '1783–1870: An Expanding Empire', in P.J. Marshall (ed.), *The Cambridge Illustrated History of the British Empire* (Cambridge, 1996).

10 Edmund Burke, 'Speech on Conciliation with America', 22 March 1775.

11 Alan Bennett, *The Madness of King George* (London, 1995), p. 70.

12 P.J. Marshall, *The Making and Unmaking of Empires: Britain, India and America, c.1750–1783* (Oxford, 2005).

13 P. J. Marshall, 'Introduction: The World Shaped by Empire', in *The Cambridge Illustrated History of the British Empire*, p. 10.

14 Bernard Smith, *European Vision and the South Pacific,* 2nd edn (New Haven, 1985).

15 On the meaning of Cook's death, see Greg Dening, *Mr Bligh's Bad Language: Passion, Power and Theatre on the Bounty* (Cambridge, 1992).

16 Robert Hughes, *The Fatal Shore: A History of the Transportation of Convicts to Australia 1787 to 1868* (London, 1987). Hughes takes his title from a nineteenth-century ballad.

17 The phrase is Simon Schama's. *A History of Britain. Vol. 3: 1776–2000: The Fate of Empire* (London, 2003), chapters five and six.

18 Catherine Hall, 'Of Gender and Empire: Reflections on the Nineteenth Century', in Phillippa Levine (ed.), *Gender and Empire (The Oxford History of the British Empire, Companion Series)* (Oxford, 2004), p. 48.

19 *Ibid.*, p. 66.

20 *Ibid.*, p. 47.

21 Among the most prominent of these voices is that of Mary Prince, a former West Indian slave whose autobiography was published through the efforts of the Anti-Slavery Society. Mary Prince, *The History of Mary Prince, a West Indian Slave, Related by Herself* (London, 1831).

22 Colley, *Britons*, p. 354.

23 Alan Lester, 'British Settler Discourse and the Circuits of Empire', *History Workshop Journal*, No. 54 (2002), pp. 24–48; Elizabeth Elbourne, 'The Sin of the Settler: The 1835–36 Select Committee on Aborigines and Debates over Virtue and Conquest in the Early Nineteenth-Century British White Settler Empire', *Journal of Colonialism and Colonial History*, Vol. 4 (2003), p. 3.

24 Catherine Hall, *Civilising Subjects: Colony and Metropole in the English Imagination, 1830–1867* (London, 2002), p. 48.

25 See William Dalrymple, *White Mughals: Love and Betrayal in Eighteenth-Century India* (London, 2002) for a recent popular history.

26 Hall, 'Of Gender and Empire', p. 47.

27 Schama, *A History of Britain. Vol. 3: 1776–2000: The Fate of Empire*, p. 241.

28 Bill Nasson, *Britannia's Empire: Making a British World* (Stroud, 2004), p. 132.

29 *Bulletin*, 2 July 1887.

30 P.J. Marshall, '1870–1918: The Empire under Threat', in *The Cambridge Illustrated History of the British Empire*, p. 71.

31 Nasson, *Britannia's Empire*.

32 *Ibid.*, p. 156.

33 A.J. Stockwell, 'Power, Authority and Freedom', *The Cambridge Illustrated History of the British Empire*, p. 182.

34 Nasson, *Britannia's Empire*, p. 201.

35 Salman Rushdie, 'Outside the Whale', in *Imaginary Homelands: Essays and Criticism, 1981–1991* (London, 1991); John Hill, *British Cinema in the 1980s: Issues and Themes* (Oxford, 1999), pp. 99–123.

36 Marshall, 'Introduction: The World Shaped by Empire'.

Chapter 7 France

BIBLIOGRAPHY

Henri Brunschwig, *Mythes et réalités de l'impérialisme colonial français* (Armand Colin, 1960).

Jacques Frémeaux, *La France et l'Islam depuis 1789* (Presses Universitaires de France, 1991).

Jacques Frémeaux, *Les Empires coloniaux dans le processus de mondialisation* (Maisonneuve et Larose, 2002).

Jacques Frémeaux, *La France et l'Algérie en guerre, 1830–1870, 1954–1962* (Economica, 2002).

Philippe Haudrère, *L'Empire des rois (1500–1789)* (Denoël, 1997).

Jacques Marseille, *Empire colonial et capitalisme français, histoire d'un divorce* (Albin Michel, 2005).

Jean Meyer, Jean Tarrade, Annie Rey-Goldzeiguer and Jacques Thobie, *Histoire de la France coloniale: des origines à 1914* (Armand Colin, 1991).

Jacques Thobie, Gilbert Meynier, Catherine Coquery-Vidrovitch and Charles-Robert Ageron, *Histoire de la France coloniale. 1914–1990* (Armand Colin, 1990).

Chapter 8 Russia

1 Richard Pipes, *Russia under the Old Regime* (London, 1974), p. 5.

2 Dominic Lieven, *Empire: The Russian Empire and its Rivals* (London, 2000), p. 262.

3 *Ibid.*, p. 278.

4 On the development of governmental structures, see George L. Yaney, *The Systematization of Russian Government. Social Evolution in the Domestic Administration of Imperial Russia 1711–1905* (Urbana, 1973). On the empire more generally, see Hugh Seton-Watson, *The Russian Empire 1801–1917* (Oxford, 1967).

5 For a short survey of each tsar, see Ronald Hingley, *The Tsars: Russian Autocrats 1533–1917* (London, 1968).

6 For a survey of nationality issues, see Lubomyr Hajda and Mark Beissinger (eds), *The Nationalities Factor in Soviet Politics and Society* (Cambridge, 1990).

7 For a survey of the post-war economy, see Philip Hanson, *The Rise and Fall of the Soviet Economy: An Economic History of the USSR from 1945* (London, 2003).

8 For an overview, see Alvin Z. Rubinstein, *Soviet Foreign Policy since World War II: Imperial and Global* (New York, 1992).

9 Archie Brown, *The Gorbachev Factor* (Oxford, 1996).

10 Robert Service, *Russia: Experiment with a People. From 1991 to the Present* (London, 2002).

Chapter 9 Austria-Hungary

1 Steven Beller, *Reinventing Central Europe* (Working Paper 92–5, Center

for Austrian Studies, Minneapolis, Oct. 1991). Internet version at http://www.cas.umn.edu/wp925.htm.

2 Moritz Csáky and Klaus Zeyringer, *Ambivalenz des kulturellen Erbes. Vielfachcodierung des historischen Gedächtnisses. Paradigma: Österreich* (Innsbruck, Vienna and Munich, 2000).

3 Even in the 1970s, both Anglo-Saxon and Austrian historiographers proceeded along these regional lines. See Adam Wandruszka and Peter Urbanitsch (eds), *Die Habsburgermonarchie 1848–1918*, 8 vols (Vienna, 1973–2006); Robert A. Kann, *A History of the Habsburg Empire 1526–1918* (Berkeley and Los Angeles, 1974); Robert J.W. Evans, *The Making of the Habsburg Monarchy, 1550–1700: An Interpretation* (Oxford, 1979).

4 Diana Reynolds, 'Kavaliere, Kostüme, Kunstgewerbe: Die Vorstellung Bosniens in Wien 1878–1900', in Johannes Feichtinger, Ursula Prutsch and Moritz Csáky (eds), *Habsburg postcolonial. Machtstrukturen und kollektives Gedächtnis* (Innsbruck, Vienna, Munich and Bolzano, 2003), pp. 243–55.

5 Claudio Magris, *Il mito absburgico nella letteratura austriaca moderna* (Turin, 1963).

6 Christiane Zintzen, '*Die österreichisch-ungarische Monarchie in Wort und Bild.' Aus dem 'Kronprinzenwerk' des Erzherzog Rudolf* (Vienna, Cologne and Weimar, 1999).

7 Richard Swartz, Preface, in Zintzen, *Kronprinzenwerk*, p. 7.

8 A detailed survey is given in Vol. 1 of Thomas Winkelbauer, *Ständefreiheit und Fürstenmacht. Länder und Untertanen des Hauses Habsburg im konfessionellen Zeitalter* (Vienna, 2003). Biography: Alfred Kohler, *Ferdinand I. (1503–1564). Fürst, König und Kaiser* (Munich, 2003).

9 Henri Pigaillem, *Le Prince Eugène (1663–1736). Le philosophe guerrier. Biographie* (Monaco, 2005).

10 For what follows, see Karl Vocelka, *Glanz und Untergang der höfischen Welt. Repräsentation, Reform und Reaktion im habsburgischen Vielvölkerstaat* (Vienna, 2001). A good survey of the economic history is to be found in Herbert Knittler, 'Die Donaumonarchie 1648–1848', in Ilja Mieck (ed.), *Europäische Wirtschafts– und Sozialgeschichte von der Mitte des 17. Jahrhunderts bis zur Mitte des 19. Jahrhunderts* (Stuttgart, 1993), pp. 880–915.

11 C.W. Blanning, *Joseph II* (London and New York, 1994); Ernst Wangermann, *Die Waffen der Publizität. Zum*

12 *Funktionswandel der politischen Literatur unter Joseph II.* (Vienna and Munich, 2004).

12 Ernst Wangermann, *From Joseph II to the Jacobin Trials. Government Policy and Public Opinion in the Habsburg Dominions in the Period of the French Revolution* (London, 1969); Walter Sauer, 'Schuster, bleib bei deinem Leisten… Politische und weltanschauliche Entwicklungen unter Wiener Handwerkern am Beispiel der Affäre des Jahres 1794', in Ulrich Engelhardt (ed.), *Handwerker in der Industrialisierung. Lage, Kultur und Politik vom späten 18. bis ins frühe 19. Jahrhundert* (Stuttgart, 1984), pp. 435–57.

13 Carsten Holbraad, *The Concert of Europe: A Study in German and British International Theory 1815–1914* (London, 1970).

14 Alan Palmer, *Metternich* (London, 1972).

15 Wolfgang Häusler, *Von der Massenarmut zur Arbeiterbewegung. Demokratie und soziale Frage in der Wiener Revolution von 1848* (Vienna, 1979); Helgard Fröhlich, Margarethe Grandner and Michael Weinzierl (eds), *1848 im europäischen Kontext* (Vienna, 1999).

16 Brandt Harm-Hinrich, *Der österreichische Neoabsolutismus: Staatsfinanzen und Politik* (Göttingen, 1978).

17 There is a detailed summary of this complex development in Helmut Rumpler, *Eine Chance für Mitteleuropa. Bürgerliche Emanzipation und Staatsverfall in der Habsburgermonarchie* (Vienna, 1997).

18 Kann, *Habsburg Empire*, p. 579.

19 Wolfram Fischer, 'Wirtschaft und Gesellschaft Europas 1850–1914', in Fischer et al (eds), *Europäische Wirtschafts– und Sozialgeschichte von der Mitte des 19. Jahrhunderts bis zum Ersten Weltkrieg* (Stuttgart, 1985), pp. 112 and 115. For a general account, see Ernst Bruckmüller, *Sozialgeschichte Österreichs* (second edition, Vienna and Munich, 2001).

20 *Österreichische Bürgerkunde. Handbuch der Staats– und Rechtskunde in ihren Beziehungen zum öffentlichen Leben I* (Vienna, 1908), p. 356.

21 Kann, *Habsburg Empire*, p. 581.

22 On this national problem, see especially Ernst Bruckmüller, *The Austrian Nation. Cultural Consciousness and Socio-Political Processes* (Riverside, Cal, 2003); for a historical perspective, see Rumpler, *Chance für Mitteleuropa*, pp. 426–523.

23 David F. Good, *The Economic Rise of the Habsburg Empire 1750–1914* (Berkeley

and Los Angeles, 1984), p. 256. With modifications, but basically in agreement: Roman Sandgruber, *Ökonomie und Politik. Österreichische Wirtschaftsgeschichte vom Mittelalter bis zur Gegenwart* (Vienna, 1995), pp. 233–313.

24 Good, *Economic Rise of the Habsburg Empire*, p. 239.

25 See case studies in Feichtinger, Prutsch and Csáky, *Habsburg Postcolonial*.

26 See Walter Sauer, 'Schwarz-Gelb in Afrika. Habsburgmonarchie und koloniale Frage', in Sauer (ed.), *k. u. k. kolonial. Habsburgmonarchie und europäische Herrschaft in Afrika* (Vienna, 2002), pp. 17–78.

27 See, *inter alia*, contributions by Wolfgang J. Mommsen and Jörg Fisch, in Stig Förster, Wolfgang J. Mommsen and Ronald Robinson (eds), *Bismarck, Europe and Africa: The Berlin Africa Conference 1884–1885 and the Onset of Partition* (London 1988).

28 Zuletzt Walter Markov, 'Die koloniale Versuchung: Österreichs zweite Ostindienkompanie. Supplementa zu F. von Pollack-Parnau', in *Österreich im Europa der Aufklärung I* (Vienna, 1985) pp. 593–603; also Malyn Newitt, *A History of Mozambique* (Johannesburg, 1995), p. 159 ff.

29 See Sauer, 'Schwarz-Gelb in Afrika', pp. 36–54.

30 On the 'Mexican adventure', which ended three years later with the execution of the Habsburg archduke, see Brian Hamnett, *Juárez* (London and New York, 1994), pp. 166–97; also Konrad Ratz, *Maximilian und Juárez*, 2 vols (Graz, 1998).

31 Quoted from Sauer, *Schwarz-Gelb in Afrika*, p. 71 ff.

32 Georg Lehner and Monika Lehner, *Österreich-Ungarn und der 'Boxeraufstand' in China* (Mitteilungen des Österreichischen Staatsarchivs, special issue 6, Innsbruck, 2002).

33 Gordon Brook-Shepherd, *Between Two Flags: The Life of Baron Sir Rudolf von Slatin Pasha* (London, 1972).

34 Harry Sichrovsky, *Der Revolutionär von Leitmeritz. Ferdinand Blumentritt und der philippinische Freiheitskampf* (Vienna, 1983).

35 A selection from the now extensive literature: Peter Berner, Emil Brix and Wolfgang Mantl (eds), *Wien um 1900* (Vienna, 1986); Emil Brix and Patrick Werkner (eds), *Die Wiener Moderne. Ergebnisse eines Forschungsgespräches der Arbeitsgemeinschaft Wien um 1900 zum Thema 'Aktualität und Moderne'* (Vienna and Munich, 1990); Alfred Pfabigan

(ed.), *Die Enttäuschung der Moderne* (Vienna, 2000).

36 Carl E. Schorske, *Fin-de-Siècle Vienna: Politics and Culture* (New York, 1980), p. xviii; for different interpretations see Albert Fuchs, *Geistige Strömungen in Österreich 1867–1918* (new edition, Vienna, 1996) or William M. Johnston, *The Austrian Mind: An Intellectual and Social History 1848–1938* (Berkeley, 1972).

37 Ernst Hanisch, *Der lange Schatten des Staates. Österreichische Gesellschaftsgeschichte im 20. Jahrhundert* (Vienna, 1994), p. 261.

38 For the development of politically dissident ideologies and organizations, see e.g. Wolfgang Maderthaner and Lutz Musner, *Die Anarchie der Vorstadt. Das andere Wien um 1900* (Frankfurt am Main, 1999); John Boyer, *Political Radicalism in Late Imperial Vienna. Origins of the Christian Social Movement 1848–1897* (Chicago, 1981); William D. Bowman, *Priest and Parish in Vienna, 1780 to 1880* (Boston, 1999).

39 Roman Sandgruber, 'Exklusivität und Masse. Wien um 1900', in Brix and Werkner, *Die Wiener Moderne*, p. 82.

Chapter 10 Belgium

1 G. Romanato, *L'Africa Nera fra Cristianesimo e Islam. L'esperienza di Daniele Comboni (1831–1881)* (Milan, 2003).

2 F. Renault, *Lavigerie, l'esclavage africain et l'Europe, 1868–1892*, Vol. 2, *Campagne antiesclavagiste* (Paris, 1971).

3 'I destroy the world and I construct the world to come' (1883), the Mahdi as reported by Slatin, *Fire and Sword*, quoted by F. Nicoll, *The Mahdi of the Sudan and the Death of General Gordon* (Stroud, 2005), p. 177.

4 There is a florilegium of Stanley's rhetorics, from his expedition to Kumasi when he expressed the hope of the Ashanti putting up some resistance and not depriving the English of a pretext for a bloody vengeance, to his downstream navigation on the Congo: 'it is a murderous world and we feel for the first time that we hate the filthy, vulturous ghouls who inhabit it.' Quoted by J.L. Newman, *Imperial Footprints. Henry Morton Stanley's African Journeys* (Washington, D.C., 2004), p. 138. The Emin Pasha relief expedition was hardly more peaceful.

5 A.-J. Wauters, *Histoire politique du Congo belge* (Brussels, 1911), pp. 57–58.

6 Four of Stanley's best-known men, E.J. Glave, W.G. Parminter, R. Casement and A.H. Ward, are united in a photogravure by A.H. Ward, *A*

Voice from the Congo (London, 1910), facing p. 204.

7 China was also a possibility. 'When we will need men, it will be in China that we will find them.' By 1888, he was thinking of five Chinese garrisons to delineate the borders. What would be their cost? R.-J. Cornet, *La Bataille du Rail* (Brussels, 1958), p. 236.

8 P. Marechal, *De 'Arabische' campagne in het Maniema-Gebied (1892–1894)* (Tervuren, 1992).

9 Between January and May 1892, the death rate among African workers reached 20 per cent (in a total workforce of 4,500, mainly from West Africa and Zanzibar), and over the whole year it was 22.5 per cent among European workers (out of a total of 120).

10 Speech by A. Thys, engineer and president of the Congo Rail Company, at the inauguration of the line, Léopoldville, 6 July 1898, *Mouvement géographique*, 1898, cols 398–99.

11 Between 1891 and 1904, the value of ivory exports fluctuated from 2.8 to 5.8 million francs p.a., while rubber exports caught up with these figures in 1896, and by 1903 had reached 47.03 million francs. The construction of the Matadi-Léopoldville railway cost 82 million francs.

12 These losses occurred when passing the Matadi escarpment, by far the most excruciating part of the work. The total number of sleepers for the line is in the order of 400,000.

13 The full text of the report is in S. Ó Síocháin and M. O'Sullivan, *The Eyes of Another Race: Roger Casement's Report and 1903 Diary* (Dublin, 2003).

14 Due to the politics of denial later adopted by the colonial administration (see below), the texts of these depositions remained long out of reach of researchers. A second wave of oral testimonies was collected fifty years later by a missionary, E. Boelaert, as part of his project of arousing a sense of collective identity against the modern capitalist economy. It remained confined to a local readership.

15 In the early generation of travellers testifying to these widespread practices, the names of Tippu Tip, a Swahili trader, of Wissmann, a German officer, and of A.H. Ward, a 'Stanley man', can be cited as examples among many. In fact, evidence for mutilations occurs as early as the first sixteenth– and seventeenth-century written sources on Central Africa, which aroused much fascination in Europe.

16 Ward, *A Voice from the Congo*, p. 286.

17 F. Cattier, *Étude sur la situation de l'État Indépendant du Congo* (Brussels, 1906); A. Vermeersch, *La Question congolaise* (Brussels, 1906).

18 K. Grant, 'Christian Critics of Empire: Missionaries, Lantern Lectures and the Congo Reform Campaign in Britain', *Journal of Imperial and Commonwealth History*, Vol. 29, No. 2 (2001), pp. 27–58.

19 W.R. Louis and J. Stengers, *E.D. Morel's History of the Congo Reform Movement* (Oxford, 1968).

20 P. Mille, 'Le Congo léopoldien', *Cahiers de la Quinzaine*, 26 November 1905; P. Mille and F. Challaye, 'Les deux Congo devant la Belgique et devant la France', *ibid.*, 22 April 1906.

21 Southern Africa and German Southwest Africa appeared to him as examples of brutality caused by racial oppression, the two Congos as victims of capitalist interests, North Africa as a political victim as much as Belgium had been in 1914. E.D. Morel, *The Black Man's Burden* (1920).

22 In 1930, two Congolese approached the Belgian consulate in Boston to complain that they were currently presented as Congo cannibals to accompany an American film, *Jango*, by Daniel Davenport, and this 'while they were Catholics'. They also pointed out that the payment of their wages was left outstanding. Correspondence Belgian Embassy, Washington, 27 February 1930, Belgian Archives Foreign Affairs, AF-I-17.

23 G.T. Mollin, *Die USA und der Kolonialismus* (Berlin, 1996), p. 129.

24 G. Vanthemsche, *Genèse et portée du «Plan décennal» du Congo belge (1949–1959)* (Brussels, 1994). Cf. the discussion in *Bulletin de l'ARSOM* (1994), pp. 349–56.

25 The period leading to independence is best analysed by Ndaywel è Nziem, *Histoire du Zaïre* (Louvain la Neuve, 1997), and J.-M. Mutamba, *Du Congo belge au Congo indépendant, 1940-1960. Émergence des évolués et genèse du nationalisme* (Kinshasa, 1998).

Chapter 11 Germany

1 Translated from Heinrich von Poschinger (ed.): *Fürst Bismarck und die Parlamentarier*, Vol. III (Breslau, 1896), p. 54.

2 There have been many attempts to account for Bismarck's U-turn on colonialism. We shall confine ourselves to the thesis propounded by Hans-Ulrich Wehler (*Bismarck und der*

Imperialismus [Köln 1969]), who viewed Bismarck's colonial policy as being motivated primarily by domestic rather than foreign affairs: 'social imperialism under the banner of domestic policy'. Even in later years, Bismarck was still firmly against the concept of colonialism, as is clear from his famous remark of 1888: 'my map of Africa lies here in Europe.' (Translated from 'Gespräche mit dem Afrikareisenden Eugen Wolf am 7. Dezember 1888 in Friedrichsruh', in *Bismarck, Die Gesammelten Werke*, Vol. 8 [Berlin, 1926], pp. 644–47, here p. 646.

3 Klaus J. Bade (ed.), *Imperialismus und Kolonialmission, Kaiserliches Deutschland und koloniales Imperium* (Wiesbaden, 1982), p. 10.

4 See surveys by Helmuth Stoecker (ed.), *Drang nach Afrika, Die deutsche koloniale Expansionspolitik und Herrschaft in Afrika von den Anfängen bis zum Verlust der Kolonien*, 2nd edn (Berlin, 1991); Horst Gründer, *Geschichte der deutschen Kolonien*, 5th edn (Paderborn etc, 2004); Winfried Speitkamp, *Deutsche Kolonialgeschichte* (Stuttgart, 2005).

5 The West Africa (or Congo) Conference of 1884–85 was attended by representatives from thirteen European countries, the USA and the Ottoman Empire, and its aim was to establish rules under international law for the further division of Africa and for free trading and missionary access to the continent. The conference is viewed today as a warning sign for the heteronomy and exploitation of Africa.

6 Good examples of area studies are those by Peter Sebald, *Togo 1884–1914. Eine Geschichte der deutschen "Musterkolonie" auf der Grundlage amtlicher Quellen* (Berlin, 1988); Hermann J. Hiery (ed.), *Die Deutsche Südsee 1884–1914. Ein Handbuch* (Paderborn etc. 2001).

7 Ulrich van der Heyden, *Rote Adler an Afrikas Küste. Die brandenburgisch-preußische Kolonie Großfriedrichsburg in Westafrika*, 2nd edn (Berlin, 2001).

8 Alexander Honold/Klaus R. Scherpe (eds), *Mit Deutschland um die Welt. Eine Kulturgeschichte des Fremden in der Kolonialzeit* (Stuttgart/Weimar, 2004), p. 20. Barth, Vogel, Rohlfs, Nachtigal and especially Eduard Robert Flegel travelled round North Cameroon.

9 In 1916 he wrote: 'If one compares, for instance, Germany's colonial acquisitions with those of other states during the same period, they are in truth ridiculously modest.' In: *Weber, Max, Gesammelte Politische Schriften*, edited by Johannes Winckelmann, 2nd edn (Tübingen, 1958), p. 154 f.

10 See Mihran Dabag/Horst Gründer/Uwe-K Ketelsen (eds), *Kolonialismus, Kolonialdiskurs und Genozid* (München, 2004).

11 Arne Perras, *Carl Peters and German Imperialism 1856–1918. A Political Biography* (Oxford, 2004).

12 Christian Geulen, 'The Final Frontier', Heimat, Nation und Kolonie um 1900. Carl Peters, in Birthe Kundrus (ed.), *Phantasiereiche. Zur Kulturgeschichte des deutschen Kolonialismus* (Frankfurt am Main/New York, 2003), pp. 35–55, here 48.

13 Jürgen Zimmerer, *Deutsche Herrschaft über Afrikaner. Staatlicher Machtanspruch und Wirklichkeit im kolonialen Namibia*, Münster 2001. See also Helmut Bley, *Namibia under German Rule* (Hamburg, 1996).

14 See Pascal Grosse, *Kolonialismus, Eugenik und bürgerliche Gesellschaft in Deutschland 1850–1918* (Frankfurt am Main/New York, 2000); Pascal Grosse, 'Zwischen Privatheit und Öffentlichkeit Kolonialmigration' in *Deutschland 1900–1940* in Birthe Kundrus (ed.), *Phantasiereiche, Zur Kulturgeschichte des deutschen Kolonialismus* (Frankfurt am Main/New York, 2003), pp. 91–109; Fatima El-Tayeb, *Schwarze Deutsche. Der Diskurs um 'Rasse' und nationale Identität 1890–1933* (Frankfurt/New York, 2001).

15 See John C.G. Röhl, *Wilhelm II. Der Aufbau der Persönlichen Monarchie 1888–1900* (Munich, 2001), p. 1027.

16 Eduard von Liebert, *Die deutschen Kolonien und ihre Zukunft* (Berlin, 1906), p. 9.

17 Sebastian Conrad/Jürgen Osterhammel (eds), *Das Kaiserreich transnational. Deutschland in der Welt 1871–1914* (Göttingen, 2004), p. 10.

18 This expression, adapted from 'the lie of war guilt', was coined by the former governor of German East Africa, Heinrich Schnee, in his book *Die koloniale Schuldlüge* (Munich, 1924). This book was reprinted twelve times and translated into many languages, and in the 1920s it was regarded as the standard work on the colonial movement.

19 Bernhard Dernburg, 'Sind Kolonien für Deutschland nötig?', in *Uhu* 2 (1926), pp. 20–25, here 22. The left-wing liberal banker Bernhard Dernburg held the office of State Secretary for Colonial Affairs from 1906 until 1910.

20 Paul von Lettow-Vorbeck (known as the 'Lion of Africa') conducted a continuous war in German East Africa from 1914 to 1918. Even among his opponents, who occupied

East Africa but were unable to conquer his territory, he enjoyed a reputation 'as the ablest soldier of World War I'. The fact that this war-within-a-war claimed countless victims and caused long-term ecological devastation in East Africa was not, of course, taken into consideration. John Iliffe (*A Modern History of Tanganyika*, Cambridge etc. 1979, p. 241) passed the following judgment: 'Lettow-Vorbeck's brilliant campaign was the pinnacle of Africa's exploitation: its use purely and simply as a battlefield.'

21 Klaus Hildebrand, *Vom Reich zum Weltreich, Hitler, NSDAP und koloniale Frage 1919–1945* (München, 1969).

22 See Conrad/Osterhammel 2004, p. 20.

23 Klaus J. Bade, Die deutsche Kolonialexpansion in Afrika: Ausgangssituation und Ergebnis, in Walter Fürnrohr (ed.), *Afrika im Geschichtsunterricht europäischer Länder, Von der Kolonialgeschichte zur Geschichte der Dritten Welt* (München, 1982), pp. 13–47, here 35. For subsequent references see ibid.

24 See for instance Marc Ferro (ed.), *Le livre noir du colonialisme. XVIe-XXIe siècle, De l'extermination à la repentance* (Paris, 2003). Many people in Africa, South America and Asia also regard globalization as colonialism by other means.

25 See Geiss, Imanuel, Die welthistorische Stellung der europäischen Kolonialherrschaft, in Wilfried Wagner (ed.), *Rassendiskriminierung, Kolonialpolitik und ethnisch-nationale Identität. Referate des 2. Internationalen Kolonialgeschichtlichen Symposiums 1991 in Berlin* (Munster/ Hamburg, 1992), pp. 21–41. Lewis H. Gann/Peter Duignan, *The Rulers of German Africa 1884–1914* (Stanford/ California, 1977), p. 239 ff. lays great emphasis on the positive effects of colonial rule. See also Heyden, 'Ulrich van der, Kolonialgeschichtsschreibung in Deutschland, Eine Bilanz ost– und westdeutscher Kolonialhistoriographie', in *Neue Politische Literatur* 48 (2003) 3, pp. 401–429.

26 On the subject of native collaboration, see Jürgen Osterhammel, *Kolonialismus, Geschichte – Formen Folgen* (München, 1995), p. 70 ff.

27 Nowadays the most important paradigms of postcolonial thinking are diaspora and nomadism, hybridization and mimicry.

28 See Tilmann Dedering, *Hate the Old and Follow the New. Khoekhoe and Missionaries in Early Nineteenth-century Namibia* (Stuttgart, 1997); Ursula Trüper, *Die Hottentottin. Das kurze Leben der Zara Schmelen (ca. 1793–1831) Missionsgehilfin und Sprachpionierin in Südafrika* (Köln, 2000).

29 Even today, Rudolf Duala Manga Bell and his fellow victims of judicial murder have still not been exonerated. Ralph A. Austen/Derrick Jonathan, *Middlemen of the Cameroons Rivers. The Duala and their Hinterland, c.1600–c. 1960* (Cambridge, 1999); Andreas Eckert, *Grundbesitz, Landkonflikte und kolonialer Wandel, Douala 1880–1960* (Stuttgart, 1999).

30 See Russell A. Berman, 'Der ewige Zweite. Deutschlands Sekundärkolonialismus', in Birthe Kundrus (ed.), *Phantasiereiche. Zur Kulturgeschichte des deutschen Kolonialismus* (Frankfurt am Main/New York, 2003), pp. 19–32, here 24.

31 Nevertheless, the genocide that took place in German South West Africa – the first in German history – was exceptional. The Maji-Maji rebellion of 1905–7 in German East Africa cost the lives of far more Africans; estimates of the number of victims vary between 75,000 and 300,000. It remains an open question whether the German military campaign against the Maji-Maji bore genocidal features, as it did in the Cameroon Mpawmanku wars of 1904 (known in colonial language as the Anyang Uprising).

32 Jürgen Zimmerer/Joachim Zeller (eds), *Völkermord in Deutsch-Südwestafrika. Der Kolonialkrieg 1904–1908 in Namibia und seine Folgen*, 2nd edn (Berlin, 2004); Jürgen Zimmerer, *Colonialism and the Holocaust. Towards an Archeology of Genocide*, in Dirk A. Moses (ed.), *Genocide and Settler Society. Frontier Violence and Stolen Indigenous Children in Australian History* (New York/Oxford, 2004); Henning Melber (ed.), *Genozid und Gedenken. Namibisch-deutsch Geschichte und Gegenwart* (Frankfurt am Main, 2005).

33 Hannah Arendt, *The Origins of Totalitarianism*, London 1986 (Chapter 7), 1st edn 1951.

34 Reinhart Kößler/Henning Melber, Völkermord und Gedenken, 'Der Genozid an den Herero und Nama in Deutsch-Südwestafrika 1904–1908' in *Völkermord und Kriegsverbrechen in der ersten Hälfte des 20 Jahrhunderts*, hrsg. im Auftrag des Fritz Bauer Instituts von Irmtrud Wojak und Susanne Meinl (Frankfurt am Main/New York, 2004), pp. 37–75, here 59.

35 Lora Wildenthal (*German Women for Empire, 1884–1945*, Durham/London 2001) examines the involvement and politics of women in the German colonial process. The two most important women's organizations were the 'Deutsche Frauenverein für Krankenpflege in den Kolonien' (German Women's Society for Nursing in the Colonies) and the 'Frauenbund der Deutschen Kolonialgesellschaft' (Women's League for German Colonization).

36 As an example of this approach, focusing on the 'periphery', see Jan-Bart Gewald, *Herero Heroes. A socio-political history of the Herero of Namibia 1890–1923* (Oxford/Cape Town/Athens, 1999).

37 Andreas Eckert, 'Konflikte, Netzwerke, Interaktionen. Kolonialismus in Afrika', in *Neue Politische Literatur* 44 (1999) 3, pp. 446–480.

38 Gesine Krüger, *Kriegsbewältigung und Geschichtsbewußtsein. Realität, Deutung und Verarbeitung des deutschen Kolonialkriegs in Namibia 1904–1907* (Göttingen, 1999); Stefanie Michels, *Imagined Power Contested: Germans and Africans in the Upper Cross River Area of Cameroon 1887–1915* (Berlin/Münster, 2004); Stefanie Michels, 'The Germans were brutal and wild': Colonial Legacies, in Stefanie Michels/Albert-Pascal Temgoua (eds), *La politique de la mémoire coloniale allemande en Allemagne et au Cameroun/Politics of colonial memory in Germany and Cameroon* (Berlin/Münster, 2005).

39 The African diaspora consisted of colonial migrants, German Africans and African-Americans. As well as people from the African colonies of the German Empire, the small group of colonial migrants also included Oceanic people from Germany's scattered possessions in the South Seas as well as China (Kiaochow). The total number of German colonial migrants and their descendants is estimated at between 500 and 1000. See Marianne Bechhaus-Gerst and Reinhard Klein-Arendt, *Die koloniale Begegnung. AfrikanerInnen in Deutschland 1880–1945, Deutsche in Afrika 1880–1918* (Frankfurt and New York, 2003); *AfrikanerInnen in Deutschland und schwarze Deutsche: Geschichte und Gegenwart* (Münster, 2004); Peter Martin and Christine Alonzo, *Zwischen Charleston und Stechschritt: Schwarze im Nationalsozialismus* (Hamburg/Munich, 2004); Heiko Möhle, Susanne Heyn and Susann Lewerenz, *Zwischen Völkerschau und Kolonialinstitut: AfrikanerInnen im kolonialen Hamburg*, Hamburg, 2006.

40 See for instance Wolfgang Fuhrmann, *Propaganda, sciences and entertainment in German colonial cinematography*, unpublished doctoral dissertation, University of Utrecht, Utrecht 2003; Wolfram Hartmann (ed.), *Hues between black and white. Historical photography from colonial Namibia 1860s to 1915* (Windhoek, 2004).

41 David M. Ciarlo, *Visualizing Colonialism and Consuming Race in German Mass Culture, 1885–1914*, unpublished doctoral dissertation, University of Wisconsin, Madison 2002.

42 See for instance Robert Young, *Postcolonialism. An Historical Introduction* (Oxford, 2001); Sebastian Conrad/Shalini Randeria (eds), *Jenseits des Eurozentrismus. Postkoloniale Perspektiven in den Geschichts– und Kulturwissenschaften* (Frankfurt am Main/New York, 2002). A kind of basic manifesto for postcolonial studies was the famous book *Orientalism* (1978) by the scholar and literary critic Edward Said, who died in 2003.

43 Sara Friedrichsmeyer/Sara Lennox/Susanne Zantop (eds), *The Imperialist Imagination. German Colonialism and Its Legacy* (Michigan, 1998); Birthe Kundrus (ed.), *Phantasiereiche. Zur Kulturgeschichte des deutschen Kolonialismus* (Frankfurt am Main/New York, 2003); Alexander Honold/Oliver Simons (eds), *Kolonialismus als Kultur. Literatur, Medien, Wissenschaft in der deutschen Gründerzeit des Fremden* (Tübingen/ Basel, 2002); Honold/Scherpe 2004.

44 Russell A. Berman, *Enlightenment of Empire. Colonial Discourse in German Culture* (Lincoln, 1998).

45 Andreas Eckert/Albert Wirz, *Wir nicht, die Anderen auch. Deutschland und der Kolonialmus*, in Sebastian Conrad/Shalini Randeria (eds), *Jenseits des Eurozentrismus. Postkoloniale Perpektiven in den Geschichts– und Kulturwissenschaften* (Frankfurt am Main/New York, 2002), pp. 372–392, here 374.

46 Susanne Zantop, *Colonial Fantasies. Conquest, Family and Nation in Precolonial Germany, 1770–1870* (London, 1997).

47 A recent opponent of the concept of 'typical German' colonialism was George Steinmetz, 'The Devil's Handwriting: Precolonial Discourse, Ethnographic Acuity and Cross Identification in German Colonialism', in *Comparative Studies in Society and History* 45, 1, January 2003, pp. 41–95.

48 Sebastian Conrad, Doppelte Marginalisierung. Plädoyer für eine transnationale Perspektive auf die deutsche Geschichte, in *Geschichte und Gesellschaft* 28 (2002), pp. 145–169, here 160.

49 For example in April 1984, on the hundredth anniversary of the beginning of German colonial expansion.

50 Joachim Zeller, *Kolonialdenkmäler und Geschichtsbewußtsein. Eine Untersuchung der kolonialdeutschen Erinnerungskultur* (Frankfurt am Main, 2000); Winfried Speitkamp, 'Kolonialherrschaft und Denkmal. Afrikanische und deutsche Erinnerungskultur im Konflikt', in Wolfram Martini (ed.), *Architektur und Erinnerung* (Göttingen, 2000), pp. 165–190.

51 Etienne Francois/Hagen Schulze (eds), *Deutsche Erinnerungsorte*, 3 vols. (München, 2001). This work followed on from Pierre Nora's ground-breaking *Lieux de mémoire* (7 vols., Paris 1986–1992). Nora, however, admitted that he had made an unforgiveable mistake by omitting colonialism from his topography of French memory.

52 Felix Driver/David Gilbert (eds), *Imperial Cities, Landscape, Display and Identity* (Manchester/New York, 1999).

53 Ulrich van der Heyden/Joachim Zeller (eds), *Kolonialmetropole Berlin. Eine Spurensuche* (Berlin, 2002); Ulrich van der Heyden/Joachim Zeller (eds), *'Macht und Anteil an der Weltherrschaft', Berlin und der deutsche Kolonialismus* (Münster, 2005).

54 Heiko Möhle (ed.), *Branntwein, Bibeln und Bananen. Der deutsche Kolonialismus in Afrika. Eine Spurensuche in Hamburg*, 2nd edn (Hamburg, 2000).

55 See Benedikt Stuchtey, Nation und Expansion. Das britische Empire in der neuesten Forschung, in *Historische Zeitschrift*, 274, 1, February 2002, pp.87–118, here 91. The thesis that the Empire formed a basic component of British culture and identity has been recently questioned by Bernard Porter, *'The Absent-Minded Imperialists'. Empire, Society and Culture in Britain*, Oxford 2004. See also Dieter Brötel ('Empire und Dekolonisation als Problem des französischen Geschichtsbewußtseins. Der Beitrag von 'kolonialer Erziehung' und Geschichtsunterricht', in Dieter Brötel/Hans H. Pöschko (eds) *Krisen und Geschichtsbewußtsein, Mentalitätsgeschichtliche und didaktische Beiträge* (Weinheim, 1996), pp. 119–158) on the formation of an 'Empire Awareness' in France.

56 Dirk van Laak, Die afrikanische Welt als Wille und deutsche Vorstellung, in *Frankfurter Allgemeine Zeitung*, 20 August 2002.

57 Black Germans and their associations have, however, been playing an increasing role in compiling the history of colonial imperialism, exposing the mechanisms of racism and discrimination. See for example *The BlackBook*, a collection published by the AntiDiskriminierungsBüro in 2004. One of the first public self-

descriptions of black people in Germany was the book by Katharina Oguntoye/May Opitz/Dagmar Schultz, *Farbe bekennen. Afro-deutsche Frauen auf den Spuren ihrer Geschichte*, 2nd edn (Frankfurt am Main, 1992), first published in 1986.

58 See for example Shalini Randeria's concept of 'entangled histories': Conrad/Randeria 2002.

59 In 2004 there were ceremonies of commemoration, conferences, exhibitions, films and publications in Namibia and Germany to commemorate the South West African colonial war. One highlight of the year was a speech made by the Federal Minister for Economic Cooperation and Development, Heidemarie Wieczorek-Zeul: in August at Waterberg/Namibia, in the name of the Federal Republic, she apologized officially for the crimes committed in the former colony. Claims for compensation by the Herero People's Reparation Corporation are still being pursued after it became known in mid November 2004 that the US Supreme Court in New York had refused to try the case, which had been pending since 2001. The law firm of Musolino & Dessel are now pursuing the claim on behalf of the Herero people in the US Southern District Court, New York. See Larissa Förster/ Dag Henrichsen/Michael Bollig (eds), *Namibia – Deuschland: Eine geteilte Geschichte. Widerstand, Gewalt, Erimerung* (Köln, 2004).

60 Charles S. Maier, *Consigning the Twentieth Century to History. Alternative Narratives for the Modern Era*, in *American Historical Review*, 105 (2000), 3, pp. 807–831.

Chapter 12 Italy

1 N. Labanca, 'History and Memory of Italian Colonialism Today', in J. Andall and D. Duncan, *Italian Colonialism: Legacies and Memories* (Bern, 2005), pp. 29–46; I. Taddia, *Memorie italiane memorie africane del colonialismo*, in S. Brune and H. Scholler, *Auf dem Weg zum modernen Athiopien. Festschrift fur Bairu Tafla* (Munster, 2005), pp. 225–46.

2 Recent work on Italian colonialism includes: Andall and Duncan, *Italian Colonialism*; R. Ben Ghiat and M. Fuller, *Italian Colonialism* (New York, 2005); P. Palumbo, *A Place in the Sun* (California, 2003). For a discussion of this new trend, see also I. Taddia, 'Notes on Recent Italian Studies on Ethiopia and Eritrea', *Africana*, Vol. 3 (2003), pp. 165–71.

3 Yemane Mesghenna, *Italian Colonialism: A Case Study of Eritrea, 1869–1934* (Lund, 1988), pp. 50–60.

4 R. Rainero, *L'anticolonialismo italiano da Assab ad Adua* (Milan, 1971), pp. 330–32.

5 R. Pankhurst, *The History of Famine and Epidemic in Ethiopia prior to the Twentieth Century* (Addis Ababa, 1985), p. 69.

6 Contemporary reports of these events in [E. Cagnassi], *I nostri errori: tredici anni in Eritrea* (Turin, 1898).

7 Tekeste Negash, *No Medicine for the Bite of a White Snake: Notes on Nationalism and Resistance in Eritrea 1890–1940* (Uppsala, 1986) and R. Caulk, 'Black Snake, White Snake': Bahta Hagos and his Revolt against Italian Overrule in Eritrea, 1894', in D. Crummey (ed.), *Banditry, Rebellion, and Social Protest in Africa* (London, 1986), pp. 293–309.

8 On the political background and the impact of the Battle of Adwa on Italian society, see N. Labanca, *In marcia verso Adua* (Turin, 1993) and I. Taddia and Uoldelul Chelati Dirar, 'Essere africani nell'Eritrea italiana', in A. Del Boca, *Adua. Le ragioni di una sconfitta* (Bari, 1997), pp. 231–53.

9 I. Taddia, 'Intervento pubblico e capitale privato nella Colonia Eritrea', *Rivista di Storia Contemporanea*, Vol. 14, No. 2 (1985), pp. 207–42; by the same author, *L'Eritrea-Colonia, 1890–1952. Paesaggi, strutture, uomini del colonialismo* (Milan, 1986), pp. 230–41.

10 Mesghenna, *Italian Colonialism*, pp. 215–16; M. Zaccaria, 'L'oro dell'Eritrea', *Africa*, Vol. 60, No. 1 (2005), pp. 65–110.

11 On Eritrean colonial troops, see particularly M. Scardigli, *Il braccio indigeno. Ascari, irregolari e bande nella conquista dell'Eritrea, 1885–1911* (Milan, 1996), A. Volterra, *Sudditi coloniali. Ascari eritrei, 1935–1941* (Milan, 2005) and Uoldelul Chelati Dirar, 'From Warriors to Urban Dwellers. Ascari and the Military Factor in the Urban Development of Colonial Eritrea', *Cahiers d'études africaines*, XLIV (3), 175 (2004), pp. 533–74.

12 T. Negash, *Italian Colonialism in Eritrea (1882–1941)* (Uppsala, 1987), pp. 79–82. See also Uoldelul Chelati Dirar, 'Church-State Relations in Colonial Eritrea: Missionaries and the Development of Colonial Strategies (1869–1911)', *Journal of Modern Italian Studies*, Vol. 8, No. 3 (2003), pp. 391–410.

13 Consociazione Turistica Italiana, *Africa Orientale Italiana Guida d'Italia della Consociazione Turistica Italiana* (Milan, 1938), p. 199.

14 Yemane Mesghenna, 'The Impact of the 1935–1941 Economic Boom on the Eritrean Labor Market', *Africa*, Vol. 58, No. 1 (2003), pp. 89–100.

15 L. Goglia, 'Sul razzismo coloniale italiano', *Materiali di lavoro*, Vol. 9, Nos 2–3 (1991), Vol. 10, No. 1 (1992), pp. 97–115; R. Pankhurst, 'Lo sviluppo del razzismo nell'impero coloniale italiano (1935–1941)', *Studi piacentini*, Vol. 3, No. 2 (1988), pp. 175–98.

16 G. Campassi, 'Il madamato in Africa Orientale: relazioni tra italiani e indigene come forma di aggressione coloniale', *Miscellanea di storia delle esplorazioni*, Vol. 12 (1987), pp. 219–60; Ruth Iyob, 'Madamismo and Beyond. The Construction of Eritrean Women', *Nineteenth-Century Contexts*, Vol. 22, No. 2 (2000), pp. 217–38; G. Barrera, 'Mussolini's Colonial Race Laws and State-Settlers Relations in Africa Orientale Italiana (1935–1941)', *Journal of Modern Italian Studies*, Vol. 8, No. 3 (2003), pp. 425–43.

17 An example of this literature is L. Robecchi Bricchetti, *Nel paese degli aromi* (Milan, 1903).

18 L.V. Cassanelli, *The Shaping of Somali Society* (Philadelphia, 1982) p. 148; K.N. Chaudhuri, *Trade and Civilisation in the Indian Ocean* (Cambridge, 1985), p. 102.

19 Cassanelli, *The Shaping of Somali Society*, p. 180. Said Samatar, *Oral Poetry and the Somaly Nationalism: The Case of Sayyd M. Abdille Hasan*, (Cambridge, 1982). Abdi Ismail Samatar, *The State and Rural Transformation in Northern Somalia* (Minneapolis, 1989). Ahmed Samatar, *The Somali Challenge* (Boulder, 1994).

20 I.M. Lewis, *A Modern History of the Somali* (Oxford, 2002), pp. 42–43.

21 R. Hess, *Italian Colonialism in Somalia* (Chicago, 1966), p. 39.

22 *Ibid.*, p. 58.

23 Abdul S. Bemath, 'The Sayyid and Saalihiya Tariqa: Reformist, Anticolonial Hero in Somalia', in Said S. Samatar (ed.), *In the Shadow of Conquest. Islam in Colonial Northeast Africa* (Trenton, NJ, 1992), pp. 33–48.

24 R. Hess, 'The Poor Man of God: Muhammed Abdullah Hassan', in N.R. Bennett (ed.), *Leadership in Eastern Africa: Six Political Biographies* (Boston, 1968), pp. 63–108; D. Laitin and S. Samatar, *Somalia. Nation in Search of a State* (Boulder, 1987), pp. 57–60

25 Lewis, *A Modern History of the Somali*, p. 86.

26 Hess, *Italian Colonialism in Somalia*, pp. 169–70.

27 G. Rochat, *Guerre italiane in Libia e in Etiopia* (Padua, 1991), pp. 100–04.

28 Laitin and Samatar, *Somalia*, p. 62.

29 Ali A. Ahmida, *The Making of Modern Libya* (Albany, 1994), pp. 57–59.

30 On the spiritual and theological aspect of the Sanusiya, see K.S. Vikør, *Sufi and Scholar on the Desert Edge: Muhammad b. Ali al-Sanusi and his Brotherhood* (London, 1995).

31 Ahmida, *The Making of Modern Libya*, p. 117.

32 L. Martone, *Giustizia coloniale* (Naples, 2002), pp. 116–20.

33 C. Moffa, 'I deportati libici nella guerra 1911–12', *Rivista di storia contemporanea*, Vol. 19, No. 1 (1990), pp. 32–56; M Missori, 'Una ricerca sui deportati libici nelle carte dell'Archivio Centrale dello Stato', in *Fonti e problemi della politica coloniale italiana. Atti del Convegno. Taromina-Messina, 23–29 ottobre 1989* (Rome, 1996), pp. 53–58; F. Sulpizi and Salaheddin Hasan Sury (eds), *Primo convegno su Gli esiliati libici nel periodo coloniale. 18–29 ottobre 2000, Isole Tremiti* (Rome, 2002).

34 Ahmida, *The Making of Modern Libya*, pp. 136–40.

35 Rochat, *Guerre italiane in Libia e in Etiopia*, p. 80.

36 A. Triulzi, 'Adwa: From Document to Monument', in Andall and Duncan, *Italian Colonialism*, pp. 143–64.

37 An example of these arguments is A. Lessona, *Verso l'Impero* (Florence, 1939)

38 H. Marcus, *Haile Sellassie I* (Berkeley, 1987), p. 179.

39 Vivid reports on this episode from the recollection of an eyewitness in C. Poggiali, *Diario AOI: 15 giugno 1936–4 ottobre 1937* (Milan, 1971).

40 Haile Mariam Larebo, *The Building of an Empire: Italian Land Policy and Practice in Ethiopia, 1935–41* (Oxford, 1994), pp. 138–40.

41 M. Fuller, 'Building Power. Italy's Colonial Architecture and Urbanism, 1923–1940', *Cultural Anthropology*, Vol. 3, No. 4 (1988), pp. 455–87.

42 I. Taddia, 'At the Origin of the State/Nation Dilemma: Ethiopia, Eritrea, Ogaden in 1941', *Northeast African Studies*, Vol. 12, Nos 2–3 (1990), pp. 157–70.

43 Ruth Iyob, 'Regional Hegemony: Domination and Resistance in the Horn of Africa', *The Journal of Modern African Studies*, Vol. 31, No. 2 (1993), pp. 257–76.

Chapter 13 USA

I am grateful to Johanna Lober, Christine Fischer and Kristof Scheller for valuable research assistance.

1 Quoted in Walter LaFeber, 'The American View of Decolonization, 1776–1920', in David Ryan and Victor Pungong (eds), *The United States and Decolonization. Power and Freedom* (New York, 2000), p. 24.

2 Rumsfeld response to a question by al-Jazeera TV network, 28 April 2003, quoted in Timothy Appleby, 'US Moves Shows Strategy Shift, Analysts Say', *The Globe and Mail*, 30 April 2003, A 11.

3 A convenient starting point to examine the various positions is provided in Andrew J. Bacevich (ed.), *The Imperial Tense: Prospects and Problems of American Empire* (Chicago, 2003); for the uses of history, see Niall Ferguson, *Colossus: The Price of American Empire* (New York, 2004); Warren Zimmermann, *First Great Triumph: How Five Americans Made their Country a World Power* (New York, 2002); Max Boot, *The Savage Wars of Peace: Small Wars and the Rise of American Power* (New York, 2002).

4 Thomas Paine, *Common Sense*, quoted in Michael H. Hunt, *Ideology and U.S. Foreign Policy* (New Haven, CT, 1987), p. 19.

5 Senator Albert Beveridge, quoted in Charles W. Kegley, Jr. and Eugene R. Wittkopf, *American Foreign Policy: Pattern and Process* (New York, 1982), p. 38.

6 For a thorough introduction to nineteenth-century processes of US expansionism, see D.W. Meinig, *The Shaping of America: A Geographical Perspective on 500 Years of History. Vol. 2. Continental America, 1800–1867* (New Haven, CT, 1993); D.W. Meinig, *The Shaping of America: A Geographical Perspective on 500 Years of History. Vol. 3. Transcontinental America, 1850–1915* (New Haven, CT, 1998).

7 As an introduction into the voluminous literature on Indian-white relations, see Francis Paul Prucha, *The Great Father: The United States Government and the American Indians* (Lincoln, NE, 1984).

8 On aboriginal policies as internal colonialism, see Jeffrey Ostler, *The Plains Sioux and U.S. Colonialism from Lewis and Clark to Wounded Knee* (Cambridge, Mass., 2004).

9 Paul Kennedy, *The Rise and Fall of the Great Powers: Economic Change and Military Conflict from 1500 to 2000* (New York, 1989), p. 243, emphases in the original.

10 Meinig, *Continental America, 1800–1867*, pp. 311–33; Meinig, *Transcontinental America, 1850–1915*, pp. 3–28 and 245–265; David Haward Bain, *Empire Express: Building the First Transcontinental Railroad* (New York, 1999).

11 Robert L. Thompson, *Wiring a Continent: The History of the Telegraph Industry in the United States, 1832–1866* (New York, 1972).

12 Michael H. Hunt, *Ideology and U.S. Foreign Policy* (New Haven, CT, 1987); for a good introduction to core convictions, see also David Ryan, *US Foreign Policy in World History* (London, 2000), pp. 19–70.

13 Anders Stephanson, *Manifest Destiny: American Expansion and the Empire of Right* (New York, 1995), p. 28, emphasis in the original; on exceptionalism, see Daniel T. Rodgers, 'Exceptionalism', in Anthony Molho and Gordon S. Wood (eds), *Imagined Histories: American Historians Interpret the Past* (Princeton, 1998), pp. 21–40.

14 David M. Fitzsimons, 'Tom Paine's New World Order: Idealistic Internationalism in the Ideology of Early American Foreign Relations', *Diplomatic History*, Vol. 19, No. 4 (Fall 1995), pp. 569–82.

15 Serge Ricard, 'The Exceptionalist Syndrome in U.S. Continental and Overseas Expansion', in David K. Adams and Cornelis A. van Minnen (eds), *Reflections on American Exceptionalism* (Keele, 1994), p. 73.

16 On the distinction between formal and informal empires, see Michael W. Doyle, *Empires* (Ithaca, NY, 1986), pp. 37–38.

17 Frank Ninkovich, *The United States and Imperialism* (Malden, MA, 2001), p. 158.

18 Some figures illustrate this dynamic: America's GNP quadrupled between 1867 and 1901 from $9,110,000,000 to $37,799,000,000. The manufacturing production index rose from 17 in 1865 to 100 in 1900. Exports mounted steadily: their value increased from $281 million to $1.3 billion between 1865 and 1900: figures in Charles S. Campbell, *The Transformation of American Foreign Relations, 1865–1900* (New York, 1976), p. 84; the China trade rose slowly and quintupled between 1890 and 1900 to $15 million. This sum constituted about 1 per cent of overall American exports: Robert L. Beisner, *From the Old Diplomacy to the New, 1865–1900* (Arlington Heights, IL, 1986), p. 17.

19 Sylvester K. Stevens, *American Expansion in Hawaii, 1842–1898* (Harrisburg, PA, 1945); Merze Tate, *The United States and the Hawaiian Kingdom: A Political History* (New Haven, CT, 1965); Thomas J. Osborne, *Empire Can't Wait: American Opposition to Hawaiian Annexation, 1893–1898* (Kent, OH, 1981).

20 Mark T. Gilderhus, *The Second Century: U.S.-Latin American Relations since 1889* (Wilmington, DE, 2000), pp. 1–36; Lars Schoultz, *Beneath the United States: A History of U.S. Policy toward Latin America* (Cambridge, MA, 1998); David F. Healy, *Drive to Hegemony: The United States in the Caribbean, 1898–1917* (Madison, WI, 1988).

21 American military interventions are analysed in Lester D. Langley, *The Banana Wars: United States Intervention in the Caribbean, 1898–1934* (Wilmington, DE, 2002).

22 Meinig, *Transcontinental America*, pp. 380–89.

23 Ninkovich, *The United States and Imperialism*.

24 Brian McAllister Linn, *The Philippine War, 1899–1902* (Lawrence, KS, 2000).

25 Richard E. Welch. Jr., *Response to Imperialism: The United States and the Philippine-American War, 1899–1902* (Chapel Hill, NC, 1979).

26 Stuart Anderson, *Race and Rapprochement: Anglo-Saxonism and Anglo-American Relations, 1895–1904* (Rutherford, NJ, 1981).

27 Bradford Perkins, *The Great Rapprochement: England and the United States, 1895–1914* (New York, 1968); William N. Tilchin, *Theodore Roosevelt and the British Empire: A Study in Presidential Statecraft* (New York, 1997).

28 Victor Kiernan has described the colonial empire as a 'logical sequel' to earlier expansion: *America, the New Imperialism: From White Settlement to World Hegemony* (London, 1980).

29 Amy Kaplan and Donald E. Pease (eds), *Cultures of United States Imperialism* (Durham, NC, 1993); John Carlos Rowe, *Literary Culture and U.S. Imperialism. From the Revolution to World War II* (New York, 2000); Amy Kaplan, *The Anarchy of Empire in the Making of U.S. Culture* (Cambridge, MA, 2002).

30 Robert W. Rydell, *All the World's a Fair: Visions of Empire at American International Expositions, 1876–1916* (Chicago, 1984); Robert W. Rydell, John E. Findling and Kimberly D. Pelle, *Fair America: World's Fairs in the United States* (Washington, DC, 2000).

31 Quoted in Neil Renwick, *America's World Identity: The Politics of Exclusion* (Houndmills, 2000), p. 106.

32 Henry R. Luce, 'The American Century', reprint in *Diplomatic History*, Vol. 23, No. 2 (Spring 1999), p. 169.

33 America's rise to global hegemony in the first half of the twentieth century is analysed in Akira Iriye, *The Globalizing of America, 1913–1945* (Cambridge, 1993); Warren I. Cohen, *Empire without Tears: America's Foreign Relations, 1921–1933* (Philadelphia, 1987); Emily S. Rosenberg, *Spreading the American Dream: American Economic and Cultural Diplomacy, 1890–1945* (New York, 1982); Emily S. Rosenberg, *Financial Missionaries to the World. The Politics and Culture of Dollar Diplomacy, 1900–1930* (Cambridge, MA, 1999).

34 Frank Ninkovich, *Modernity and Power: A History of the Domino Theory in the Twentieth Century* (Chicago, 1994); Frank Ninkovich, *The Wilsonian Century: U.S. Foreign Policy since 1900* (Chicago, 1999).

35 On the concept of 'soft power', see Joseph S. Nye, 'Soft Power', *Foreign Policy*, Vol. 80 (Fall 1990), pp. 153–71.

36 Theodore Roosevelt, May 1904, quoted in Andrew J. Bacevich, *American Empire. The Realities and Consequences of U.S. Diplomacy* (Cambridge, MA, 2002), p. 141.

37 Mary Renda, *Taking Haiti: Military Occupation and the Culture of Imperialism* (Chapel Hill, NC, 2001); Michael Gobat, *Confronting the American Dream: Nicaragua under U.S. Imperial Rule* (Durham, NC, 2005).

38 Alfred E. Eckes, Jr. and Thomas W. Zeiler, *Globalization and the American Century* (Cambridge, MA, 2003), p. 9.

39 *Ibid.*, p. 82.

40 I have borrowed this term from Emily Rosenberg, whose path-breaking study *Spreading the American Dream* remains the best introduction to the rise of American communication power in the interwar years; for the wider context, see Daniel R. Headrick, *The Invisible Weapon: Telecommunications and International Politics, 1851–1945* (New York, 1991).

41 James R. Mock and Cedric Larson, *Words That Won the War: The Story of the Committee on Public Information, 1917–1919* (Princeton, NJ, 1939); Stephen Vaughn, *Holding Fast the Inner Lines: Democracy, Nationalism, and the Committee on Public Information* (Chapel Hill, NC, 1980).

42 Rosenberg, *Spreading the American Dream*, p. 81.

43 Quoted in *ibid.*, p. 101.

44 The London *Morning Post*, quoted in Renwick, *America's World Identity*, pp. 105–06.

45 Edward G. Lowry, 'Trade Follows the Film', in *Saturday Evening Post* 198 (7 November 1925), p. 12, quoted in Rosenberg, *Spreading the American Dream*, p. 103.

46 Gore Vidal's novel *Washington D.C.*, quoted in Thomas J. McCormick, *America's Half Century: United States Foreign Policy in the Cold War* (Baltimore, 1989), p. 47.

47 Madeleine K. Albright, 'The Testing of American Foreign Policy', *Foreign Affairs*, Vol. 77, No. 6 (November–December 1998), pp. 50–64.

48 The evolution of America's containment strategy is analysed in John Lewis Gaddis, *Strategies of Containment: A Critical Appraisal of Postwar American Security Policy* (New York, 1982).

49 Ernest R. May (ed.), *American Cold War Strategy. Interpreting NSC-68* (Boston, MA, 1993), p. 26.

50 *Ibid.*, pp. 28–29.

51 *Ibid.*, p. 55.

52 Monnet quoted in Geir Lundestad, *'Empire' by Integration: The United States and European Integration, 1945–1997* (Oxford, 1998), p. 3.

53 See also Lundestad's *The American 'Empire' and Other Studies of US Foreign Policy in a Comparative Perspective* (Oxford, 1990).

54 Peter C. Stuart, *Isles of Empire: The United States and its Overseas Possessions* (Lanham, MD, 1999); Peter L. Hahn and Mary Ann Heiss (eds), *Empire and Revolution. The United States and the Third World since 1945* (Columbus, OH, 2001).

55 John Prados, *The President's Secret Wars: CIA and Pentagon Covert Operations since World War II* (New York, 1986).

56 Walter L. Hixson, *Parting the Curtain: Propaganda, Culture, and the Cold War, 1945–1961* (New York, 1997); Scott Lucas, *Freedom's War: The American Crusade against the Soviet Union* (New York, 1999); on cultural exports, see e.g. Giles Scott-Smith and Hans Krabbendam (eds), *The Cultural Cold War in Western Europe, 1945–1960* (London, 2003).

57 Francis Fukuyama, *The End of History and the Last Man* (New York, 1992).

58 Acheson address at West Point, 5 December 1962: 'Great Britain has lost an empire and has not yet found a role', quoted in Douglas Brinkley, *Dean Acheson: The Cold War Years, 1953–1971* (New Haven, CT, 1992), p. 176.

59 Stephen G. Brooks and William C. Wohlforth, 'American Primacy in Perspective', *Foreign Affairs*, Vol. 81, No. 4 (July–August 2002), pp. 21–22.

60 Brooks and Wohlforth, 'American Primacy', p. 22.

61 On American information power, see Joseph S. Nye, Jr and William A. Owens, 'America's Information Edge', *Foreign Affairs*, Vol. 75, No. 2 (March–April 1996), pp. 20–36.

62 Bacevich, *American Empire*; William G. Hyland, *Clinton's World: Remaking American Foreign Policy* (Westport, CT, 1999); Bob Woodward, *The Commanders* (New York, 1991); David Halberstam, *War in a Time of Peace: Bush, Clinton, and the Generals* (New York, 2001); Ivo H. Daalder and James M. Lindsay, *America Unbound: The Bush Revolution in Foreign Policy* (Hoboken, NJ, 2005).

63 Quoted in Susan M. Matarese, *American Foreign Policy and the Utopian Imagination* (Amherst, MA, 2001), p. 89.

64 The National Security Strategy of the United States of America (hereafter referred to as NSS), September 2002, at www.whitehouse.gov/nss.html, accessed 30 December 2005; John Lewis Gaddis has argued that NSS 'could represent the most sweeping shift in U.S. grand strategy since the beginning of the Cold War': 'A Grand Strategy of Transformation', *Foreign Policy*, Vol. 133 (November–December 2002), pp. 50–57; Joseph S. Nye, Jr., 'U.S. Power and Strategy after Iraq', *Foreign Affairs*, Vol. 82, No. 4 (July–August 2003), pp. 60–73.

65 NSS, 6.

66 Winston Churchill speech at Harvard University, 6 September 1943, at: http://www. winstonchurchill.org, accessed 12 April 2006.

67 William Appleman Williams, *Empire as a Way of Life: An Essay on the Causes and Character of America's Present Predicament, Along with a Few Thoughts about an Alternative* (New York, 1980), p. ix.

Sources of illustrations

1 The Ottoman Empire

26 Attributed Gentile Bellini, *The Sultan Mehmet II*, 1480. National Gallery London

27 Manuscript *du Voyage d'outremer de Bertrandon de la Broquiere* 1455. Bibliothèque Nationale, Paris

28 School of Muhammad Siyâh-Qalam, *A dismounted prince listens to a dervish*, Tabrîz, 1478–90. Topkapi Sarayì Museum, Istanbul, H.2153, fol iv

29 German School, *The Church of Saint Sophia transformed as a Mosque*, 16th century. Bridgeman Art Library

30 Le Hay, *Janissary Officer*, early 18th century. Corbis/Historical Picture Archive

31 *Battle of Mohács* from the *Süleymannane* of Arifi transcribed in 1558. Topkapi Sarayì Museum, Istanbul. H.1517, fol 220a

32 Romain de Hooghe, *View of Vienna during the Siege, bombardment by the Turkish Artillery*, c.1683.

33 Miniature from Nusretname,*Ottoman camp in Georgia*, 1582. British Museum, London

34 Ingres, Jean-Auguste-Dominique, *The Turkish Bath*, 19th century. Bridgeman Art Library/Musée du Louvre, Paris

35 *Turkey's first Parliament*, 1876. Corbis/Bettmann

36 Political cartoon, 1877. Corbis/Bettmann

37 Anton von Werner, *Congress of Berlin*, from *Bismarck Album*, 1878. British Museum, London

38 Crowds on the Galata Bridge, c.1880. Corbis/Austrian Archives

41 A patriotic mass demonstration in Constantinople as a result of the abolition of capitulations, 7 October 1914. Corbis/Bettmann

42 Kaiser Wilhelm II of Germany travelling with the Sultan of Turkey in a carriage during the First World War, 1916. Corbis/Hulton Archive

43 President Mustafa Kemal, who took the name Atatürk, 'Father of the Turks', c.1923

2 Spain

44 Leone Leoni, *Emperor Charles V*, 1555. Sammlung für Plastik und Kunstgewerbe, Kunsthistoriches Museum, Vienna

45 Theodore de Bry, *Peruvians forced into slavery by the Spanish* from *America*, 1590

46 Conquistador Francisco Pizarro meeting Atahualpa, last Inca emperor, in Cajamarca, 1532. Cajamarca, Peru. Mosaic, 1880. The Art Archive/Mireille Vautier

47 Anon, *Hernán Cortés*, 16th century. Museo Naval, Madrid

47 Fanciful drawings of the New World in a Swiss edition of Columbus' report to his patron, King Ferdinand of Spain, 1493. Rare Book Division, The New York Public Library, Astor, Lenox and Tilden Foundations

49 *Entrance of the Triumphant Army of Cortes into Tlaxcala after the Victory of Otumba*, 19th century. Bridgeman Art Library/Museo de América, Madrid

50 Amerindian smallpox victim, from Baltasar Jaime Martínez Compañón, *Trujillo del Peru*, 18th century, Vol. 2, plate 197. Patrimonio Nacional, Real Biblioteca del Palacio Real, Madrid

51 Anonymous, *Bartolomé de las Casas*, 1560. Museo de Bellas Artes, Seville

52 Theodore de Bry, *Gold mining in Potosí*, from *America*, 1590, plate 3

53 Fray Pedro de Gante, *Catechism*, c.1525–28; Ministerio de Educación, Cultura y Deporte. Archivo Histórico Nacional, Madrid (Códice 1257).

54–55 Gaspar Miguel Berrio, *Despicion de Zerro Rico e Ymperial Villa de Potosi*, 1758. Charcas Museum, Sucre, AKG/Gilles Mermet

56 Anonymous, *Dominicans baptize Indians*, Castillo de Chapultepec, Mexico. Bridgeman Art Library

58–59 *Casta* paintings, 18th century, Mexico. Museo de América, Madrid

60 Vincente Alban Quito, *Lady with slave and fruit* 1783. The Art Archive/Museo de América, Madrid

62 Machine for sifting tobacco leaves in the Royal Cigar Factory, 1787. Archivo de Indias, Seville

63 *Cultivation of cochineal in Peru*, 17th century. Biblioteca Publica de Toledo, Coleccion Borbon-Lorenzana

64 Jose Gil de Castro, *Simon Bolivar*, 1783–1830. Instituto de Cultura Hispánica. Madrid

65 Walter Yeager, *Cuban farmers harvesting sugar cane on the plantation of Las Canas*. Corbis/Bettmann

66 Gillam, *Uncle Sam: "I've had my eye on that morsel for a long time, guess I'll have to take it in!"* from *Judge*, volume 29, 10 August 1895

3 Portugal

68 A. Castrioto, *Don João V drinking chocolate*, 18th century. Museu Nacional de Arte Antiga, Lisbon

69 Carlos Juliao, *Diamond mining in Brasil*, c.1775. Art Archive/Biblioteca National do Rio de Janeiro, Brazil/Dagli Orti

70 *Rua Direita, Goa*, from Jan Huygen Von Linschoten, *Itinerarium ofte Schipvarert naer Oost ofte Portugaels Indien*, 1623. Biblioteca Nacional, Lisbon

71 Anon, *Missionary activity in Congo, Angola and neighbouring countries*. Turin, Biblioteca Civica, MS 457

71 Nicolas Antoine Taunay, *Largo de Carioca, Rio de Janeiro, Brazil*, 1816. The Art Archive/Museu Nacional de Belas Artes Rio de Janiero Brazil/Dagli Orti

72 *Vasco da Gama disembarking at Calcutta, Southern India, 28 May 1489*, early 16th century. Flemish

74 *A group of Portuguese dining in a Water-Tank*, from the *Codice Casanatense*, c.1540. Biblioteca Casanatense, Rome

75 Fray Juan Bautista Maino, *Relief of Bahia, Brazil*, detail, 17th century. The Art Archive/Museo del Prado Madrid

76 *Portuguese offering presents to Shah Jahan in Agra, after capture of Ugulim by the Mogols*. Royal Library, Windsor Castle

76 Attributed to Kano Domi, Kano School, *Portuguese (Namban-jin) recently disembarked from the great black ship which traded with China, bearing gifts to the Shogun of Nagasaki*, detail, 1593–1600. Museu Nacional de Arte Antiga, Lisbon.

77 Pier van der Aa, *View of Macau* beginning of the 18th century. Biblioteca Nacional, Lisbon.

78–79 Attributed to Alberto Cantino, *Planisphere*, 1502. Biblioteca Estense e Universitaria, Modena

79 Joaquim Jose Codina, *Two Jurispixuna Indians of Amazonia with masks*, 1787. Museu Bocage, Lisbon

81 Theodore de Bry, *Natives attacking Colonial Villages in the French and Portuguese Colony of Brazil*, 1562. Corbis/Archivo Iconografico, SA

82 *Property of S. Ramao de Jesus Maria, Quane do Marral, Quelimane Mozambique*, from *O Ocidente* 11-4-188. Biblioteca Nacional, Lisbon

84 Morais Carvalho, *Mouzinho de Alburquerque surprises and captures Gungunhana at Chaimité, 26 December 1895*. Museu Militar, Lisbon

85 *Members of Portuguese Royal Commission charged with defining frontiers of Mozambique with Rhodesia*, c.1900. Jill Dias

87 Henrique Galvão, '*Portugal is not a small country*', 1934. Album Comemorativo da Primeira Exposição Colonial Portuguesa, Porto

88 *Labourers belonging to a plantation*, c.1900. Jill Dias/photo AC de Sobral

89 Poster advertising film *Feitiço do Império, (The Enchantment of Empire)*, 1940. Cinematecca Portuguesa, Lisbon

90 African-Portuguese mission and school-teacher, early 20th century. Jill Dias

91 *Portuguese missionaries baptizing Africans in Barwe, Mozambique, c.*1895. Jill Dias/Photo Souza Machado

91 Boy soldier, Cover of *Escola Portuguesa*, 24 October 1960. Biblioteca Nacional, Lisbon

4 The Netherlands

92 Fabric from Surinamese Independence anniversary, 1976. Tropenmuseum, Amsterdam

93 Maria Sibylla Merian, *Flos Pavonis*, (Peacock flower) from her book *Metamorphosis Insectorum Surinamensis*, 1705

94 Jacob Jansz Coeman, *The Family of Pieter Cnoll*, 1665. Batavia, Rijksmuseum, Amsterdam

96 An Islamic pilgrim who has been to Mecca, 1854. Tropenmuseum, Amsterdam

97 Exterior of the Mosque on Aloeng Aloeng, Bandoeng, Java, Indonesia, *c.*1920. Corbis/Bettmann

98 Anon, *Jan Pieterszoon Coen*. Westfries Museum, Hoorn

98–99 Ivan Rynne, *City of Batavia, Java, c.*1780. The Art Archive

100 *A Negro hung alive by the Ribs to a Gallows*, 1806, from *Narrative of a Five Years Expedition against the Revolted Negroes of Surinam* by John Gabriel Stedman. TopFoto/HIP/The British Library, London

100 Coffee establishment from *Het Kamerlid van Berkensteinin Nederlandsch, Indie*, 1870. India Office, London

101 J.D. Herlein, *Chop sugar cane*, 1718. Universiteits bibliothek van de Universiteit Amsterdam, Tropenmuseum

102 *Battle of Lombak, batik, c.*1920. Collectie Galerie Rudolf G. Smend Keulen

103 Anon. *Paramaribo River, Suriname*, 19th century. The Art Archive/Maritem Museum Prins Hendrik, Rotterdam/Dagli Orti

104 Potentate of Surakarta with Dutch Resident, 19th century. British Museum/Archives Koninklijk Instituut voor de Tropen, Amsterdam

105 Beeckman, Andries, *The Castle of Batavia, as seen from Kali Besar West, c.*1656. Bridgeman Art Library/Rijksmuseum, Amsterdam

106 D.K. Bonatti, *Slave Rebellion in Surinam, c.*1832–1834. Corbis/Historical Picture Archive

107 Children from an orphanage await arrival of Princess Juliana of Netherlands in Paramaribo, Suriname, 1955. Tropenmuseum, Amsterdam

108 Shell oil tank, drawn by buffaloes in a factory for the distillation of crude oil in the Netherlands Indies, December 20, 1941. Corbis/Bettmann

109 Musical instrument makers at work in workshops of J.H. Seeling, early 20th century, Corbis/Hulton

110 Eurasian family strolling the streets in Arnhem outside Chinese restaurant, *c.*1960. Esther Captain

111 Eurasian and Dutch women in traditional Dutch clothing from Volendam *c.*1960. Esther Captain

5 Scandinavia

112 Anon, *Two Women and a Girl from Greenland with the Dutchman David Danell*, 1654. National Museum of Denmark, Copenhagen

113 Anon. *The Danish colonist in Africa September 17, 1817 with black slave in background*. The Art Archive/City Museum Copenhagen/Dagli Orti

114 Hans Egede, *Whaling and Seal Hunting amidst the Eskimos*, 19th century. Det Kongelige Bibliotek, Copenhagen

114 Anon, *Danish Merchant ships on Icelandic Coast*, 19th century. Private Collection

115 *Unamark in Northern Greenland*, from *Hans Willumsen*, 1819. Private Collection

116 The *New Testament* translated by Poul Egede into the Inuit language of Greenland, published 1766. Ny Carlsberg Glyptotek, Copenhagen

117 Abraham Wuchters, *Frederik III's Queen Sofie Amalie with her Negro boy and other Exotic Accoutrements, c.*1650. Museum of National History, Frederiksborg Castle, Denmark

118 Peter Lindeström, *Map of New Sweden*, late 17th century. The Royal Library, Stockholm

119 *View of the Harbour Streets in Gustavia*, 1800. Statens Sjohistoriska Museet, Stockholm

120 A woodcut from Danish explorer Jens Munk's account of his 1619 voyage. Private Collection

120–121 *View of Tranquebar, India*, after 1650. The Skokloster Collection, Sweden

122 The first Bible in Tamil language, printed in Tranquebar, 1715. By permission of the Syndics of Cambridge University Library and of the British and Foreign Bible Society

123 Anon, *Copenhagen from the water showing British and Danish ships*, 1786. The

Art Archive/Sofarts Museum, Elsinore, Denmark/Dagli Orti

124 Paul Erdmann Isert, *Otho's Camp at Volta*, 1784. Private Collection

125 Johann Friedrich Fritz, *Christiansted, Saint Croix, West Indies*, 1837. The Art Archive/Maritime Museum, Kronborg Castle, Denmark/Dagli Orti

126 H. G. Beenfeldt, *A Prospect of the Harbour Square in Christiansted Viewed from the Sea*, 1815. Rigsorkivet, Copenhagen

127 Vilhelm Hammershøi, *The Asiatic Company's Buildings in Copenhagen*, 1902. Private Collection

6 Britain

128 A Mughal artist, *Warren Hastings, c.*1782. British Library, London

129 Richard Collins, *A Family At Tea, c.*1800. The Art Archive/Victoria and Albert Museum, London/Eileen Tweedie

130 J.M.W. Turner, *Harewood House from North East*, 1797. Harewood House, reproduced by the kind permission of the Earl and countess of Harewood and Trustees of the Harewood House Trust

131 *The East offering her riches to Britannia*. A painted ceiling from East India House currently on display in the Foreign Office, London

132 Catherine Prestell after Richard Westhall *A view taken near Bain on the West Coast of Guinea in Africa, c.*1789. Bridgeman Art Library/Private Collection/Michael Graham-Stewart

132 *Best Tobacco* advertised on labels, mid-18th century. Private Collection

133 Francis Hayman, *Clive meeting Mir Jafar after the Battle of Plassey in 1757, c.*1761–2. National Portrait Gallery, London

134–135 After Jan Van Ryme. *Fort St George on the Coromandel coast, Madras, India*, 1794. akg images

136 Currier, *Boston Tea Party*, 1846. akg images

137 George Carter, *Death of Captain Cook*, 1781. Rex Nan Kivell Collection, National Library of Australia, Canberra

138 Group of slave boys and men on the lower deck of the British ship, HMS Daphne, after being rescued from a dhow, 1 November 1868. National Archive, Kew, Richmond

139 *Governor Davey's proclamation to the Aborigines*, 1816. Rex Nan Kivell Collection, National Library of Australia, Canberra

140 Thomas Watling, *A Direct North General View of Sydney Cove*, 1794. Bridgeman Art Library/Dixson Galleries,

State Library of New South Wales, Sydney

141 Tommy McRae, *An Aboriginal of the Wahgunyah tribe on the River Murray*, 1880. From *Drawings by Tommy McCrae, an Aboriginal of the Wahgunyah tribe on the River Murray*, National Library of Australia, Canberra

141 Henry Brewer, attributed The Port Jackson Painter, *Australian Aborigine, c.*1790. Rex Nan Kivell Collection, National Library of Australia, Canberra

142 *A Village in Pukapuka under Heathenism*, 19th century. Rex Nan Kivell Collection, National Library of Australia, Canberra

142 *A Village in Pukapuka under Christianity*, 19th century. Rex Nan Kivell Collection, National Library of Australia, Canberra

143 Felice Beato, *Execution of Delhi mutineers, c.*1850. akg images

144 Bauer, *A Sugar Plantation in the South of Trinidad, c.*1850. Bridgeman Art Library/Private Collection

145 Baxter, *The Ordinance of Baptism, Brawns Town, Jamaica*, 1842. Victoria and Albert Museum, London

146 Woman and child at British concentration camp during the Boer War, *c.*1900. akg images

147 Dead British soldiers in trenches of Natal, South Africa, following the battle of Spions Kop, 24 January 1900. Corbis/Hulton Archive

148 Field Marshal Kitchener, Earl of Khartoum, reviews Indian troops during First World War, *c.*1914–1915. akg images

149 Mahatma Gandhi on the Salt March, India, 1930. Corbis/Hulton Archive/Walter Bosshard

150 Interned Mau Mau suspects held by the British government, Kenya, 1 December 1952. Ullstein bild

151 Immigrants from West Indies disembark from ship in Britain to seek a new life in the UK, 1 July 1962. Popperfoto

7 France

152 Jean-Michel Moreau-Lejeune, *C'est à ce prix que vous mangez du sucre en Europe*, illustration from Voltaire *Candide*, Paris, 1787. Engraving by Baquoy (fils), Cabinet des Estampes, Bibliothèque Nationale, Paris

153 Colonist teaching African children to tell the time in African colony, *c.*1920. Kharbine –Tapabor, Paris

155 Valentin Foulquier, *Slaves gather sugar cane, c.*1860. Kharbine – Tapabor, Paris/Jonas

156 Anne-Louis Girodet, *Citizen Jean-Baptiste Belley*, 1797. The Hermitage, St. Petersburg

157 *A qui le Maroc ?* 1906. Kharbine–Tapabor, Paris

158 Anonymous, *Rencontre du Radeau par le brick L'Argus*, 1818. Cabinet des Estampes, Bibliothèque Nationale, Paris

159 *French taking of Algiers*, 4 July 1830. Bibliothèque Nationale, Paris

161 Laveran, *Various stages of malaria parasites as seen on fresh blood*, late 19th century. Service de Santé des Armées, France

162–163 *Algiers, North Africa*, 1905. Roger-Viollet, Paris

164 French school textbook depicting various products of the colonies, *c.*1920–30. Kharbine-Tapabor, Paris

165 Louis Remy Sabattier, *A European woman in Algeria*, 1910. Bridgeman Art Library/Private Collection

166 French intervention in Morocco. Moroccan prisoners await their interogation at a camp in Dar-Debibals, after the revolt in Fez, 1911. Roger-Viollet, Paris

167 Captain Marchand and a small detachment of French troops nearly precipitated an Anglo-French war when they raised the tricolor over Fashoda on the Nile in 1898

169 Poster for the Paris Colonial Exposition, 1931. Bridgeman Art Library/Bibliothèque Historique de la Ville de Paris, Paris

170 Tribunal de conciliation des differentes races, province d'Alger, 1858. Bibliothèque Nationale, Paris/Photo FJA Moulin

171 Algerian infantrymen in the French army prepare to board trains, a few months before the First World War, 1 January, 1914. Getty Images/Roger Viollet

172 Eric Castel, Poster for the French Empire *Trois couleurs, Un drapeau, Un empire, c.*1940. Bridgeman Art Library/Private Collection

173 Theodor Baumgartner, *Two Algerians* from *Die Feinde Deutschlands* (The Enemies of Germany), 1916. Mary Evans Picture Library

174 French prisoners of war, escorted by Vietnamese soldiers, walking to a camp in Dien Bien Phu, 7 May 1954. Getty Images/AFP

175 Demonstrators outside Government House, during Algerian War of Independence, 23 May 1958. Getty Images/Hulton Archive/Meacher

8 Russia

177 Heinrich Vogeler, *For Increased Production in Karelia*. Staatliche Museen zu Berlin

178–179 Vitus Bering's epic journey from Tobolsk to Kamchatka, map of 1729. Universitätsbibliothek, Göttingen

180 A street in Semipalátinsk, 19th century. From George Kennan, *Siberia and the Exile System*, 1891

180 A Yurt of the Káchinski Tatárs, 19th century. From George Kennan, *Siberia and the Exile System*, 1891

181 The peoples of Russia. From Johann Gottlieb Georgi, *Beschreibung alle Nationen der Russischen Reiches*, St. Petersburg, 1799

182 Achille Beltrame, *Nicholas II, Tsar of Russia, signing ukase* (edict) *concerning reform of institutions of Russian Empire*. From Italian newspaper, *La Domenica del Corriere*, 1905, The Art Archive/Domenica del Corriere/Dagli Orti

183 The First Duma, opening ceremony, 24 May 1906. Hutchison Library/Anatoly Therei

184 A Tholander, *Peter the Great*, 1874. Museum of Fine Arts of the Republic of Karelia, Petrovodsk

185 *Caricature of Peter the Great's reforms depicting a boyar having his beard cut off, c.*1700. akg images

186 *Alexander II with his manifesto on the emancipation of the serfs*. Novosti

187 Railway construction, late 19th century. Private Collection

188 Nikolaj Semenovic Samokis, *Cavalry Engagement at Mukden, 25th February 1905*. Bridgeman Art Library/Bibliothèque Nationale, Paris

189 Red cross orderlies view 600 dead after battle during the Russo-Japanese War, 1904. Private Collection

190 Vladimir Ilyich Lenin walking through Red Square, Moscow with a group of military commanders, 1 May 1919. Frank Lane Picture Library/Silvestris

191 Yury Ivanovich Pimenov, *Heavy Industry*, 1928. Tretyakov Gallery, Moscow

191 M. Voron, *Give first priority to gathering the Bolshevik harvest*, 1934. Moscow

192 *We Smite the Lazy Workers*, 1931. Hoover Institution, Stanford University

193 *What Siberia is giving to Soviet Russia*. The Art Archive/Musée des Deux Guerres Mondiales, Paris/Dagli Orti

194 A Romanian worker stands atop the statue of Lenin, after it was removed from its pedestal in Bucharest, 5 March 1990. Getty Images, AFP/André Durand

9 Austria-Hungary

196 Hapsburg insignia, 1848

197 Bernard Strigel, *Maximilian I of Austria*. The Art Archive/Academia Fernando Madrid/Dagli Orti

199 *Emperor Joseph at the Plough*, 1765. akg images/Wien Museum/Erich Lessing

200–201 *Second defenestration of Prague*, May 22nd, 1618. The Art Archive/Eileen Tweedy

203 Engelbert Seiberts, *Assembly of important statesmen at the time of the Congress of Vienna*, after fresco in the conference room of the Maximilianeum, 1815. akg images/Maximilianeum Collection, Munich

204 *Fraternity between workers, students, citizens and guards*, 1848. akg images

205 *Demonstration at factory gate Vienna, March 13, 1848*. The Art Archive/Museum der Stadt Vienna

206–207 *Venetian delegation arriving in Turin, Italy, 1866,* 19th century. The Art Archive/Museo Nazionale di San Martino Naples

208 Franz Xaver Winterhalter, *Emperor Franz Joseph I of Austria in the gala uniform of a Field Marshal*, 1865. Bridgeman Art Library/Kunsthistorisches Museum, Vienna

208 The bodies of Franz Ferdinand and his wife, Sofie, murdered in Sarajevo on June 28, 1914. akg images

209 Anti-Serbian riots after the assassination of the Archduke Franz Ferdinand in Sarajevo on 28th June 1914. akg images

210 L. Garfasjeng, *Feudal Landlord*, Szekley county, Transylvania, 1900. From Kronprinzenwerk, *Ungarn VI*, 1902, Austrian National Library, Vienna

211 Riots in the Vienna Parliament over the dismissal of the Prime Minister, Count Badeni. from *Leipziger Illustrierte Zeitung*, Dec 9th 1897. British Newspaper Archive, London

212–213 Mihaly Munkascy, *Before the Strike*, 1895. Magyar Nemzeti Galeria, Budapest, Bridgeman Art Library

215 Archduke Ferdinand Maximilian. Photo by Imagno/Getty Images

216 Heinrich von Angeli, *Rudolf Carl Von Slatin*. The Royal Collection, photo 2007, Her Majesty Queen Elizabeth II

217 Gustav Klimt, Poster for Secession I, 1898. Private Collection, courtesy Barry Friedman Ltd, New York, photo courtesy Lee Stalsworth

218 Stuarts Island. Photo by Imagno/Getty Images

10 Belgium

221 Henri Meyer, *Cardinal Lavigerie and the White Fathers*, illustration to an article on the repression of slavery from *Le Petit Journal,* April 1891. Bridgeman Art Library/Private Collection

223 King Leopold II, late 19th century. Corbis/Hulton Archive

224 HM Stanley, *The Congo and the Founding of its Free State*, jacket of book, 1885. Jean-Luc Vellut

225 Pende chair, 1948. Made by sculptor Mulende. Royal Museum for Central Africa, Tervuren, Belgium. Photo J.-M. Van Dyck

227 Bridge on first Congo railway, 1897. Royal Museum for Central Africa, Tervuren, Belgium, Photo Aumôniers du Chemin de Fer

228 Luluabourg. Early days of state outpost, 1887. Royal Museum for Central Africa, Tervuren, Belgium

229 Ch. Kuck, *Belges! Connaissons Notre Congo*, 1918. Belgian Ministry of Colonies

230 Interior of a Belgian Mission school in the African Congo, *c.*1900. The Art Archive

231 Baptism in Congo, *c.*1907. Mary Evans Picture Library

232 *Chicotte*, early 19th century. Royal Museum for Central Africa, Tervuren, Belgium

233 Ivory in Antwerp wharehouse, early 19th century. Royal Museum for Central Africa, Tervuren, Belgium. From Congo-Noël, 1902

234 From J. Perraudin, *Le Beau Métier de Missionnaire*, Namur, Grands Lacs

236 Dignatories on Independence Day, 1960. Royal Museum for Central Africa, Tervuren, Belgium

11 Germany

238 Franz Seraph von Lenbach, *Chancellor Otto Von Bismarck*, 1890. Bridgeman Art Library, Walters Art Museum, Baltimore

239 *The March of Kaiser Wilhelm II*, 1914. Corbis/Rykoff

240 Prince Von Bülow, late 19th century. Getty Images/Hulton Archive

240 The West Africa Conference Berlin 1884–85. From: *Die Gartenlaube*, Collection Joachim Zeller

241 The German colonial army in Togo, published by Calwey Verlagsverein, Stuttgart, 1904. Collection Joachim Zeller

242 Postcard showing an advertisement for the company 'Th. Moskopf of Fahr, Rhineland' pre-1914. Collection Joachim Zeller

243 Rudolf Hellgrewe, *Victoria, Cameroon,* 9 February 1909. Collection Joachim Zeller

243 The German colonial army soldier, Richard von Bentivegni, with Africans at Nyassa Lake in German East Africa, *c.*1912. Joachim Zeller/Michael von Bentivegni

244 Locally recruited troops under German command in Dar es Salaam, German East Africa, *c.*1914. Getty Images/Hulton Archive

245 Journeys in the colonial style – in a slope mat and with sun protection. Bpk

246 Djombe natives working on tobacco plantation, German South West Africa, 15 April 1918. Corbis/Bettmann

246 Ketteler killed, Boxer Rebellion, China, *c.*1900. Mary Evans Picture Library

247 Detail of east frieze of Great Altar of Pergamon; *c.*165–156 BC. Pergamon Museum, Berlin, Corbis/Bettmann

248 Africa as visualized by Rome and Berlin, 1941. From *Kolonie und Heimat* published Berlin, 1941. Collection Joachim Zeller

249 Manga Bell (sitting right) of Cameroon and his Duala delegation, visiting the Baptist missionary Scheve. From *Die Woche,* 1902. Collection Joachim Zeller

249 Professor Robert Koch giving injections in Africa, 1940. From *Berliner Morgenpost,* 1940. Collection Joachim Zeller

250 The hanging of a ringleader by the German colonial army during the Maji-Maji-War in German East Africa, 1905. Collection Joachim Zeller/*East Africa,* 27 May 1926

251 The German garrison of Windhoek besieged by the Hereros. Published in *Le Petit Journal* 21 February, 1904. Bridgeman Art Library

252 Herero prisoners of war at train station, 1905. Collection Joachim Zeller/Bernd Labenski

253 Herero prisoners of war at a concentration camp in Windhoek near the colonial fort, 'Alte Feste', *c.*1905–06. Collection Joachim Zeller/Bernd Labenski

12 Italy

255 W. Roveroni, propaganda poster on behalf of the overseas colonization scheme in Ethiopia, reproduced in *Penrose Annual,* 1939. Mary Evans Picture Library

256 Troops prepare to leave Messina for Eritrea and Italian Somaliland, 12 October 1935. Topham

257 An Italian military encampment in Eritrea, *c.*1935. Topham

258 Front Line of the People's Liberation Front of Eritrea, *c.*1935. Topham

259 Italian planes in flight, Massawa, Eritrea, October 10, 1935. Corbis/Bettmann

261 Emperor Menelik at Battle of Aduwa. Mary Evans Picture Library

262 A street of Massawa, full of Italian soldiers in readiness for action against Abyssinia 1935. Topham

263 An Ethiopian general surrenders to the Italians, from *Illustrazione del Popolo,* 26 October 1935. Mary Evans Picture Library

264–265 Attributed Haili Berhan Yemene, *The Abyssinians routing the Italian troops, scene from the Italian invasion of Abyssinia in 1896,* 20th century. Bridgeman Art Library/Private Collection

266 Ristorante Italia in Tripoli, April 29–May 11, 1914. Topham

267 Italian ships in Tripoli, 1911. Topham

268 Tobruk with fires burning, 23 January 1941. Topham

269 Karl Arnold *The Italians in Ethiopia,* 1935. From *Simplicissimus* 1935. Mary Evans Picture Library

270 Mussolini receiving the sword of Islam, Tripoli, April 1937. Topham

271 Crowd greeting Victor Emanuel III and Queen Elena on a visit to Tripoli. Topham

272 *The Italian Army against Ethiopia in 1935–36,* 1937. Bridgeman Art Library/Private Collection

273 Possibly Haili Berhan Yemene, *Two scenes from the Italian invasion of Abyssinia,* 20th century. Bridgeman Art Library/Private Collection

274 Muslim and Christian fellow countrymen march to fight for Ethiopia, *c.*1935. Corbis/Bettmann

275 Ethiopians in the Tigre Province of Ethiopia give the Fascist salute to a poster of the 'Great White Father', Mussolini, 19 November 1935. Corbis/Bettmann

276 Former Fascist headquarters, Asmara, Eritrea

277 Haile Selassie Speaking at League of Nations, 1936. Corbis/Bettmann

13 USA

279 George A. Crofutt, *American Progress,* 1873. After the painting by John Gast of 1872, Library of Congress, Washington DC

281 Bayot after C. Nebel, *General Scott's entrance into Mexico City.* From George W. Kendall *The War between the United States and Mexico,* 1851. Library of Congress, Washington DC

282–283 Fanny Frances Palmer, *Across the Continent. Westward the Course of Empire Takes Its Way,* 1868. Bridgeman Art Library/Private Collection

284 Robert Lindneux, *Trail of Tears,* 1942. Woolaroc Museum, Bartlesville, Oklahoma

285 *Commodore Matthew Perry Meets Royal Commissioner at Yokahama,* 1853. Corbis/Bettmann

286–287 Japanese print, *Commodore Matthew Perry's paddle-steamer arriving in Yokahama 1853.* Bridgeman Art Library/British Museum, London

288 Poster advertising the Great American Tea company, importers and Jobbers of Teas, 19th century. Bridgeman Art Library/Collection of the New-York Historical Society

289 Marines boarding U.S.S.Connecticut for Haiti to aid Admiral Caperton's men, 31 July 1915. Corbis/Bettmann

290 Native Americans riding horses at the St. Louis Exposition, 1904. Corbis

291 A promenade on the grounds of the Saint Louis Exposition in 1904 leading past pools, gardens and exhibition halls, *c.*1905. Corbis

293 Ford Model T ready for delivery from the factory, *c.*1925. Corbis/Bettmann

295 American fighter planes fly in formation over the USS Missouri in Tokyo Bay on 2 September 1945. Corbis

296 A mushroom cloud from an atomic bomb rises over Nagasaki, August, 1945. Corbis/Nagasaki Atomic Bomb Museum/EPA

299 *Something for Everybody,* a box of groceries and supplies is opened by a family in England, *c.*1946. Library of Congress, Washington DC

300 Vice President Richard Nixon and Soviet Premier Nikita Khrushchev during their Kitchen Debate at Sokolniki Park, Moscow, USSR, 24 July 1959. Corbis

301 'McLenin's', Moscow, *c.*1999. Corbis/Steve Raymer

302 Burning oilfields in background with US Marines in truck after operation Desert Storm, Kuwait, 1991. Magnum/Bruno Barbey

303 World Trade Center's Twin Towers burning following attack on 9/11. Empics/AP Photos

Index

Page numbers in **bold** indicate illustrations